NORMATIVITY AND THE WILL

Normativity and the Will

Selected Papers on Moral Psychology and Practical Reason

R. JAY WALLACE

CLARENDON PRESS · OXFORD

OXFORD
UNIVERSITY PRESS

Great Clarendon Street, Oxford OX2 6DP

Oxford University Press is a department of the University of Oxford.
It furthers the University's objective of excellence in research, scholarship,
and education by publishing worldwide in

Oxford New York

Auckland Cape Town Dar es Salaam Hong Kong Karachi
Kuala Lumpur Madrid Melbourne Mexico City Nairobi
New Delhi Shanghai Taipei Toronto

With offices in

Argentina Austria Brazil Chile Czech Republic France Greece
Guatemala Hungary Italy Japan Poland Portugal Singapore
South Korea Switzerland Thailand Turkey Ukraine Vietnam

Oxford is a registered trade mark of Oxford University Press
in the UK and in certain other countries

Published in the United States
by Oxford University Press Inc., New York

British Library Cataloguing in Publication Data

Data available

Library of Congress Cataloging in Publication Data

Wallace, R. Jay.
Normativity and the will: selected papers on moral psychology and
practical reason / R. Jay Wallace.
p. cm.
1. Normativity (Ethics)   2. Will.   3. Practical reason.   I. Title.
BJ1458.3.W35 2006   153.8—dc22   2005033114

Typeset by Newgen Imaging Systems (P) Ltd., Chennai, India
Printed in Great Britain
on acid-free paper by
Biddles Ltd., King's Lynn, Norfolk

ISBN 978–0–19–928748–2
ISBN 978–0–19–928749–9 (Pbk.)

For Mom and Dean

Acknowledgments

The Introduction was written, and the collection as a whole prepared, with the generous support of a Research Award from the Alexander von Humboldt Foundation. Nicola Helferich provided helpful research assistance, and Gerardo Vildostegui prepared the index.

Contents

Introduction

Moral philosophy has turned increasingly to topics in moral psychology and the theory of normativity in recent years. But there are very different ways of approaching both of these clusters of issues. Some philosophers treat moral psychology as a largely empirical domain, dedicated to the description and explanation of human thought, emotion, and behavior, through methods that are broadly continuous with those of the sciences. The moral psychologist, on this conception, tries to get clear about what people are like as a matter of fact, ignoring for these purposes normative questions about how people ought to behave or what it would be valuable for them to do. On the other side, normativity is sometimes taken to constitute an autonomous intellectual realm, one that can be studied largely in abstraction from questions about human psychology. Normative considerations define ideals for human thought and action, and it is natural to suppose that our conception of the ideal should not be held hostage to messy facts about what human beings actually think and do.

There is no doubt something importantly right about the distinction between fact and value on which these approaches rely. It is one thing to ask what people are like, quite another to consider how they ought to behave. While acknowledging the distinction between these questions, however, I myself do not believe that they can effectively be addressed in isolation from each other. Normativity in the domain of practice is fundamentally about reasons for action, the considerations that count for and against actions in the perspectives of deliberation and advice. But reasons can be normative in this sense only if they are considerations that agents are able to acknowledge and to comply with, insofar as they are rational and are otherwise deliberating correctly. To the extent this is the case, the study of normativity in practice must attend to the psychological capacities that undergird normative response, and that make it possible for normative reasons to figure properly in the deliberations of the agents to whom they apply. Conversely, human motivational psychology distinctively involves capacities to respond to considerations whose normative significance for action the agent acknowledges, as well as motivations and emotions that can interfere with these forms of rational response. These reciprocal connections between normativity and motivation raise a series of large and difficult questions for philosophy, centering on the interpretation of our capacities for rational agency, the nature and conditions of normativity in general, and the possibilities for motivated departures from our own judgments about what we have reason to do.[1]

The present volume collects fourteen papers on these central questions in moral psychology and the theory of practical reason. All of the papers reflect my commitment to the general idea that normativity and moral psychology are best pursued together. They might be thought of as advertisements for this idea, attempts to explore the interpenetration of the normative and the psychological in a series of debates that lie at the heart of moral philosophy.

Substantively the essays are united in their allegiance to three broad claims:

(a) Rationalism in ethical theory, which holds that moral considerations are reasons for action.

(b) Realism in the theory of normativity, the thesis that there are facts of the matter about what we have reason to do that are prior to and independent of our normative convictions.

(c) An anti-Humean approach to motivational psychology, which denies that desires have a substantial role to play in explanations of rational action.

The essays that have been selected pursue these central philosophical issues from a variety of perspectives. I have organized them into three parts, to emphasize thematic continuities between individual papers; a brief account of each part follows.

1. REASON, DESIRE, AND THE WILL

This part addresses general issues about the relation between normative considerations and motivation. It collects five papers on these issues.

Chapter 1, 'How to Argue about Practical Reason', was written as a survey of contemporary approaches to practical reason. A main focus here is the relation between normative reasons for action and the dispositions and desires of the agents to whom they apply. Many philosophers, taking their inspiration from a perhaps inaccurate reading of Hume, have held that normative reasons for action must be grounded in the antecedent desires and dispositions of the agents to whom they apply. (This is what Bernard Williams has called the internal reasons model,[2] or 'internalism', as I shall refer to it.) Chapter 1 traces the intuitive appeal of this approach to the ideas that normative reasons must be capable of being acted on in deliberation, and that intentional action in turn involves states of

---

[1] For more on the interpenetration of normative and psychological issues in these domains, see my 'Moral Psychology', in Frank Jackson and Michael Smith (eds.), *The Oxford Handbook of Contemporary Philosophy* (Oxford: Oxford University Press, 2005), and 'Practical Reason', in Edward N. Zalta (ed.), *The Stanford Encyclopedia of Philosophy*, URL = http://plato.stanford.edu/entries/practical-reason/.

[2] See Bernard Williams, 'Internal and External Reasons', as reprinted in his *Moral Luck* (Cambridge, England: Cambridge University Press, 1981), 101–13.

desire. But the paper goes on to show why these considerations do not in fact support the internalist approach to normative reasons, identifying the more specific question that properly divides Humeans and their opponents about the conditions of normative reasons. This question concerns the explanation of motivation: internalists maintain that deliberation can give rise to a new motivation only if it begins in some sense from desires that are already to hand (in accordance with what I call the principle of 'desire-out, desire-in'), while externalists deny that practical reflection must accord with this principle.

Chapter 2, 'Three Conceptions of Rational Agency', is a later exploration of the basic idea that deliberation on our normative reasons must be capable of giving rise to corresponding motivations to action. The paper begins by noting that rational agents are not merely motivated in accordance with their normative reasons, but guided in their deliberation by their reflection on those reasons. The question is, what must be true about rational deliberation if it is to satisfy this 'guidance condition'? I identify and assess three frameworks for answering this question. Internalists hold that normative reasons are grounded in the antecedent desires of the agent, and they appeal to these desires to make sense of the capacity of deliberation to generate new motivations and actions (in accordance with the principle of 'desire-out, desire-in'). I argue, however, that this approach does not really do justice to the guidance condition, insofar as it leaves no room for genuinely normative thought to figure in deliberation. A second approach, which I call 'meta-internalism', does better in this respect, tracing deliberated revisions in our motivating attitudes to the operation of abstract or second-order dispositions that are partly constitutive of our standing as (rational) agents. But this approach comes to grief over cases of irrationality, in which we act in ways that conflict with our own judgments about our normative reasons. A third alternative, 'volitionalism' as I call it, rejects the empiricism about motivation that is implicit in the other two approaches, postulating motivating attitudes with respect to which the agent is fundamentally active. I offer a tentative defense of this approach, arguing that volitionalism can account for the guiding role of normativity in the deliberative reflections of rational agents, while leaving the right kind of space for cases in which we freely defect from our own normative views in action.

Chapter 3, 'Explanation, Deliberation, and Reasons', offers a slightly different perspective on the role of normative considerations in deliberation and action. The paper is a critical response to Jonathan Dancy's contention—developed in his book *Practical Reality*[3]—that the considerations we cite to explain motivation and action are not psychological states or facts, but rather normative considerations, as they struck the agent at the time of action. Dancy is correct to stress the role of normative reasons in relation to rational agency, but I argue that we can do justice to their significance without denying that explanations of action are a kind of

---

[3] Jonathan Dancy, *Practical Reality* (Oxford: Oxford University Press, 2000).

psychological explanation. To this end, I distinguish between the prospective standpoint of practical deliberation and advice, within which normative considerations are front and center, and the retrospective standpoint of explanation. From the latter standpoint, we consider an action that has already been performed, and ask why the agent carried it out. I suggest that the general form of an answer to this explanatory question will cite the agent's normative beliefs or convictions; these are psychological considerations, but ones that precisely capture or constitute the agent's normative point of view. (The discussions in Chapters 1 and 2 might be construed as addressing the question, what *further* psychological conditions must be satisfied in order for normative convictions of this kind to guide reflection and generate corresponding motivations to action?)

Chapters 4 and 5 continue the focus on the general connection between motivation and normativity, but they approach the connection from the other direction. Here the question is not about the role of normative considerations in guiding deliberation, but about the normative significance and implications of motivation itself. Chapter 4, 'Normativity and the Will', discusses the constructivist approach to the sources of normativity that has recently been developed by Christine Korsgaard. The basic constructivist idea is that normative principles are not prior to and independent of the will, but somehow constituted by it; but how should we understand the metaphor of construction that is central to this approach? I offer an interpretation of Korsgaard's constructivist program, and contrast it with a realist approach to normativity. According to the interpretation I propose, constructivists hold that a commitment to comply with principles of practical reason is built into every act of will, and that this element of commitment accounts for the idea that such principles are binding or normative for the agent. I argue, however, that a conception of commitment adequate to this theoretical task is elusive, and suggest that we do better to think about the will within the framework of a realist conception of normativity.

Chapter 5, 'Normativity, Commitment, and Instrumental Reason', continues to explore the interplay of the normative and the psychological in volition. The paper begins where Chapter 4 leaves off, with Korsgaard's claim that volition is to be understood in terms of principles that are essentially normative. Korsgaard contends that our activity as agents can be made sense of only if we take normative principles to be implicit in each act of willing. I show that the argument from activity fails, appealing to cases of *akrasia* to support the conclusion that one can be committed actively to achieving some end or goal, without believing that the end or goal would be valuable or justified. The remainder of the paper considers the principle of instrumental reason, which specifies that one should take the means that are necessary relative to one's ends. The challenge for an account of this principle is to explain why it applies even to acts of will that are not normative in Korsgaard's sense—why, that is, even *akratic* agents are subject to a kind of internal irrationality if they fail to take means that they know to be necessary for the attainment of their *akratic* ends.

My response to this challenge builds on the idea that intention or volitional commitment involves an element of belief: the belief, namely, that it is possible that one will attain the end one has set for oneself. If (as I contend) this idea is plausible, we can see why a minimally reflective agent would be subject to a kind of incoherence in belief if they failed to take the necessary means to their chosen ends. The instrumental principle thus derives from basic requirements of theoretical rationality, together with a plausible assumption about the nature of volition or intention. In a new postscript to this chapter I develop this cognitivist account of the instrumental principle further, defending it against some objections and alternatives that have recently been proposed. I emphasize in particular the role of the instrumental principle as a source of rational pressure that we feel and respond to when we recognize that a given means is necessary if we are to achieve the ends we have set ourselves to pursue.

2. RESPONSIBILITY, IDENTIFICATION, AND EMOTION

This part too collects five papers. Here the general focus is on issues of responsibility and identification, especially as they intersect with questions about the norms that apply to our actions and the rational and volitional capacities that enable compliance with such norms.

Chapter 6, 'Reason and Responsibility', takes as its starting point the general approach to moral accountability defended in my book *Responsibility and the Moral Sentiments*.[4] This approach holds that accountable agency is to be understood not in terms of freedom of will, but rather in terms of general rational powers or capacities, specifically those that enable us to grasp and respond to moral principles. But what if an agent who possesses these general powers of reflective self-control should lack compelling reason to do what morality prescribes? I argue that such agents would not be fully responsible for their failure to comply with moral principles in that case. The rational powers approach takes responsible agency to be grounded in our general capacities for critical reflection and self-determination. But if a given agent has no compelling reason to do the right thing, then even the most conscientious application of their general rational powers would not bring them to comply with the requirements of morality. I then address the question of whether people in general have good reason to comply with moral demands. I suggest that even if moral reasons are in some sense inescapable, that alone would not secure their normative grip on all agents. There

---

[4] R. Jay Wallace, *Responsibility and the Moral Sentiments* (Cambridge, Mass.: Harvard University Press, 1994).

is a further dimension of practical reason to consider, having to do with the relation between moral requirements and the demands of a good or a meaningful human life. If these two sources of norms cannot be reconciled with each other, then practical reason will be divided within itself; the result of such a division in practical reason would be that we are not fully to blame when we sacrifice morality for the sake of ends that are personally of great human significance.

Chapter 7, 'Moral Responsibility and the Practical Point of View', looks at the powers or capacities that underwrite moral responsibility, on the approach I favor, and in general make it possible for agents to comply with the normative requirements. I begin by suggesting that these capacities should be understood as including an active power of self-determination, in line with the volitionalist conception of rational agency sketched in Chapter 2. But this volitionalist picture seems potentially problematic. It will perhaps be surprising to readers of *Responsibility and the Moral Sentiments*, which argued that responsible agency does not require the kind of metaphysical freedom that incompatibilists have traditionally insisted on. Doesn't the postulation of an active power of self-determination make responsibility hostage to questions of freedom of the will, in ways that the book attempted to resist? Furthermore, whether or not it is compatible with the argument in *Responsibility and the Moral Sentiments*, the volitionalist conception of the will might appear independently implausible. It is reminiscent, for instance, of the problematic theory of agent-causation, according to which agents intervene in the causal order of nature from a position indeterminately external to it.

Chapter 7 addresses these worries. To this end, it invokes the distinction between the practical standpoint of deliberation and the theoretical standpoint of explanation drawn in Chapter 3, arguing that the capacity for volitional self-determination—like the other powers of reflective self-control—should be understood in relation to the distinctively practical point of view. Once we are clear about this, I contend, concerns about the mysteries of agent-causation can be disarmed. The theory of agent-causation goes wrong in supposing that the volitional capacities with which agents are equipped constitute a framework for explaining actions by reference to the agent who performed them; but this is not the right way to understand volitionalism. The paper goes on to consider whether the volitional picture involves a commitment to the kind of freedom that would be threatened by determinism. I argue, first, that the association of our volitional powers with the practical point of view does not automatically insulate them from any possible conflict with deterministic approaches to explanation. But I contend, second, that the only real threat from this direction would be posed by a distinctively psychological version of determinism, such as we have no real reason to take seriously.

This general way of conceptualizing the will involves a distinction between two classes of desire: the volitional forms of intention, choice, and decision that are themselves paradigms of agency, and states of inclination, longing, and attraction with respect to which we are merely passive. If we accept this distinction, questions naturally arise about the role of the second class of desires—given desires, as

we might call them—in relation to agency and intentional action. These questions are addressed in Chapters 8 and 9. Chapter 8, 'Addiction as Defect of the
Will', looks at the kinds of desires involved in addiction, and asks how we should
think about their influence on our capacities for deliberated agency. The paper
makes the case that the basic features of addiction can best be accommodated
within the framework of volitionalism, which rejects the assumption that intentional action is a simple causal function of the agent's beliefs and given desires,
operating in accordance with a 'hydraulic' conception of the mind. On the volitionalist alternative I favor, states of given desire involve, *inter alia*, the direction of
one's attention onto possibilities for action, as attractive or potentially valuable
along some dimension (e.g. as an opportunity for pleasure or visceral satisfaction).
Addiction renders one susceptible to given desires of this kind that are both
resilient and strong, but it is not clear how these notions of resilience and strength
are to be interpreted. I reject the causal understanding of them that is latent in the
hydraulic conception, defending in its place a phenomenological interpretation of
the phenomena of strength and resilience of given desire. This phenomenological
account is then deployed to explain the ability of addictive desires to interfere with
the good functioning of our deliberative capacities. In particular, I show that
addictive desires may affect the volitional as well as the cognitive side of rational
agency, and trace some implications of such 'defects of the will' for questions of
responsibility in this domain.

Chapter 9, 'Caring, Reflexivity, and the Structure of Volition', turns to a different phenomenon, that of identification. The pioneering work of Harry Frankfurt
has drawn attention to many important complexities of human agency, including
above all the possibilities for desire and intentional action from which the agent is
estranged. Frankfurt himself favors an approach to the twin phenomena of identification and estrangement that makes use of the notions of reflexivity and of
a hierarchy of desire. Chapter 9 is an extended response to Frankfurt's approach.
I argue that the idea of a hierarchy of desire, taken literally, distorts more than it
illuminates the phenomena with which Frankfurt is concerned. To improve on it,
we need to move away from the noncognitivism about given desire that seems
implicit in much of Frankfurt's work (and that has, I contend, contributed to its
appeal and influence). In its place, I recommend the quasi-perceptual conception
of given desire sketched in Chapter 8, and show how this conception leads to an
improved understanding of identification and estrangement. To identify with
a given desire is to affirm through reflection the normative content that the desire
presents, in ways that would remain stable if subjected to further critical scrutiny.
With this account in place, I turn next to the notions of caring and reflexivity that
have figured prominently in Frankfurt's more recent work. Among other things,
the paper argues that there is a distinctive context of eudaimonistic reflection—
already anticipated in the argument of Chapter 6—in which we deliberate reflexively
on the things that we care about, reflecting on their contribution to the goodness
of our own lives. I suggest, however, that we cannot capture the potential critical

force of this kind of reflection unless we depart from the noncognitivist assumptions about caring that Frankfurt evidently favors.

Questions about the relation between desire, emotion, and value are pursued within a very different context in Chapter 10, '*Ressentiment*, Value, and Self-Vindication: Making Sense of Nietzsche's Slave Revolt'. As its title suggests, this paper offers a sustained interpretation of Nietzsche's idea that modern moral consciousness has its origin in a slave revolt. This episode or process, as Nietzsche describes it, involves strong feelings of *ressentiment* that build to monstrous proportions in the psyches of the powerless masses, eventually giving birth to a new table of values—a democratic, leveling, universalistic conception of morality that challenges the older aristocratic values of good and bad. The fundamental question that is raised by this account concerns the relation it posits between *ressentiment* and the values to which that emotion is said to give birth. Most commentators interpret this causal nexus in strategic terms, assuming that the new moral values are adopted by the slavish masses as part of a plan to achieve revenge against the masters who have oppressed them. I argue that this way of thinking about the slave revolt is deeply problematic, and propose in its place an expressive interpretation of the slave revolt. The *ressentiment* of the masses gives them an emotional orientation to the social world that does not fundamentally make sense, so long as they accept the aristocratic values of good and bad. *Ressentiment* involves profound hostility to the very people who are, in terms of the aristocratic value scheme, paradigms of the good, and this combination of attitudes is essentially unstable and conflicted. According to the expressive account, the adoption of new values by the slavish serves to resolve this psychic tension, and the slave revolt can in this way be construed as the expression of slavish *ressentiment*.

The paper aims in the first instance to reconstruct Nietzsche's position, but it is not possible to pursue this goal without addressing systematic issues of independent interest in moral psychology and the theory of value. Reflection on Nietzsche's account helps us to understand how unconscious emotions can distort and corrupt evaluative reflection, leading to forms of moral thought that amount to ideology and false consciousness. Important in these processes, I suggest, is the widespread need people have to understand themselves and their world in ways that provide a kind of vindication of their position within it.

3. MORALITY AND OTHER NORMATIVE DOMAINS

This part collects four papers in which morality is in the foreground. Issues that are addressed include the structure and normative significance of morality, the relation between moral and other reasons, and the distinctive sources of moral motivation.

Chapter 11, 'Virtue, Reason, and Principle', grapples with John McDowell's account of the nature of moral reasons and moral reasoning. In a series of challenging and influential papers McDowell has drawn on both Wittgenstein and the Aristotelian tradition to defend an interpretation of morality as a domain of considerations that make rational claims on agents. Central to McDowell's approach is his denial that the deliberations of the virtuous agent can be reconstructed in terms of general principles that capture the rational requirements to which the agent responds. Grasp of the reasons provided by morality requires habituation into a comprehensive form of life, one whose requirements resist discursive formulation. Virtue, on this account of it, involves a responsiveness to reasons that are not fully intelligible to those who are not themselves virtuous already.

I offer an interpretation of this central idea, proposing that McDowell's conception of practical reason be understood on analogy with the phenomenon of connoisseurship. The virtuous agent, like the connoisseur, has a refined, quasi-perceptual capacity to make reasoned discriminations of a kind that can be justified on a case-by-case basis, but that resist capture in a set of general principles or norms applicable across the board. I argue that this represents a legitimate model of rational discrimination and response, but raise some questions about its applicability to morality as a normative domain. The connoisseurship model seems most plausible if we think of virtue as involving a comprehensive conception of how to live, something that would require a corresponding capacity for responding to a range of normative considerations too diverse and complex to permit perspicuous representation through general discursive principles. At least since the modern period, however, there has been a tendency to think of morality as a distinctive subdomain within the broader normative landscape, involving reasons that are binding on and accessible to people who accept a plurality of comprehensive conceptions of the good. This modern conception of the moral remains attractive, and I suggest that it goes together with the idea that moral requirements admit of discursive formulation in terms of principles accessible equally to all the members of pluralistic communities.

On the Aristotelian conception implicit in McDowell's approach, morality does not constitute a unified subdomain within the landscape of reasons. Virtuous agents have a special, habituated capacity for responding to the normative considerations that bear on their choices, but there is nothing presumptively moral about this capacity, nor is there any nonsuperficial way of carving up the reasons to which the virtuous respond into moral and nonmoral classes. This deeply pluralistic understanding of normativity contrasts with the conception implicit in such modern theories as utilitarianism and Kantianism, which take morality to collect a unified set of reasons for action. Among the most impressive and influential recent unifying theories of this kind is the contractualism of T. M. Scanlon, which forms the subject of Chapter 12 ('Scanlon's Contractualism'). According to Scanlon, the unity implicit in morality should be understood in terms of the notion of justification to others; moral considerations are genuine reasons for action, and what these reasons have in common is their connection to principles for the general regulation of behavior that permit us to justify our actions to those potentially affected by them. Actions are morally wrong, for instance, if they are prohibited by principles of this kind that nobody could reasonably reject, and their being wrong in this way is something that constitutes a strong reason against them.

My discussion of Scanlon's theory focuses on four different sets of issues. I begin with the conception of rational agency that forms the background to Scanlon's account. This conception—a version of what I call 'meta-internalism' in Chapter 2—holds that intentions, like beliefs, are attitudes that are intrinsically sensitive to our normative judgments. I argue that this approach exaggerates the continuities between theoretical and practical reason, in a way that does not do full justice to the kinds of irrationality that seem possible in the practical sphere.[5] It also, I contend, leads to a distorted interpretation of our responsibility for the kinds of wayward desires and emotions discussed in Chapter 9, which persist in the face of one's reflective rejection of their contents. Scanlon treats such attitudes as fully attributable to us, insofar as they are open to assessment in terms of reasons; but in cases in which wayward desires and emotions resist our best efforts at reflective scrutiny and control, it seems to me they do not constitute a ground for moral blame. A further element in Scanlon's comprehensive theory is his 'buck-passing' account of the value, which holds that goodness is not to be understood as a substantive property that grounds reasons for action. Though broadly sympathetic to this way of thinking about the relation between the normative and the evaluative, I raise some questions about the specific version of the buck-passing account that Scanlon seems to favor.

The core of Scanlon's contractualism is his suggestion that the contractualist formula accounts for the reason-giving force of what he calls the morality of right and wrong, in a way that supports the idea that morality in this sense is a unified normative domain. Scanlon himself traces moral reasons to the value of the distinctive kind of relationship with other people that compliance with moral principles makes possible. I develop this suggestion by situating the appeal to what Scanlon calls mutual recognition within the context of the kind of eudaimonistic reflection identified in Chapters 6 and 9. Attention to the valuable forms of human relationship made possible by compliance with moral principles helps us to see how compliance with such principles can make our own lives better. But it is not clear that this line of thought alone vindicates the basic thought that the morality of right and wrong is a unified normative realm. Scanlon himself accepts a pluralistic account of the broader domain of reasons, and against this

---

[5] Compare the discussion of theoretical and practical irrationality in Chapter 5, section 2 of this volume.

background the question can be pressed of whether morality is just a convenient way of collecting a variety of reasons that exhibit no interesting substantive unity. I propose some tentative answers to this question on behalf of contractualism, which seems to me the most promising unifying story about morality on the contemporary scene.

Among the most important recent defenders of a thoroughgoing pluralism about the normative is Joseph Raz. According to what he calls the 'classical view', there is no context-independent way of categorizing reasons as distinctively moral in nature. Normative reasons are grounded in values, and there is a diversity in the realm of the normative that reflects the deep variety of ways in which the actions open to us can be valuable. It is a consequence of this picture, as Raz develops it, that there is no interesting global contrast to be drawn between morality and self-interest, a position that seems to undermine the challenge to morality that is posed by one traditional form of skepticism about its normative significance. I take Raz's view as my starting point in Chapter 13, 'The Rightness of Acts and the Goodness of Lives'. This paper develops further the idea—presented in Chapters 6, 9, and 12—that there is a distinctive perspective of eudaimonistic practical reflection, and that the normative importance of morality may be threatened if moral considerations cannot be justified from this point of view. I offer an interpretation of the terms in which eudaimonistic reflection is framed, distinguishing it from the standpoint of narrowly egoistic concern about our own interests and well-being. Against Raz, I contend that the eudaimonistic perspective collects a significant set of normative considerations, and show that an appeal to such considerations lies behind the important challenge to morality presented in the work of Bernard Williams. To respond adequately to this challenge, it needs to be shown that compliance with moral requirements can make a direct contribution to the goodness or meaning of the agent's own life. I argue that part of the appeal of traditional unifying approaches to morality, such as utilitarianism and Scanlon's contractualism, is that they help us to understand how acting morally can contribute along this important dimension of normative assessment.

Chapter 14, 'Moral Reasons and Moral Fetishes', explores the interplay of the normative and the psychological as it bears on the interpretation of distinctively moral motivation. Rationalists hold that morality is a set of unconditional (or external) reasons for action, considerations that have normative significance for agents in a way that is not dependent on their subjective interests and desires. Proponents of this approach have held that its denial would render the concern to act rightly a kind of fetish. I take up this charge, with the aim of getting clear about what the fetishism objection comes to, and assessing its force against anti-rationalist accounts of morality. A form of motivation may be said to be fetishistic, I suggest, when it cannot be understood as a response that is merited by its proper object. I develop this interpretation, contrasting it with Michael Smith's contention that the concern to act rightly is fetishistic if it is understood *de dicto* rather than *de re*. I argue that the objection, on the account of it I favor, poses a significant challenge to anti-rationalists. To parry it, the anti-rationalist must either defend a global nihilism about normative reasons, or abandon the distinctively anti-rationalist account of moral motivation. Normative and psychological issues are thus revealed, once again, to be inextricably intertwined, insofar as a plausible and attractive conception of moral motivation rests on normative assumptions about the character and conditions of moral reasons.

PART I

REASON, DESIRE, AND THE WILL

1

How to Argue about Practical Reason

What are the comparative roles of reason and the passions in explaining human motivation and behavior? Accounts of practical reason divide on this central question, with proponents of different views falling into rationalist and Humean camps. By 'rationalist' accounts of practical reason, I mean accounts which make the characteristically Kantian claim that pure reason can be practical in its issue. To reject this view is to take the Humean position that reasoning or ratiocination is not by itself capable of giving rise to a motivation to act. This alternative position is most famously expressed in Hume's polemical assertion that 'reason is, and ought only to be the slave of the passions' in influencing the will or moving us to act.[1]

To fix terms, let us say that a process of thought is an instance of reasoning or ratiocination just in case it is governed by the principles or norms of rationality. To say that a principle or norm *governs* a process of thought is in turn to make an explanatory claim: it is to say, not just that the process of thought is in accordance with the rational principle or norm, but that the process of thought occurs *because* the person believes it to be in accordance with the principle or norm. Thus, if we say that it is a principle or norm of rationality that people should not hold inconsistent sets of beliefs, this does not just mean that they revise those sets of beliefs which they know to be inconsistent, but that they revise them *because* they know those sets of beliefs to be inconsistent.

In these terms, the dispute between the Humean and the rationalist is a dispute about the capacity of rational principles or norms to contribute to explanations of motivation. The rationalist holds that such rational principles have a *primary* role to play in the explanation of motivation, that the psychological processes which originally give rise to motivation can be processes which are governed—in the sense I have specified—by the principles or norms of reason. By contrast, the

Originally published in *Mind*, 99 (July 1990), 355–85. Copyright © Oxford University Press 1990. Reprinted by permission of Oxford University Press. I have had helpful comments on predecessors of this paper from Simon Blackburn, John Collins, Samuel Freeman, Gilbert Harman, Sally Haslanger, Katharina Kaiser, Wolfgang Mann, and an audience at the University of Pennsylvania. I owe a special debt to Michael Smith, with whom I have had the benefit of many stimulating discussions about practical reason. Work on this paper was partially supported by a grant from the Research Council of the University of Pennsylvania.

[1] See Hume, *A Treatise of Human Nature*, ed. Selby-Bigge, 2nd edn. (Oxford: Clarendon Press, 1978), 415.

Humean maintains that such rational principles never have a primary role to play in the explanation of motivation or the fixing of our ends. Rather, the explanatory contribution they make is exclusively secondary, accounting for the extension of motivational influence (for example, along means/end lines), but never explaining the original formation of motivation.

The significance of this dispute about practical reason lies in its connection with central issues in moral philosophy, concerning the nature and scope of moral requirements. It is a common thought that moral requirements, if they are to provide reasons for action, must be capable of guiding behavior, leading those who are aware of the requirements to be motivated in accordance with them. (This is, presumably, one thing that is meant by the multiply ambiguous word 'internalism'.) If we combine this internalist position with the Humean picture of practical reason, however, it seems to follow that moral requirements can only provide an agent with reason to act if they are appropriately related to the agent's antecedent desires; for all motivation and behavior, on the Humean view, must be explained by reference to the agent's given, prior desires. The resulting account represents moral behavior as dependent on the agent's existing dispositions, in a way that could restrict the scope of moral reasons (since the required prior desires may not be universally distributed). A Kantian approach to practical reason, by contrast, suggests a different picture of the psychological bases of moral behavior, and a straightforward development of the idea that moral requirements are universal or inescapable in their scope. It does this by opening up the possibility that there are processes of pure reasoning or ratiocination which can explain moral behavior by themselves, and which could equally lead all agents, regardless of their background desires, to be motivated to act on moral requirements.

All of this should be familiar to students of the history of philosophical ethics since Hume. Indeed, so familiar has it become that one might reasonably be skeptical whether there is anything to be contributed on the topic which has not already been said. In the event, however, such skepticism has not deterred contemporary philosophers from entering the fray, and recent years have seen a flurry of philosophical discussions purporting to defend or refute the different approaches to practical reason. My aim in this essay is to sort through these recent discussions, with an eye to reaching a clear assessment of the current state of argument between the opposing camps. I hope to show that recent work has in fact helped to advance the old debate between Humeans and rationalists. For one thing, it has become increasingly clear that the appeal of the Humean position is linked to the teleological character of intentional action, consideration of which suggests an *a priori* argument for the Humean claim that action must be explained ultimately in terms of desires. Rationalists have generally not paid sufficient attention to these teleological considerations and the *a priori* arguments they suggest, and this has made their pronouncements about the possibility of pure practical reason vulnerable. Or so I will suggest.

My own view is that the rationalist position can, in the end, be sustained against the challenge of these Humean arguments. To see why, however, it will be necessary to get clear about what is really at stake in the debate about practical reason. A further aim of my discussion will accordingly be to sharpen our understanding of the issue that divides Humeans and rationalists. Here, I think it will be helpful to turn to the somewhat less recent work of Thomas Nagel, which contains important suggestions about how the issue dividing Humeans and rationalists should be conceived. This is, or ought to be, familiar territory—Nagel's work has hardly wanted for readers. But the issues are complicated, and Nagel himself has neither explained nor developed his proposals adequately. Hence, despite the influence his work has enjoyed, its significance for the debate about practical reason remains rather poorly understood. A clearer account of what is at stake in the debate, which draws on and develops Nagel's suggestions, should help to reveal the inadequacy of recent arguments for the Humean view, and lead to an improved understanding of how we should be thinking, and arguing, about practical reason.

1.

Rationalist accounts of practical reason claim that principles or norms of reason can play a primary role in the explanation of action and motivation. In an incisive recent discussion, Christine Korsgaard has distinguished two kinds of skepticism about this rationalist position.[2] *Content* skepticism, as she describes it, is doubt about whether specific principles or norms of rationality are sufficient, by themselves, to guide practical reflection and to explain motivation and action. *Motivational* skepticism, by contrast, is not directed at specific proposals about the content of rational principles and norms. Rather, it purports to offer general grounds for doubting whether there could be such a thing as pure practical reason, grounds which are antecedent to consideration of rationalist proposals about the norms or principles of reason, and which turn on the alleged incapacity of reason to give rise to motivation.

Korsgaard herself rejects motivational skepticism. She says: 'motivational considerations do not provide any reason, in advance of specific proposals, for skepticism about practical reason'.[3] In support of this conclusion, Korsgaard suggests that motivational skepticism typically rests on a misinterpretation of the internalist requirement on practical reasons.[4] Humeans, she contends, often construe internalism as the requirement that rational considerations (or reasons) necessarily succeed in motivating us. So construed, internalism would lead fairly

---

[2] Christine M. Korsgaard, 'Skepticism about Practical Reason', *Journal of Philosophy*, 83 (1986), 5–25. [3] Ibid. 25.
[4] Ibid. 15.

directly to motivational skepticism, since it is doubtful that there are any rational considerations which *necessarily* succeed in motivating us, independently of our desires. Korsgaard argues, however, that this is a misinterpretation of internalism, which does not require that reasons necessarily succeed in motivating us, but only that they 'succeed in motivating us insofar as we are rational'.[5] This, however, is a fairly trivial condition on reasons, which does not place any *a priori* constraints on the possible norms of practical rationality. Whether a candidate principle could motivate rational agents depends on what it is to be rational, and that in turn depends on what the norms or principles of reason are. Hence, Korsgaard concludes, 'motivational skepticism must always be based on content skepticism';[6] it has no independent force.

This conclusion, if correct, would already be a kind of victory for the rationalist approach. Motivational skepticism, as Korsgaard describes it, purports to offer a general argument against the very possibility of a principle or norm of pure practical reason. But if there is no such argument, then it is already possible that pure reason might be practical in its issue, and this, in its weakest form, *is* the rationalist position. A more substantial victory for the rationalist, however, would require specification of the norms or principles of practical reason. Here, as Korsgaard notes, the internalist requirement entails that rationalist proposals about the norms or principles of practical reason will have psychological implications, telling us something about what it would be like to be rational.[7] Some proponents of the rationalist approach, notably including Thomas Nagel, have seen in these psychological implications of internalism a fertile source of arguments in favor of specific rationalist proposals. Focusing on the case of prudence, Nagel argues that this class of motivations can better be explained in terms of principles or norms of reason than on the Humean assumption that motivation always has desire at its source.[8] His strategy is to show that the psychological implications of rationalist accounts, for the motivation of ideally rational agents, are more plausible than those of alternative, Humean accounts.

If we are to conceive the debate in this way, however, it must indeed be the case that there is no reason for questioning the very possibility of a rationalist explanation of motivation. On this point, Korsgaard's own argument seems to me too swift. She takes it that internalism will be seen as innocuous, for the rationalist, once it is correctly interpreted as a thesis about the motivations of the fully rational agent.

---

[5] 'Skepticism about Practical Reason', 15.   [6] Ibid. 6.   [7] Ibid. 23–5.

[8] Thomas Nagel, *The Possibility of Altruism* (Princeton: Princeton University Press, 1978), chs. vi–viii. Nagel's discussion of prudence is guardedly endorsed by Philippa Foot, in 'Reasons for Action and Desires', as reprinted in her *Virtues and Vices* (Oxford: Blackwell, 1978), 148–56; and there is a similar account of the rationality of prudence in Martin Hollis, *The Cunning of Reason* (Cambridge, England: Cambridge University Press, 1987), ch. 6. Derek Parfit offers some powerful objections to accounts of this sort in his discussion of the self-interest theory of practical rationality, in *Reasons and Persons* (Oxford: Oxford University Press, 1984), pt 2. See also Richard Kraut, 'The Rationality of Prudence', *Philosophical Review*, 81 (1972), 351–9; and Janet Broughton, 'The Possibility of Prudence', *Philosophical Studies*, 43 (1983), 253–66.

But rationalism is not simply a stipulative claim, about the motivations that the fully rational agent will happen to have; it also makes an explanatory claim, to the effect that the rational agent's motivations can be explained in terms of norms or principles of correct reasoning. As I show in what follows, there is something about the teleological character of motivation that has seemed to rule out the possibility of such explanations in principle, and so to provide an *a priori* argument for motivational skepticism about the rationalist approach. It is this argument, and not simply a misunderstanding of the internalist requirement, that accounts for the persistence of Humean skepticism about the very possibility of pure practical reason. Only once this argument is understood, and conclusively laid to rest, can we proceed to assess the plausibility of specific rationalist proposals about the content of the principles or norms of reason.

2.

The *a priori* argument I want to consider may be called the teleological argument, because it takes as its starting point the essentially teleological character of both motivation and intentional action. In saying that these are teleological phenomena, I mean that the person who acts intentionally, or who is motivated so to act, is in a goal-directed state. Any psychological explanation of these phenomena must account for the fact that to act intentionally, or to be motivated so to act, is necessarily to be in a goal-directed state. The teleological argument aims to show that conformity to rational principles cannot alone account for this fact.

The argument—which has been given its clearest and most vigorous statement in a recent discussion by Michael Smith[9]—proceeds as follows. To be in a goal-directed state, it is claimed, is to be in a distinctive kind of psychological condition. Specifically, it is to be in a state whose content is not meant to match or represent the way things are in the world, but which is such that the world is to be made to match or fit the content of the state.[10] This reflects itself in the fact that people who are in a goal-directed state will not, in general, give up the goal, upon learning that it has not been realized in the world, but will instead take steps to change the world so that the goal can be realized. The question arises, however, as

---

[9] See Michael Smith, 'The Humean Theory of Motivation', *Mind*, 96 (1987), 36–61. Smith's article makes the significant contribution (which I have followed) of formulating the argument in terms of claims about the 'direction of fit' of psychological states, vis-à-vis the world. I suspect that similar considerations, less cogently expressed, have historically tended to move proponents of the Humean approach. They also seem to lie behind the common thesis that intention entails desire; for a recent discussion of this idea, see Robert Audi, 'Intending, Intentional Action, and Desire', in Joel Marks (ed.), *The Ways of Desire* (Chicago: Precedent Publishing, 1986), 17–38.

[10] On the idea that psychological states may be differentiated according to their 'direction of fit' with the world, see e.g. G. E. M. Anscombe, *Intention* (Ithaca: Cornell University Press, 1963), sects. 36, 40; Bernard Williams, 'Consistency and Realism', as reprinted in his *Problems of the Self*

to what it is to be in a psychological state which has this peculiar direction of fit vis-à-vis the world; and a plausible answer to this question must hold that, whatever else is involved in being in a goal-directed state, it cannot simply be a matter of having a certain belief or set of beliefs. Beliefs are precisely those psychological states which aim to match or represent the world, and their direction of fit is therefore just the converse of that which characterizes goal-directed states. Some other kind of state must thus be present, whenever one acts intentionally or is motivated so to act. Moreover, it is plausible to suppose that these further goal-directed states will characteristically be constituted by desires; for there is a general conception of desires according to which they are the psychological states one is in whenever one is in a state such that the world must be made to fit the content of the state (rather than vice-versa).[11]

This argument, which looks fairly strong as far as it goes, establishes that beliefs alone cannot account for motivations to action, but that desires must also be present whenever an agent is so motivated. The Humean, however, wishes to draw the stronger—or at any rate, different—conclusion that we cannot account adequately for motivation and intentional action solely in terms of the following of rational principles or norms, and to reach this conclusion on the basis of the teleological argument it is necessary to make some further assumptions.[12] The most important such assumption is the following: that rational principles will only be capable of contributing to the explanation of motivation to the extent that desires are not implicated in motivation. This assumption seems to be part of a broader picture of rationality, according to which reasoning and ratiocination are associated exclusively with the cognitive side of human psychology—that is, with beliefs and relations among one's beliefs—and contrasted with such nonrational

(Cambridge, England: Cambridge University Press, 1973), 187–206, at 203–5; John Searle, *Intentionality* (Cambridge, England: Cambridge University Press, 1983), 7–9; and Richard Wollheim, *The Thread of Life* (Cambridge, Mass.: Harvard University Press, 1984), 52–3. Talk about 'direction of fit' applies literally to propositions; its application to psychological states may seem metaphorical or otherwise problematic. For attempts to explain and to defend talk about the 'direction of fit' of propositional attitudes, see Andrew Woodfield, 'Desire, Intentional Content and Teleological Explanation', *Proceedings of the Aristotelian Society*, 82 (1981–2), 69–88, at 82–6; and Smith, 'The Humean Theory of Motivation', sect. 6.

[11] The conception in question is dispositional (but nonbehaviorist). See e.g. the dispositional conceptions of desire sketched by Richard B. Brandt and Jaegwon Kim, in 'Wants as Explanations of Actions', *Journal of Philosophy*, 60 (1963), 253–66; and by William P. Alston, in 'Motives and Motivation', in Paul Edwards (ed.), *The Encyclopedia of Philosophy* (New York: Macmillan and Free Press, 1967). Apparent counter-examples to the claim that goal-directed states are always realized by desires—such as hopes and wishes—are plausibly understood as involving an element of desiring; on this point, see Wayne Davis, 'Two Senses of Desire', in Joel Marks (ed.), *The Ways of Desire*, 63–82, at 64. Some philosophers, such as Brandt and Kim, find it more felicitous to use the term 'want' to refer to the general, dispositional conception of desire, reserving the term 'desire' for appetitive states which have a distinctive phenomenology; but nothing significant hangs on this terminological issue.

[12] This gets obscured in Smith's discussion, because he is content for the most part to represent the Humean view as the claim that explanatory reasons for action are partly constituted by desires. This formulation, however, does not bring out adequately the central point at issue between the Humean and the rationalist, which is the extent to which rational processes of thought—those which are governed by rational principles or norms—can contribute to the explanation of motivation.

states as desires and emotions (what Hume refers to collectively as 'the passions'). Hume himself endorses some version of this picture in the *Treatise*.[13] He distinguishes between the passions, as 'original existences', and those states of the understanding which admit of truth and falsity, suggesting that the latter states are alone the province of rationality. But this picture, when combined with the teleological argument, appears to make the Humean conclusion irresistible: if desires are necessarily present on occasions of motivation, and if desires are not themselves rational psychological states, what scope can there possibly be for the rational explanation of motivation and intentional action?

This, in outline, is the teleological argument for the Humean position. If sound, it would constitute an *a priori* argument against the very possibility of a rationalist account of practical reason, for it would show that rational principles or norms cannot contribute to the primary explanation of motivations, in the way the rationalist supposes. Motivation, being a teleological phenomenon, requires the presence of desire, and desires are simply beyond the range of explanation in terms of rational principles or norms.[14]

3.

If we are to leave open the possibility of a rationalist account of practical reason, some response to the teleological argument will have to be made. In fact I think there are two strategies that might be followed in responding to the teleological argument. One strategy would be to question the conception of desire that figures in the argument. In particular, we might challenge the Humean assumption that to be in a teleological or goal-directed state is necessarily to be in a state of desire. Though some have followed this strategy, it does not seem a very promising line to take, because the conception of desire underlying the teleological argument is independently more plausible than the alternative accounts that have been proposed.[15] For this reason, I think that a different strategy will have to be pursued.

---

[13] Bk. II, pt. III, sect. iii (p. 415). I assume here that when Hume describes the passions as original existences, he is not necessarily denying that they have propositional content, but only denying that their content is 'representational'—such as aims to fit the way the world is. For discussion of this and other possible interpretations, see Mark Platts, 'Hume and Morality as a Matter of Fact', *Mind* 97 (1988), 189–204, sects. 6–9.

[14] This teleological aspect of action-explanations is entirely left out of account in the argument which Richard Warner gives for the coherence of a rationalist account of motivation, in *Freedom, Enjoyment and Happiness* (Ithaca: Cornell University Press, 1987), 42–5. Warner describes a thought experiment in which we are to imagine a creature which takes thoughts as inputs and produces behavior as output; the coherence of the description is then taken to show that a rationalist account is at least possible. But the description is coherent only if we interpret the creature's behavior as mere bodily movement rather than as intentional action. The point of the teleological argument is that it is *not* coherent to suppose that intentional action could take place in the absence of a state of desire.

[15] The alternative accounts treat desires—or at any rate, 'genuine' desires, as opposed to mere formal desires—as states that have a distinctive phenomenology: see e.g. Mark Platts, *Ways of Meaning* (London: Routledge and Kegan Paul, 1979), ch. 10; and Don Locke, 'Beliefs, Desires and

The immediate conclusion of the teleological argument, it should be recalled, is that a person cannot simply be in a state of belief, on an occasion when he acts intentionally or is motivated to act intentionally; some state of wanting or desiring is additionally required. As I said earlier, however, this conclusion by itself is not yet damaging to the rationalist, or supportive of a Humean account of practical reason. To derive a Humean moral from the teleological argument, it is necessary to make the further assumption that the presence of desire precludes the rational explanation of motivation; that because the desires involved in motivation are themselves nonrational states, there is no scope for distinctively rational principles to enter into the explanation of motivation. The second and more promising strategy for challenging the Humean is to question this crucial assumption.

To understand the problem with this assumption, however, it will be necessary to provide a clearer account of what the debate between the Humean and the rationalist is all about. Now I suspect—though I am not certain about this—that the key to a proper understanding of the debate is to be found in chapter V of Thomas Nagel's book, *The Possibility of Altruism.* I say I am unsure about this, because Nagel's account of the debate turns on distinctions and concepts that are not adequately explained; certainly, his discussion has not prevented his readers from continuing to misunderstand the issue that divides Humeans and rationalists. In what follows I shall develop an interpretation of that issue which is at least broadly inspired by Nagel's discussion, with the aim of making more perspicuous than Nagel himself succeeded in doing the flaw in the Humean appropriation of the teleological argument.

Nagel starts by accepting the immediate conclusion of the teleological argument, and the associated conception of desires as states that realize one's having of an aim or goal. He says, for instance, that '*whatever* may be the motivation for someone's intentional pursuit of a goal, it becomes in virtue of his pursuit *ipso facto* appropriate to ascribe to him a desire for the goal'.[16] Desires, then, must always be present on occasions of motivation and intentional action. But a further issue arises, concerning the explanatory role of desires in accounting for motivation, and the resolution of this issue is absolutely crucial to the Humean interpretation of the teleological argument. Nagel raises this further issue by drawing a distinction between two broad categories of desires, which he calls 'motivated' and 'unmotivated'.[17] He explains the distinction in the following terms. Unmotivated desires are desires which simply assail us or come over us (Nagel cites as examples the appetites and certain emotions); whereas motivated desires are '*arrived at* by

---

Reasons for Action', *American Philosophical Quarterly*, 19 (1982), 241–9. Smith effectively criticizes the idea that all genuine desires are states with a distinctive phenomenology, in 'The Humean Theory of Motivation', sect. 5. See also Alston, 'Motives and Motivation', 402–3.

[16] *The Possibility of Altruism*, 29.

[17] Ibid. Various historical precedents for this distinction have been cited. Nagel himself now claims that it has affinities with the Kantian distinction between inclination and interest; see his *The View from Nowhere* (New York: Oxford University Press, 1986), 151 n. 3. N. J. H. Dent suggests a

decision and after deliberation'.[18] Desires of both types are presumably susceptible of explanation—we can, for instance, explain the onset of an unmotivated desire to eat by citing the physiological factors associated with a lack of food. But only motivated desires admit of what Nagel calls 'rational or motivational explanation'.[19]

Now this account of the difference between motivated and unmotivated desires is not very helpful. It suggests that motivated desires will always be formed after a prior episode of deliberation, and that all unmotivated desires are like bouts of animal lust in 'assailing' the agent unfortunate enough to be in their grip; but I do not think this can have been the kind of distinction that Nagel was trying to draw. For one thing, Nagel's distinction looked like offering a comprehensive typology of desires; but a great many of the desires that we ascribe to people are neither states that simply assail the person who has them, nor states that the person goes into following an episode of deliberation. Consider, for instance, the important class of long-term or dispositional desires that are formed as a result of moral education, and help to constitute a person's overall character: these can hardly be said to 'assail' the person who has them, like lust or thirst, but at the same time they are not arrived at by decision and after deliberation, either.

More promising, in my view, is Nagel's suggestion that what marks the difference between motivated and unmotivated desires is the kind of explanation to which each is susceptible; in particular, the idea that motivated desires are distinctive in admitting of what he calls 'rational or motivational explanation'. So far, however, this idea is merely a suggestion, for Nagel's own discussion does nothing to clarify the important notion of rational or motivational explanation. Moreover, without a precise explanation of this notion, the significance of the distinction between motivated and unmotivated desires is apt to remain obscure—a point which I shall have occasion to illustrate, later in my discussion. Let me now offer my own account of the notion of rational or motivational explanation, and say in terms of it what is significant about the distinction between motivated and unmotivated desires.[20]

The basic idea, I would suggest, is that when a person has a motivated desire, it will always be possible to explain that desire in a way that shows it to be *rationalized* by other propositional attitudes that the person has. That is, psychological

different parallel between Nagel's distinction and the distinction in Aristotle and Aquinas between 'deliberated appetites' and 'sense appetites', in *The Moral Psychology of the Virtues* (Cambridge, England: Cambridge University Press, 1984), ch. 4. I am myself doubtful how close Nagel's distinction really is to either of these antecedents—the category of motivated desires is much more encompassing than the earlier counterparts, at least on the interpretation of it I shall go on to offer.

[18] *The Possibility of Altruism*, 29.   [19] Ibid.

[20] There is, in fact, a variety of ways of distinguishing between different kinds of desires, many of which are close to being coextensive with the distinction between motivated and unmotivated desires, as I shall construe it. Consider, e.g., Stuart Hampshire's distinction between desires which are, and desires which are not, mediated by descriptions or conceptions, in *Freedom of the Individual*, expanded edn. (Princeton: Princeton University Press, 1975), ch. 2; Stephen Schiffer's distinction

explanation of motivated desires is not restricted to causal claims, about the states or conditions that trigger the onset of the desire. Rather, motivated desires also (and *necessarily*) admit of a different kind of psychological explanation, in which the propositional content of the desire is shown to be rationalized or justified by the content of other of the person's attitudes.[21] Of course, it is possible for one propositional attitude to be rationalized by other attitudes of the agent's, without the rationalizing attitudes *explaining* the formation of the state that is rationalized; a rationalizing explanation requires, more strongly, that the person should be in the rationalizing state *because* he has certain other attitudes that rationalize that state. But it is plausible to think that motivated desires can be explained in this distinctive, rationalizing way. Thus—to take Nagel's own simple example—if Wotan's desire to shop for groceries is a motivated desire, then there will be an explanation of it that reveals it to be rationalized by other propositional attitudes that Wotan has: for example, a desire to eat something, a belief that there is nothing at home to eat, plus various other beliefs of Wotan's (about grocery stores, shopping, etc.). It is because Wotan has these rationalizing attitudes that he forms the motivated desire to shop; but at the same time those rationalizing attitudes provide *reasons* for Wotan's motivated desire.[22]

To put the point this way, however, is potentially misleading. Rationalizing explanations, as I have introduced the notion, explain propositional attitudes in terms of other attitudes whose content rationalizes the state which is to be explained, where rationalization is construed as the provision of reasons or justifications. Strictly speaking, however, the *contents* of desires never provide reasons or justifications for other propositional attitudes; nor do they themselves appear directly susceptible of rationalizing explanation. For example, the propositional content of Wotan's desire to shop for groceries—that is, 'that he (Wotan) shop for groceries'—simply seems to have the wrong form either to justify, or be justified by, other propositions; read literally, it is not even in the indicative mood.[23]

---

between reason-providing and reason-following desires, in 'A Paradox of Desire', *American Philosophical Quarterly*, 13 (1976), 195–203; and the distinction Wayne Davis draws between volitive and appetitive desires, in 'Two Senses of Desire'. The near coextensiveness of these various distinctions may make it tempting to suppose that they are all, at bottom, different ways of marking the same basic difference between kinds of desires; but I suspect that this is not in fact the case. At any rate, my discussion in the text is meant only to give a sharper interpretation of a single distinction which is especially important for the debate about practical reason, that between what Nagel has called motivated and unmotivated desires.

[21] I do not mean to suggest that rationalizing explanations may not also be cause-giving explanations. For a useful recent discussion of this point, and of the nature of rationalizing explanation more generally, see Philip Pettit, 'Broad-Minded Explanation and Psychology', in Pettit and John McDowell (eds.), *Subject, Thought, and Context* (Oxford: Clarendon Press, 1986), 17–58.

[22] There is an obvious analogy here with the case of beliefs. Many of a person's beliefs are held for reasons, where the reasons are other propositional attitudes which both rationalize the belief and explain the holding of it.

[23] Michael Smith made me see this point. It raises a potential problem for all accounts which hold that some desires are held for reasons, such as those of Stephen Schiffer, in 'A Paradox of Desire', and Wayne Davis, in 'Two Senses of Desire'.

It would be a mistake to conclude from this, however, that desires cannot enter into rationalizing explanations at all. To see how they can, we need only note that desires are characteristically associated with evaluative beliefs. Thus, if Wotan wants to shop for groceries, it will—in the normal case, at least[24]—be legitimate to ascribe to him an evaluative belief, to the effect that shopping for groceries is (*prima facie*) desirable.[25] The content of this evaluative belief, however, can straightforwardly enter into relations of rationalization and justification with other contents of propositional attitudes. For example, we might deploy the schema of the practical syllogism to explain the belief that shopping for groceries is (*prima facie*) desirable in terms of the following, further propositional attitudes: the evaluative belief that eating is (*prima facie*) desirable; and the belief that in order to eat it is necessary to go shopping for groceries.[26] The content of these propositional attitudes justifies or provides a reason for the conclusion that shopping for groceries is (*prima facie*) desirable. And, a person might have reached this conclusion *because* that person holds these further, rationalizing beliefs.

Evaluative beliefs can in this way straightforwardly enter into relations of rationalizing explanation. If this much can be admitted, however, then we have a way of drawing the distinction between motivated and unmotivated desires in terms of the notion of rationalizing explanation. We may say, to start with, that motivated desires are desires whose associated evaluative beliefs admit of a rationalizing explanation. Furthermore, when the evaluative belief associated with a desire admits of a rationalizing explanation in this way, the factors which justify and support the belief can equally be said to justify and support the desire associated with the belief; so that the reasons for the belief may be considered reasons for acquiring the desire as well. To give a rationalizing *explanation* of the desire in terms of these reasons, it need only be supposed in addition that the desire has

---

[24] The abnormal cases are those in which one desires something which one does not value at all, not even instrumentally. Such cases are discussed by Harry Frankfurt, in 'Freedom of the Will and the Concept of a Person', as reprinted in his *The Importance of What We Care About* (Cambridge, England: Cambridge University Press, 1988), 11–25; and Gary Watson, 'Free Agency', as reprinted in Watson (ed.), *Free Will* (Oxford: Oxford University Press, 1982), 96–110. See also Frankfurt's more recent discussion 'Identification and Wholeheartedness', as reprinted in *The Importance of What We Care About*, 159–76. For present purposes it is enough to acknowledge that such desires exist, and to observe that they cannot, strictly speaking, provide material for practical reasoning or deliberation. (Reasoning or deliberation involving such desires requires the *pretence* that their objects satisfy some evaluative predicate or other.)

[25] The predicate 'is (*prima facie*) desirable' is meant only as an example; it should be construed as ranging over both instrumental and intrinsic kinds of desirability. Similar points might be made, with appropriate modifications, in terms of other specific evaluative predicates; or in terms of 'ought'-judgments, or judgments about reasons for action.

[26] That these apparently simple syllogistic explanations mask the complexity of even instrumental reasoning is a point made by Jaakko Hintikka, in 'Practical vs. Theoretical Reason—An Ambiguous Legacy', in Stephan Körner (ed.), *Practical Reason* (Oxford: Blackwell, 1974), 83–102; see also David Wiggins, 'Deliberation and Practical Reason', in Amélie Oksenberg Rorty (ed.), *Essays on Aristotle's Ethics* (Berkeley and Los Angeles: University of California Press, 1981), 221–40. The point does not seem to me to detract from the usefulness of the practical syllogism, as a framework for certain kinds of rationalizing explanations.

been formed *because* the agent has endorsed the evaluative judgment and the reasons that directly support it. This would often seem to be a plausible assumption to make.

A distinction can thus be drawn between two broad classes of desires—the motivated and the unmotivated—in terms of whether the evaluative beliefs associated with the desires admit of a distinctively rationalizing explanation. Moreover, it should be clear that this distinction has some relevance to the Humean appropriation of the teleological argument. The Humean concludes, from the fact that desires are always present on occasions of motivation, that motivation cannot be explained rationally, assuming that the presence of desires necessarily limits the scope for explanation in terms of rational principles or norms. But Nagel's distinction, at least on the interpretation of it I have offered, calls this assumption into question. Many of the desires that figure in motivation are themselves motivated propositional attitudes—in my terms, states which admit of a further rationalizing explanation, via their associated evaluative beliefs. Their presence on occasions of motivation therefore does not necessarily preclude the purely rational explanation of motivation. For all that the teleological argument shows, the rationalizing explanation of motivated desires may sometimes rely solely on the agent's beliefs, together with rational principles or norms, and in such cases it would be possible to give a purely rational explanation of both motivation and the desires necessarily implicated in it.

4.

It will be well to pause over the distinction between motivated and unmotivated desires, to get clearer about its implications for the debate between the Humean and the rationalist. On the interpretation I have urged, a motivated desire is one whose associated evaluative belief admits of a rationalizing explanation, where the desire is formed *because* the agent has arrived at the evaluative belief. A crucial assumption here is that the rational explanation for an evaluative belief may account for the formation of the motivated desire as well, so that the reasons which explain the belief will equally be reasons for the motivated desire. To say this, it seems, is to admit that it is an independent principle or norm of rationality that one should desire in accordance with one's evaluative beliefs, where this means that one should desire those ends and activities one takes to be desirable, to the extent one takes them to be desirable. Only on this assumption are we entitled to maintain that the rational explanations and justifications of evaluative beliefs may extend as well to the motivated desires associated with them.

This would seem to be a plausible minimal assumption to make about the content of the principles or norms of practical reason, since we do in fact try to adjust our desires to our evaluative beliefs, and take ourselves to be subject to rational criticism when we fail. Officially, of course, Hume himself would deny that this is a legitimate assumption, since he is on record as holding that rational criticism is restricted to the theoretical sphere of beliefs and the relations between them. But as Nagel and Korsgaard have persuasively suggested, Hume's own discussion of practical reason appears to take for granted some irreducible principles of practical rationality, such as the principle that one should adjust one's desires to one's evaluative beliefs.[27] Thus, Hume notes that people who cease to believe that a certain action or object is a means to some valued end will immediately desist from desiring that action or object.[28] But how are we to understand this tendency? Behind it, there seems to lie the assumption (or something equivalent to it) that it is rational to adjust one's desires at least to one's beliefs about what is instrumentally valuable; plus the assumption that people are, in this respect, characteristically rational. Hume himself thus seems poorly placed to reject out of hand the principle that rational agents adjust their desires to their evaluative beliefs.

This has important implications for the debate about practical reason. It shows that if we are to make sense of the notion of a motivated desire—a desire, that is, which is explicable in terms of the agent's reasons—then we must deny the most extreme Humean claim that there are no irreducible principles or norms of practical reason, only principles or norms of theoretical rationality. To deny this claim, however, is not yet to settle the issue between the Humean and the rationalist. That issue concerns the possibility of explaining motivation and intentional action in purely rational terms. But for all that has been established so far, it might be that the irreducible principles of practical reason are exclusively principles of instrumental or derivative rationality, accounting for the rational extension of motivational influence, but not capable of explaining the original formation of motivation or the original fixing of an agent's ends.

Rationalists, of course, deny this. They maintain that the principles or norms of practical reason are such that reasoning in accordance with them can explain, not just the extension of given motivations, but the original formation of motivation and the fixing of one's ends. If I am right, explanations of this sort would have to be capable of yielding explanations of an agent's motivated desires, since, by the teleological argument, desires are invariably present on occasions of motivation. What would a distinctively rationalist explanation of motivated desires look like?

For purposes of illustration, we may consider two possibilities. The rationalizing explanation of desires, I have suggested, will proceed via the rationalizing explanation of their associated evaluative beliefs. One way we might provide these explanations is to deploy the schema of the practical syllogism, relating specific evaluative conclusions to more general evaluative premises, by way of intervening factual beliefs, until we arrive at basic principles about what is intrinsically valuable. The rationalist might then attempt to establish that these basic evaluative principles can themselves be given a rational justification, one which shows them

[27] Nagel, *The Possibility of Altruism*, 33–4; Korsgaard, 'Skepticism about Practical Reason', sect. III.
[28] Hume, *A Treatise of Human Nature*, 416.

to be valid independently of considerations about the desires that particular agents may happen to have.

Consider, for example, Nagel's argument in part III of *The Possibility of Altruism*.[29] We might reconstruct Nagel's rationalist position, in accordance with the model I have just sketched, in the following terms. Suppose someone has a desire to perform a specific action of type *r*, and an associated evaluative belief that doing that action is (*prima facie*) desirable (where *r* = an act of relieving someone's pain). On one reading of Nagel's account, the rationalizing explanation of this evaluative belief may relate it to a basic evaluative principle that the agent accepts, to the effect that *any* action which would relieve someone's pain is (*prima facie*) desirable. This basic evaluative principle may then in turn be given a rational justification, on the reading of Nagel's argument now under consideration, in so far as rejection of the principle would commit one to the constitutively irrational doctrine of solipsism.[30] But if such a justification can successfully be carried through, then the rational considerations which figure in it could be invoked to explain, not just the basic evaluative principles and the specific evaluations derived from them, but also an agent's desires in accordance with these (basic and derived) evaluations. For we are assuming that it is an independent principle of rationality that one should desire in accordance with one's evaluative beliefs.

This is not, however, the only way that a rationalist explanation of motivated desires might be developed. A second possibility is that the rationalizing explanation of specific evaluative beliefs may depart from the schema of the practical syllogism; so that we are sometimes able to explain a specific evaluation rationally by relating it *directly* to further beliefs that the agent holds, together with background principles of rational reflection. To return to the example of Nagel's argument, this model suggests a different way of explaining the specific evaluative belief that it is (*prima facie*) desirable to perform a particular action of type *r* (where *r* = an act of relieving someone's pain). In particular, we might rationally explain the belief by relating it, simply, to the agent's belief that the action is of type *r*; for on a second interpretation of Nagel's argument, background principles of rationality license a *direct* inference from the belief that an act would relieve someone's pain to the evaluative conclusion that the act is (*prima facie*) desirable.[31] Furthermore, this

---

[29] What follows is based only very loosely on Nagel's complicated discussion, but I hope the parallels will be apparent. It should be stressed, too, that I am not trying to argue for Nagel's position, but only trying to see what a rationalist position might look like, by considering how Nagel's claims might variously be formulated.

[30] Nicholas Sturgeon seems to interpret Nagel this way, as trying to provide a *justification* for a basic evaluative principle in favour of altruistic motivation, in 'Altruism, Solipsism, and the Objectivity of Reasons', *Philosophical Review*, 83 (1974), 374–402 esp. 375, 393–4. Aristotle's ethical theory is sometimes interpreted as an attempt to provide a similar rational justification for such basic evaluative principles (fixing the ends of action). See e.g. T. H. Irwin, 'Aristotle on Reason, Desire, and Virtue', *Journal of Philosophy*, 72 (1975), 567–78, esp. 574–6; and Norman O. Dahl, *Practical Reason, Aristotle, and Weakness of the Will* (Minneapolis: University of Minnesota Press, 1984), pt. 1.

[31] An interpretation on these lines seems the more proper way of reading Nagel's argument. The burden of the argument is not to provide a rational justification for some basic evaluative premise, such as figures in the first model of the rationalist position which I sketched. Rather, it is to provide an

rationalizing explanation of the evaluative belief may carry over to the desire which is associated with it, since (again) we are assuming the rational requirement that one should desire in accordance with one's evaluative beliefs.

We have, then, two models for explaining motivated desires in accordance with the rationalist claim that pure reasoning can be practical in its issue. What, on the other side, would a Humean position look like? Here, the simplest approach would be to deploy the schema of the practical syllogism to explain specific evaluative beliefs. That is, we should suppose that, when specific evaluative beliefs admit of a rationalizing explanation, the explanation offered will relate the beliefs to more general evaluative premises, by way of factual beliefs, until basic principles are reached about what is intrinsically desirable. So far, the Humean approach would follow the first model for a rationalist account which I sketched above. Unlike the rationalist, however, the Humean must deny that the basic evaluative principles with which syllogistic explanations terminate can be given an independent rational justification. Rather, the Humean will suppose that these basic evaluative principles are fixed by the agent's intrinsic desires, desires which cannot themselves be given a further, rationalizing explanation.[32] Only if we make this assumption will it be the case—as the Humean claims—that practical reason is restricted to accounting for the extension of motivational influence from fixed, antecedent ends.

To put the issue in these terms is to admit that, even on a Humean account, rational explanations of motivation can be given exclusively in terms of the agent's (evaluative) beliefs. For on the kind of Humean position I have sketched, the rational explanation of motivation terminates with citation of the agent's basic principles or beliefs about what is intrinsically valuable. It is true that, on the Humean account, these basic beliefs will in turn be fixed by the agent's intrinsic desires; but those desires do not *rationalize* or *rationally* explain the basic evaluative beliefs. To think that they do is to suppose that it is a basic principle of practical rationality that one should adjust one's evaluative beliefs to one's (intrinsic) desires. But in fact rationality does not require that we adjust our evaluative beliefs to our desires in this way (it can be perfectly rational to hold that one's intrinsic desires sometimes aim at objects or activities which are not valuable at all). Still,

---

interpretation of the inference patterns characteristic of moral reflection, showing those inference patterns to be rational by displaying their connections with broader patterns of inference that are paradigmatically rational. See Nagel's remarks about the 'method of interpretation', in *The Possibility of Altruism*, 4, 18–23.

[32] The most straightforward way to develop this claim would be to say (with Hobbes) that a person's basic values are, simply, those things which the person desires for their own sakes. A more plausible proposal would allow room for discrepancies between a person's actual, first-order desires and the person's values, treating values (for instance) as some function of the agent's second-order desires (cf. Frankfurt, 'Freedom of the Will and the Concept of a Person' and 'Identification and Wholeheartedness').

Note too that it will often be possible to provide *non*-rationalizing explanations of an agent's intrinsic desires. For instance, in some cases they might be taken to result from a process of Aristotelian habituation or training.

even if intrinsic desires do not rationally explain an agent's basic evaluative beliefs, on the Humean view, there is a looser but more important sense in which they determine the starting points for practical reasoning and deliberation. So long as basic evaluations are fixed by an agent's intrinsic desires, rational criticism of the agent's ends will not be a possibility, and practical reason will be restricted to accounting for the extension of motivational influence from given, antecedent ends.[33]

This discussion may be summarized by saying that Humeans are committed to a distinctive thesis about the form taken by rationalizing explanations of desires. In particular, they are committed to the view that rationalizing explanations of desires must terminate, at some point, with the citation of a basic evaluative belief of the agent's which cannot itself be justified or explained in rational terms. An agent's particular evaluative beliefs and motivated desires may be explained, in the first instance, by being related to basic evaluative principles that the agent holds; but on the Humean view these basic principles are always fixed or determined by the agent's intrinsic desires, and so beyond range of rational justification or explanation. This thesis about the form taken by rationalizing explanations of desires might be called the 'desire-out, desire-in' principle, since it maintains that processes of thought which give rise to a desire (as 'output') can always be traced back to a further desire (as 'input'), one which fixes the basic evaluative principles from which the rational explanation of motivation begins. An adequate defence of the Humean position must provide a reason for accepting this distinctive thesis about the form taken by rationalizing explanations of desires.

Once the issue is seen in this way, however, it becomes apparent that the teleological argument by itself has no direct bearing on the dispute between the Humean and the rationalist. That argument establishes only that desires must be present on occasions of motivation. It leaves it an open question whether the present desires are themselves motivated or unmotivated; and, still more significantly, it says nothing at all about the form that must be taken by rationalizing explanations of motivated desires. An *a priori* argument for the Humean account would have to be a defense of the desire-out, desire-in principle, and the teleological argument sketched earlier does not by itself provide a defense of that crucial principle.

I would suggest, then, that the significance of the distinction between motivated and unmotivated desires is that it sharpens our conception of the debate

[33] This point seems to be neglected by Don Locke, in 'Beliefs, Desires and Reasons for Action'. Locke argues against the Humean approach by insisting that rational explanations of motivation can be given exclusively in terms of an agent's evaluative beliefs (in particular, he suggests explanations in terms of what he calls 'sufficient reason' beliefs: see 'Beliefs, Desires and Reasons for Action', 246–7; also Locke's 'Reasons, Wants, and Causes', *American Philosophical Quarterly,* 11 (1974), 169–79, at 170–2). But Locke admits that these sufficient reason beliefs may simply 'derive from' the agent's desires ('Beliefs, Desires and Reasons for Action', 247). In the terms I have proposed, however, this is not an admission which it is open to an anti-Humean to make, since the distinctive Humean claim is precisely the claim that the evaluative beliefs in terms of which we explain desires are themselves 'derived from' or fixed by the agent's desires.

between the Humean and the rationalist. Interpreting this distinction as I have done, we see that the real burden on the Humean is to defend a claim about the rationalizing explanation of desires, the claim I have called the desire-out, desire-in principle. It is because the teleological argument by itself lends no support to this crucial principle that it fails to settle the issue between the Humean and the rationalist.

5.

Of course, the failure of one attempted *a priori* argument for the Humean position does not rule out other strategies that might be pursued in support of the Humean approach. In this section I wish to consider, briefly, three further arguments that purport to offer general support for a broadly Humean account. The interpretation of the debate I have developed in the preceding sections should help us to see why none of these further arguments succeed.

An assumption commonly made about rationalist accounts is that they end up identifying desires and beliefs, saying that there are certain beliefs which are desires, or which serve as desires, or which are necessarily connected with desires.[34] But the idea that desires might be identified with beliefs in this way has recently come under attack, on grounds that it is incompatible with the accounts of belief and desire provided by decision theory.[35] The idea, roughly, is that on decision-theoretic accounts, beliefs and desires should evolve in different ways, when new information is added to an existing set of attitudes, thus precluding the identification of desires with beliefs. If this is right,[36] it should provide a general reason for anyone who accepts decision theory to resist the identification of desires with beliefs.[37] It is doubtful, however, whether this result has any direct

[34] See e.g. Warner, *Freedom, Enjoyment and Happiness*, ch. I, where it is suggested that, on a rationalist view, certain thoughts may 'serve as' desires; and Philip Pettit, 'Humeans, Anti-Humeans, and Motivation', *Mind*, 96 (1987), 530–3, who proposes a version of rationalism on which the presence of desires is sometimes entailed by the presence of beliefs.

[35] See David Lewis, 'Desire as Belief', *Mind*, 97 (1988), 323–32, where the argument is presented using Bayesian decision theory; and John Collins, 'Belief, Desire, and Revision', *Mind*, 97 (1988), 333–42, who reaches a similar conclusion using nonquantitative decision theory.

[36] For some doubts, see Huw Price, 'Defending Desire-as-Belief', *Mind*, 98 (1989), 119–27. A better objection, found in very recent work by John Collins, challenges the argument's premise that rational belief-revision is always by conditionalization (or its nonquantitative analogue). Collins now thinks that there are independent reasons for holding that belief revision follows two, distinct methods: conditionalization, which is appropriate for genuine updating of belief; and the merely *hypothetical* revision implicit in the decision theoretic definition of expected value, which has quite different formal properties. The theorems proved in the papers by Collins and Lewis (see n. 35, above) give us further reasons for acknowledging these two distinct methods of belief revision; but they do not rule out the possibility that beliefs and intrinsic desires are necessarily connected. Collins's new position is developed in his paper 'Updating and Supposing', read at the A.A.P. Conference in Canberra in July 1989.

[37] Stephen Darwall has argued from decision theory to the opposite conclusion that the Humean approach must be wrong, in *Impartial Reason* (Ithaca: Cornell University Press, 1983), ch. 6. He maintains that we can only make sense of the decision-theoretic requirement of transitivity of

bearing on the debate between the Humean and the rationalist, as I have reconstructed it. For on neither of the models of a rationalist account which I have sketched is the rationalist committed to identifying desires and beliefs, or to holding that they are necessarily connected. What the rationalist does maintain is that certain kinds of desires can be given a rational explanation, in terms of an agent's beliefs (together with principles or norms of practical rationality). This would establish, perhaps, a *rational* connection between certain beliefs and certain desires. But to conclude, on this basis, that the beliefs and desires in question are identical, or necessarily connected, is to confuse the rational connections of explanation and justification with laws of psychological necessity. People are irrational, much of the time, and for this reason alone no rationalist account should identify beliefs with desires, or hold that they are necessarily connected.[38]

Still, the rationalist must establish the claim that there is at least a rational connection between beliefs and desires, and attempts to make out such a connection might appear to run into a different kind of problem. To see this, observe that the two models for a rationalist account which I sketched above both apparently license an inference from *factual* premises to an *evaluative* conclusion. On the first model, this occurs at the point at which a rational justification is provided for basic evaluative principles; on the second model, it occurs in the allegedly rational inference from specific factual beliefs to specific evaluative conclusions. Noticing this feature of rationalist accounts, Mark Platts has recently suggested that the force of Hume's own argument against the rationalist rests on his famous strictures against deducing 'ought'-conclusions from 'is'-premises.[39] For the ban on such inferences, if it could be sustained, and extended to all inferences from factual premises to evaluative conclusions, would indeed seem to rule out the rationalist explanation of motivated desires.

As an interpretation of Hume, however, this seems to me to get things the wrong way around: coming long after the Hume's discussion of the influencing motives of the will,[40] and lacking any independent support, the is-ought considerations appear simply to reflect Hume's basic anti-rationalist convictions, not to

individual preferences on the assumption that an agent's preferences are criticizable in terms of reasons. Even if this is correct, however, it does not yet establish that the terms for criticism of desires conform to a rationalist rather than a Humean pattern: the basic values which lie behind an agent's preferences, and render them commensurable, may themselves merely reflect the agent's intrinsic desires.

[38] This is the moral of Korsgaard's discussion of internalism, in 'Skepticism about Practical Reason'. See also Nagel, *The Possibility of Altruism*, 20–2, 65–7; Michael Smith, 'On Humeans, Anti-Humeans, and Motivation: A Reply to Pettit', *Mind*, 97 (1988), 589–95, at 591–2; and Michael Smith, *The Moral Problem* (Oxford: Blackwell, 1994), ch. 3.

[39] Platts, 'Hume and Morality as a Matter of Fact', 201–3. It should be stressed that Platts offers this as an interpretation of Hume, not as an argument he himself endorses. In discussing Platts's suggestion, I shall put aside the question of whether Hume's intent in the is-ought passage was really to propose a strict ban on deriving 'oughts' from 'is'-premises.

[40] The is-ought passage is in bk. III, pt. I, sect. iii of the *Treatise*, a full fifty pages after the discussion of the influencing motives of the will, which appears in bk. II, pt. III, sect. iii.

provide an argument for them. The point, moreover, is a general one. *Any* argument against rationalist accounts which merely invokes the alleged gap between is and ought (or between facts and values) seems bound to fail, because Humean strictures against deriving 'oughts' from 'is'-premises are not independent of Humean accounts of practical reason. An argument for accepting the ban on deriving 'oughts' from 'is'-premises would already *itself* be an argument for rejecting the rationalist approach to practical reason. But then the Humean needs to show us what that argument is; it is no use simply invoking the is-ought strictures, as if they had the status of an independent and established conclusion in the context of the debate between the Humean and the rationalist.

A third general argument against the rationalist approach has recently been suggested by Michael Smith.[41] Like the argument I presented in section 2, above, this argument turns on the teleological character of reason explanations. The apparent aim of Smith's new argument, however, is to show, not just that desires must be present on occasions of motivation, but that the explanation of motivated desires must conform to the principle of desire-out, desire-in. As we have seen, this is precisely what a general argument for the Humean account must establish.

Smith's own presentation of his position is succinct enough to be quoted virtually in its entirety:

A motivated desire is a desire had for a reason; that is, a desire the having of which furthers some goal that the agent has. The agent's having this goal *is*, in turn, *inter alia*, the state that constitutes the motivating reason that he has for having the desire.... But if the state that motivates the desire is itself a reason, and the having of this reason is itself constituted by his having a goal, then, given that the having of a goal is a state with which the world must fit rather than *vice versa*..., so it follows... that the state that motivates the desire must itself be a desire. Thus, the Humean will say, the idea that there may be a state that motivates a desire, but which is not itself a desire, is simply implausible.[42]

The structure of this argument is extremely straightforward. A motivated desire, Smith notes, is one that is explicable in terms of reasons. But reason explanations are essentially teleological, attributing a goal to the person who has the reason; and to have a goal is already to be in a state of desire. Of course that further desire may itself be motivated by a reason, but simple iteration of Smith's teleological argument suffices to show that the chain of explanations must eventually terminate in an unmotivated desire. Hence it is not an open question whether explanations of desires themselves always terminate in a desire. On the contrary, teleological considerations concerning the nature of reason explanations suffice to establish the Humean principle of desire-out, desire-in.

---

[41] See Smith, 'The Humean Theory of Motivation', 58–60; the argument is repeated in Smith's book *The Moral Problem*, ch. 4. A different argument, which like Smith's assumes that the states which rationally explain a desire must themselves be motives, may be found in Joel Marks, 'The Difference between Motivation and Desire', in Marks (ed.), *The Ways of Desire*, 133–48, at 136–42; my remarks about Smith's argument tell equally against the one that Marks offers.

[42] 'The Humean Theory of Motivation', 59.

So Smith argues; but his argument seeks to prove too much. It turns on the claim that reason explanations are necessarily teleological, in the sense that the psychological states which constitute one's reasons are always goal-directed states. But if this were true, then to have a reason for *believing* something would equally be to have some desire which enters into the explanation of the belief. This is clearly not the case, however, since rationalizing explanations of beliefs are ordinarily given exclusively in terms of further beliefs that the agent holds (together with principles or norms of theoretical rationality). Thus, when Smith confronts the rationalist with what is supposed to be a dilemma—that is, a choice between denying that to have a reason is necessarily to have a goal, and denying that desires are the states that realize one's having a goal[43]—the appropriate response is to grasp the first horn. Far from its being, as Smith suggests, a conceptual truth, the principle that 'to have a reason is to have a goal' is simply *false*, on the interpretation of it that is relevant to the dispute between the Humean and the rationalist. What the Humean needs to establish is something at once less general and more difficult: not that to have a reason which explains a propositional attitude is always to have a goal, but that it is to have a goal whenever the attitude to be explained is itself a goal-directed state. That is the desire-out, desire-in principle, and there is nothing in the considerations Smith adduces that would support this crucial claim.

In fairness, however, it should be mentioned that Smith's apparent misinterpretation of the rationalist position is one that is directly encouraged by Nagel's own presentation of that position. As I explained in section 3, above, Nagel attaches great significance to the distinction between motivated and unmotivated desires, without making it adequately clear what it is for a desire to be motivated. Taking the terminology of 'motivated' and 'unmotivated' states quite literally, Smith seems to have assumed that a motivated desire is one that is formed for something like an *ulterior* motive.[44] That is, he interprets motivated desires as states which are precisely *not* rationalized by other of the agent's propositional attitudes, but rather formed under pressure of some further aim or goal that the agent has (as in a case of wishful thinking). This is what leads him to suppose that explanation of motivated desires has to postulate some further, goal-directed state of desire. Once we are quite clear about what is at stake in the debate between the Humean and the rationalist, however, it also becomes clear that teleological considerations are not going to determine the outcome of the debate.

6.

To this point, I have offered an interpretation of the debate between the Humean and the rationalist, and in light of this account I have tried to show why teleological

---

[43] 'The Humean Theory of Motivation', 59–60.

[44] On this point, see Smith's more recent paper 'Reason and Desire', *Proceedings of the Aristotelian Society*, 88 (1987–8), 243–56, at 251–2.

and other considerations do not provide general grounds for preferring the Humean to the rationalist account. We are, I would submit, now in a much stronger position to accept Korsgaard's contention that motivational skepticism about the rationalist position cannot be sustained. Still further support for this conclusion may be provided by considering one additional and extremely influential discussion of practical reason, that found in Bernard Williams's paper 'Internal and External Reasons'.[45] Williams's discussion has widely been interpreted as an attempt to raise a quite general problem for rationalist accounts of practical reason, and while there is now some evidence that Williams himself does not share this interpretation,[46] it will be useful to take up his argument on the assumption that it does in fact aim to support the Humean account.

Williams's argument starts from what might be called an internalist view of practical reasons. That is, Williams assumes that a person's reasons for action must be deliberatively accessible to the person, in the sense that it must be possible for the person to become motivated by her reasons for action as a result of purely rational reflection.[47] Given this assumption, Williams goes on to distinguish two positions about the conditions under which one may have a given practical reason. On the first view—in Williams's slightly confusing terminology,[48] the 'internal reasons theory'—people may only have a given reason if they could come to be motivated to act on the reason by deliberating *from* some desire in their 'subjective motivational set'. On an 'external reasons theory', by contrast, one's reasons are not required to stand in this kind of deliberative relation to one's antecedent desires.

Williams correctly takes the decision between these two positions to depend crucially on the question of the possibilities for rational explanation of motivations—the question, that is, that divides Humean and rationalist accounts of practical

---

[45] Reprinted in his *Moral Luck* (Cambridge, England: Cambridge University Press, 1981), 101–13.

[46] See his book *Ethics and the Limits of Philosophy* (Cambridge, Mass.: Harvard University Press, 1985), 223–4 n. 19, where Williams attributes to Kant the denial 'that there can be an absolutely "external" reason for action, one that does not speak to any motivation the agent already has'. The clear implication here is that the internal reasons theory which Williams has defended is something to which *both* Humeans and (Kantian) rationalists are committed; so that the difference between Humeans and rationalists would become a difference about the content of the dispositions which are to be included in the subjective motivational sets of rational agents. (See also Korsgaard, 'Skepticism about Practical Reason', sect. vi, where a similar reading of the internal reasons model is offered as part of an argument against Williams's position in 'Internal and External Reasons'.) If this is Williams's present view, however, it is difficult to reconcile with the text of 'Internal and External Reasons', which connects the internal reasons theory much more closely with the Humean approach to practical reason.

[47] 'Internal and External Reasons', 108–9. Actually Williams attributes this assumption to the 'external reasons' theorist, rather than endorsing it *in propria persona*; but it seems clear from the course of his argument that he takes the assumption to describe a genuine condition on practical reasons for action.

[48] The terminology is confusing because both Williams's 'internal reasons theory' and his 'external reasons theory' are, in a more conventional sense, *internalist* accounts, postulating a necessary connection between agents' reasons for action and their motivational capacities.

reason. Given the general internalist assumption, the external reasons theorist must hold that agents can acquire the motivation to act on their reasons as a result of rational reflection. At the same time what is distinctive about this view is precisely the denial that one's reasons need be restricted by one's prior desires, as considerations one could come to be motivated on by deliberation *from* those prior desires. The external reasons theorist thus needs to defend a rationalist account of practical reason, to show that rational reflection can give rise to new motivations without taking the form of deliberation *from* prior desires in the agent's subjective motivational set. Once these requirements arc clearly set out, however, Williams apparently finds the external reasons theory easy to dismiss. He says, simply: 'I see no reason to suppose that these conditions could possibly be met.'[49]

The real problem, however, is to see how, at this level of generality, any such statement about the prospects for an external reasons account could possibly be defended. Williams may be taking for granted here some version of the teleological argument, correctly assuming that the explanation of motivation requires the postulation of a desire on the part of the agent who is motivated, and inferring from this that practical deliberation must be deliberation *from* the desires in one's prior motivational set. But the inference is unsound, as we have seen: the desire implicated in motivation, by the teleological argument, may itself be a motivated desire, in which case it will constitute not the starting point for practical deliberation but its conclusion. General skepticism about the possibility of pure practical reason would have to be based on a defence of the desire-out, desire-in principle, in rationalizing explanations of desires. But Williams, in line with most proponents of the Humean view, provides no grounds for this crucial Humean principle.

He does, it is true, at one point allege that there is a circularity in what he presumably takes to be the most plausible version of an external reasons theory.[50] This is an account according to which agents can come to be motivated in a certain way simply by coming to believe that they have reason to act in that way, where coming to believe such a thing is not necessarily a matter of deliberating *from* the motives in one's prior subjective motivational set. About this proposal, Williams demands to know in what the content of such a belief could possibly consist. Answering this question himself, he suggests that the content of the belief must consist in 'the proposition, or something that entails the proposition, that if [the agent] deliberated rationally, he would be motivated to act appropriately'.[51] But this answer, Williams observes, merely takes for granted the possibility of pure practical reason, without showing us how reasoning which does not start from the agent's prior desires can generate by itself a new motivation.

To see why this is a weak objection, consider the following analogy with a case of theoretical reasoning, or reasons for belief. Presumably, everyone would agree

  [49] 'Internal and External Reasons', 109.
  [50] Ibid. 109–10. Cf. Brad Hooker, 'Williams' Argument against External Reasons', *Analysis*, 47 (1987), 42–4, for a similar criticism of this part of Williams's discussion.
  [51] 'Internal and External Reasons', 109.

that an agent could come to draw a new theoretical conclusion by coming to believe that there is reason to draw that conclusion. But suppose we now ask the question that is the analogue of Williams's question in the practical case: namely, in what might the content of the belief possibly consist? Here, it appears, there are any number of answers that might be given, such as that the new conclusion is a logical consequence of other beliefs of the agent's which she is not prepared to give up. To follow Williams's treatment of the practical case, this propositional content may indeed *entail* (in conjunction with some minimal assumptions about theoretical rationality) that if the agent were to reason correctly, she would draw the new theoretical conclusion. But this does nothing to show that the original answer was circular, or question-begging, or otherwise uninformative.

Perhaps Williams was misled here by an ambiguity in his formulation of the rationalist position. It is, he says, the view that an agent can acquire a new motivation as a result of coming to believe that there is reason for him to act in a certain way. But the existential proposition that gives the content of this belief may be read in two different ways: either as the claim that there is some such reason for action or other, where the agent does not necessarily know what that reason is; or as the claim that there is a particular practical reason which the agent grasps and understands.[52] Naturally the first interpretation of the proposition would leave us unsatisfied about the possibility of a purely rational explanation of motivation and motivated desire, if it were indeed all the rationalist had to say about the matter. But as the analogy with belief shows, the interpretation to opt for would anyway be the second. That is, the rationalist should say that pure practical reason is possible, because agents can acquire both new motivations, and the motivated desires implicated in such motivations, by coming to grasp and understand the particular reasons that they have for acting in certain ways. Of course, for this to be a satisfying account we will need to be convinced that the motivated desires involved here really are explicable solely in terms of the agent's new beliefs, plus principles or norms of rationality; otherwise what is represented as 'coming to grasp and understand the particular reason for action that one has' will not be a genuine case of *pure* practical reflection. But again, Williams has said nothing that would rule out this form of explanation in principle.[53]

7.

My topic in this essay has been a question about the explanation of motivation and action, the question, namely, whether we can explain motivation and action

---

[52] Williams himself, in a different context, notices precisely this ambiguity in existential claims about reasons; see ibid. 107.

[53] For further discussions of Williams's account, see Rachel Cohon, 'Are External Reasons Impossible?', *Ethics*, 96 (1985–6), 545–56; John McDowell, 'Might There Be External Reasons?', in J. E. J. Altham and Ross Harrison (eds.), *World, Mind, and Ethics: Essays on the Ethical Philosophy of Bernard Williams* (Cambridge, England: Cambridge University Press, 1995), 68–85; and Martin Hollis, *The Cunning of Reason*, ch. 6.

in distinctively rational terms. To provide explanations of this kind—particularly explanations of moral motivation and behaviour—has been a characteristic aspiration of Kantian approaches to moral philosophy, and I have urged that there is no reason to think that this aspiration would be impossible to satisfy. Some recent work, however, has suggested a different way of developing a Kantian (or at any rate, anti-Humean) approach to practical reason, one which is not committed to the possibility of explaining motivation and action in purely rational terms. This possibility requires brief consideration.

Even if, as I have argued, rational explanations of action could in principle be carried through, it might be that they would add nothing significant to the formulation of a Kantian position in ethics. This, in effect, has been suggested by Michael Smith.[54] Smith distinguishes between two ways of understanding the Kantian claim that moral requirements are, or are based on, norms or requirements of practical reason. 'Belief-rationalism', as he calls it, takes the norms or requirements of practical reason to be capable of explaining motivation and motivated desire, in line with my depiction of the rationalist position in this paper. What Smith calls 'desire-rationalism', by contrast, holds that explanations of motivation and desire conform to the Humean principle of desire-out, desire-in. Unlike the Humean, however, Smith's desire-rationalist maintains that certain basic desires are intrinsically rational, in the sense that all rational agents must have those basic desires. On this view, the norms or requirements of reason tell us that certain intrinsic desires are rationally required, without being able to explain the formation of such desires.[55]

Having introduced these two rationalist positions, Smith proceeds to question the significance of the differences between them, and hence to raise a doubt about the importance of the aspiration to explain motivation in rational terms. He notes that both positions will be able to identify the same sorts of behavior as irrational: where the belief-rationalist says (for instance) that the amoral person is failing to reason correctly, in accordance with norms or principles of rationality, the desire-rationalist will say that the person lacks a basic desire which is intrinsically rational.[56] The same conclusion holds for rational behavior, on Smith's view. On the belief-rationalist account, the rational agent will have specific moral desires which can be explained rationally in terms of principles or norms of reason. But Smith argues that any agent who has such specific moral desires could equally be credited with a basic dispositional desire with moral content, which the desire-rationalist may characterize as intrinsically rational.[57]

This seems to me correct, as far as it goes, but Smith is wrong to conclude from it that the differences between his two forms of rationalism are insignificant.[58]

[54] See Smith, 'Reason and Desire', sect. 4.

[55] Smith suggests that the critical present aim theory discussed by Derek Parfit might be a version of desire-rationalism, in so far as it claims that certain desires are rationally required, certain others intrinsically irrational; see Parfit, *Reasons and Persons*, pt. 2 (esp. sect. 46).

[56] Smith, 'Reason and Desire', 253–4.

[57] Smith, *'The Moral Problem'*, Oxford University D. Phil. (1989), ch. 8, sect. 4.

[58] Still less does it seem correct to say that belief-rationalism 'collapses into' desire-rationalism, as Smith suggests, ibid.

Take the case of the fully rational agent It is true that on both views, such an agent may be credited with the same standing or dispositional desires. But these desires will have very different explanatory roles in the two kinds of account. For the desire-rationalist, they fix the starting points for the rational explanation of any specific moral desires that the rational agent may have, since the desire-rationalist only admits explanations of desires that satisfy the Humean desire-out, desire-in principle. On a belief-rationalist account, by contrast, it is possible to explain specific intrinsically moral desires in purely rational terms; and these explanations may equally account for the dispositional or standing desires that we ascribe to rational agents in virtue of their specific moral desires.[59]

Thus, Smith's two kinds of rationalist position continue to differ in their implications for the rational explanation of motivation. Nor is this difference an insignificant one. Its importance is clearest in cases where a formerly amoral agent comes to acquire the desires and motivations characteristic of virtue. On both of the rationalist positions Smith describes, this transition will mark a change from irrationality to rationality. But if desire-rationalism is correct, the transition cannot itself be explained in rational terms; rather it must be described as something akin to a conversion—the acquisition of a new motivation which is constitutively rational, but which does not admit of a rational explanation. Belief-rationalism, on the other hand, would enable us to see the transition from amoralism to virtue as a *reasoned* change in the agent's motivations, the result of a process of reasoning or reflection in accordance with the norms or principles of practical rationality. Thus belief-rationalism promises to offer terms for a rational discussion with the amoralist, terms which—in principle, at least—the amoralist might be persuaded by, leading to a reasoned adjustment of or addition to the amoralist's motivations.[60] There is no such possibility on the view that Smith calls desire-rationalism.

I conclude that the aspiration to explain motivation and behavior in purely rational terms makes a distinctive contribution to the Kantian approach to ethics. Once this is granted, however, a further question arises, concerning the extent to which other characteristically Kantian or anti-Humean claims about practical reason can be made by a theory which renounces the aspiration to provide purely rational explanations of motivations. This question is posed, albeit in very different ways, by the recent work of John Rawls, T. M. Scanlon, and John McDowell.[61] These philosophers reject the Humean claim that practical reason is

---

[59] I take it this is the possibility Nagel is suggesting, when he offers the following comparison with the beliefs involved in deductive inference (in *The Possibility of Altruism*, 31): 'If someone draws conclusions in accordance with a principle of logic such as *modus ponens*, it is appropriate to ascribe to him the belief that the principle is true; but that belief is explained by the *same* thing which explains his inferences in accordance with the principle.'

[60] It need not be supposed that such reasoned discourse with the amoralist would be an easy thing to bring off in practice; only that it would be possible.

[61] See John Rawls, 'Justice as Fairness: Political Not Metaphysical', *Philosophy and Public Affairs*, 14 (1985), 223–51; T. M. Scanlon, 'Contractualism and Utilitarianism', in Amartya Sen and Bernard Williams (eds.), *Utilitarianism and Beyond* (Cambridge, England: Cambridge University Press, 1982), 103–28; and John McDowell, 'Virtue and Reason', *The Monist*, 62 (1979), 331–50.

exclusively instrumental in its function, restricted to identifying means to the sat-isfaction of individual ends; and they reject equally the modern development of the instrumentalist approach, according to which practical reason is directed toward maximizing the joint satisfaction of sets of desires or preferences. Instead, Rawls, Scanlon, and McDowell all contend that there are noninstrumental pat-terns of practical reasoning in terms of which we can criticize actions and social institutions morally, and explain distinctively moral kinds of motivation and con-cern. And yet, none of these philosophers seems to suppose that the morally dis-tinctive patterns of practical reasoning are equally accessible to all agents, regardless of those agents' antecedent desires.[62]

If this is right, it suggests that there may be considerable work for a Kantian or anti-Humean[63] approach to ethics, even if it renounces or suspends the aim of explaining motivation and action in purely rational terms. The work would con-sist in showing that there are patterns of reasoning *from* an agent's desires—to use Bernard Williams's expression[64]—which are not forms of instrumental or maximizing reasoning. This seems to me a fertile area for further research and dis-cussion: questions arise, for instance, concerning the explanatory *role* that desire plays in forms of practical reasoning that are neither instrumental nor maximiz-ing, but that nevertheless, in some sense, begin from an agent's desires. But how-ever these questions are answered, the possibility that reasoning from one's desires need not take a maximizing or instrumental form is an important one. It does not undermine the aspiration to provide purely rational explanations of motivation, or show it to be misguided. But it suggests that rather less may hang on the satisfaction of the aspiration than some Kantians have supposed.

8.

I have argued that Humeans have so far failed to give us good reasons for accepting motivational scepticism about the rationalist approach. To support this conclu-sion, it has been necessary to get clearer about what is at stake in the debate

---

[62] On this point, see Rawls's remarks about the role of consensus in political justification, in 'Justice as Fairness: Political Not Metaphysical', 229, 246–7; Scanlon's suggestion that the desire to be able to justify one's actions may be the basis of moral motivation, in 'Contractualism and Utilitarianism', 116–18; and McDowell's denial that those who lack the desires characteristic of virtue need be irrational, in 'Are Moral Requirements Hypothetical Imperatives?', *Aristotelian Society,* suppl. vol. 52 (1978), 13–29, at 13, 24.

[63] Rawls's and Scanlon's accounts are broadly Kantian, whereas McDowell's is more directly inspired by his reading of Aristotle.

[64] See 'Internal and External Reasons', 104–5, where Williams too contends that reasoning from the elements in one's subjective motivational set need not take an instrumental or maximizing form. I do not mean to suggest that Rawls, Scanlon, and McDowell would all agree with Williams's way of putting the point (see McDowell, 'Might There Be External Reasons?', for some objections). Whether disagreements on this point are significant, however, will depend on how the notion of reasoning *from* one's desires is developed.

between Humeans and rationalists. Developing a suggestion of Thomas Nagel's, I have proposed that the Issue turns on the form taken by rationalizing explanations of desires and motivations; in particular, the question is whether such explanations conform to the Humean principle of desire-out, desire-in. Once the question is correctly seen in this way, however, it becomes clear that recent arguments, purporting to offer general support for the Humean approach, do not succeed.

How are we to proceed beyond this point? One approach that suggests itself is to turn to phenomenology to settle the issue. The idea would be that, once we see that there is nothing to rule out or determine either kind of account on general or *a priori* grounds, we may appeal to the evidence of the moral life to see what kinds of explanations of motivation are actually accepted in practice. Evidence of this sort, however, seems to me of extremely limited value in the context of the debate between the rationalist and the Humean. The main reason for this is that the conception of desire with which the Humean operates is a dispositional rather than a phenomenological conception, a conception, that is, on which one may be in a state of desire without being aware that one is in such a state. But if desires are not phenomenological states, it is unclear how phenomenological or experiential evidence could possibly settle the issue of whether desires always serve as the ultimate source of our motivations.

Indeed, so long as the issue is joined in experiential terms alone, it is open to the Humean to confront the rationalist with a dilemma. The rationalist will want to say that certain motivations and motivated desires may be explained in terms of beliefs, because in moral experience it seems (for instance) as if the desire to perform a given action may be both justified and explained by the agent's belief that the action would be, say, helpful, or just. If this is an ordinary belief, however, then it should be equally open to an amoral agent to have the belief; and yet the belief that an action would be helpful or just will not give rise, in the amoralist, to the motivated desire to perform the action.[65] Pointing to this difference, the Humean will say that it can best be explained by supposing that the virtuous agent has, while the amoral agent lacks, a dispositional desire to perform actions that are helpful or just, where this dispositional desire is the real source of the virtuous person's motivations. Phenomenological evidence, in other words, seems rather to support the Humean approach than to confute it. The rationalist may try to avoid this outcome, perhaps, by denying that the beliefs which seem to explain motivations and motivated desires are ordinary beliefs, available equally to those who are

---

[65] Richard Warner offers an experiential argument against the Humean which allows for this possibility (namely, that the very same beliefs which motivate may sometimes fail to serve as motives), in *Freedom, Enjoyment and Happiness*, 46–51. His anti-Humean position is different from the one I am considering in the text in holding, not that beliefs explain desires, but that they sometimes 'serve as' desires (see sect. 5, above, for a discussion of this proposal). I am supposing, however, that an experiential argument similar to Warner's could be mounted in support of the conclusion that beliefs may sometimes explain desires; and that both arguments would be subject to the same objection.

not motivated by them.[66] But this conception of 'extraordinary' beliefs seems questionably coherent; and in any case, its invocation is completely *ad hoc* so long as the debate is being conducted on phenomenological or experiential grounds alone.

What the rationalist needs to establish is that it is *irrational* to have certain sorts of beliefs, but lack the corresponding desires and motivations. To show this, it is necessary to go beyond phenomenology, by specifying the relevant principles or norms of reason, or by offering a conception of rationality in terms of which the inferences in question can be shown to be rationally required. The real burden of the rationalist position is to find a way of defending such a conception of rationality or of the specific principles or norms of reason. One strategy, adverted to in section 1, above, would proceed by showing that a rationalist account of the principles or norms of reason yields a more plausible ideal of rational attainment than alternative, Humean accounts. Or, rationalists might try to establish that their conception of practical rationality develops or extends certain aspects of theoretical rationality (such as impersonality, consistency, or universality) that may be taken as paradigmatic.

Much work remains to be done, before we can definitively judge the outcome of these strategies (which are themselves rather poorly understood). At this point, I would only venture to say that the success of the rationalist strategies is likely to be affected by the increasing sophistication of accounts which deny that pure reason can be practical in its issue (or which at least remain noncommittal on this question). Thus, to the extent that such accounts can be freed from an instrumental or maximizing conception of practical reason (see section 7, above), it will become correspondingly difficult to show that rationalist accounts provide a uniquely plausible ideal of rational attainment. Difficult, but not impossible: further progress with this debate is only going to be made once we give up the thought that there must be something wrong in principle with the attempt to explain motivation in rational terms, and begin assessing particular rationalist and Humean proposals on their merits.

---

[66] See John McDowell, 'Are Moral Requirements Hypothetical Imperatives?', 16–17, for this suggestion. The extraordinary character of the beliefs McDowell here takes to be explanatory of moral behaviour is revealed by his admission that ascription of the beliefs is independent of 'ordinary' tests for mastery of the language in which the content of the beliefs is expressed (Ibid. 22). Doubt about the coherence of this notion is suggested by Sabina Lovibond in *Realism and Imagination in Ethics* (Minneapolis: University of Minnesota Press, 1983), sect. 12. (I take it that in 'Virtue and Reason', referred to in sect. 7, above, McDowell offers further, nonexperiential support for his anti-Humean conception of practical reason.)

2

Three Conceptions of Rational Agency

At the center of philosophical debates about normative reasons for action are questions about the relation between such reasons and motivation. Many philosophers hold—rightly, in my view—that normative reasons must satisfy what I shall call the motivation requirement.[1] This requirement may be formulated (with deliberate vagueness) as follows: if agent A has reason r to perform action x, and A is properly aware that r obtains, then A must be motivated to do x, on pain of irrationality.[2]

Among those who accept some version of the motivation requirement, there is controversy as to its implications for the substantive theory of reasons for action. Proponents of internalism in Bernard Williams's sense—the thesis that all reasons for action are grounded in an agent's antecedent desires—typically appeal to the requirement in support of their position. Thus Williams himself points to the 'dimension of possible explanation' latent in normative reasons claims, or

Originally published in *Ethical Theory and Moral Practice*, 2 (1999), 217–42. Copyright © 1999 Kluwer Academic Publishers. Reprinted with kind permission of Springer Science and Business Media. I have profited greatly from discussion of the ideas in this paper on the following occasions: the Workshop on Practical Reason held in Munich in July 1998; the annual meeting of the British Society for Ethical Theory, held in Canterbury in September 1998; and departmental colloquia held at Rutgers University and Stanford University in February 1999. I owe a special debt to Angela Smith, David Velleman, and Ralph Wedgwood for extensive and extremely valuable written comments, and to Logi Gunnarrson and Kirsten Petzold for stimulating discussion.

[1] The motivation requirement, in my terminology, is commonly referred to and discussed under the rubric of internalism. But the term 'internalism' has been given so many divergent interpretations that it no longer seems to me helpful to introduce it in discussion of these issues. The problem is complicated by the fact that 'internalism' has increasingly been used to designate the thesis that all reasons for action are internal in Williams's sense; see e.g. Bernard Williams, 'Internal Reasons and the Obscurity of Blame', as reprinted in his *Making Sense of Humanity and Other Philosophical Papers 1982–1993* (Cambridge, England: Cambridge University Press, 1995), 35–45, and Derek Parfit, 'Reasons and Motivation', *Aristotelian Society*, suppl. vol. 77 (1997), 99–130. This is confusing, since many of us who oppose that thesis also accept the motivation requirement (or 'internalism' in the more traditional sense). For useful summary discussions of internalism in this traditional sense, see esp. Christine Korsgaard, 'Skepticism about Practical Reason', as reprinted in her *Creating the Kingdom of Ends* (Cambridge, England: Cambridge University Press, 1996), 311–34; Stephen Darwall, *Impartial Reason* (Ithaca: Cornell University Press, 1983), pt 1; and Thomas Nagel, *The Possibility of Altruism* (Princeton: Princeton University Press, 1978), ch. 2.

[2] The vagueness of the formulation reflects ambiguities in such phrases as 'proper awareness that r obtains' and 'motivation'. The vagueness is deliberate, since the issues I wish to address are raised by virtually all interpretations of the motivation requirement. For the record, I believe the requirement is

the 'interrelation of explanatory and normative reasons',[3] as considerations that speak in favor of internalism. Opponents of internalism, on the other hand, maintain that normative reasons may perfectly well satisfy the motivation requirement even if they are not grounded in an agent's antecedent desires.[4] They contend, for instance, that from the fact that agent A lacks a motivation to do x, it cannot be inferred that r is not a reason for A to do x, since the possibility remains that A is irrational in virtue of lacking the relevant motivation.

But there is a further dimension of normative reasons that is obscured in this exchange. When we say that a given consideration is a reason for A to x, we are apparently suggesting that it is a requirement of reason that A be moved to do x. Rational requirements on action, however, are connected with our conception of persons as capable of deliberative agency. They are not merely classificatory norms that stipulate what it is for people to be good in some respect (defining an ideal of rational virtue, so to speak). They are norms of reasoning, which can be grasped and applied in a way that directly gives rise to action. The point may be expressed as follows. As formulated above, the motivation requirement specifies that rational agents who grasp that they have reason to do x will be motivated accordingly.[5] But it does not say anything about the connection between the agent's grasp of their reasons and the corresponding motivation. It is important to our conception of persons as rational agents, however, that practical deliberation be correctly related to motivation. In particular, the motivations and actions of rational agents are guided by and responsive to their deliberative reflection about what they have reason to do. Unless this guidance condition (as we may call it) can be satisfied, we will not be able to make sense of the idea that persons are genuine agents, capable of determining what they shall do through the process of deliberation.[6]

I believe that the guidance condition has been insufficiently appreciated in discussions of normative reasons for action. Taking the requirement seriously, we see that an interpretation of such reasons must at the same time offer an interpretation of rational agency; reasons must be such that deliberative reflection on them is capable of controlling directly our motivations and actions. My topic in this paper are the connections between conceptions of normative reasons and conceptions of rational agency. I shall begin with the internalist thesis that an agent's

only plausible if 'proper awareness of reasons' is interpreted in terms of the agent's normative judgment about what they have most reason to do, or what it would be best to do on the whole, and if 'motivation' is interpreted in the volitional terms I shall go on to sketch in the present essay.

   [3] See Bernard Williams, 'Internal and External Reasons', reprinted in his *Moral Luck* (Cambridge, England: Cambridge University Press, 1981), 101–13, at 102, 106, for the 'dimension of possible explanation', and his 'Internal Reasons and the Obscurity of Blame', 38, for the 'interrelation of explanatory and normative reasons'.

   [4] See Korsgaard, 'Skepticism about Practical Reason'.

   [5] I assume, here and throughout my discussion, that the 'proper awareness' clause of the motivation requirement is to be interpreted in terms of the agent's *normative* beliefs—about what they have reason to do, or what it would be good to do in the circumstances of action.

   [6] Compare Christine Korsgaard, 'The Normativity of Instrumental Reason', in Garrett Cullity and Berys Gaut (eds.), *Ethics and Practical Reason* (Oxford: Clarendon Press, 1997), 215–54.

reasons must be grounded in that agent's antecedent motivations. As mentioned above, defenders of this thesis argue that it alone can account for the motivational dimension of normative reasons. I shall argue, however, that this is precisely the weakness of internalist accounts; consideration of the guidance condition reveals that these accounts deny the very possibility of action that is controlled by the agent's own deliberative reflection.

I then turn to externalist approaches (in sections 2 and 3), distinguishing two alternative externalist accounts of rational agency—what I call meta-internalism and volitionalism—and arguing in favor of the latter. It will emerge that a satisfactory approach to rational agency must equally yield an adequate understanding of the kinds of irrationality to which human action is distinctively subject. Only then can we make sense of the important idea that rational requirements on action can be normatively binding even on occasions when they are deliberately flouted.

Recent discussion of normative reasons has focused predominantly on specific arguments for and against the internalist position. It has neglected what is to my mind the ultimately more important question of how we are to conceive of rational agency once we have abandoned internalist assumptions. A larger aim of my discussion is to raise this question, and to sketch some virtues of the volitionalist answer to it.

1. INTERNALISM

The motivation requirement is often thought to support a fairly direct argument in favor of internalism about normative reasons. In the case of internal reasons, it is suggested, we have a more or less clear idea how deliberation in terms of those reasons might reliably produce a new motivation.[7] Internal reasons presuppose that some disposition to action is already to hand, and reflection on such reasons can therefore generate a new motive by tapping into the agent's preexisting motivations (so to speak). But matters are not so simple with external reasons. These reasons precisely do not presuppose that an appropriate source of motivation is already present. So it must be explained how reflection in terms of external reasons could generate by itself a new motivation to action. Internalists such as Williams claim that this burden of argument cannot be met.[8]

It is not entirely clear, however, what the force of this challenge is supposed to be. One is initially tempted to respond on behalf of the externalist with a reminder that there are no *a priori* constraints on causal relations. If the question is, how could reflection by itself produce a new motivation to action?, the answer might

---

[7] Compare Williams, 'Internal Reasons and Obscurity of Blame', 39 (emphasis mine): 'Internalist theory explains how it is that the agent's accepting the truth of "There is a reason for you to φ" could lead to his so acting, and the reason would thus explain the action. It is *obvious* on the internalist view how this works.'

[8] The objection is most clearly articulated by Williams in 'Internal and External Reasons', 108–9. Compare his 'Internal Reasons and the Obscurity of Blame', 38–9.

simply be that there is no general reason to suppose that it could not.[9] That is, in advance of empirical inquiry we have no more reason to exclude the possibility that externalist reflection might generate a new motive than we have to rule out any other kind of causal consequence. Nor would it be a convincing response to this point to observe that anyone who acquires a motivation to do x in circumstances c must, as a matter of conceptual necessity, already have had a corresponding disposition to be so motivated. For one thing, for reasons that will emerge later I find it highly misleading to characterize rational motivation in terms of standing *dispositions* to action. But even if we choose to speak in these terms, the sense in which motivation presupposes a prior disposition to action is the truistic sense in which it is conceptually impossible to acquire through deliberation a motivation that is independent of the dispositions to which one was antecedently subject. So interpreted, however, the claim fails to rule out any of the interesting options in the theory of rational motivation that one might wish to endorse.[10] In particular, it does not rule out the idea that correct reflection on one's moral reasons might suffice to generate a corresponding motivation, even if, prior to the episode of deliberation, one lacked any identifiable desire from which the new motivation might have derived. So the question remains, why should one suppose, prior to empirical inquiry, that reflection alone must be incapable of giving rise to entirely new motivations to action?

But perhaps there is a more interesting idea at the root of the internalist position. Consider the guidance condition. This says that deliberation on our reasons must be capable of controlling directly our motivations and actions. This was the point of insisting that reasons for action are norms of reasoning, connected with our understanding of persons as rational agents. Emphasizing this condition, however, it does indeed begin to seem problematic to suppose that reflection on external reasons could satisfy that requirement. At least this seems problematic if we accept two further and apparently widespread assumptions.

The first is the assumption that motivations are not the kinds of states that are under our direct control. To be motivated in a certain way is to be subject to a desire of some kind, and desires in turn are psychological states with respect to which we are ultimately passive. In the terms of this essentially empiricist conception of motivation, desires may be considered the active principles in the human psychological economy, insofar as they provide an original impetus to action. But *we* are not active in regard to our desires. At the end of the day, whether or not we are subject to a given form of motivation is simply not up to us; rather we *find* that we take an interest in certain kinds of object and activity, while others seem to

---

[9] This line of response is pressed in my paper 'How to Argue about Practical Reason', Chapter 1 in this volume; see in particular the discussion there of the 'desire-out, desire-in' principle. Though I still agree with the conclusions defended in that paper, its focus on questions about the rationalizing explanation of *desires* now seems to me not to do full justice to the considerations I have here summarized under the heading of the guidance condition.

[10] Compare Parfit, 'Reasons and Motivation', 118–19.

leave us cold. A second assumption is that motivational states, if they are to have any chance of being effective in moving the agent to action, must be substantive. They must be focused, that is, not on abstract or purely formal ends, but on specific modalities of value that are directly relevant to action—the sorts of categories that are typically expressed by means of so-called 'thick concepts'.[11]

Combining these assumptions with the guidance condition, we can begin to appreciate the attraction of internalist approaches. The guidance condition can only be satisfied in the right way if it is possible for us, through the activity of reasoning, to acquire a motivation that corresponds to our views about what we ought to do. But motivation is not the kind of state that is under our direct control in this way. Hence it is not so much as possible for us to bring ourselves to be motivated appropriately solely through reflection on allegedly external reasons for action; practical reason can move us to action only if it taps into substantial motivating states to which we are already subject. Here we have a challenge that is worth taking seriously. It does not rest on implausible *a priori* constraints on causal relations, but rather on a natural and widely accepted interpretation of what it is to be subject to a motivation to action.

As stated, however, the argument threatens to prove too much; if sound, it would render problematic not only externalist practical reasoning, but internalist reasoning as well. To see this, we need to look more closely at the internalist interpretation of rational agency in terms of the empiricist conception of motivation. Consider a clear example of the kind of practical deliberation that internalists approve of, namely a case in which one arrives at the conclusion that going to the opera tonight would would make for an entertaining evening.[12] In this example we are to suppose that the agent already has the substantive desire for an entertaining evening. So the deliberated solution to the problem of what would constitute an entertaining evening can generate a corresponding motivation by tapping into this substantive desire. Presumably, the background desire for an entertaining evening is to be understood as a dispositional state, involving in particular the disposition to engage in those activities that one takes to be entertaining, and to have occurrent desires focused on such activities. Reasoning correctly about the entertaining, so to speak, can thus combine with one's standing dispositions to produce new motivations, in a way that is characteristic of the operation of dispositional states more generally.

This is probably the best way to think of deliberation, if we adopt the conception of motivation in terms of substantive desires. The proposed account, however, does not really show us how reflection on internal reasons can satisfy the

---

[11] On thick concepts, see Bernard Williams, *Ethics and the Limits of Philosophy* (Cambridge, Mass.: Harvard University Press, 1985), 129, 140, 143–5. I should stress here that, though the two assumptions I have identified have some echoes in Williams's writings, they are not assumptions that he himself explicitly endorses. The argument I am sketching is thus not meant as an interpretation of Williams's own views; it is rather an attempt to identify some widely held assumptions in motivational psychology that would motivate the kind of position he advocates.

[12] Williams, 'Internal and External Reasons', 104.

guidance condition. The problem we were faced with was to understand how one could come through the activity of reasoning to be motivated in accordance with one's views about what there is reason to do, where rational activity involves a kind of deliberative self-determination. But the internalist account just sketched offers no solution to this problem. Reflection on a reason gives rise to a new motivation by causally triggering a standing disposition whose presence is a condition of one's having the reason in the first place. Accounted for in this way, however, the motivational effects of reasons are not traceable to our deliberative activity as agents, but to the operation of causal forces within us. The guidance condition turns out not to be satisfied after all.

The difficulties with the internalist conception of deliberative agency begin to emerge when we think about cases in which reflection on an apparently internal reason fails to generate a new motivation of the appropriate type. There are two things one might say about a case of this kind, and both of them make trouble for the internalist. First, one might suggest that the failure of reflection to generate a new motivation entails that a dispositional desire of appropriate strength was not to hand after all. Suppose, for instance, that having reached the conclusion that going to the opera would be the most entertaining way to spend the evening, one finds oneself with no particular occurrent desire to do that. This could be taken to indicate that one lacks the dispositional desire to do something entertaining in any form. If a dispositional desire for entertainment is understood as a disposition to desire occurrently whatever one believes would make for entertainment, then the absence of such an occurrent desire in the circumstances must show that the disposition was not really present after all.[13]

This line of response, however, threatens to banish deliberate practical irrationality from the scene, making it impossible for one to grasp that one has reason to do x, and yet to fail to be motivated accordingly. Error would still be possible in the domain of theoretical rationality (in reflection, for instance, about what would make for an entertaining evening). But the distinctive defects of practical reason, such as *akrasia* and accidie, would not be possible. The absence of an occurrent desire to do x, given that one believes that x would be entertaining, reveals that one's subjective motivational set is not such as to give one reason to do something entertaining in the first place. In effect, one would always be motivated to do what one has reason to do, relative to one's beliefs; the motivation requirement, which says that we should be motivated in accordance with our beliefs about what we have reason to do, would thereby become inviolable. But if it is not so much as

[13] One might instead content that the dispositional desire for an entertaining evening must generate an occurrent desire to do what one believes would be entertaining only in the absence of other standing desires of greater strength. This position yields the view that one always does what one most strongly wants to do. On the natural assumption that the force of one's reasons is proportional to the strength of one's desires, the position would encounter difficulties analogous to the ones discussed in the text. Compare Simon Blackburn's discussion of the decision-theoretic conception of revealed preference, in his 'Practical Tortoise Raising', *Mind*, 104 (1995), 695–711.

possible to violate the motivation requirement, our conception of ourselves as self-determining agents becomes correspondingly deflated.

Suppose, on the other hand, that the failure of reflection to generate a corresponding motivation does not call in question the underlying motivational basis of one's reason. One sees that it would be entertaining to go to the opera, and remains disposed to do something entertaining, but the relevant connection somehow isn't made—the opera-option simply leaves one cold. If this is possible, then it would also be possible to violate the motivation requirement. But now we encounter a different problem, namely that it is obscure how it would be possible for the agent in the situation described to *comply* with the motivation requirement. To comply with the requirement, one would need to acquire a desire to go to the opera. But desires, on the empiricist conception of them with which we have been operating, are states with respect to which one is fundamentally passive. It follows that if a desire of the required sort is not present in the circumstances, there is precious little one can do about it. Perhaps one could try to focus one's attention on the considerations that led one to conclude that going to the opera would be entertaining, hoping that by doing so, one might trigger an occurrent desire of the relevant kind. But if it is possible to violate the motivation requirement, it should also be possible that focusing one's attention in this way will not give rise to the occurrent desire that is required. In that case, compliance with the guidance condition would become impossible. There would be no way for agents to control their behavior directly by deliberative reflection on what they have reason to do.

This discussion might be summarized by saying that practical irrationality and rational agency are two sides of the same coin. Either internalism renders it impossible to flout deliberately rational requirements that we ourselves acknowledge, thereby restricting artificially the range of ways in which we can exercise our capacities for self-determination. Or it renders it impossible for us to control our behavior in accordance with rational requirements that we deliberately flout, thereby calling in question the normative authority of such requirements. We may surmise that an adequate conception of rational agency must also provide the resources to make sense of such paradigmatically irrational phenomena as *akrasia*, accidie, and the like.

The more immediate problem with the internalist account, however, is that it renders the guidance condition unsatisfiable even on occasions on which agents succeed in acting in accordance with their reasons. According to the guidance condition, rational activity should be directly controlled by the agent's own deliberative grasp of what they have reason to do. That is, one's understanding of considerations *r* as normative—as recommending or speaking in favor of doing, say, *x*—should itself be what governs one's consequent motivation to do *x*. On the internalist account, however, it turns out that there is no room for grasp of reasons in this sense at all. Rational motivation is causally triggered by the agent's beliefs, but the beliefs in question are not normative beliefs about what it would be good or desirable to do, but beliefs about the availability of things that, as a matter of contingent psychological fact, one happens to want.[14]

Consider our earlier example, in which the rational agent acquires the motivation to go to the opera as a result of thinking about what would make for an entertaining evening. Deliberative reflection is here exclusively a matter of specifying a substantive end that is taken as given. As far as the generation of rational motivation is concerned, there is no role to be played by distinctively normative thoughts to the effect that it would be *good* to go in for some entertainment, or that this is what one *ought* to be up to. Rather we are to picture the agent as equipped with a disposition to do something entertaining, which gets engaged causally by their thoughts about what would count as an entertaining evening under the circumstances. Rational motivation is controlled by one's grasp of considerations that count as reasons for action, but not by one's grasp *that* they have this normative status, recommending or speaking in favor of what one ends up doing. The result, I would contend, is a distorted conception of our standing as rational agents, capable of determining what we do as the result of our own deliberative reflection.

In fairness to internalists, however, it might be said that their position provides at least a minimal, base-line account of the motivational side of reasons for action. Internalism might not satisfy the guidance condition, on its most attractive interpretation, or vindicate our understanding of ourselves as persons who are capable of deliberative self-determination. But it provides an explanation of the undeniable fact that reflection on the alternatives that are open to us typically gives rise to new motivations, an explanation moreover that is compatible with the empiricist conception of motivation. In deliberating about what to do, we think about possibilities for action that we are disposed to find attractive in some way or other, and the fact that we are so disposed renders it intelligible that deliberation should routinely generate new motivations to action. The production of new motives through reflection is simply an example of the general phenomenon whereby standing dispositions are causally triggered in particular circumstances. If externalists find this explanation of the motivation requirement unsatisfactory, as I have argued that we should, it is up to them to sketch a superior account of the capacities that render us rational agents.

2. META-INTERNALISM

The internalist position presented in the preceding section rests on two foundations: the empiricist assumption that motivation is a state with respect to which

---

[14] Another way to put this point would be to say that the internalist interpretation of rational motivation seems to imply a kind of noncognitivism about the normative judgments arrived at through practical deliberation. These function not to ascertain independent truths about (say) what we have reason to do, but rather to express our motivating attitudes. (Again, the aim here is not to interpret Williams's own views, but to articulate assumptions that would clearly motivate the internalism he favors.)

we are basically passive, and the further assumption that motivations to action must be substantive, focused on specific modalities of value that are directly relevant to action. By departing from the latter assumption, however, it is possible to construct an externalist account of rational agency that is compatible with the broadly empiricist conception of motivation.

Accounts of this kind have become increasingly prominent in recent work on practical reason. Their hallmark is the reapplication of the empiricist conception of motivation to account, at the most abstract level, for the operations of reason itself. The basic approach can assume a variety of forms, but the idea common to them all is that there is a disposition or desire, subjection to which is constitutive of our being rational or (alternatively) of our being agents, and that it is this abstract disposition or desire that ultimately both makes possible and explains action in accordance with our conception of our reasons. Thus it has been suggested that we are only rational to the extent we exhibit a disposition to coherence in our attitudes, or to do what we believe we ought to do;[15] while our status as agents has been identified with the desire to be autonomous, or to act for reasons, or to do what makes sense to us.[16]

This general strategy differs importantly from the internalist conception of rational agency sketched above. Internalists hold that the particular considerations that provide our reasons must stand in an appropriate relation to elements in our subjective motivational set. But the proponents of the strategy just outlined all agree in rejecting internalism in this form. That is, they agree that a given consideration can count for me as a reason even if I do not have an antecedent substantive disposition to respond appropriately to considerations of that kind. Like Williams himself, however, they are exercised by the question of how reflection whose content is provided by our beliefs about what we have reason to do could reliably generate appropriate motivations on the part of the agent. The internalist answer is that what gives our practical reflection its specific content must be such as to guarantee that corresponding empirical motivational resources will already be to hand. If one rejects this view, however, then it might start to seem mysterious that practical reason should be capable of moving us to act. If

---

[15] The tendency to coherence is appealed to by Michael Smith, most fully in 'The Definition of "Moral"', in Dale Jamieson (ed.), *Singer and his Critics* (Oxford: Blackwell, 1999), 38–63; see also Michael Smith, *The Moral Problem* (Oxford: Blackwell, 1994), sect. 5.10; and Michael Smith, 'In Defense of *The Moral Problem*: A Reply to Brink, Copp, and Sayre-McCord', *Ethics*, 108 (1997), 84–119, sect. 5–6. The disposition to do what one believes one ought is discussed by John Broome, in 'Reasons and Motivation', *Aristotelian Society*, Suppl. vol. 77 (1997), 131–46.

[16] These proposals—which are meant to be equivalent to each other—are all due to J. David Velleman. See his *Practical Reflection* (Princeton: Princeton University Press, 1989), for the desire to do what makes sense; his 'What Happens When Someone Acts?', as reprinted in his *The Possibility of Practical Reason* (Oxford: Clarendon Press, 2000), 123–43, for the desire to act in accordance with reasons; and his 'The Possibility of Practical Reason', as reprinted in his *The Possibility of Practical Reason*, 170–99, and 'Deciding How to Decide', as reprinted in his *The Possibility of Practical Reason*, 221–43, for the desire for autonomy. The basic strategy of posulating a tendency to rationality that is causally responsible for rational action is anticipated in C.G. Hempel, 'Rational Action', *Proceedings and Addresses of the American Philosophical Association*, 35 (1961–2), 5–24.

considerations of fairness, for example, are external reasons for action, then we would be reasoning correctly in concluding that we ought to do *x* because it would be fair, even if we have no antecedent concern whatsoever for fairness. What then provides the impetus for us to act on this conclusion about what we ought to do? The answer is given by the basal disposition that makes us rational agents in the first place: for instance, by the desire to do what we believe we ought to do.

The resulting position differs from internalism in not placing any substantive constraints on what might count for a given agent as a reason.[17] Like internalism, however, it assumes that the motivation requirement can only be satisfied by persons who are subject to an appropriate desire or disposition—not, to be sure, by a substantive desire corresponding to each of our specific classes of reasons, but by the basal desire that distinguishes us as (rational) agents. In this respect, the position sketched amounts to a kind of internalism of last resort. Though our substantive reasons do not require to be backed up individually by corresponding elements in our antecedent motivational profile, our status as persons who are subject to reasons for action in the first place does require the presence of an appropriate disposition.[18] Only if such a disposition is present, the thought seems to be, can we explain how practical reason can be practical not just in its subject matter but also in its issue.

Meta-internalism, as it might be called, offers an interesting alternative to the internalist conception of rational agency. My discussion to this point has been structured by appeal to the guidance condition. This says that genuinely rational motivation would be the expression of our activity as reasoners, guided by our awareness of particular considerations as having normative significance for what we do. As we saw, it is a defect of internalism that it apparently leaves no role for normative reflection on our reasons to play in the etiology of rational action. If we are to repair this defect, we shall need a way of making sense of the idea that rational action is governed by the agent's distinctively normative reflection. Meta-internalism offers a direct and appealing response to this problem.

Thus, to say that one is guided by one's recognition of normative considerations is apparently to offer a certain kind of explanation. The guidance condition would not be secured merely by the copresence of a belief that one ought to do *x* and an instance of *x*-ing intentionally; it is required, beyond this, that the action and the belief stand in the right relation, where one does *x* *because* one recognizes that one ought to. Meta-internalism seems to do justice to this aspect of rational agency, offering a

[17] Compare Williams's remarks about the 'reapplication of the desire and belief model' to account for the operations of reason, in 'Internal and External Reasons', at 109–10. Williams complains that this move takes for granted specific beliefs about what we have reason to do, and so cannot solve the problem of fixing the content of those beliefs. Externalists would agree that the basal desire they appeal to cannot fix a content for our beliefs about what we have reason to do. But they would insist that this is not the role assigned to that desire. Its job is not to fix the content of our reasons, but to explain how beliefs about our reasons can generate a corresponding motive.

[18] These are in fact exactly the terms in which Velleman characterizes his position, in 'The Possibility of Practical Reason'.

straightforward causal interpretation of the relation between normative reflection and motivation. According to this position, our normative beliefs succeed in guiding our behavior when, in combination with the standing disposition that makes us (rational) agents in the first place, they cause us to act in an appropriate way.

Now, different versions of meta-internalism will yield different interpretations of the notion of rational guidance, depending on how the disposition constitutive of (rational) agency is understood. On some accounts, this disposition is like ordinary desires in that it produces effects in a way that is mediated by beliefs. Take for instance the claim that what makes us rational is the disposition to do what we ought. On the most natural way of unpacking this claim, practical reason is pictured as reaching cognitive verdicts about what one ought to do, and these verdicts then combine with the basal desire to do what one ought, producing behavior in compliance with the rational verdicts.[19] This version of meta-internalism yields a comparatively robust interpretation of the guidance condition. Rational agents are credited with an awareness that what they are doing is required by reason, reflected in their judgments about what they ought to do, and this awareness is causally effective in producing corresponding behavior. Rational guidance becomes guidance by one's own acknowledgment that one's actions are requirements of reason.

Other interpretations of the basal disposition yield different and weaker conceptions of rational guidance. Thus it has been suggested that the tendency that makes us rational is unlike ordinary desires in not being mediated by beliefs.[20] It is a tendency to coherence, a disposition to make transitions from overall sets of attitudes that are less coherent to sets that are more coherent, by addition and subtraction of beliefs, desires, and other attitudes. On this picture, it is the fact that acquisition of (say) a new desire would enhance the coherence of one's overall set of attitudes that makes it a requirement of reason that one do so. But the rational agent need not be aware, at any level, that acquisition of the new desire would contribute to coherence in this way. One's rationality is displayed in one's having a tendency to change one's views in ways that, as a matter of fact, enhance coherence; but no causal role is played by the agent's own acknowledgment that transitions of this kind are requirements of reason. This is the sense in which the basal tendency to coherence is not mediated by beliefs. Even on this account, however, it remains the case that rational agents are guided by rational requirements. They are not guided by their *acknowledgment* of inferences and actions as rationally required. But they are guided by the considerations of coherence that make inferences and actions rationally required, in the sense that they are counterfactually responsive to those considerations. This minimal, causal interpretation of the idea of rational guidance is simply a corollary of the claim that it is the basal tendency to coherence that explains our activities as reasoners.

[19] This is basically Broome's suggestion, in 'Reasons and Motivation'.
[20] See Smith, 'The Definition of Moral'.

The strength of meta-internalism thus lies in its interpretation of the guidance condition, as a constraint on normative reasons. The position offers an account of how deliberative reflection on external reasons can control our behavior as rational agents, without departing from the basic empiricist assumption that motivational states are not subject to our immediate control. Its commitment to this empiricist assumption, however, ultimately renders meta-internalism inadequate as an account of deliberative agency, as I shall now proceed to explain.

The difficulty I have in mind emerges most clearly when we think about the distinctive forms of practical irrationality mentioned in the preceding section, such as *akrasia*, accidie, and the like. These are cases in which we do intentionally what we ourselves believe we do not have most reason to do.[21] In situations of this kind, meta-internalism entails that the agent must have lacked the basic capacity to act in accordance with reason. This in turn undermines the important assumption that the requirements of practical reason apply even where they are violated.

Consider a familiar example of practical irrationality in the above sense: a case of *akrasia*, in which one believes (say) that one ought to get to work on the stack of student papers sitting on one's desk, but one chooses instead to watch a football game on television. Let us assume that this really is a genuine, hard case of *akrasia*, where one's practical judgment that one ought to start on the papers is not interpreted in an 'inverted commas' sense, but instead expresses one's sincere assessment of what one has most reason to do under the circumstances. What can the meta-internalist say about a case of this kind? The distinctive claim of the meta-internalist is that the operations of practical reason can be traced back to the causal effects of the basal desire or tendency that makes us (rational) agents in the first place, such as the desire to do what we ought.[22] In the case under consideration, however, this basal disposition is by definition not strong enough to motivate the agent to act rationally. The agent judges that they ought to grade the student papers, but watches the football game instead. If we interpret the basal disposition to do what one ought as an ordinary psychological state that competes with other states of the agent's for causal influence, then we must conclude that the agent's desire to watch the game was stronger than the disposition to do what they ought.

---

[21] Some might prefer to characterize *akrasia* differently, as involving action contrary to one's judgment about what it would be best to do. I shall assume, however, that these formulations are equivalent: in the context of practical deliberation, judgments about what it would be good to do are, in effect, judgments about what one has reason to do.

[22] The remarks that follow apply most directly to the verions of meta-internalism proposed by Broome and Smith. Velleman's variant is more complicated, since the higher-order desires he postulates are meant to be constitutive not of rational agency in particular, but of agency across the board. (The desire to act for reasons might seem to be a constitutively rational desire that one acts against in cases of *akrasia*, but only if it is given a *de dicto* interpretation, which Velleman himself rejects.) *Akratic* action, on his account, will be motivated by the desire(s) constitutive of agency, and what makes this possible is the fact that the agent's normative beliefs about what it would be best to do fail to engage properly with those constitutive desires. I suspect that this strategy for explaining *akrasia* ends up tracing it to defects in the agent's normative understanding, in a way that is false to the potential perversity of the phenomenon; but there is not the space to go into this problem here.

It follows that, in a quite straightforward sense, the *akratic* agent was incapable of acting rationally under the circumstances. This in turn calls in question the important assumption that the agent really ought to have graded the papers in the first place. For how can it be required rationally that one do what one lacks the basic capacity to do? Doesn't ought imply, in this sense, can?

To this it might be responded that, though the ought of practical reason does indeed imply can, there are different ways of interpreting the notion of rational capacity. The meta-internalist should concede that the *akratic* agent could not have acted rationally, *given* the nature and strength of the desires and tendencies to which they were actually subject at the time of action. This much is implied by the contention that the operations of reason can be explained causally in terms of such desires and tendencies. To allow that the agent could have done otherwise, even holding fixed the content and strength of the beliefs and desires to which the agent was subject, would be to abandon a governing commitment of meta-internalism, *viz.*, the conviction that our inferences and actions are causal consequences of psychological states to which we are (merely) subject.[23] It is this commitment that makes it appropriate to think of meta-internalism as a form of empiricism in the philosophy of mind and action. More specifically, meta-internalism shares with internalism what might be called a hydraulic interpretation of human motivational psychology, tracing our actions and inferences to the causal operations within us of psychological forces with respect to which we as agents are essentially passive.[24]

Even if meta-internalism entails this kind of hydraulicism, however, the proponent of that position might rightly insist that there remains a sense in which the irrational agent could have done otherwise. True, one could not have done otherwise, given the nature and strength of the psychological states to which one was subject at the moment of action. But one could still have acted rationally, in the familiar, conditional sense that one would have done so, had one's basal tendency to

---

[23] This commitment is suggested by the 'motivational perspective' sketched and defended by Philip Pettit and Michael Smith, 'Backgrounding Desire', *Philosophical Review*, 99 (1990), 565–92 and 'Practical Unreason', *Mind*, 102 (1993), 53–79; see also Alfred Mele, *Autonomous Agents* (New York: Oxford University Press, 1995), ch. 2. According to the motivational perspective, what agents do, when they act intentionally, depends on what they are most strongly motivated to do. (Of course, if 'motivation' is interpreted in such a way as to allow what I shall later call a volitionalist interpretation, the commitment in question would not amount to hydraulicism in the sense I have in mind; but the authors in question evidently do not interpret motivation in volitionalist terms.)

[24] I discuss the hydraulic conception of desires as vectors of force in 'Addiction as Defect of the Will: Some Philosophical Reflections', Chapter 8 in this volume. I should stress that hydraulicism in this sense goes well beyond the bare commitment to mental causation. Any plausible account of rational agency will be committed to mental causation in some form, insofar as it holds that deliberation and decision give rise to intentional action. The hydraulic picture interprets the psychological states involved in these processes as comprising a system of causal forces to which we are subject, where the states of the system at any one time are a function of the system's states at earlier times. If we make the further assumption that these causal relations entail that there are strict psychological laws governing our beliefs, desires, and actions, then hydraulicism amounts to a form of psychological determinism.

rationality (e.g., the desire to do what one ought) been somewhat stronger. Given the truth of a counterfactual statement of this kind, it seems that there is a perfectly respectable sense in which the *akratic* agent was nevertheless able to act rationally. The proponent of meta-internalism might contend that this is the can implied by the ought of practical reason.[25]

This response is unconvincing, however. The basic reason is that it fails to capture our conception of ourselves as potentially rational agents, within the practical point of view. When we deliberate about what to do, we take it that we have it in our power to determine for ourselves how we shall act, by exercising our capacity for self-control. That is, we take it that we are not simply determined to act by the strength of the desires to which we are antecedently subject, but that it is up to us to choose what we shall do.[26] This is the basis for the familiar conceit that the capacity for self-control involves an ability to rise above the desires to which one is subject, and to take the reins in one's own hands.

Moreover, it seems we need to conceive of agency in something like these terms if we are to make sense of the idea that the requirements of reason apply even in those cases in which one irrationally fails to comply with them. For suppose that one's successfully rational inferences and actions are in general due to the operations of a basal disposition, such as the desire to do what one ought, and that at time t this disposition is simply not strong enough to motivate one to grade the student papers rather than watch the football game. The natural thing to say about the situation so described is that the agent in that situation lacked the power to act rationally. This is the natural thing to say, because according to the conception of agency on offer, our powers and capacities as agents are essentially defined in terms of the desires and beliefs to which we are actually subject. One is tempted to say that there is nothing else for the agent to be other than a person who is subject to beliefs and desires of various strengths. But this may be misleading.[27] My complaint is not that the hydraulic approach can give no sense to the thought that a given agent might have been subject to a different configuration of desires; presumably conditions of agent-identity could be specified that would underwrite counterfactual claims of this sort. The problem is that the truth of such counterfactuals would not by itself suffice to vindicate our conception of ourselves as self-determining

[25] Compare Philip Pettit and Michael Smith, 'Freedom in Belief and Desire', *Journal of Philosophy*, 93 (1996), 429–49. Of course, the conditionalist approach has deep roots, extending at least to Hobbes, in empiricist work on freedom and responsibility. For a general statement—one that is also explicit in endorsing the empiricist assumption that the desires on which action depends are not subject to the agent's direct volitional control—see Donald Davidson, 'Freedom to Act', as reprinted in his *Essays on Actions and Events* (Oxford: Clarendon Press, 1980), 63–81, esp. 72–3.
[26] According to nondeterministic versions of hydraulicism, it would perhaps be false to say that actions are strictly determined by the desires that cause them; the laws linking desires and beliefs to actions might, for instance, leave some small probability that the agent subject to a given configuration of beliefs and desires might perform any of a range of alternative actions. This alone, however, would obviously not vindicate our conception of our capacity to control our behavior through deliberation.   [27] Thanks to Logi Gunnarsson and Ernest Sosa for helping me to see this.

agents, capable of complying with rational requirements even when we in fact violate them. In a nutshell, the hydraulic interpretation of rational agency leaves no room for the kinds of powers or capacities presupposed by the normativity of rational requirements on action.

The point becomes clear if we think about a different kind of case, in which an agent performs an irrational action out of compulsion—perhaps the television network, after spending enormous sums to secure the broadcast rights to the game, has introduced a subliminal signal that causes viewers to become mesmerized by the images. About this kind of case, we could presumably say that the agent would have done what they believed they had most reason to do, had their basal disposition to be rational only been stronger. After all, the compulsive desire induced by the mesmerizing images was presumably not unlimited in its causal strength, and so there must be a conceivable variant of the disposition to rationality such that, had the agent been subject to a disposition of that kind, they would have succeeded in wrenching themselves from the television. Yet the truth of this counterfactual would hardly license the conclusion that the agent, in the actual situation described, had the power to resist the temptation to watch the game—it is, after all, a case of compulsion. Similarly, the truth of the counterfactual claim that the ordinary *akratic* agent would have done the rational thing, had their basal disposition to rationality been stronger, would equally not ground a conclusion about what that agent was actually capable of doing.

The meta-internalist might respond by pointing to a salient difference between the cases of compulsion and weakness, namely that a basal tendency toward rationality sufficient to overcome the compulsive temptation is virtually never met with in human beings, whereas a basal tendency sufficient to overcome temptation in the case of ordinary weakness is part of the normal human repertoire (as it were).[28] This is indeed an interesting difference between the cases, and it might motivate us to classify the temptation as a compulsion in one case but not the other. What is harder to grasp is why this basically classificatory move should entail a difference in the powers of the particular agents in the two cases. For all that has been said so far on behalf of the meta-internalist, there is nothing that would differentiate the robust disposition to rationality from, say, a disease to which human beings are in general susceptible. One can distinguish the compulsive from the noncompulsive temptation by appeal to the idea that a rational tendency sufficient to defeat the latter temptation is sometimes met with in human beings—just as one can distinguish between diseases to which humans are susceptible, and diseases that do not affect people. But if being in the relevantly diseased condition were a causally necessary condition for acting rationally, we would not say that a given agent A has the power to act rationally just in virtue of belonging to a species that is susceptible to the disease. It would be necessary to

[28] Compare Gary Watson, 'Skepticism about Weakness of Will', *Philosophical Review*, 84 (1977), 316–39.

claim, in addition, that A has the power to induce the state of disease directly. Similarly, if we wish to credit A with the power to act rationally in a case of *akrasia*, it will not suffice to appeal to the fact that A belongs to a species whose members are routinely subject to desires that cause them to act rationally in the face of similar temptations. We will need, beyond that, to establish that A had the power to generate a desire of this kind directly.

3. VOLITIONALISM

The discussion to this point may be summarized as follows. First, an adequate conception of rational agency must account for the phenomenon of rational guidance, the fact that our behavior is controlled by our deliberative understanding in cases in which we succeed in complying with our judgments about what there is reason to do. In this respect, meta-internalism proves clearly superior to internalism. Second, a conception of rational agency must also allow for cases of practical irrationality; in particular, it must make sense of our subjection to rational requirements even in cases in which we knowingly fail to comply with them.

As far as this second desideratum is concerned, internalism and meta-internalism seem equally inadequate. Neither conception provides a convincing interpretation of the idea that we are capable of acting in accordance with our deliberative understanding on occasions when we fail to do so, and for this reason both accounts render mysterious the common assumption that rational requirements can retain their normative force for agents who deliberately flout them. Furthermore, given that both internalism and meta-internalism share the empiricist conception of motivation, it is natural to suppose that this common assumption may be the culprit. I now want to pursue this suggestion, presenting a third conception of rational agency that departs from the basic idea that motivation is a state with respect to which we are passive.

What is the alternative to empiricism in the theory of motivation? We need, to coin a phrase, a *volitionalist* conception of rational agency. On the volitionalist conception, there is an important class of motivational states that are directly subject to our immediate control. Familiar examples from this class of motivations are such phenomena as decision and choice. Ordinarily we think of decisions and choices not merely as states to which we happen to be subject. Rather they are states for which we are ourselves directly responsible, primitive examples of the phenomenon of agency itself. It is most often in our power to determine what we are going to do, by deciding one way or another. Furthermore, when we exercise our power of self-determination by actually making a decision, the result is something we have done, not something that merely happens to us. Examples of these kinds suggest that in our self-understanding as agents we take for granted that there is a kind of motivation that is directly subject to our own control. My contention is that we need to acknowledge such volitionalist motivations if we are to make sense of reasons for action as norms of reasoning, capable both of guiding our activity through deliberation and of retaining their normative force when such guidance breaks down.[29]

It is important to be clear that what is at issue here is not merely whether our intentional actions always involve desires. Proponents of the volitionalist conception can agree that in a technical sense of the word 'want', agents *always* do what they want to do. This is the sense, commonplace in philosophical discussions, in which it follows from the fact that S did *x* intentionally that *x* was something S wanted to do.[30] If we adopt this way of speaking, however, we must be careful not to think of the desires that are necessarily implicated in intentional actions in exclusively empiricist terms, as states with respect to which we are ourselves passive. There is room in our conception of the etiology of action for a moment of self-determination through choice or decision. To be an agent is to be equipped with the capacity for this kind of self-determination, a capacity that in turn precludes what I earlier referred to as hydraulicism in the theory of motivation: the thesis that what one does is solely a function of the causal strength of psychological states to which one is passively subject. Self-determining agents can choose for themselves what they are going to do, independently of the strength of the desires to which they are passively subject, indeed independently of whether they are subject to any phenomenologically identifiable desires at all.[31]

Moreover, that we are capable of self-determination in this volitionalist sense is a condition for the normativity of rational requirements that we deliberately flout. Agents who are equipped with what we might as well call a will—that is, with the capacity for self-determination independently of the desires and dispositions to which they are merely subject—can retain the capacity to comply with reasons that they knowingly act against. When they act *akratically*, for instance, it is not merely true of them that they would have done what they believe they ought had they been subject to a different configuration of desires and dispositions. It is true, more strongly, that they could have done what they ought, holding fixed the desires and dispositions to which they were subject when they chose to do otherwise. For the volitionalist capacity for choice is, as we have seen, precisely a capacity to determine

---

[29] Compare my *Responsibility and the Moral Sentiments* (Cambridge, Mass.: Harvard University Press, 1994), sect. 5.2. Similar ideas are interestingly developed in Korsgaard, 'The Normativity of Instrumental Reason'—with the important difference that Korsgaard interprets the stance of volitional commitment in *essentially* normative terms, whereas I do not. I discuss this difference in my paper 'Normativity, Commitment, and Instrumental Reason', Chapter 5 in this the volume.

[30] Compare the discussion of desire in the pro-attitude sense in G.F. Schueler, *Desire* (Cambridge, Mass.: MIT Press, 1995), 29–38.

[31] This capacity for self-determination is among the general powers of reflective self-control discussed in my book *Responsibility and the Moral Sentiments*. As such, it can assume a place in a compatibilist interpretation of agency and responsibility. The general capacity for self-determination through choice would not necessarily be undermined by determinism at the level of physical description—though it is, as I shall argue here, incompatible with psychological determinism and (more generally) with hydraulicism. For more on these issues, see my paper, 'Moral Responsibility and the Practical Point of View', Chapter 7 in this volume.

what one shall do in ways independent from one's merely given psychological states. In this way, the volitionalist conception represents a clear improvement over both internalism and meta-internalism. Those approaches picture rational agency as a system consisting wholly of causally interconnected beliefs, desires, and desire-like dispositions, and a system of this kind leaves no room for the kind of rational powers that our subjection to requirements of practical reason presupposes.

But what about the guidance condition? According to this condition, deliberative reflection on normative reasons must be capable of controlling our activity as rational agents. We saw in the preceding section that meta-internalism offers an appealing account of this phenomenon, cashing out the idea of rational guidance in straightforwardly causal terms. Our behavior is relevantly sensitive to our deliberative reflection when our beliefs about what we have reason to do combine with the dispositions that make us rational in the first place to cause us to act in accordance with those beliefs. Rational guidance, it thus emerges, is a matter of the causal pedigree of our actions. If this is right, however, it suggests that we can only understand the capacity of external reasons to satisfy the guidance condition by cleaving to the empiricist assumption about the source of rational motivation, in the style of meta-internalism.

But the volitionalist approach I favor has resources of its own for understanding this dimension of normative reasons. That approach places such volitional states as choices and intentions at the center of our conception of agency. These are not states with respect to which we are merely passive, but rather direct expressions of our agency, and they are criterially connected with appropriate bodily movements. States of these kinds, however, admit of sophisticated forms of intentionality. In the Kantian tradition (with which I would associate volitionalism), the content of the intentions that are expressed in our actions are specified by maxims. These may be thought of as having, potentially, the following, schematic form: 'I shall do x, in circumstances c, in order to y/as a way of y-ing'. By filling in the slots in this schematic representation of a maxim, we provide information about what agents take themselves to be up to in acting as they do. Above all, the last slot in the maxim-schema can be filled in ways that specify the agent's conception of the reason on which they are acting. This suggests an intentional rather than a causal interpretation of the image of rational guidance. A person is guided by their conception of their reasons when that conception is reflected in the content of the intention on which they act; in that case, one will be able to understand what the agent is doing only by grasping what speaks in favor of so acting, from the agent's own point of view.

An example may help to illustrate how this might work. Consider the situation discussed by Kant in the first section of the *Groundwork*, in which actions of a single kind are performed for different reasons.[32] Agent A may act beneficently because it is the right thing to do, whereas B does does so in order to collect a

---

[32] In discussing this example I sketch the internalist style of causal explanation rather than the kind to which meta-internalism is committed; but the example could equally be developed in meta-internalist terms. Doing so, we would treat the two agents A and B as motivated by the same formal desire (e.g. to do what they ought), but as differing in their beliefs about what it is they ought to do.

financial reward. The causal theorist would treat this situation as one in which two agents perform an action of the same type—an act of helping someone, say—which is rationalized and caused by different sets of attitudes in the two cases: in A's case, by the desire to do what is morally required, together with the belief that it would be wrong not to help, and in B's case by the desire for financial gain, together with the belief that helping the needy person will most likely bring a reward. Indeed, the causal theorist will insist that it is only by thinking of acting for reasons along these lines that we can make sense of a possibility that seems real enough, namely that there is a fact of the matter about what one's reasons for action are, although several competing sets of rationalizing attitudes are present.[33] Agent A, for instance, might have the same desire for financial gain that motivates agent B, and the same belief that the helping action will prove lucrative, without it being the case that A performs the helping action for these reasons. How else to account for this possibility, if not by supposing that the reasons on which we act are causally responsible for bringing those actions about?

On the alternative I have sketched, this possibility is captured by assuming that there is a fact of the matter about the content of the intention with which the agent acts. Those intentions, I have suggested, can incorporate information about the agent's conception of their reasons for acting as they do. Thus in the original example we may suppose that A's intention is to provide assistance as a way of doing what is morally required, while B acts on the different intention of providing assistance as a way of collecting a financial reward. In just the same way, we can also make sense of the thought that A's real reason for performing the helping action is that it is the right thing to do, even though A believes the action would also prove lucrative, and wants to acquire more money. We need only suppose that A might act on the first of the two intentions specified above—the intention to help as a way of doing what is morally required—despite the presence of the desire for financial gain. It need hardly be added that in granting this possibility, we do not for a minute need to think that it is necessarily a simple matter, even for agents themselves, to ascertain what their real intentions in acting are.[34] In this respect, the intentional account I have sketched is in no worse shape than the causal account of guidance by one's conception of reasons. At issue is not the epistemological question of the conditions under which one can have knowledge of the true reason on which one acts; it is whether a non-causal approach to reason explanations has the conceptual resources to make sense of the phenomenon of rational guidance. I believe the answer to this question is clearly yes, once we have a suitably sophisticated understanding of the content of an agent's maxims of action.

[33] The classic statement of this line of thought is Donald Davidson, 'Actions, Reasons, and Causes', as reprinted in his *Essays on Actions and Events*, 3–20.

[34] Compare Kant's remarks at the beginning of the second section of the *Groundwork* (p. 407 in the Akademie edition) about the impossibility of knowing with certainty the true motive on which one acts.

Crucial to this reconstruction of rational guidance is the assumption that our understanding of what we are doing as agents can reflect our implicit conception of the reasons that support the action we are performing. Rational action is in this way an inherently intelligent phenomenon. Indeed, once the possibility of this kind of account is brought into focus, it begins to seem obscure how any other approach could do justice to the idea that we are guided by our conception of our reasons, while also leaving appropriate room for the kinds of irrationality in action manifested by *akrasia*. On the volitionalist account I have sketched, the relation between reason and action is internal, in the sense that one's intentional representation of what one is doing incorporates as well an understanding of the reason for acting in that way.[35] When this internal relation is present, our choices acquire an inherently normative content, and in terms of this kind of normative content we can make sense of the idea that rational agents are guided by their conception of their reasons.

The volitionalist conception thus offers an appealing account of rational agency, showing how rational activity can be controlled by the normative reflection of the agent. The key to this conception is the rejection of the empiricist account of motivation. The volitionalist maintains that rational motivation is a matter of self-determination through choice or decision, the exercise of a basic capacity to fix what one is going to do in a way that is independent of the desires to which one is antecedently subject. It is independent of the substantive desires that internalists take to be conditions for having normative reasons in the first place. And it is independent as well of the abstract dispositions that meta-internalism postulates to account for our rational activity as agents. This enables the volitionalist to do justice not only to cases in which we are guided by our understanding of our reasons, but also to cases of practical irrationality, in which we deliberately go astray by our own lights.

But if rational agents are equipped with the capacity for active self-determination, there is no problem whatsoever in understanding how external reasons could satisfy the guidance condition. Compliance with such reasons requires simply that one choose to do what one believes one has reason to do, and the capacity for this kind of choice is what makes us agents in the first place.

---

[35] I find myself in agreement here with some points made by Annette Baier in 'Actions, Passions, and Reasons', as reprinted in her *Postures of the Mind* (Minneapolis: University of Minnesota Press, 1985), 109–34. I should like to stress, however, that it is no part of volitionalism as I understand it to deny that the intentional states that incorporate our understanding of our reasons can *cause* the bodily movements we make in acting. What volitionalism denies is not the causal efficacy of such states as choice or decision, but the idea that those states are in turn caused by our antecedent desires and beliefs.

3

Explanation, Deliberation, and Reasons

Jonathan Dancy's *Practical Reality* defends a strikingly nonpsychologistic account of motivating reasons for action.[1] When we explain what people do by citing their reasons, we are trying to isolate the considerations that were actually effective in moving them to act. But it is crucial, Dancy contends, that these considerations be understood in a way that preserves their connection to the normative contexts in which the concept of a reason also has a place. The considerations that move agents to act are considerations that agents take to cast a favorable light on the actions they perform, and it is at least sometimes the case that peoples' motivating reasons are also good reasons for action, considerations that really do recommend or speak in favor of the action that was undertaken. If we make the plausible further assumption that these normative reasons are typically not psychological states of the agents to whom they apply, it follows that motivating reasons equally cannot be understood in essentially psychological terms. The reasons for which people act are not psychological states to which they are subject, but (real or purported) facts or states of the world of the sort that are capable of counting in favor of actions, and that in successful cases render sensible or reasonable the very actions that agents in fact perform.

Dancy agrees that we may distinguish, if we like, between motivating and normative reasons. But he insists that we must be careful not to misunderstand the distinction that is drawn in these terms. In particular, the distinction is not a distinction between two different kinds of reason, but rather between two different *questions* that the concept of a reason may be used to answer (p. 2). Motivating reasons are cited in answer to the question of motivation, which Dancy understands as an invitation to specify the considerations in light of which a given agent acted as she did. Normative reasons, by contrast, provide an answer to the different question of whether there is (or was) good reason for a given agent to act in a certain way. Once we are clear about this, the way will be open for us to acknowledge that one and the same consideration can sometimes serve both as a motivating and as a normative reason. And if, as Dancy rightly contends, the considerations that are fit to answer the normative question about good reasons

Expanded version of a contribution to a symposium on Jonathan Dancy's book *Practical Reality* published in *Philosophy and Phenomenological Research*, 67 (2003), 429–35. Reprinted by permission.

[1] Jonathan Dancy, *Practical Reality* (Oxford: Oxford University Press, 2000). All page references in the text of this chapter refer to Dancy's book.

are seldom themselves psychological states, the possibility of a nonpsychologistic account of motivating reasons begins to come into view.

I agree wholeheartedly with Dancy that normative reasons should not in general be understood to consist in psychological states or attitudes. There are indeed cases in which the considerations that recommend or speak in favor of a person's doing something are conditioned in some way by that agent's dispositions and states of mind. That a certain activity—say, bungee jumping—would be pleasant or thrilling for Angie can count in favor of her going in for it, and this is a consideration that depends, in intelligible and familiar ways, on Angie's subjective constitution. Even in these cases, however, it would be a distortion to say that the agent's reason *consists* in the psychological conditions that are thus conceded to be relevant to deliberation; what speaks in favor of bungee-jumping is the prospective pleasure or thrill that it would provide, and not Angie's present desires and dispositions, even if the latter are apt to condition and color her future experiences.

I also agree with Dancy that motivating reasons should be understood in a way that preserves and renders intelligible their connection to the kinds of normative consideration that recommend or speak in favor of actions. As Dancy helpfully puts the point, our aim in answering the question as to why a given agent did something is to reveal the favorable light in which the agent saw what he was doing (p. 97). The considerations we cite in explaining action must be such as to enable us to understand the normative factors that were salient from the agent's point of view. This important dimension of motivating reasons goes missing when we construe them as psychological states whose contribution to the explanation of what the agent does derives exclusively from their causal role in bringing about the action to be explained.

Despite these important points of agreement, however, I find myself stubbornly resisting Dancy's nonpsychologistic approach to motivating reasons. More precisely, I find his main argument for the approach he favors inconclusive. The argument appeals to an idea that is both simple and compelling: the idea, namely, that it must be possible for people to act for good reasons. Dancy calls this idea the 'normative constraint' (p. 103), and he interprets it as a requirement on motivating reasons, to the effect that the very considerations that provide or constitute an agent's motivating reasons must themselves be capable of being good reasons for action (pp. 96–7). Dancy argues effectively that the normative constraint, on the interpretation of it he favors, precludes a psychologistic understanding of motivating reasons, as consisting either in psychological states of the agent, or in facts *about* the agent's psychological states.

But Dancy's extremely literal interpretation of the normative constraint leads to a strained understanding of cases in which people do not act for good normative reasons, because (for instance) things are not in fact as they take them to be. If Peter's investment decision did not turn out to lead to an increase in his pension, then it seems to me strange and misleading to explain his action by saying: 'His reason for doing it is that it would increase his pension, though as it happened it failed to do so' (cf. pp. 132–3). A more felicitous thing to say would be: 'He did it because he thought it would increase his pension, though he was mistaken in thinking that.' Dancy attempts to defuse this kind of worry by arguing that explanation need not be factive (pp. 131–7), and by developing two potentially complementary accounts of the reference to agents' beliefs in colloquial explanations that cite their motivating reasons. The first of these accounts treats states of belief as enabling conditions for reason explanation, rather than as constituents of the reason that is postulated by such explanations (pp. 127–8); the second interprets the reference to belief in these contexts appositionally, as a kind of paratactic commentary on the considerations that are cited to explain what agents have done (pp. 128–30). But these seem to be *ad hoc* devices for coping with the peculiar consequences of Dancy's interpretation of the normative constraint with regard to situations in which people fail to act for good reasons. His insistence on a literal interpretation of the normative constraint (cf. pp. 106, 114) results in a somewhat artificial treatment of these failure cases, insofar as it seems natural to mention psychological states in answering the question as to the agent's distinctively motivating reasons in such cases.

I do not think this is a decisive argument against Dancy's position, but it does at least raise a doubt about his appeal to the normative constraint. If acceptance of his interpretation of the constraint forces us to explain away the reference to psychology in the failure cases, then it no longer seems such an advantage of his position that it is fastidiously faithful to the letter of our practice of ascribing motivating reasons to people. Instead of reinterpreting the reference to psychological states in the failure cases, we might equally look for a different way to interpret the normative constraint, one that allows psychological states or facts to play a role in reason explanations across the board. A first thing to note in this connection is that some of Dancy's most appealing formulations of the constraint do not require a literal identity of motivating and normative reasons. At one point he glosses the constraint, for instance, as saying that 'it must... be possible to act for a good reason' (p. 103). This seems utterly compelling, but it does not entail that in the success cases (as we might call them), agents' motivating reasons must consist exclusively in the nonpsychological considerations that provide their good normative reasons for doing what they do. When we act for good reasons, the explanation of what we do might make essential if sometimes implicit reference to our psychological condition at the time of action, reference of a kind that is explicit and completely natural in the failure cases. If that is so, then we could embrace the normative constraint—the idea that it must be possible to act for a good reason—without abandoning a generally psychologistic approach to the explanation of action in terms of reasons.

In support of this possibility, I would now like to call attention to an important feature of the distinction between motivating and normative reasons, one that should lead us to expect that reasons of these two kinds, despite the important and acknowledged connections between them, are never strictly identical. As I noted above, Dancy himself suggests that motivating and normative reasons do not represent two distinct categories of reason; rather, the distinction drawn in these terms is better understood as a distinction between two different questions that the concept of a reason may be used to answer. This seems to me correct, but it has implications that Dancy fails to come to terms with. In particular, the two questions that the concept of a reason may be used to answer are characteristically posed from very different points of view, and the differences are highly relevant to the issue of psychologism about motivating reasons.

When we address the question of motivation, we typically focus on an action that has already been performed, and we think about the action from a distinctively third-person perspective. The aim is to arrive at a certain kind of explanation, taking the explanandum as a given. Of course, I can ask about my own motivating reasons, reflecting back on something that I have already done, in the hope of understanding better what led me to do it; but in posing this question I am viewing my action from a point of view that is disconnected from my present capacities for agency, and that is therefore in principle accessible to anyone. By contrast, the perspective within which normative reasons have their place is characteristically prospective, first-personal, and deliberative. It is the point of view from which I weigh the considerations for and against the various courses of action that are open to me, with the aim not of explaining something that has already occurred, but of resolving for myself the question of what is to be done and acting accordingly. It is possible, again, for other persons to reflect on and assess my normative reasons; in doing so, however, they are naturally described as adopting sympathetically my deliberative point of view, trying to get clear about the force and weight of considerations whose primary place is in the kind of reflection undertaken by an agent. For this reason, the deliberative point of view within which the question of normative reasons is posed can be described as presumptively first-personal.

Dancy sometimes acknowledges that a distinction between points of view might be relevant to the contrast between normative and motivating considerations, but he does not characterize the distinction in the terms I have proposed. When he introduces the notions of a normative and motivating reason, he takes as an example an action that has already been performed, and poses—from a third-person point of view—two different questions about that action: 'There is the question what were the considerations in the light of which, or despite which, he acted as he did. . . . There is also the question whether there was good reason to act in that way . . .' (p. 2). But this way of putting it obscures the real differences between the contexts within which the two questions are paradigmatically addressed. The question to which normative considerations answer is above all the agent's question, asked about the merits of prospective actions that deliberation is to decide between, whereas motivating reasons answer to the spectator's request for an explanation of something already done. This last point is subtly camouflaged in later discussions, where Dancy represents agents as reporting authoritatively on their own motivating reasons, even as they perform the actions whose motivations they are reporting (pp. 108–12, 135).[2] There are perhaps a few situations in which agents report on their reasons while in the heat of action (e.g. when they are caught doing something that is apparently incriminating, and asked to give an account of themselves). But much more typically the agent's perspective in action is continuous with the deliberative point of view, and focused accordingly on the merits of the actions that are being undertaken; whereas the question to which motivating considerations are relevant is at home in a retrospective or detached perspective that is not presumptively that of the agent in question.

Once we are clear about the distinctive points of view within which motivating and normative reasons have their place, it seems utterly plausible that these two kinds of reason should systematically diverge in the way adumbrated above. This remains true even if we accept Dancy's characterization of reasons in terms of the metaphor of a 'favorable light' in which actions may be seen. This favorable light is the light that is, so to speak, cast onto prospective actions in the deliberative perspective of agency, as the agent reflects directly on the considerations that recommend those actions. Since I agree with Dancy that these normative considerations are rarely if ever to be understood as psychological states of the agent's, I believe we should accept a generally nonpsychologistic account of normative reasons. But things change when we adopt the distinct perspective of third-person explanation in terms of reasons. Here we are contemplating an action that has already been performed, and asking why it was done; in posing this question, we abstract from the immediate deliberative horizon of the agent, and adopt a standpoint that brings the agent herself into view, as an object of reflection. Whereas the psychological states of an agent are typically transparent to the agent herself, when she is deliberating about what to do, they are very much in the picture when we pose the explanatory question to which motivating reasons provide an answer. It thus seems perfectly natural that we should explain action by citing not the normative considerations that cast a favorable light on the action performed, but the fact that the agent saw what she was doing in the light of those considerations.[3] The motivating reason, in other words, admits of a psychological interpretation, whereas the normative reason does not.

But what about the essential connection between motivating and normative reasons—a connection that I affirmed above, and that Dancy expresses in the form of the normative constraint? Here is one way we might understand this connection. The psychological states that are cited in explanatory contexts, to account for the agent's motivation, can achieve their explanatory aim only if they *render*

---

[2] The general form of the agent's explanation in these passages is taken to be: 'I am doing it because . . .' (e.g. p. 108); and the authority of such explanations is suggested when Dancy remarks: 'our third-person explanation of the agent's action should be, so far as possible, the agent's explanation' (p. 110).

[3] In practice, of course, we often explain what people do without mentioning explicitly their psychological states—'she left without saying goodbye because the store was about to close and there was something she needed to pick up'. In the explanatory context, however, statements of this kind are naturally taken as abbreviated ways of characterizing the agent's state of mind.

intelligible the agent's deliberative point of view. Our ultimate objective in occupying the explanatory standpoint is to make sense of the agent's action. But an explanation in terms of reasons achieves this objective in a distinctive way: situating the action that was performed in relation to features of the agent's psychology, so that we come to understand the action as the performance of an agent with a distinctive point of view. If, within the deliberative perspective, considerations *c* present themselves to the agent as casting some prospective action *x* in a strong favorable light, and the agent proceeds to do *x* on this basis, then our explanation of the agent's *x*-ing should point to the fact that he saw things in this favorable light. It is *the agent's seeing* some consideration as recommending or speaking in favor of her action that is the generic form of a motivating reason, construed as the fact or state of affairs that provides the answer to the explanatory question as to what moved the agent to act. But psychological facts or states of this kind[4] can count as motivating reasons *only because* they connect in the right way to the normative considerations that the agent reflected on in deliberating about what to do.

It is an attraction of this way of understanding the relation between motivating and normative reasons that it helps us to make sense of Humean models of motivation, which can otherwise seem puzzling. For suppose there is no normativity in the world, no fact or truth of the matter about which considerations really do 'recommend' or 'speak in favor' of particular actions. From the deliberative perspective of agency, it will nevertheless seem to us that there are normatively significant features of our situation, features that cast prospective actions in a favorable light. The explanatory task to which the theory of motivating reasons is a response will accordingly be to cite psychological states of agents that render intelligible their seeing things this way in the deliberative point of view, compatibly with the denial of genuine normativity in the world. The strategy that naturally suggests itself in this context is to appeal to the agent's desires, in the standard philosophical sense of generic pro-attitudes, understanding states of these kinds to be involved whenever agents view the actions they perform in a favorable light. On this broadly noncognitivist approach, seeing what one does in a favorable light cannot be understood as a kind of responsiveness to normative facts that are anyway there to be grasped, since by hypothesis there are no such normative facts. What renders the agent's deliberative point of view intelligible must therefore be some noncognitive state of desire or pro-attitude, a kind of affect that gets projected onto the world, in a way that is experienced by the agent as an encounter with normatively significant features of her situation.

---

[4] I ignore here the distinction between the psychological state of my seeing something as a reason, and the psychological fact that I see something as a reason, a distinction that Dancy discusses at some length. Dancy is of course correct that this distinction becomes significant if we assume that motivating and normative reasons must be 'capable of being identical' (p. 106); but I think it is less significant within the context of explanation appropriate to motivating reasons. We typically explain action by citing psychological facts, but the motivation or 'motivating reason', strictly speaking, is the psychological state picked out by descriptions of such facts.

I don't for a minute want to endorse this kind of picture. The point is just that the interpretation I have offered of the relation between motivating and normative reasons helps us to understand its appeal. It is not that Humeans in the theory of motivation are realists about the normative who mistakenly think that normative reasons are constituted by desires. For reasons that Dancy articulates forcefully, a position of this kind would represent an odd and unstable compromise. In particular, it would not succeed in rendering the agent's deliberative point of view intelligible, since it would suggest—contrary to our own experience—that the characteristic focus of deliberation is reflexive, directed onto the agent's own states of desire, as considerations that are themselves seen to count in favor of prospective actions. A Humean approach to motivation is better understood as a response to the wholesale rejection of realism about the normative. By the same token, the account I have sketched also helps us to see that for those of us who are comfortable with normative realism, there is nothing at all to recommend the identification of motivating reasons with desires. If we accept that there can be facts or truths of the matter about the ways in which various considerations speak in favor of actions that are open to a given agent, then there is no reason not to take at face value the agent's seeing such actions in the favorable light that is cast by those considerations. It is this way of viewing or grasping one's situation that can be cited in the third-person perspective of action explanation, to render intelligible to the spectator the agent's deliberative point of view and the intentional action to which it gave rise.[5]

What are we to make, finally, of Dancy's normative constraint, the idea that it must be possible for agents to act for good reasons? This possibility is realized, I believe we can say, when there really are good reasons for a given agent to act in a certain way, and the agent acts accordingly *because* he appreciates that those reasons obtain. Dancy objects that an account along these lines 'simply awards itself the concept of a good motivating reason, without really doing anything to show that it makes sense' (p. 119). But this objection misunderstands the proposed response. The idea is not that the agent's motivating reason itself becomes a good reason when the condition I have mentioned is satisfied, but that the agent acts for a good reason when that condition is satisfied. Strictly speaking, the only good reason in the offing here is the normative reason that is salient in the deliberative perspective of agency. The motivating reason—the consideration we cite in the perspective of explanation, to make sense of what the agent has already done—is the agent's seeing that normative consideration as counting in favor of the action

---

[5] To this it may be objected that cognitive states are motivationally inert, incapable by themselves of giving rise to action. The short answer to this worry is that explanations that appeal to psychological states succeed only on the assumption that the agent is possessed of other powers or capacities—such as a disposition to coherence in attitudes, or a capacity for self-determining choice or decision. But these powers and capacities should be understood as generic enabling conditions of rationality in action (to borrow Dancy's term), rather than as conditions that themselves *explain* why the agent acted as she did. Compare Chapter 7 in this volume.

performed, a normative consideration that, as it happens, was also a good reason for so acting. What we give up, on this way of understanding motivating reasons, is the idea that motivating and normative reasons can strictly be identical, such that the very same consideration that speaks in favor of my doing *x* might itself also explain my doing *x*. Once we are clear about the distinct contexts that the tasks of explanation and deliberation define, however, this no longer seems a surprising or peculiar result.[6]

---

[6] I myself believe that nothing significant would be lost, and some clarity might be gained, if we dropped talk of motivating reasons altogether, reserving the term 'reasons' for the considerations that are significant within the standpoint of deliberation, counting for or against particular courses of action. What are called 'motivating reasons' are really explanations of action in terms of reasons in the normative sense—as I have put it, psychological explanations that render intelligible agents' normative understanding of the action they were performing. Talk of 'motivating reasons' invites us to make the mistake of thinking that the psychological states cited in these explanations are themselves potentially identical with the normative considerations salient from the agent's deliberative point of view. It would perhaps be better, and anyway more colloquial, simply to speak of 'motivation' in this context.

4

Normativity and the Will

If there is room for a substantial conception of the will in contemporary theorizing about human agency, it is most likely to be found in the vicinity of the phenomenon of normativity. Rational agency is distinctively responsive to the agent's acknowledgment of reasons, in the basic sense of considerations that speak for and against the alternatives for action that are available. Furthermore, it is natural to suppose that this kind of responsiveness to reasons is possible only for creatures who possess certain unusual volitional powers, beyond the bare susceptibility to beliefs and desires necessary for the kind of rudimentary agency of which the higher animals are arguably capable.

But what exactly is the relation between normativity and the will? In this paper I want to discuss an influential contemporary answer to this question, due to Christine Korsgaard. This answer holds that normativity itself must be accounted for in terms of the movements of the will. On the constructivist position that Korsgaard favors, what makes a given principle normative for me is my volitional commitment to comply with it in action. The primary role for the will in understanding rational action is thus to serve as what she calls the 'source' of normativity, providing an account of what makes principles binding on us in the first place, as reasons for action. Constructivism in this sense may fruitfully be contrasted with a realist framework for thinking about the normative principles that specify what we have reason to do. According to the realist approach, such principles are not made normative for us by our commitment to comply with them, rather their normative force is taken to be prior to and independent of our particular decisions about what to do. The distinctive role for the will, on the second approach, is to explain the striking capacity of rational agents to be guided in their activity by their conception of what they have reason to do.

Originally published in John Hyman and Helen Steward (eds.), *Agency and Action* (Cambridge, England: Cambridge University Press, 2004), 195–216. Reprinted by permission. This version does not include section 2 of the paper as it appeared in *Agency and Action*, which covers ground that is discussed more extensively in Chapter 2 of the present volume. I received helpful feedback on earlier versions of this paper from audiences at the following occasions: an APA session on the future of moral philosophy in December 2001, the 2002 Riverside Conference on the history and future of the will, and the 2002 Royal Institute of Philosophy conference on action and agency. I have particularly benefited from written comments by Michael Bratman, Christine Korsgaard, and Helen Steward.

I myself reject the first, constructivist conception of the work that is done by the notion of the will, and accept the second, realist approach to this question. My aim in this paper, which will of necessity be sketchy and incomplete, will be to offer an interpretation of the constructivist position, and to raise some questions about its prospects for success, focusing on the demands that it makes on the theory of the will.

In a series of influential recent writings Christine Korsgaard has developed a constructivist approach to the fundamental issues in moral philosophy, which includes a distinctive and important account of the sources of normativity in our volitional activity.[1] Korsgaard presents her approach as an alternative to realism in ethics. I want to begin by considering some interpretations of moral realism, in the hope that this will provide an illuminating foil for the reflections that follow about the relation between normativity and the will.

It sometimes seems as if there are as many versions of moral realism as there are moral realists. But one thing that most realist positions have in common is the following. They can be understood as attempts to give expression to the idea that discourse in a certain domain is answerable to a reality that is in some sense prior to and independent of us. Korsgaard herself endorses a similar thought when she characterizes moral realism as 'the view that propositions employing moral concepts may have truth values because moral concepts describe or refer to normative entities or facts that exist independently of those concepts themselves' (p. 100). The difficulty is that talk about the concept or agent independence of entities or facts is rather dark, and admits of a variety of incompatible interpretations.

One way to make out the independence and priority of moral reality would be to take seriously Korsgaard's reference to 'normative entities'. That is, we might adopt an objectual paradigm of the real, assuming that discourse is realistic if it makes reference to objects or events that are both independent of us, and capable of standing in causal relations to us. To be a moral realist, on this conception of realism, would be to hold that the furniture of the world includes, in addition to the ordinary physical objects with which our senses put us in contact (medium-sized dry goods and the like), an array of concrete normative entities or values, conceived perhaps as particulars of some kind or other. Actually, I believe that the objectual conception of realism underlying this position is more often adopted by opponents than by proponents of realism in ethics.

Thus anti-realists often assume the objectual interpretation of reality, and then proceed to argue that realism is not a tenable position in ethics, because of the utter implausibility of the view that moral discourse makes reference to a realm of concrete normative entities that are anything like the physical objects and events

[1] Korsgaard's reflections on this topic are presented most recently in a paper written for a special APA session on the state of moral philosophy at the turn of a new century; see Christine M. Korsgaard, 'Realism and Constructivism in Twentieth-Century Moral Philosophy', APA Centennial Supplement to the *Journal of Philosophical Research* (2003), 99–122. Page numbers in the text to follow refer to passages in Korsgaard's article.

with which we make causal contact in experience,[2] Nevertheless, we may agree that if a defender of realism in ethics wished to adopt this objectual interpretation of reality, the resulting position would not be very plausible. Moral discourse, on this objectual construal of it, would be conceived basically as a way of characterizing a peculiar set of normative entities, whose independence from us is modeled on the independence of ordinary physical objects.

There is a second class of positions in ethics that more interestingly develop the basic realist idea. This class of positions is distinguished by the following two commitments. There is, first, a factive as opposed to an objectual conception of independent reality. That is, moral realists of this stripe would claim that the reality to which moral discourse is answerable is not a realm of concrete particular entities or objects, but a set of distinctive facts about what is the case. The independence of moral reality, on this conception of it, finds expression in the idea that moral facts obtain in a way that is prior to and independent of our judging that they obtain. Second, the class of realist positions I am envisaging is further distinguished by what is sometimes referred to as an externalist conception of the relation between moral facts and reasons for action. According to this kind of conception, the question of whether a given moral fact does or does not obtain is strictly independent from the question of whether any given agent has reason to act accordingly. Even if moral facts are conceived in such a way that their linguistic characterization requires apparently normative vocabulary (as in: 'It is wrong to torture the innocent'), it does not follow from the truth of such claims that any particular agent has reason to comply with them. Instead, the legitimacy of talk about an independent realm of moral facts might be established by making out the explanatory significance of such facts (for instance, in accounting for large-scale processes of social change).

This variety of factive moral realism seems a good bit more plausible than the objectual version sketched earlier. It is, for one thing, a view that a number of actual philosophers have been tempted to hold and to defend (examples might be Richard Boyd, David Brink, and Peter Railton[3]). What this position shares with objectual moral realism, however, is its rejection of the practical conception of ethics that Korsgaard—in common with others influenced by Kant—has advocated. Korsgaard herself presents the practical conception by contrasting two different accounts of the function of moral concepts: as serving to describe an independent reality, on the one hand, and as working out solutions to practical problems, on the other (pp. 105, 116). I must confess that I am a little uncomfortable with talk about the 'function' of 'concepts'. But I think I understand well

---

[2] Cf. Gilbert Harman, *The Nature of Morality* (New York: Oxford University Press, 1977), ch. 1 and J. L. Mackie, *Ethics* (Harmondsworth: Penguin Books, 1977), ch. 1.

[3] See Richard Boyd, 'How to be a Moral Realist', as reprinted in Stephen Darwall, Allan Gibbard, and Peter Railton (eds.), *Moral Discourse and Practice* (New York: Oxford University Press, 1997), 105–35; David Brink, *Moral Realism and the Foundations of Ethics* (Cambridge, England: Cambridge University Press, 1989); and Peter Railton, 'Moral Realism', as reprinted in Darwall et al. (eds.), *Moral Discourse and Practice*, 137–63.

enough what Korsgaard is driving at. On the practical conception she favors, the normativity of moral discourse has to do with its suitability to answer the questions that we pose in the first-person standpoint of practical deliberation. A claim is normative, in this sense, insofar as it identifies a reason, a consideration that speaks for or against a given agent's acting in some specific way or other.

In these terms, the practical conception of ethics interprets moral discourse as discourse about an autonomous domain of reasons for action. Of course, we must leave open the possibility that ethics comes to nothing, insofar as there might turn out to be no distinctively moral reasons for acting one way or another. But the practical conception interprets moral discourse as essentially aspiring to identify a distinctive class of normative considerations, in the sense sketched above. It follows that an account of moral reality or objectivity that leaves open the question of whether anyone ever has reason to comply with moral demands would fail to capture the kind of normativity that is essential to and distinctive of moral discourse, as the practical conception conceives it. In this respect, the second kind of moral realism sketched above resembles the first version that we considered: both forms rest on an 'essentially theoretical' conception of ethics (cf. p. 118).

Let us now consider a third variety of moral realism, one that accepts the factive rather than the objectual interpretation of the real, but that abandons the thesis that questions about the obtaining of moral facts are independent from questions about their standing as reasons for action. Thus, a factive moral realist might agree with Korsgaard that moral discourse essentially aspires to normativity in her sense, characterizing or purporting to characterize a domain of distinctive reasons for action. According to this kind of realist position, the priority and independence of moral facts is a matter of their obtaining prior to and independent of our judging that they obtain. But the appropriate kind of moral fact will obtain only if (say) rightness and wrongness are genuine reasons for action, considerations that can and should count for and against prospective courses of action in the perspective of practical deliberation. I believe that a position of roughly this shape—we might refer to it as normative moral realism, or NMR for short—is implicit in the work of a number of contemporary philosophers, including Thomas Nagel, Derek Parfit, Joseph Raz, and T. M. Scanlon.[4]

As I said above, it would seem to be a touchstone of realist positions that they take our discourse to be answerable to a reality that is in some sense prior to and

---

[4] See Thomas Nagel, *The View from Nowhere* (New York: Oxford University Press, 1985), ch. 8; Derek Parfit, 'Reasons and Motivation', *Aristotelian Society*, suppl. vol. 77 (1997), 99–130; and T. M. Scanlon, *What We Owe to Each Other* (Cambridge, Mass.: Harvard University Press, 1998), ch. 1. Actually Scanlon is a constructivist of a sort about moral reasons, and a realist about normative reasons of other kinds; one could also be a realist about normativity, but a skeptic about morality, denying that moral considerations constitute genuine reasons for action. For my purposes in what follows, the more important position is general realism about the normative, rather than the specific view that moral reasons are prior to and independent of the will, since it is the more general position that fundamentally contrasts with Korsgaard's brand of constructivism. I shall understand NMR in what follows in this more general sense.

independent of *us*. This is an idea that NMR accepts. It holds that when we project ourselves into the practical point of view, and set our minds to the question of what we ought to do, our deliberation is an attempt to get clear about an objective and appropriately independent fact of the matter, namely what an agent in our deliberative situation has most reason to do. Offhand, the assumption that the will is answerable to independent and irreducibly normative facts of this kind would seem neither metaphysically extravagant, nor otherwise implausible. To paraphrase Thomas Nagel, some unchosen constraints on choice may be among the conditions of its possibility.[5]

If NMR is a promising approach to the relation between normativity and the will, why does Korsgaard reject it in favour of her constructivist alternative? She seems to hold that NMR does not come to grips with the fundamental philosophical problem of normativity, and that in this respect constructivism is distinctly superior. Korsgaard's most fundamental complaint about NMR is that it doesn't in the end *explain* the normativity of the concepts and judgments to which it applies. NMR says that there are independent normative truths about what we have reason to do (including truths about our moral reasons), and that deliberative reflection is an attempt to get clear about this independent normative realm. But NMR does not itself provide any global account of why the normative considerations it countenances are genuine reasons for action, considerations that advance a justified claim to govern our deliberative reflections. Thus Korsgaard represents the moral realist as postulating normative rules or standards that are to be applied by us when we engage in practical deliberation. But this way of conceiving of normativity, she argues, is unable to account for the authority of the postulated rules to tell us what we must do. 'If we think of rules of action as something we may or may not *apply* when we deliberate about what to do, then either we are obligated to apply them or we are not' (p. 112). In the first case, the realist will have to suppose that 'the notion of obligation [is] prior to the existence of the rule' (p. 111); this is tantamount to giving up the suggestion that normativity is fixed by independent rules that are potential objects of knowledge. In the second case, the realist will have abandoned the idea that the postulated rules are genuinely normative principles, and the fundamental problem of practical philosophy will remain unsolved.

Actually, this dilemma seems to be escapable by the proponent of NMR, as I have presented it. We should concede that the normative principles that the theory postulates are ones that we may or may not apply in practice. To admit this much is to acknowledge what is in any case extremely plausible, namely that people are only imperfectly rational, and that we often fail to do what we ourselves see to be normatively required. It doesn't follow from this, however, that there is a further normative question that can be raised in regard to any given normative principle, of whether we are obligated to comply with it. The normativity or

---

[5] See Thomas Nagel, *The Possibility of Altruism* (Princeton: Princeton University Press, 1970), 23.

bindingness is built into the content of the principle, its standing as a principle that specifies what we have reason to do. The question whether we are obligated to comply with a given principle is already settled by whatever considerations establish it, in the first place, as an expression of the independent truth of the matter about what there is reason to do. These considerations, I take it, will primarily be the deliverances of first-order deliberative reflection about action. Thus, if it is not incoherent to suppose that there can be independent normative truths about what we have reason to do, then there is nothing implausible about supposing that knowledge of those truths might guide our deliberative reflection.

Nevertheless, I think I have some idea of what Korsgaard is objecting to in this realist picture. Her complaint must be that the realist assumes that there are independent normative facts or truths, without doing anything to explain philosophically how the normative truths it postulates are possible. And indeed, if we conceive realism in ethics as an attempt to provide a unified philosophical *account* of normativity, then we must agree with Korsgaard that it does not succeed in shedding much light on the matter. If realism is to yield an explanation of this kind, then we should expect its distinctive feature—the postulation of a body of truths that are prior to and independent of us—to illuminate the capacity of those truths to legislate to us how we are to act and to live. But Korsgaard is surely correct in thinking that the independence of the moral truths does not itself explain their normative grip on us. On the contrary, in the context of the search for a global explanation of how normativity is possible, the postulation of an independent body of moral truths threatens to multiply questions rather than to answer them. Morality will start to look like an objective structure that is completely independent of the will, and consequently presumptuous in its aspiration to prescribe to us how we are to behave.

Let us now turn to Korsgaard's constructivism, to see whether it offers a more satisfactory approach to this explanatory issue. The idea that is central to constructivism is that we, as agents, construct or bring about a reality that is not prior to and independent of our volitional activity, but rather its product. If this is to help with the present problem, then the reality that is constructed must be the realm of the normative. Thus, whereas a realist view such as NMR has it that there are normative truths that are prior to and independent of the will, a constructivist position might hold that such truths are distinctively the result of our volitional activity. The question is, can we really make sense of the idea that the realm of the normative is itself constructed through our deliberative activity as agents?

There is one class of positions in moral and political philosophy that offers a comparatively clear account of the idea of constructing a normative realm, namely contractualist positions. These accounts represent the basic normative principles of justice or morality as the result of the choices of hypothetical agents under carefully circumscribed conditions. Thus Rawls defines justice by reference to principles defining the basic structure of society that a self-interested chooser would select from behind a veil of ignorance. Similarly, Scanlon takes morality to be specified by principles for the general regulation of conduct that could not reasonably be rejected by persons who are informed about their situation, and motivated by the concern to arrive at a set of principles that no one could reasonably reject. But it is striking that these theories attempt to construct only a part of the larger realm of normative concepts: in Rawls's case, the realm of justice, and in Scanlon's the morality of right and wrong.[6] The contractualist apparatus that gives a content to the metaphor of construction is in each case embedded within a larger context of normative concepts that are not themselves explicated in terms of a hypothetical choice situation, including reasons for action that are grounded in agents' projects, life plans, relationships, aspirations, conceptions of the good, and so on.

Korsgaard herself acknowledges this feature of contractualist views. She raises the interesting question of whether a form of constructivism can be conceived that goes all the way down, or whether instead constructivist approaches always presuppose more basic normative notions that are to be understood in realist rather than in constructivist terms (p. 118). She does not herself defend a definite answer to this question. But for my part, it seems that constructivism has to go all the way down if it is to represent a genuine alternative to the kind of position in ethics represented by NMR. So long as a constructivist theory takes for granted normative notions that are not themselves accounted for in constructivist terms, it loses its title to be the approach that is uniquely adequate to make sense of the characteristically *practical* dimension of normative thought and concepts. At the same time, so long as contractualism provides our paradigm for a constructivist approach, it is unclear that constructivism really could go all the way down. For I doubt that we can really make sense of the idea that *all* normative principles are the result of a hypothetical choice under specified conditions. To render this idea coherent, we would need to imagine agents making choices under parameters that can be represented without recourse to any normative concepts whatsoever, and our ideas of agency and choice would arguably give way under those conditions. Again, some unchosen normative constraints on choice would seem to be among the conditions of its possibility.

If I understand Korsgaard's position, it would seem to move in a rather different direction from these familiar contractualist accounts. Her version of constructivism rests ultimately on the idea that the normative principles that govern the will are the very same principles that are constitutive of the will in the first place. In a sympathetic discussion of Kant's views on freedom and morality, Korsgaard writes that 'the categorical imperative is a principle of the *logic* of practical deliberation, a principle that is constitutive of deliberation, not a theoretical premise applied in practical thought' (p. 115). The idea seems to be that the normativity of practical principles is to be accounted for by showing that we necessarily commit

---

[6] Thus as I mentioned above, Scanlon's NMR is a form of realism about normativity in general (including what he would call morality in the broader sense), within which his constructivism about the 'morality of right and wrong' (or morality in the narrower sense) is embedded. I discuss this aspect of his position in my paper 'Scanlon's Contractualism', Chapter 12 in this volume.

ourselves to complying with them whenever we undertake to act; commitment to such principles is, indeed, constitutive of willing anything at all. The element of construction in this account is to be understood not in terms of the hypothetical choice of principles (as in contractualist theories). It refers, more basically, to the fundamental role of practical activity in grounding the principles that regulate that very activity. Principles of practical reason are not principles whose normative force is prior to and independent of the will. Rather they are principles that are rendered normative for us *by* our act of willing itself, insofar as they describe constraints that we aspire to comply with in willing anything at all.

This is, of course, a bracingly audacious philosophical program. Korsgaard may be correct in thinking that it is the only approach that stands a chance of providing a unified account of the source of normativity, and she herself has done more than anyone to articulate its merits as an option in contemporary moral philosophy.[7] But I am skeptical that the normative force of all principles of practical reason can be accounted for by showing that we are committed to complying with them through the very act of willing. I shall mention two reasons for doubt on this score. First, there is the striking diversity of considerations that appear to have normative weight when people deliberate about what to do. Taken together, the things that can recommend or speak in favor of (or against) the potential actions of any given agent form a remarkably heterogeneous group. They include, to take only a few examples, considerations about the bodily and mental states of the agent (that a prospective action would be harmful, or cause pleasure or pain); considerations about the agent's relationships and status (that it would be unbecoming to do *x*, given one's professional role); and considerations of an aesthetic and moral nature that are themselves highly diverse and multifaceted. Korsgaard's constructivist thesis is that the normativity of all these different reasons can be accounted for in the very same way, by appeal to the basic idea of volitional commitment. But the project of providing a unified account of the normativity of such a heterogeneous range of considerations seems implausible on its face. It is far more natural to suppose that there is no unified account to be given of what renders the variety of considerations that count as reasons for action normative, what makes them significant for our practical deliberation.

Second—and more importantly—there are problems surrounding the interpretation of the notion of the will, as it figures in Korsgaard's constructivism. The unitary source of normativity, according to that account, is the commitment to comply with such normative requirements as the instrumental principle and the categorical imperative, a commitment that is in turn built into all concrete determinations of the will. But how are we to understand this important idea? There seem to be two possible interpretations, and neither of them is very plausible. We

---

[7] Especially significant in this connection is her book *The Sources of Normativity* (Cambridge, England: Cambridge University Press, 1996), and her 2002 John Locke lectures on 'Self-Constitution: Action, Identity and Integrity'.

might take volitional commitments to be brute motivational tendencies of some kind to comply with the principles whose normativity is in question. According to this interpretation, a basic tendency to act in accordance with those principles is partly constitutive of willing or choosing to do any particular action. But how can a brute tendency to comply with a given principle render that principle normative for me, a source of *reasons* for doing that which I am committed to doing? It could do so, I should have thought, only if some antecedent normative principle is operative that tells us that we have reason to comply with those principles that we are ineluctably inclined to act in accordance with. But a normative principle of this kind would not seem very plausible—it hardly seems to follow from the fact that I have a brute inclination to do something that it would be good or valuable to do so.[8] More to the point, postulation of such a principle would anyway explode the framework of constructivism, introducing at a crucial juncture in the account a principle whose normative force is not after all explained in terms of the idea of volitional commitment.

Alternatively, we might try to interpret such commitments not as brute motivational tendencies, but rather in essentially normative terms. Thus, Korsgaard might understand the commitments that are necessary to any individual determination of the will as states with normative content rather than as mere tendencies to act. But this proposal seems to introduce normativity at the wrong place. We need an account that shows how the commitment to comply with a principle can render that principle normative for the agent. For these purposes, it would seem necessary to attach normativity to the stance or state of commitment itself, and not merely to the content of that stance or state. From the fact that I am, say, committed to the normative principle that it would be good to thwart my enemy, it cannot be inferred that it really would be good for me to thwart my enemy. This would follow only if the stance of commitment is normative not merely in its content but in its essence. The problem is that there seems to be no way to make out the latter claim without presupposing some normative principle of the sort that the constructivist was supposed to be accounting for in terms of the idea of commitment itself.

Korsgaard might respond that this argument fails to take seriously the first-personal character of the perspective of deliberation. The normative commitments that are constitutive of individual acts of willing are commitments of the first-personal standpoint of practical reason. The objection broached in the preceding paragraph is that those commitments, even if necessary, might turn out to be false. But to affirm the falsity of such a first-order normative claim is itself to make a move from within the deliberative point of view. Korsgaard might contend that a move of this kind is ruled out by her argument for the necessity of the commitment to the normative principles that determine what we have reason to do

---

[8] I assume, here and in what follows, that an agent will have reason to do *x* only if their doing *x* would be good or valuable in some way.

(such as the categorical imperative and the principle of instrumental reason). If these commitments are genuinely constitutive of the standpoint of practical reason, there is no position from which we could intelligibly challenge them—any attempt to do so will lead to a performative contradiction.

This interpretation treats constructivism as a kind of transcendental argument, about the conditions for the possibility of willing. When we recall that the approach is meant to provide a unified explanation of the normative force of *all* reasons for action, it becomes clear just how ambitious it really is, and how unlikely it is to succeed on its own terms. But even putting this problem to the side, a difficulty remains concerning the interpretation of the notion of commitment. We have been supposing that commitments are normative in their content, and this amounts to treating them in essentially cognitive terms, namely as commitments to *believe* or *accept* that it would be good or valuable to act in compliance with certain principles. But this interpretation leaves unexplained the *motivation* of rational agents to comply with their reasons for action. Korsgaard covers over this problem by using ambiguous terms like 'commitment' to present her constructivist position, terms that can be understood either in a cognitive or in a conative sense. This encourages us to suppose that the states that are implicit in all deliberation and choice can explain at once the truth of normative claims about what we have reason to do, and our determination to comply with those truths in practice. But when we put pressure on this notion, and start to consider more carefully what exactly it might mean, an interpretation capable of discharging these dual tasks appears elusive. At the very least, more needs to be said about the notion of the will before we can make sense of the constructivist idea that it functions as the unified source of normativity.

The considerations adduced above make me skeptical about the prospects for Korsgaard's constructivism about normativity. The alternative approach that I myself favor is NMR. This approach holds that there are normative truths that are prior to and independent of the individual human will. In the version of NMR that I am attracted to, no attempt is made to provide a unified account of the normative force of the variety of reasons that are relevant to practical deliberation; in particular, there is no assumption that the postulated priority and independence of the normative truths is the common feature that makes them all normative. NMR should therefore not be construed as aspiring to rival Korsgaard's unifying explanation of the sources of normativity. It is rather a framework for thinking about practical normativity, one within which the aspiration to trace all normativity to a unified source is eschewed.

Among the advantages of this framework, to my mind, is the way it promises to illuminate the structure of rational agency. Agency of this kind, as I understand it, exhibits precisely the feature that Kant singled out when he characterized practical reason as the capacity to act not only in accordance with laws, but in accordance with one's conception of laws. This feature goes beyond the bare capacity for intentional action, construed as bodily movement that is both aimed at some goal, and causally sensitive to the agent's conception of the goal, as that which the agent is aiming to bring about. Activity can be intentional in the latter sense without being rational, and it is natural to locate the difference in the idea of responsiveness of action to the agent's conception of distinctively normative 'laws' or principles. By postulating that there are independent normative truths of the matter about what agents have reason to do in the situations they encounter, NMR secures a condition for the possibility of rational agency in this sense. Rationality in action can be understood as a matter of thinking clearly about the independent normative facts regarding one's reasons, and acting in a way that is both in accordance with and guided by one's grasp of those independent normative truths.

If this picture is to have application, however, then normative knowledge alone will not suffice. In addition, rational agents will require capacities that enable them to translate their normative insights into action, and to do so in ways that are genuinely guided by their normative understanding of what it would be best to do. This, in my view, is where the will comes in. The role that the will should play in relation to normativity is not as the unified source of normative principles, but rather as that which enables agents to act in the light of their grasp of such principles. The will, in this sense, is part of what sets distinctively rational creatures apart from other creatures that are capable only of more rudimentary intentional agency.

5

Normativity, Commitment, and Instrumental Reason

There are two tendencies in our thinking about instrumental rationality that do not seem to cohere very well. On the one hand, the instrumental principle—enjoining us to take the means that are necessary relative to our ends—does not seem to apply indifferently to any end that we might be motivated to pursue. There is, for instance, no genuine requirement to take the means that are necessary for realizing ends that one merely happens to desire. This encourages what we might call a moralizing tendency in reflection about instrumental reason: the supposition that instrumental requirements come on the scene only in relation to ends that have themselves been endorsed in some way by the agent, as ends that it would be good or desirable to achieve.

On the other hand, it seems undeniable that agents can display a kind of instrumental rationality in the pursuit of ends that they do not themselves endorse, when for instance they are in the grip of *akrasia*. People sometimes exhibit great intelligence and skill in executing plans that they view as dubious or questionable—think, for instance, of the extraordinary talent many of us display at procrastinating when it comes to tasks that we regard as worthy but difficult. It seems plausible to regard this kind of intelligence—cleverness, as we might call it[1]—as a form of instrumental rationality, relative to the ends that we are in fact pursuing.

Originally published in *Philosophers' Imprint*, 1/3 (Dec. 2001), URL = http://www.philosopher-simprint.org/001003. Reprinted by permission. The Postscript is new to this collection. Earlier versions of this paper were presented to the Jowett Society of Oxford University, to the Berliner Workshop zur praktischen Vernunft, to the Philosophy Department of the University of California at Berkeley, to the section on metaethics and methodology of the Netherlands School for Research in Practical Philosophy in Utrecht, and to a workshop on moral and social philosophy at the Australian National University; many thanks to the audiences on all these occasions for very helpful feedback. A list of the numerous people whose probing and constructive questions led to improvements would have to include at least the following: Karin Boxer, Jan Bransen, Ruth Chang, Stephen Darwall, Hannah Ginsborg, Brad Hooker, Joanna Perkins, Joseph Raz, Samuel Scheffler, and Theo van Willigenberg. Lengthy written comments by John Brooms and a second reader for *Philosophers' Imprint* (who has since identified himself to me as Michael Bratman) were especially helpful, and prompted extensive changes during the last round of revisions. My interest in the phenomenon of cleverness grew out of memorable discussions with Michael Smith held in Princeton in the 1980's.

[1] I borrow this term (loosely) from English translations of Aristotle. In the Aristotelian context 'cleverness' means instrumental effectiveness with respect to ends that are in fact bad; I shall use it to refer to effectiveness relative to ends the agent believes to be bad.

This verdict, however, conflicts with the moralizing tendency in our reflection about the instrumental principle, since the cases at issue are precisely ones in which people do not endorse the ends they are pursuing as good or worthwhile on the whole. There thus appears to be a latent tension in our thinking about instrumental rationality.

My ultimate aim in this paper will be to resolve this latent tension. The key to doing so, I shall argue, is to arrive at an improved understanding of the options in moral psychology that are available to us for conceptualizing both rational and irrational motivation. My thesis will be that we can account adequately for instrumental rationality only if we depart from a motivational psychology that makes do with the elements of belief and desire. In particular, we need to suppose that rational agents are equipped with a capacity for active self-determination that goes beyond the mere susceptibility to desires and beliefs.[2] On this volitionalist picture, as I shall call it, rational agency is made possible when we choose or decide what to do in ways that align with our own reflective verdicts about the reasons that bear on our deliberative situation.

Before we can see how this volitionalist account helps us with the problem of instrumental rationality, however, it will be necessary to take a detailed look at the nature of the volitional commitments involved in human agency. In particular, we must consider the extent to which such commitments are to be understood in normative terms. I shall argue against the interpretation of volitional commitment as an essentially normative stance. This issue is of substantial interest in its own right, with important implications in regard to the possibility of irrationality in action. But consideration of the issue will also point the way to an improved understanding of instrumental reason, enabling us eventually to resolve the latent tension in our thinking about the instrumental principle to which I called attention above.

The paper divides into four sections. In the first, I consider a number of arguments that have recently been advanced in favor of the normative interpretation of self-determination. These arguments purport to establish that genuine agency and self-determination presuppose the agent's commitment to normative principles. But I show that the arguments do not succeed: there is no general reason why agents should not be able to commit themselves to ends that they do not really endorse. Section 2 considers some differences between practical and theoretical reason. I contend that the proper counterpart of belief in the realm of action is not desire but choice or decision; but I suggest that the latter states do not involve the normative commitments characteristic of belief. In the third and

---

[2] There are other strategies for capturing the distinctive intelligence of human agency without departing from a belief-desire motivational psychology. For instance, some philosophers postulate higher-order desires with normative content—such as the desire to do what one ought—to explain how rational agency can reflect the agent's grasp of their reasons. I discuss this strategy (under the rubric of 'meta-internalism'), and contrast it with the volitionalist motivational psychology that is more conventionally associated with the Kantian approach, in my paper 'Three Conceptions of Rational Agency', Chapter 2 in this volume. In the present paper I focus primarily on the more conventional, volitionalist version of the Kantian approach, though many of the points I make against normative interpretations of the will apply equally to meta-internalism.

fourth sections, I return to the problem of instrumental rationality. Drawing on the version of volitionalism defended in sections 1 and 2, I develop a nonmoralizing account of the normativity of instrumental reason. In particular, I show how we can explain the normative force of the instrumental principle without supposing that the ends to which the principle applies need be endorsed by the agent, as good or worthy of pursuit. Among the advantages of this strategy, it will emerge, is the attractive interpretation it makes possible of the phenomenon I referred to above as cleverness.

1. CHOICE AND NORMATIVE ENDORSEMENT

Let us begin with some issues in motivational psychology. I suggested above that we should reject the belief-desire model of human motivation and postulate a distinctive capacity for self-determining choice, as a precondition of rational agency. It is not my intention to argue directly for this suggestion in the present paper. Instead I want to raise an interpretative issue about the volitionalist strategy: how are we to understand the choices that, on the volitionalist picture, are characteristic of rational agency?

Christine Korsgaard has recently offered a normative interpretation of volitionalism, as a framework for understanding the binding force of principles of practical reason.[3] She takes choice to be a matter of first-personal commitment to pursue an end, where this commitment is essentially normative. To choose to do *x* is, in effect, to accept a 'law' or normative principle specifying, in general terms, which features of one's circumstances give one reason to do *x*. This stance commits one, in turn, to complying with a supreme unconditional principle of practical reason, the Kantian moral law, as well as with principles of instrumental reason instructing one to take necessary means to one's ends. This extremely ambitious approach can be understood as an attempt to extract from an interpretation of what we are doing when we act an account of the normative force of basic principles of practical reason.[4] Moral and instrumental principles are binding on us as agents, insofar as we necessarily commit ourselves to complying with them through the normative act of choice.

---

[3] For the normative interpretation of choice, as involving acceptance of a 'law', see Christine M. Korsgaard, *The Sources of Normativity* (Cambridge, England: Cambridge University Press, 1996), 97–100 and 222–33; see chs. 3 and 4 for the argument that this stance commits one to complying with the moral law; and for the argument that this commits one to complying with a principle of instrumental rationality, see Korsgaard, 'The Normativity of Instrumental Reason', in Garrett Cullity and Berys Gaut (eds.), *Ethics and Practical Reason* (Oxford: Clarendon Press, 1997), 215–54, esp. 243–54.

[4] A similar strategy is adopted by J. David Velleman, who holds that our understanding of the nature of reflective agency can deliver a substantive criterion for normative reasons. See his *Practical Reflection* (Princeton: Princeton University Press, 1989), ch. 7, and 'The Possibility of Practical Reason', as reprinted in his *The Possibility of Practical Reason* (Oxford: Clarendon Press, 2000), 170–99, at 188, 193, 198.

Notice that there are two kinds of normative commitment involved in human action, on this account of it. There are, first, specific normative commitments regarding the value of the actions we set out to perform; these commitments are enshrined in normative principles that specify our reasons for acting as we do, in the particular circumstances that confront us. But action on the basis of such principles involves, secondly, commitment to comply with more general principles of moral and instrumental rationality, principles whose normative force is explicated in terms of this second moment of commitment. I shall consider this second variety of normative commitment in sections 3 and 4, below, when I return to the question of instrumental rationality; for the moment, I want to focus on the specific kind of normative commitment involved in ordinary choices or intentions to act, on Korsgaard's interpretation of them.

To be clear, the issue is not whether choosing or intending to do something necessarily gives one reason to do it. A view of this sort, to the effect that intention and choice are what we could call objectively normative states, might seem to be the most promising basis for a moralizing approach to instrumental rationality. But this is not the view from which Korsgaard begins, and it is therefore not the view that I shall engage with here. Korsgaard's starting point is that intention and choice are subjectively normative states, involving our acceptance of a law that identifies, in general terms, our reason for acting in a given way. We must consider this thesis on its merits, including the very suggestive arguments that Korsgaard has advanced for thinking that choice and intention can be made sense of only on the assumption that they represent subjectively normative attitudes.

It is useful to think of the content of choices as specified by something like Kantian maxims. These may be treated as having the following schematic form: 'I shall do x, (under circumstances c), in order to y/as a way of y-ing'. Interpreted in this way, maxims articulate an agent's more or less provisional plan; choosing or deciding to do something can thus be thought of as committing oneself to a plan of action, the details of which can range from sketchy to quite complete.[5] Moreover, when one has reached a settled view about what one has reason to do, or which course of action it would be best to pursue, this view may be reflected in the content of one's choice. If, for instance, I believe it would be best to stop at a café after touring a new city for several hours, on account of my aching feet, my actual decision about what to do will ordinarily give expression to this normative belief. That is, I will commit myself to a maxim or plan of action with the following content: 'I shall stop at a café, in order to rest my weary feet'. When our intentions in acting rest on our conception of our reasons in this way, we should agree that the choices reflect normative commitments.

It is unclear, however, why choice should be thought of as necessarily normative, in the subjective sense distinguished above. In cases of *akrasia*, for example, we

---

[5] I am indebted here—and indeed throughout my discussion of the volitionalist approach—to Michael E. Bratman's pioneering work on planning agency; see his *Intention, Plans, and Practical Reason* (Cambridge, Mass.: Harvard University Press, 1987).

certainly appear to choose to act in ways that we ourselves do not regard as justified or best. What normative 'law' is supposed to be implicit in choices of this
kind? It cannot be the principle that we ought to be doing the action that we have
chosen to perform, on pain of simply denying that *akrasia*, in the strong and
philosophically interesting form, is so much as possible.[6] Perhaps, then,
Korsgaard has in mind a normative 'law' in a somewhat weaker sense—a principle, for instance, specifying that the action one has chosen to perform is at least
pro tanto good.[7] But offhand, even this seems to go too far. There are cases in
which we choose to do things without believing that there is anything genuinely
good about them, in the actual circumstances at hand—the apparent value of the
action we perform has the status of a *prima facie* good, not a *pro tanto* good. And
there appear to be other, more alarming cases in which we choose to do things that
we believe to be bad, precisely on account of their seeming badness.[8]

Here it is important to distinguish between the normative judgments that an
agent genuinely accepts, and the normatively structured thoughts that may be
prompted by the agent's desiderative and emotional states. It is states of these latter kinds that generally incite us to act at variance with our settled views about
what there is most reason to do. Moreover, I believe that such desiderative and
emotional states typically involve normative cognitions of one kind or another.
Thus, on the first warm day of the summer term one may find that one wants to
head off to the beach, and this desire will show itself in the thought that it would
be good (because, say, pleasant) to spend the day amidst the surf and sand.
I believe further that the connection between desiderative and emotional states
and such normative cognitions helps to explain the fact that it occurs to us at all to
perform actions that we do not really believe to be good. Thus, if I am angry or
embittered, the fact that a prospective course of action would be bad may appear
to render it attractive, and I will be tempted to opt for the course of action on
account of its badness. But normatively structured thoughts of this kind are not to
be confused with normative judgments or beliefs. Our intellectual capacities
include the ability to entertain thoughts that we do not genuinely accept as true,
and the gap between normative thought and normative judgment makes possible
akratic action in the absence of a belief in the (*pro tanto*) goodness of what one is

---

[6] In *The Sources of Normativity*, sect. 3.3.2, Korsgaard provides an explanation of how *akrasia* is
possible, turning on the idea that we can 'make an exception of the moment or the case' (p. 103). The
question, however, is how this is to be reconciled with her claim about the normative 'law' implicit in
the stance of choice. Either 'making an exception' is construed in normative terms, as endorsement of
the principle that it is permissible to give in to temptation under the circumstances, in which case we
are no longer dealing with a case of acting against one's better judgment. Or 'making an exception'
amounts to intentionally violating a normative principle we accept, in which case the claim about the
normative 'law' implicit in choice seems to go out the window.

[7] On the importance of *pro tanto* reasons and values in accounting for cases of *akrasia*, see
S. L. Hurley, *Natural Reasons: Personality and Polity* (New York: Oxford University Press, 1989), pt. 2.

[8] For insightful discussion of cases of this kind, see Michael Stocker, 'Desiring the Bad', *Journal of
Philosophy*, 76 (1979), 738–53, and J. David Velleman, 'The Guise of the Good', as reprinted in his
The Possibility of Practical Reason, 99–122.

doing. One may act on one's desire to go to the beach, for instance, without really accepting that the pleasures thus made available provide a reason to skip the class one is scheduled to teach.[9]

Of course, in what is doubtless the more common variety of *akratic* action, the agent accepts that there is something that is *pro tanto* good about the action that is performed. Furthermore, it is the fact that the action is believed to be genuinely good in some way that renders it an eligible candidate for choice, from the agent's point of view. Even when this is the case, however, we must be careful to distinguish between the agent's normative beliefs and the act of choice itself. After all, in many of the situations in which we judge that there is something *pro tanto* good about the action we are performing, we also judge that that action is not the one that it would be *best* to perform, on the whole. This is the general normative judgment that is authoritative for our practical reflection about what to do, and yet we choose to do something else instead. If we are to leave open the possibility of this kind of *akratic* action, we cannot understand choice exclusively in normative terms. Choice may often reflect or be based on normative commitments that the agent accepts, but it cannot be *identified* with such commitments without foreclosing genuine possibilities in the theory of action. There has to be something in the act of choice that distinctively goes beyond normative commitment if we are to leave room for *akrasia* and the other forms of irrationality to which action is characteristically subject.

Korsgaard offers two main arguments against this line of thought. The first of these appeals to the important idea that, as agents, we are not merely determined to act by the states of desire to which we are subject.[10] We are, as other proponents of volitionalism should agree, active with respect to our motives, and Korsgaard contends that this makes sense only on the assumption that when we act, we endorse a universal normative principle. Thus she writes: 'the special relation between agent and action, the necessitation that makes that relation different from an event's merely taking place in the agent's body, cannot be established in

---

[9] I elaborate on these suggestions about the cognitive structure of desire and emotion in my paper 'Addiction as Defect of the Will: Some Philosophical Reflections', Chapter 8 in this volume. Note that if my remarks here are on the right lines, there will be a different sense in which all choice might be said to be 'subjectively' normative, insofar as choice or commitment always presupposes at least the *apparent* value of the ends chosen. I take it, however, that Korsgaard wishes to affirm the subjective normativity of choice in the different and stronger sense discussed in the text.

[10] What follows is an interpretation of Korsgaard's remarks in the 'Reply' chapter of *The Sources of Normativity*, 222–33. The task of interpretation is complicated by the fact that, when Korsgaard introduces the notion of a 'law' in her argument for what she calls the categorical imperative, she does not explain or even give an example of what she has in mind (see ibid., sects. 3.2.3–3.2.4). But in the 'Reply' it seems clear that she takes the universal laws to which we commit ourselves in acting to be normative principles, specifying our conception of our reasons. She opens her discussion there by raising the question of 'why the dictates of the free will must be universal in any sense at all' (p. 222). A little later, however, she characterizes 'the point we were supposed to be establishing' as the thesis that '*reasons* are general' (pp. 224–5, my emphasis); and she begins talking about 'the *normative* principles of the will' (p. 229, my emphasis). This strongly supports my assumption that 'law' is to be understood throughout in the sense of a normative principle of action, specifying in general terms the agent's conception of their reason for acting.

the absence of at least a claim to law or universality'.[11] This claim is to be understood as 'a claim that the reasons for which I act now will be valid on other occasions, or on occasions of this type—*including this one, conceived in a general way*'.[12] Without a claim of this kind, Korsgaard suggests, agency effectively dissolves, insofar as we lose the conceptual resources for distinguishing between the choices of the agent and the results of psychological forces to which the agent is subject. Choice is intelligible only on the assumption that it is at least possible to fail to follow through on one's choice. This in turn supports the identification of choice with the act of commitment to a general principle, a universal law by reference to which some possible performances can be interpreted as failures.[13]

This argument seems to me correct in the following respect: when our choices to act are based on our conception of what we have reason to do, they will entail that we accept some general normative principle. The reason for this is that the conclusions of normative reflection are best understood as implicitly general judgments.[14] If I conclude that my being in the mood for an action movie gives me reason to see the latest John Woo film, I commit myself thereby to a normative principle that is general, insofar as it could apply to other situations besides the present one: for example that—other things being equal—one has reason to go to the kind of movie one is in the mood for, when it is a question of what would make for an entertaining evening.[15]

For present purposes, however, the relevant question is why one should identify the act of choice with the acceptance of a normative judgment of this kind. Korsgaard is surely correct to insist that our choices are recognizable as expressions of our agency only on the condition that it is in principle possible for us to fail to follow through on them. This means, perhaps, that their content— the plan of action given expression in a maxim—must be specifiable in terms that are to some extent general.[16] But there is no reason to suppose that the general specification must amount to a normative principle. Thus, in a spiteful and nasty mood I might resolve to burn all my roommate's books, without really supposing that what I am doing is best, on the whole; indeed, I might not really believe that it is good or justified in any way at all. In this case, the information supplied

---

[11] *The Sources of Normativity*, 228.   [12] Ibid. 232.   [13] Ibid. 228–33.

[14] Compare T. M. Scanlon, *What We Owe to Each Other* (Cambridge, Mass.: Harvard University Press, 1998), 73–4.

[15] As this example illustrates, the commitment to generality that is at issue is a fairly modest one. Note in particular that the general judgment I have formulated incorporates an 'other things equal' clause that the agent probably would not be able to unpack in nontrivial terms at the time of action. It is unclear whether this is at odds with Korsgaard's intentions, but it does make the talk about 'universal laws' seem somewhat overblown. For discussion of this issue, see Michael Bratman, 'Review of Korsgaard's *The Sources of Normativity*', as reprinted in his *Faces of Intention* (Cambridge, England: Cambridge University Press, 1999), 265–78, sect. 4.

[16] Again, the commitment to generality at issue is fairly minimal; there is nothing to rule out such indexically formulated intentions as the intention to catch *that man* in order to return his hat to him.

about the content of my resolution is enough to undergird the attribution of the resolution to me, as agent; it specifies a goal that I might in principle fail to reach—by, say, neglecting to burn the roommate's cookbooks in the kitchen. But identification of me as the agent of the choice does not require that I accept a normative principle justifying the action chosen, and in the case under consideration it would seem implausible to construe the choice as a commitment to a principle of this kind. Even if I accept that what I am doing is *pro tanto* good (insofar as it causes my roommate distress, say), my choice cannot be identified with acceptance of such a principle without rendering mysterious the phenomenon of *akratic* choice in the face of normative judgments about what it would be best to do on the whole. If an agent really accepts that a given action would be best, the identification of choice with normative commitment should entail that that is the action that is chosen, in fact—an apparent denial of the very possibility of clear-eyed *akrasia*.

On Korsgaard's behalf, it might be suggested that we can leave open this possibility by distinguishing between normative judgments and normative commitments. *Akratic* agents judge that some action *y* would be best, but commit themselves to an alternative action *x*, which they thereby affirm to be good along some dimension. But this just concedes the point I have been at pains to make in this section. The distinction between normative judgment and normative commitment can be drawn only if there is something in the act of commitment that distinctively goes beyond acceptance of a normative principle or judgment, and this assumption calls into question the identification of volitional commitment with the acceptance of a normative principle or judgment. In any case, the example above makes clear that we do not need to identify choice with normative commitment in order to make sense of our authorship of our actions. So long as choices are interpreted in terms of an implicitly general plan of action, we have resources enough to render intelligible the attribution of them to the agent.

Korsgaard's second argument seems to take for granted that choices might be intelligible as such even if their agent does not accept an antecedent normative principle that justifies them. Thus, she imagines a 'heroic existentialist' who chooses to pursue an end without supposing that there is anything independently good about the end to be pursued.[17] This sounds like the kind of case I have just described, except that Korsgaard goes on to add that the existentialist must at least view their own act of will as normative, as creating a reason to act where there was none before. In effect, it seems, the heroic existentialist endorses a general normative principle whose content is that one has reason to pursue those ends one has

---

17 'The Normativity of Instrumental Reason', 250–3. It is not clear that Korsgaard herself understands this case as opening up a new line of argument, in part because she seems in some doubt as to whether the attitude of the heroic existentialist is a real possibility (see esp. p. 251). But if it is conceded to be a possibility, the case calls in question the strong conclusion of her first argument, namely that choice is intelligible only if it is justified by a universal normative judgment the agent accepts.

chosen to pursue; it is only that this principle does not and cannot provide an independent justification for the initial act of choice.

But why must one accept a normative principle of this kind in support of the action one has chosen to perform? As I cart the books out to the back yard and fling them onto the pyre, must I really suppose that the bare fact of my having resolved to do such a silly thing makes it a good thing for me to be doing? Korsgaard answers such questions as follows: 'If I am to will an end, to be and to remain committed to it even in the face of desires that would distract and weaknesses that would dissuade me, it looks as if I must have something to *say to myself* about why I am doing that—something better, moreover, than the fact that this is what I wanted yesterday.'[18] Well, in the case we have been imagining I do have something better to say to myself than that burning the books is what I wanted yesterday, namely that it's what I have resolved to do. Unless one is a heroic existentialist, this doesn't by itself count as a justification for the action; but why should it be thought psychologically impossible to carry out one's intentions if one doesn't have a way of justifying them to oneself?

The reasonable point to which Korsgaard is calling attention is that intentions that diverge from one's normative judgments will not form a reliable basis for long-term planning about the future. If I really believe that it would be best to go into the office next Saturday to work on admissions files, it would be peculiar for me nevertheless to say that I intend to stay home on Saturday and watch the game; my normative judgment about what I ought to do would lead me to hope that I do not come to act on the intention, and this would undermine the role of the intention in my planning for the future. Since future-directed intentions are plausibly understood in part in terms of the role they play in such planning agency,[19] it may be doubted whether we would really want to speak of intention in a case such as this.

But this good point does not rule out the possibility of short-term intentions to act—still less intentions in acting—that diverge from our normative commitments. Granted, an agent who encounters large obstacles on the way to executing an *akratic* intention of this kind will find it hard to follow through on their intention, and will probably give up. But not necessarily: thinking that I really shouldn't do so, I might nevertheless choose to go out and buy a bottle of rum—and persist, despite discovering that the first shop I drive to is closed, and the second out of stock. In any case, there are plenty of situations in which we don't encounter any unusual additional obstacles on the way to carrying out our short-term *akratic* intentions. To suppose that the execution of such intentions must be impossible is, it seems to me, to neglect a large and interesting spectrum of cases of

---

18 'The Normativity of Instrumental Reason', 250.

19 Here I am drawing on Bratman, *Intention, Plans, and Practical Reason*. Also relevant are some of the considerations raised by Gregory Kavka in 'The Toxin Puzzle', *Analysis*, 43 (1983), 33–6; for a sophisticated recent discussion of these issues, see Michael Bratman, 'Toxin, Temptation, and the Stability of Intention', as reprinted in his *Faces of Intention*, 58–90.

freely chosen human action, encompassing such phenomena as sheer willfulness, stubbornness, lethargy, habit, blind self-assertion, thoughtlessness, and various actions expressive of emotional states.[20]

To be sure, in not all cases of this kind is it equally plausible to suppose that agents really choose or commit themselves to acting in a way they do not endorse. People quite often decide on a course of action that they take to be supported by good reasons, and continue on that course in the face of subsequent doubts or new reasons to reconsider their original normative assessment of what they are up to. There is a kind of 'volitional inertia' that enables us to carry on as before, despite our having revised our judgment about whether what we are doing is well advised. (Thus we may continue to flip through the channels on the television long after it has become clear to us that there is nothing on, and that it would be better to go back to work.) In these cases we may speak of practical irrationality in the absence of a deliberate choice that goes against normative principles we ourselves accept.[21] My point, however, is that there is also room for a more extreme kind of irrationality in action, in which we deliberately *choose* to act in a way that is at variance with our own normative beliefs about what it would be best to do. (We sometimes choose to turn on the television while knowing in advance that there is nothing on, and that it would be better to get back to work.) Furthermore, the same phenomenon of volitional inertia implicated in cases of irrationality without choice can help us to execute short-term intentions that exhibit this kind of extreme irrationality. Thus, if we can carry out even fairly complicated activities in the face of a revised normative assessment of their value, we should equally be able to carry out such activities when the choice to engage in them was not one that we initially endorsed—provided, perhaps, that we do not encounter too much resistance along the way.[22] One would need a powerful philosophical argument to establish that appearances must be deceptive in this area, that we can follow through on our immediate intentions in the face of potential resistance only if we initially viewed them as justified.

[20] Compare Velleman, 'The Guise of the Good'. Velleman himself supposes, however, that agents who have chosen to do something precisely because it is bad must take the badness of the chosen action to be a reason for performing it, something that contributes to the intelligibility of what they are doing (see ibid. 121–2). This further claim seems strained to me, given the rest of what Velleman says about the cases he discusses: a person completely unconcerned about the goodness of what they are doing would presumably be equally unconcerned about whether what they are doing is fully intelligible, or otherwise makes sense. The claim is connected with Velleman's account of full-blooded human action as motivated by a basal desire of the agent's that provides a criterion for something's being a normative reason (see e.g. his 'The Possibility of Practical Reason').

[21] See Hilary Bok, 'Acting Without Choosing', *Noûs*, 30 (1996), 174–96, for an illuminating discussion of cases of this kind.

[22] It is interesting to note here that cases of carrying on in the face of 'external' obstacles (the closed liquor shop) are more easily conceivable than cases of carrying on in the face of such 'internal' obstacles as laziness, boredom, and distraction. If I believe sincerely that there is nothing to be said for burning my roommate's books, then—barring a particularly strong case of 'volitional inertia'—I will almost certainly stop burning them when I become interested in a football game on television (thanks to Ruth Chang for this example). The reason for this, I would suggest, is that *akratic* action

Korsgaard's first argument aims to establish a conclusion of this kind, but as we have seen that argument does not succeed. Beyond that, I can merely venture a diagnosis of her position. Korsgaard seems to assume that there are only two options in the theory of the will: either we assume that the ends we pursue are fixed by our desires, or we grant that persons are capable of choosing for themselves what they shall do, where choice in turn is a matter of normative endorsement.[23] Since I agree with her that the first option is unattractive, I concede that we would have grounds for preferring the second, if it is the only alternative. But it should by now be apparent that I do not believe this to be the only alternative. Human agents have the capacity for a sophisticated kind of rational agency, insofar as they can reach independent normative conclusions about what they have reason to do, and then choose in accordance with such normative conclusions. This capacity presupposes that we are equipped with the power to choose independently of the desires to which we are subject.[24] Once we have this power, however, it can be put to use in ways that are at odds with our own practical judgments about what we have reason to do. That is, we can treat our disposition to do what we ought as a further desire from which we set ourselves apart, choosing to act in a way that is at variance with our reflective better judgment. This may be regarded as a hazardous by-product of the capacity for self-determination that makes rational agency possible in the first place.

2. INTENTION AND BELIEF

Reflecting on this side of agency, we see that there are important dissimilarities between our capacities in the practical and the theoretical spheres. In much writing about practical reason it is customary to press very hard an analogy between

presupposes an emotional or desiderative state—involving, as I explained above, normative thoughts about the action one is performing—that is contingently incompatible with such states as boredom and distraction. Thus, the kind of intense anger or spite that might lead me to want to burn my roommate's books leaves little psychological space for (say) interest in a football game on TV; by the time I become interested in the game, my anger will have abated to the point where I am no longer even tempted by the prospect of burning the books.

[23] See e.g. 'The Normativity of Instrumental Reason', 251 n. 74, where Korsgaard writes: 'The heroic existentialist's ends are not merely the objects of his desires, but rather of his will, so he is not merely given them by nature: he has endorsed them, and to that extent he does see them as things he has reason to pursue.' What I am questioning is why an object of one's will must necessarily be something one endorses, as reason-giving in any sense. For a different challenge to Korsgaard's conception of the options in the theory of action, see Bratman, 'Review of Korsgaard's *The Sources of Normativity*', 276–7.

[24] I understand by desire here an occurrent state of being attracted or drawn to a course of action, which can become an object of reflective self-awareness. I discuss the volitional capacity to choose independently of desire in this sense in the following papers: 'Three Conceptions of Rational Agency', Chapter 2 in this volume, sect. 3; 'Addiction as Defect of the Will', Chapter 8 in this volume; and 'Moral Responsibility and the Practical Point of View', Chapter 7 in this volume.

reasons for belief and reasons for action.[25] Korsgaard's treatment of the will provides an example of this trend. Thus, she rejects the assumption that the proper
counterpart of belief in the practical sphere is desire; pointing out that believing is
an essentially normative act, she suggests that the right analogue in the practical
sphere must involve a similarly normative commitment, arguing that volition or
choice is suited to play this role.[26] I would agree with Korsgaard that it is a mistake
to attempt to reconstruct agency in terms of the concept of desire, but disagree
that agency is like believing in being essentially normative.

The inherent normativity of believing is reflected in the fact, to which
G. E. Moore famously called attention, that first-person assertions of the following forms are paradoxical: '*P* is true, but I don't believe it' and 'I believe that *p*, but
p isn't true.' Moore's paradox brings out that to believe a proposition is to be committed to its truth,[27] and this normative aspect of believing, as we might call it, is
connected with the further fact that there are clear limits, of a conceptual nature,
on the possibility of believing something at will.[28]

Against this suggestion, it might be objected that normativity has to do with
reasons, not with truth.[29] To say that belief is an inherently normative stance is
to say that it is specially connected to conceptions of what one has reason to
believe, and nothing would seem to follow from the considerations relevant to
Moore's paradox about whether this is or is not the case. I agree that it is natural to understand normativity as a matter of reasons, and that the considerations just adduced do nothing to suggest that belief is intrinsically connected
to reasons in a way that intention is not. In fact, as I shall suggest below, neither
belief nor intention is an intrinsically normative stance, if normativity is
construed in terms of the idea of intrinsic and necessary responsiveness to
(judgments about) reasons. But belief is intrinsically and necessarily responsive
to (judgments about) truth, and this yields a different sense in which belief—
by contrast to choice or intention—can be claimed to be an essentially normative
stance.

---

[25] For examples of this tendency, see Philip Pettit and Michael Smith, 'Freedom in Belief and
Desire', *Journal of Philosophy*, 93 (1996), 429–49; Peter Railton, 'On the Hypothetical and Non-
Hypothetical in Reasoning about Belief and Action', in Cullity and Gaut (eds.), *Ethics and Practical
Reason*, 53–79; Scanlon, *What We Owe to Each Other*, ch. 1; and Velleman, 'The Possibility of
Practical Reason'.

[26] 'The Normativity of Instrumental Reason', 248–9, esp. no. 69.

[27] For a much fuller presentation of the thought that this is one of the lessons of Moore's paradox,
see Richard Moran, 'Self-Knowledge: Discovery, Resolution, and Undoing', *European Journal of
Philosophy*, 5 (1997), 141–61. I have formulated the paradoxical Moore-sentences in terms of the
truth predicate to emphasize what Moran refers to on p. 157 of this paper as 'the internal relation
between belief and truth'.

[28] See Bernard Williams, 'Deciding to Believe', in his *Problems of the Self* (Cambridge, England:
Cambridge University Press, 1973), 136–51. For a nuanced discussion of the precise nature of the
commitment to truth implicit in belief, see Velleman, 'The Guise of the Good', 110–15, and 'The
Possibility of Practical Reason', 182–6.

[29] I am indebted to John Broome and Hannah Ginsborg for pressing me to be clearer about the
sense in which belief is an inherently normative attitude.

We may think of theoretical reason as a capacity to modify our beliefs directly, through reflection on the question of what we should believe.[30] Considerations pertaining to the truth of propositions are normative for theoretical reason, in this sense, insofar as they are immediately and constitutively relevant to theoretical reflection about what we should believe. Presumably we do not have reason to believe every proposition whose truth is epistemically accessible to us—many truths are too trivial or tangentially related to our interests to be the sorts of things we should bear in mind, or keep track of consciously, in the ways characteristic of belief. But when we do have reason to believe that p, the considerations that provide us with reason to do so will be considerations that speak in favor of the truth of p, and their status as reasons for belief will be connected crucially to the fact that they point in this way toward the truth.[31] Reasons for action, on the other hand, are considerations that bear on the question of the goodness or value of action. Truth and goodness are thus the normative aims of belief and action, respectively: those aims by reference to which we make sense of considerations as reasons for belief and for action. But if believing that p is (*inter alia*) a commitment to the truth of p, it follows that there is a sense in which belief can be considered an inherently normative stance. It involves our acceptance that the aim by which theoretical reflection is properly governed has been achieved, and this in turn places constraints on our capacity to believe things at will. By contrast, we do not ordinarily suppose that our capacity to *intend* or *choose* is similarly constrained by the aim that is normatively regulative of practical deliberation, regarding the value of the alternatives open to us. The question of what action we are going to perform is not necessarily answered by our having determined to our own satisfaction what it would be best to do.[32]

This intuitive disanalogy between the practical and theoretical cases is reflected in the fact that first-person utterances of the following statements do not appear to be paradoxical at all: 'I really ought to do x, but I'm going to do y instead,' 'X would be the best thing to do under the circumstances, but I intend to do y,' 'I've chosen to do y, though it's not in fact the best alternative open to me,' etc. Of course, if one has a thesis to maintain about the essentially normative character of choice, it would be possible to interpret the normative vocabulary deployed in

---

[30] Some may object to this characterization that 'oughts' and reasons have a comparatively modest role to play in theoretical reasoning, insofar as changes in our beliefs are often effected without reflection on the question of what we ought to believe. Nothing in the argument to follow hangs on my characterization of theoretical reason. For the record, however, it seems to me important to bear in mind that many of our beliefs are not arrived at through reasoning. Once we are clear about this, it becomes quite plausible to suppose that the cases of belief-revision that do involve reasoning are precisely cases in which there is at least implicit consideration of reasons.

[31] Of course, other kinds of considerations are sometimes brought to bear in assessment of our beliefs, as when it is said that we would be happier if we believed that our colleagues loved us. This kind of consideration is not however itself a reason for *believing* that our colleagues love us—though it might be a reason for *acting* in some way or other (e.g. for undertaking to induce the relevant belief by hypnosis or other indirect means).

[32] Compare Rogers Albritton, 'Freedom of Will and Freedom of Action', *Proceedings of the American Philosophical Association*, 59 (1985–6), 239–51, at 246–48.

such statements in an 'inverted commas' sense. But no thesis of this kind can be motivated by reflection on those statements alone. Our sense that they are not paradoxical does not rest on our recognition of the possibility that the speaker might be deploying evaluative vocabulary insincerely. It rests, rather, on the conviction that our capacities for agency and choice can be exercised in a way that does not automatically align with our normative convictions. We do not think of choice as an essentially normative stance, and this is connected with our feeling that our active powers of self-determination in the practical domain present us with a set of alternatives for action that is wider than the set of actions we ourselves approve of.

The disanalogy between the theoretical and the practical cases is further reflected in the fact that, whereas *akrasia* in the practical sphere is an intelligible and even familiar phenomenon, strong *akrasia* of belief is rather harder to imagine.[33] The latter would be a case in which one judges that a given conclusion—say, *p*—is true, and yet one consciously and without self-deception believes that not-*p*.[34] But how can one believe that not-*p* in this way, if at the same time one consciously judges that *p* is true? T. M. Scanlon, who presses in a different way the analogy between theoretical and practical reason, has proposed an answer to this question. Drawing on the plausible assumption that belief involves an interconnected network of dispositions over time (including dispositions to recall the proposition one believes and to feel convinced about it, to use it as a premise in further reasoning, etc.), Scanlon suggests that *akrasia* is no less conceivable in connection with belief than in the practical realm: 'I may know, for example, that despite Jones's pretensions to be a loyal friend, he is in fact merely an artful deceiver. Yet when I am with him I may find the appearance of warmth and friendship so affecting that I find myself thinking, although I know better, that he can be relied on after all.'[35]

There is no doubt that cases of this kind are possible, perhaps even common. The question is whether they qualify as cases of *akrasia* of belief in the strong sense defined above. I am not convinced that they do; here it is necessary to recall the distinction introduced above between normatively structured cognitions and normative judgments. Certainly Jones's appearance of warmth and conviviality can prompt in me the thought that he is a decent friend. But do I really *believe* that this is the case, if at the same time I know that his appearance of friendship is nothing more than an artful pretence? This seems highly implausible. Of course, the thought that Jones is reliable might turn into a belief, if the force of his warm appearance prompts me to reconsider my judgment that he is merely a deceiver. But if I remain committed to that judgment—if, as Scanlon puts it, I *know* that Jones is merely an artful deceiver—then the thought that he is reliable cannot be

[33] On this point, I agree with Hurley, *Natural Reasons*, 130–5, 159–70.

[34] We might contrast strong *akrasia* of belief in this sense from weak *akrasia* of belief, in which one merely fails to accept *p* in the face of the judgment that *p* is (very likely to be) true.

[35] Scanlon, *What We Owe to Each Other*, 35.

considered a proper belief. The reason, again, is that belief is an inherently normative stance, in the special sense distinguished above.

Granted, belief is probably best understood as involving a network of dispositions that extends over time. It follows, perhaps, that the normative judgment that *p* is true does not entail that one actually forms the sustained belief that *p*, in the full sense of the word.[36] Much of the trivial but presumably reliable information one reads about in the daily *Times*, for instance, is not retained in memory, deployed in future episodes of reasoning, associated in one's thought with a feeling of conviction, and so on. Normative commitment to the truth of *p* may thus not be sufficient to ensure that one actually comes to believe that *p*. Nevertheless, normative commitment of this kind does seem necessary to the stance of believing that *p*. That is, when one believes that *p*, one is thereby committed to the truth of *p*. This is what rules out strong *akrasia* of belief, in which one consciously believes that not-*p* while also judging that *p* is true.

There is a different phenomenon that is often discussed under the heading of *akrasia* of belief.[37] This is the phenomenon whereby one believes that not-*p*, while also accepting that the available evidence speaks overwhelmingly in favor of *p*. To take a clear if somewhat hackneyed example: parents may find themselves clinging to the belief that their daughter is still alive, while granting that all indications point toward the conclusion that she went down with the other passengers in the shipwreck. What makes this phenomenon possible, despite the kind of normativity I have argued to be inherent in belief, is the logical gap between theoretical reasons and the truth of the propositions for which those reasons speak. Even when the available evidence points overwhelmingly to the truth of *p*, it is still possible that *p* is false, and the person who hangs onto the belief that not-*p* in the face of massive evidence to the contrary is exploiting this possibility. For this reason, belief resembles intention in respect to the different sense of normativity distinguished above: neither attitude is intrinsically and necessarily responsive to (judgments about) reasons. But there is no similar logical gap to exploit in the case in which one accepts not merely that the evidence speaks in favor of *p*, but that *p* is true; this is what rules out the possibility of strong *akrasia* of belief such as I have described. Nor is there any need to appeal to a gap of this kind to account for the possibility of *akrasia* in the sphere of action.[38] The *akratic* agent may choose to do *x*, while believing not merely that the evidence speaks in favor of the conclusion that some alternative action *y* would be better, but that *y* would in fact be better.

[36] Some cases of this kind will be cases of weak *akrasia* of belief. But not all cases: there are many contexts, such as the one I go on to describe in the text, in which considerations such as intellectual clutter-avoidance make it perfectly rational not to believe (in Scanlon's dispositional sense) all of the propositions whose truth one is prepared to grant. Compare Gilbert Harman, *Change in View* (Cambridge, Mass.: MIT Press, 1986), 56.

[37] See e.g. Alfred R. Mele, *Irrationality: An Essay on Akrasia, Self-Deception, and Self-Control* (New York: Oxford University Press, 1987), ch. 8.

[38] Thus, I would dispute Mele's claim that 'strict incontinent believing is possible for roughly the reason that strict in continent action is', *Irrationality*, 119.

This is the respect in which theoretical reason seems disanalogous to practical reason. I have contended that there is no paradox involved in choosing to pursue an end that one acknowledges to be bad, tracing this to the idea that volition differs from belief in not being an essentially normative commitment. Having said that, however, I should also like to reiterate that there are complex and important connections between choice and normative *concepts*. Thus, in cases in which we choose at variance with our better judgment there must be something that makes the action chosen seem attractive, an eligible candidate for performance from the agent's point of view, and this will typically be a function of our normative cognitions. We might believe, for instance, that what we are doing is *pro tanto* good, while judging that it is not really best on the whole. Alternatively, states of emotion or desire can make it *seem* to us as if our actions are valuable in some dimension, even if we are aware that they are not valuable in fact. Furthermore, citing these kinds of evaluative thoughts and cognitions can help us to understand *akratic* actions retrospectively, making it at least partially intelligible why the worse act was freely chosen, what made it seem attractive to the agent at the time. In this sense, evaluative cognitions can illuminate the reason why *akratic* agents act as they do.[39]

In practice, of course, cases of nonnormative choice are the exception rather than the rule. Our capacities for self-determining choice are what make possible deliberate practical rationality in the face of temptation, and in a vast range of cases we exercise them in ways that we believe will facilitate rather than thwart the realization of aims we endorse. Exemplary in this connection is the phenomenon of decision, which we ordinarily understand as the deliberative resolution of uncertainty on an agent's part about what is to be done. In ordinary decision-making, the agent arrives through reflection at the decision *that* (say) *x* would be the best thing to do, where this in turn involves a corresponding orientation of the will—a decision *to* do *x*. There is no phenomenological gap between the two sides of decision, the normative judgment, on the one hand, and the formation of a corresponding intention on the other, and this is reflected in the use of a single term to refer to both aspects. In cases of this kind, the content of the intention with which the agent acts, specifying what it is that the agent decides to do, will be a maxim of the subjectively normative sort discussed in the preceding section, one that reflects the agent's judgment about their grounds for doing what they have chosen to do.

Furthermore, even when we fail to do what, by our own lights, we ought to do, there is plenty of room for the kinds of errors and mistakes in reasoning familiar from theoretical contexts. We often neglect to focus on the relevant considerations

[39] It has become something of a truism in philosophical discussions of *akrasia* that the *akratic* agent acts 'for a reason'. This way of speaking is harmless enough, if it is only meant to call attention to the fact that *akratic* agents act intentionally, and that their choices can be made sense of retrospectively in light of their other psychological states. It should not however be taken to imply that *akratic* agents necessarily endorse what they are doing, as even *pro tanto* good.

as the time for action approaches; or we revise our normative judgment under pressure of the temptation to which we are subject, telling ourselves that it's really all right to have just one more drink, watch one more series of plays, smoke one more cigarette, and so on. My point in this section has merely been that irrationality in the practical domain is not necessarily traceable to errors and mistakes of these kinds. We are familiar with a kind of deliberate, self-conscious irrationality in action that has no direct analogue in cases of belief. This is connected with our understanding of our own powers of action as agents, our sense that what we do is in some ultimate way up to us, and it shows that the volitions on which we act are not essentially normative in their commitments.

3. CLEVERNESS AND NORMATIVE REQUIREMENTS

It is time to bring these reflections about motivational psychology to bear on the question from which I began in this essay, that of the normativity of instrumental reason. The instrumental principle introduced at the start of this paper enjoins us to take the means that are necessary relative to our ends. A central problem that is posed by this principle is to define the class of ends to which it applies—what we might refer to as the class of ends that are *privileged* with respect to instrumental reason.

On the one hand, it will not do to interpret this class of privileged ends as the ends that are fixed by an agent's desires. There is simply nothing irrational about wanting a given end—even wanting it very strongly—and failing to take the means that are necessary relative to the end. On the other hand, it equally will not do to interpret the class of privileged ends as fixed by the agent's normative beliefs. Thus, consider a case of *akrasia*, in which you believe that it would be best on the whole to do *x*, but you do *y* instead. In a case of this kind, you of course fail to take the means that are necessary to bring about the ends that you believe it would be best to pursue. Yet it would seem peculiar to characterize the problem in this scenario as a breakdown of instrumental rationality.[40] *Akratic* agents do not go wrong in failing to take the means that are necessary relative to their ends, but in failing to have the right ends in the first place.

Now, Korsgaard's interpretation of the instrumental principle promises an improved account of the class of privileged ends, building on the basic idea of volitional *commitment*. According to Korsgaard, the instrumental principle tells us to adopt those means that are necessary in regard to the ends we have actively accepted or endorsed, as normative. Her contention is that the force of the instrumental principle—its bindingness on us, as a principle of practical reason—derives from

[40] That is, if instrumental rationality is construed as a matter of adopting necessary means to one's ends. As I explain later, there are broader norms of means-end coherence that often are violated in cases of *akrasia*, and that can help to explain what is ill-advised, from the agent's own point of view, about the course of action that is chosen.

the active nature of the stance of commitment to an end we endorse.[41] To be committed actively in this way is, among other things, to endeavor to bring about the end that one endorses as good, and this orientation of the will requires that one adopt the means that are (believed) necessary with respect to that end. The principle of instrumental rationality is thus construed as a constitutive principle of the will, a principle we necessarily commit ourselves to complying with through the normative act of choice.[42]

Of course, this account of the instrumental principle is couched in terms of the normative interpretation of the will that was criticized extensively above. The present question, however, does not concern the general adequacy of Korsgaard's account of volition, but the conditions for the application of the instrumental principle. Even if I am right that there can be intentional human action in the absence of normative commitment, it might still be the case that means-end rationality gets a grip on us only when the condition of normative commitment to an end of action has been satisfied.

But I believe we should reject this moralizing assumption. The reason is that it neglects the phenomenon I referred to earlier as cleverness, or effectiveness in the pursuit of ends one does not endorse. In cases of *akrasia*, for instance, agents often exhibit great practical intelligence in the pursuit of ends that they do not themselves accept as good—tracking down the one shop in town, for instance, where it is possible to purchase at midnight the bottle of rum they have just decided, against their better judgment, to acquire. Furthermore, this kind of practical intelligence seems correctly characterized as a matter of rationality, relative to the *akratic* agents' ends. Given their determination to achieve the chosen ends, it seems a requirement and not merely an option that such agents should take the means that are necessary to bring their ends about, and those who fail to do this exhibit a characteristic breakdown of rationality. Indeed, they display a lapse precisely in regard to the instrumental principle. This strongly suggests the need for an account of the normative requirement expressed in the instrumental principle

---

[41] See Korsgaard, 'The Normativity of Instrumental Reason', esp. 245–51. I interpret Korsgaard in these pages as arguing for the instrumental principle from the distinctive features of the subjective attitude of commitment to an end that you normatively endorse. John Broome has suggested that Korsgaard is better interpreted as arguing from the assumption that the attitude of intention is (objectively) a reason to do what you intend (see his 'Normative Requirements', *Ratio*, NS 12 (1999), 398–419, sect. 11). But Korsgaard never endorses this objective normative relation, nor would it be particularly plausible for her to do so (since intending an end does not itself seem to give you reason to adopt it). Her 'constructivist' argument is best understood as building on the distinctive features of the stance of commitment to realize an end, a stance that Korsgaard believes to involve an element of normative endorsement. (For further discussion, see 'Normativity and the Will', Chapter 4 in this volume.) My contention will be that this general strategy is on the right track, though Korsgaard's own development of the strategy is flawed: it is not the stance of normative endorsement of an end that introduces rational constraints on our other attitudes, but the distinct and independent stance of commitment to realize the end (a point I believe Broome would also accept, as I go on to explain below).

[42] This is what I referred to in sect. 1, above, as the second moment of normative commitment in Korsgaard's reconstruction of rational agency.

that will apply both to cases in which agents take their ends to be well grounded, and to cases in which they do not do so.[43]

But the phenomenon of cleverness helps to bring into focus a different aspect of the instrumental principle that is equally significant. This is that the principle imposes rational constraints on the attitudes of agents without entailing either that they have reason to take the means necessary relative to their ends, or that they are rationally required to believe that they should adopt the necessary means.[44] Thus, in cases of this kind agents do not believe an objective normative relation to obtain between the overall goodness of the ends under pursuit and the necessary means to the attainment of those ends. It is precisely the hallmark of cases of *akrasia* that the agents involved in them do not believe their ends to be the best, and the pressure to adopt the necessary means therefore cannot be accounted for by assumptions about the transmission of normativity across the relation of ends and means. We should accordingly balk at saying either that *akratic* agents have a normative *reason* for taking the means that are necessary relative to their ends, or that they are rationally required to believe that they have such a reason. On the other hand—and this is the point emphasized above—the fact that an agent has chosen to pursue x introduces rational constraints on their other attitudes and intentions that go beyond the constraints imposed by the mere desire for x, and that are independent of the agent's normative commitments in regard to the desirability of x-ing. These constraints amount to a requirement of instrumental consistency, and what I have referred to as cleverness is a matter of responsiveness to this requirement.

We thus arrive at the following position: an adequate account of the instrumental principle must explain its applicability even to cases of cleverness, but without delivering the questionable conclusion that the deliberate pursuit of an end always yields a reason to take the means that are necessary relative to the end. I now want to sketch the outlines of a response to this problem, proceeding in two steps. The first step concerns the kind of requirement represented by the instrumental principle. We are looking for an interpretation of this principle according to which it imposes constraints on the attitudes of agents, without giving them reason to take the necessary means to their ends. A natural way to achieve this result is to construe the principle as governing combinations of attitudes—as a normative

---

[43] Earlier (in n. 9) I suggested that even *akratic* choice could be said to be subjectively normative, insofar as it is prompted by emotional and desiderative states that present options as attractive along some dimension or other. Stephen Darwall has suggested to me that one might appeal to this phenomenon to account for the grip of instrumental requirements even in contexts of *akrasia*, treating *akratic* actions as actions that are chosen 'on the hypothesis' that the chosen end is valuable. But I doubt whether this strategy can render cleverness fully intelligible. If instrumental requirements operate relative to the hypothesis that the end chosen is good or valuable, it is obscure why they should retain their force in cases of *akrasia*, since in these cases the agent precisely rejects the hypothesis that is supposed to be their basis.

[44] This is related to the 'bootstrapping' problem identified and discussed by Bratman in *Intention, Plans, and Practical Reason*, 24–7, 86–7; see also his 'Intention and Means-End Reasoning', *Philosophical Review*, 90 (1981), 252–65.

requirement, in the specialized sense recently distinguished by John Broome.[45] The distinctive features of a normative requirement, in this sense, can be illustrated by considering the relevance of logical principles, such as *modus ponens*, to theoretical reasoning. Suppose you believe p and you also believe $p{\to}q$. *Modus ponens* clearly applies to the contents of your beliefs in a situation of this sort, and it therefore imposes constraints on what you should believe. But it would be a mistake to interpret these constraints as licensing you to conclude that you ought to believe q, or even that you have reason to believe q. If for instance your belief that p is itself poorly grounded (by comparison with the considerations that speak against the supposition that q), it may be that the best way to comply with the relevant constraints on belief would be to give up your belief that p, rather than to form the new belief that q. The principle of theoretical reasoning based in *modus ponens*, in other words, functions as a constraint on combinations of your attitudes. We might put this by saying that its normativity is nondetachable, and of wide scope. The requirement could be expressed by saying that you ought to bring about the following: that you believe q, if you believe p and $p{\to}q$. It would be incorrect to understand the requirement as saying, or entailing, that if you believe p, and you believe $p{\to}q$, then you ought to believe q.

I submit that we would do well to interpret the instrumental principle along similar lines, as a constraint on combinations of attitudes that does not license detached normative judgments to the effect that we have reason to take the necessary means to our ends. Thus if you intend to do x, and believe that you can do x only if you do y, then the instrumental principle imposes a normative constraint on your attitudes. You can comply with this constraint either by giving up the intention to do x, or by forming the intention to do y. But it does not follow from the constraint, together with the fact that you intend to do x and believe that you can do x only if you do y, that you ought to intend to do y. In the cases of cleverness that we have been considering, for instance, this would seem to be precisely the wrong thing to say. If the instrumental principle is to apply in the right way to cases of this kind, we will need to understand it as a normative requirement in Broome's sense, imposing strict and nondetachable restrictions on sets of attitudes that include the intention to do x, and the belief that one can do x only if one does y.

This is the first step toward an adequate understanding of the instrumental principle that I announced above. The second step is to elucidate the normative force of the requirement that is embodied in the instrumental principle. Given the

---

[45] See esp. Broome's 'Normative Requirements'. Gilbert Harman makes a related point about the bearing of logic on theoretical reasoning (*Change in View*, ch. 2). The basic idea that instrumental requirements constrain combinations of attitudes is also implicit in some of the literature on hypothetical imperatives: see e.g. Stephen L. Darwall, *Impartial Reason* (Ithaca: Cornell University Press, 1983), 14–16; P. S. Greenspan, 'Conditional Oughts and Hypothetical Imperatives', *Journal of Philosophy*, 72 (1975), 259–76, sects. 4 and 5; R. M. Hare, 'Wanting: Some Pitfalls', as reprinted in his *Practical Inferences* (Berkeley and Los Angeles: University of California Press, 1972), 44–58, esp. 45–9; and Thomas E. Hill, Jr., 'The Hypothetical Imperative', as reprinted in his *Dignity and Practical Reason in Kant's Moral Theory* (Ithaca: Cornell University Press, 1992), 17–37, esp. 23–4.

understanding of this principle as a strict and nondetachable constraint on combinations of attitudes, what is it that makes it a rational constraint? We can appreciate
the task to be addressed here by recalling the comparison of desires with intentions.
As I noted above, the fact that you desire that you do *x*, and believe that you can do
x only if you do *y*, does not seem to have the same rational implications for your
further attitudes as the fact that you intend to do *x*. So there must be something
about the attitude of intending to do *x* that goes beyond the attitude of desiring
that one do *x*, in a way that brings a distinctively rational requirement into play.

To understand what this additional distinctive feature of intention might be, it
may help to return to Korsgaard's elucidation of the instrumental principle. On
her account, as we have seen, the ends to which the instrumental principle applies
are those that agents have actively committed themselves to realizing, where the
stance of active commitment is in turn taken to involve an attitude of normative
endorsement. There are two distinct parts to this account. One is the idea that
normative endorsement of an end by the agent is a condition for the applicability
of the instrumental principle. The second is the volitionalist idea that the ends to
which the principle applies are ones to whose realization the agent is actively committed. Korsgaard evidently supposes that these two ideas stand or fall together,
contending that the stance of commitment to an end must be cashed out in terms
of the different notion of endorsement of a normative principle. But I have argued
that Korsgaard is wrong to link these ideas in the way she does: the volitionalist
capacity for the distinctive stance of commitment to realize an end can be exercised independently from the kind of normative endorsement to which Korsgaard
appeals. Once we are clear about this, perhaps we can define in terms of the notion
of active commitment the privileged class of ends to which the instrumental
principle applies.

This suggestion certainly has an air of plausibility about it. If you are actively
committed to doing *x*, in the way characteristic of the stance of intention, then it
seems that you must also be committed to taking the steps that you believe to be
necessary to your doing *x*, on pain of irrationality. The question, however, is this:
why would you be irrational if you failed to intend the means that you believe to
be necessary, relative to some end that you intend to realize? What in particular is
it about the stance of commitment to realize the end that makes this combination
of attitudes rationally required, even in the absence of normative endorsement?
Until we have answered this question, we will not really have explained the force
of the normative requirement embodied in the instrumental principle.

Now, Broome has proposed a straightforward response to this problem.[46] The
normativity of the instrumental principle, he suggests, may be traced to the very
same logical constraints that underlie the requirement to adjust one's beliefs in
accordance with *modus ponens*. Suppose you intend to do *x*, and believe that *y* is a

---

[46] See John Broome, 'Practical Reasoning', in José Bermúdez and Alan Millar (eds.), *Reason and
Nature: Essays in the Theory of Rationality* (Oxford: Clarendon Press, 2002), 85–112; also Broome,
'Normative Requirements', esp. sect. 6.

necessary means to bringing it about that you do *x*. In this scenario, the objects of your intention and your instrumental belief can be represented as propositions to which *modus ponens* applies, as follows:

(a) You will do *x*.

(b) For you to do *x*, it is necessary that you do *y*.

Modus ponens tells us that these two propositions can be true only if a third proposition is also true, namely:

(c) You will do *y*.

The validity or truth-preserving character of this pattern of inference is what grounds the rational requirement that we should adjust our beliefs in accordance with it. Beliefs are essentially attitudes toward the truth of propositions, as we saw in section 2, above; the internal aim of the attitude of belief, as we might put it, is to track the truth. It follows that we are not rational in our beliefs if we do not arrive at them in a truth-preserving way, and this explains the relevance of logical principles such as *modus ponens* to theoretical reasoning.

But Broome suggests that intentions are equally attitudes toward the truth of propositions. They are not, to be sure, attitudes whereby we take propositions to be true; but they can be understood as attitudes whereby we are set to *make* propositions true. Once we grasp this point, Broome contends that we will see the direct relevance of the very same logical principles to practical reflection that involves intentions and beliefs about necessary means to our ends. If you intend to bring it about that (a) is true, and you believe that (b) is true, then you must intend to bring it about that (c) is true on pain of irrationality. For to fail to do this is to thwart the internal aim that is constitutive of your initial state of intention— the aim, namely, of bringing it about that (a) is true.

This is an elegant response to the present problem. It builds on the plausible idea that intention involves a commitment to bringing something about, cashing this out in terms of the attitude of being set to make a proposition true, in a way that renders considerations of validity immediately relevant to the assessment of the rationality of intentions. On closer inspection, however, it may be wondered how much this proposal really explains. One difficulty with it is that it does not seem to distinguish in the right way between our attitudes toward the means that are believed necessary to realize our ends, and our attitudes toward necessary but unintended consequences or side-effects of our pursuit of our ends. In the schema above, (b) could characterize equally either of these two relations. For instance, given my end of getting to work in time for my 11.00 a.m. class, I may believe both that it is necessary that I set off in the car before 10.30 a.m., and that I crush numerous acorns (which are littering the street at this time of year).[47] Following Broome, if I am set to make it true that I get to work in time for my 11.00 a.m. class, then these two beliefs of mine would seem to require that I be set to make it

---

[47] It is an interesting question how the notions of possibility and necessity relevant to instrumental rationality are to be understood; I come back to this issue in sect. 4, below.

true both that I drive off in the car before 10.30 a.m., and that I crush numerous acorns. But it would be odd, to say the least, to suggest that an intention to do the latter is rationally required by the other attitudes that have just been ascribed to me.

Broome responds to this difficulty by distinguishing between things that are necessary as consequences of my x-ing and things that are necessary as means to my x-ing.[48] Items of both kinds fall within the purview of the attitude of being set to make true. In the example just sketched, for instance, given my beliefs and my initial intention, I must be set to make it true both that I set off in the car before 10.30 a.m., and that I crush numerous acorns. But Broome suggests that not all the things that I am set to make true are things that I intend. If I intend to x, then I must rationally be set to make true anything that I believe to be necessary to my x-ing; but I must intend only those things that are believed to be necessary as *means* to my x-ing. But this proposal raises two new and very challenging questions. First, how are we to distinguish necessary means from necessary consequences of our actions? And second, how are we to distinguish the distinctive attitude of intending that p from the more generic attitude of being set to make it true that p? Broome's initial appeal to the idea of being set to make something true looked to be a way of elucidating the distinctive stance of intention, showing how it goes beyond the attitude of merely desiring that p, in a way that renders transparent the relevance of logical principles to the assessment of the rationality of our intentions. But now we discover that being set to make something true is not sufficient for intending it: what then is the further feature of intentions that distinguishes them from cases in which we are set to make something true without intending it?

4. THE COGNITIVE CONDITIONS OF INTENTION

Perhaps satisfactory answers to these questions can be devised. But I do not wish to pursue that issue here, because it seems to me that there is an alternative account of the instrumental principle available, one whose plausibility does not depend on such controversial matters as these. We may begin by returning to the comparison of intentions with desires. I have already suggested that to intend an end is to be committed to realizing it or bringing it about, in a way that goes beyond the attitude involved in merely desiring the end. One specific respect in which these attitudes differ is that the commitment to realize an end is constrained by one's beliefs about the possibility of realizing the end, whereas desires are not similarly constrained. One could want the process of global warming to stop immediately, without believing that this is so much as possible, given the rest of what one believes about the current state of the world. But intentions are different in this respect. Some philosophers have gone so far as to suggest that intentions

---

[48] See 'Practical Reasoning', sect. 3.

presuppose (or may in part be identified with) the belief that what one intends will in fact come to pass;[49] but this thesis is controversial, and anyway unnecessary to account for the principle of instrumental rationality. It will suffice to maintain what is at any rate more plausible, namely that the intention to do *x* requires at least the belief that it is *possible* that one do *x*.

It is worth pausing to compare this suggestion to the assumptions implicit in Broome's account of the instrumental principle. Broome suggests, in effect, that the stance of intending to do *x* is rationally answerable to considerations regarding the possibility of one's *x*-ing. To intend to do *x* is to be set to make true the proposition that one *x*'s, and this internal aim of intention will be thwarted if the proposition in question cannot be true, given the rest of what one believes. There is an assumption here about the possibility of realizing the aim of intention; but the assumption is made by the theorist of instrumental rationality, not necessarily by the agent. Given the characterization of the internal aim of intention, the theorist assumes that this aim will be thwarted if the propositional object of intention cannot be true together with other propositions that the agent believes, about necessary means. By contrast, I have suggested that agents who intend to do something must *themselves* believe that it is possible for them to do what they intend. The difference between these proposals can be brought out by reflecting on the attitudes of agents who firmly believe that they cannot do something (say, *x*). For all Broome says, it might be the case that such agents intend to do *x*, though their intentions would then be irrational. By contrast, if I am right in suggesting that intention presupposes the belief that it is possible for one to do what one intends, then agents who believe that they cannot do *x* should not even be described as intending to do *x* in the first place.

Once we are clear about this, it seems to me that intuition and reflection support the proposal I have put forward.[50] For it seems to me that we simply do not describe people as intending to do *x* in circumstances in which it is clear that they do not believe it to be possible for them to do *x*. Nothing the agent might do under these circumstances, we might say, would correctly be described as intending to do *x*.[51] If this is on the right lines, however, it suggests a different account of the normative force of the instrumental principle. For consider now a situation in which the following attitudes can be ascribed to you: you intend to do *x*, you

---

[49] See e.g. Gilbert Harman, 'Practical Reasoning', as reprinted in Alfred R. Mele (ed.), *The Philosophy of Action* (Oxford: Oxford University Press, 1997), 149–77. The basic account of instrumental rationality that I am about to offer owes much to Harman's discussion of practical reasoning in this paper, and in his *Change in View*. But of course I work out the basic strategy in a way very different from Harman, starting (for instance) from much weaker, and hence more plausible, assumptions about the cognitive conditions of intention.

[50] I do not mean that Broome would necessarily disagree—he does not take a stand on the issue I have raised, nor does his account of instrumental rationality require him to do so. But if he agrees with me about this point, then he should be open to the suggestion that intentions introduce rational constraints on our attitudes that operate via independent rational constraints on coherence of beliefs.

[51] This is one of the lessons of Albritton's 'Freedom of Will and Freedom of Action'.

believe that your doing *y* is necessary if *x* is to be brought about, and you believe that you will do *y* only if you intend to do *y*.[52] Given that the intention to do *x* brings with it the belief that it is possible for you to do *x*, your further beliefs about *y*-ing and its relation to your doing *x* entail that you will be subject to an incoherence in beliefs if you do not either abandon the original intention to do *x*, or adopt a new intention to do *y*. Failing to take either of these steps, you will be left in effect with the following incoherent set of beliefs (assuming you are minimally self-aware): the belief that it is possible that you do *x*, the belief that it is possible that you do *x* only if you also intend to do *y*, and the belief that you do not intend to do *y*. The incoherence of these beliefs is a straightforward function of the logical relations among their contents, suggesting that the normative force of the instrumental principle can be traced to independent rational constraints on your beliefs—in particular, to constraints on certain combinations of beliefs (a normative requirement, in the specialized sense discussed above).

To this it will be replied that theoretical constraints on rational belief formation cannot by themselves account for the requirement to intend to do *y*, even given the intention to *x* and the other beliefs about the relation between *x*-ing and intending to *y* specified above.[53] Granted those other attitudes, you will be subject to an incoherence in belief if you do not form the belief that you intend to do *y*. But from the rationality of this belief it does not follow that it would be rational for you to intend to do *y*. Theoretical constraints on rational belief can get you only as far as the *belief* that you intend to do *y*; to go beyond that, to a rational requirement that you form the intention to *y*, we need an additional principle of distinctively practical reason. Moreover, without an additional principle of this kind, we will not have succeeded in accounting for the force of the instrumental principle. This can be seen by considering the (slightly comical) situation in which you intend to do *x*, and believe that your intending to *y* is necessary to your doing *x*, but mistakenly or wishfully come to believe that you intend to *y*. In this scenario you seem to have satisfied fully the constraints on rational belief spelled out above. But we should presumably want to say that you have not yet complied with the instrumental principle, which remains in force and says that your attitudes are not in rational order so long as you do not in fact form the intention to do *y*. Conversely, a situation is imaginable in which you fully comply with the demands expressed in the instrumental principle while violating the requirements of theoretical reason appealed to above. Thus you might intend to *x*, and believe that your intending to *y* is necessary to your *x*-ing, and also intend to *y*; but if you mistakenly or carelessly believe that you do not intend to *y*, you will be subject to the kind of incoherence in belief characterized above.

---

[52] I do not mean, of course, that these beliefs must be explicitly and articulately present to the consciousness of the agent who is engaged in instrumental reasoning, only that they are implicit in the agent's understanding of their situation and their possibilities for action.

[53] I am grateful to John Broome and Michael Bratman for pressing me to think about the line of objection sketched in this paragraph. Compare Bratman, 'Intention and Means-End Reasoning', 255–6 (n. 4).

This line of objection turns on the possibility of divergence between your intentions and your beliefs about what you intend. But what, in practice, does this possibility amount to? Ordinarily, future-directed intentions are fairly accessible to consciousness. This is connected to the distinctive role that intentions play in shaping our deliberations. Someone who is entirely unaware of their alleged intention to do *x*, or who has completely forgotten that this is what they intend to do, cannot really be described as having the intention to do *x* any longer. In what would the distinctive commitment to bringing it about that one *x*'s consist, under the circumstances described? We can imagine an unconscious *desire* that is expressed in some course of behavior that a person performs, fixing the real point of the behavior (as opposed to the account of it that the agent would be inclined to provide when asked). But a fully unconscious desire cannot amount to the kind of commitment to realize a plan of action that is represented by intentions, for the simple reason that it is inaccessible to consciousness, and so incapable of attaining the functional features implicit in talk of *commitment* (as opposed to mere desire).[54] By the same token, it is equally difficult to imagine a scenario under which you sincerely believe that you intend to do *x*, while utterly failing to have this intention in fact. Your belief about what you are committed to—if it is sustained and sincerely held over time (as opposed to being a passing vivid impression or hallucination)—will itself start to shape your deliberations and reflections in the ways characteristic of intention.

In light of these considerations, I would suggest the following answer to the objection sketched above. First, assume, as I have been suggesting, that intentions are readily accessible to consciousness. In this situation it would indeed seem independently irrational for you to have false beliefs about the content of your intentions. You may of course be momentarily distracted or forgetful, but reflection at the level of minimal self-awareness can bring you to see or recall what you are really intending to do. It follows that you will be subject to rational criticism if you believe that you intend to do *y* without really so intending, or if you form such an intention without believing that that is the case. Indeed, the rational requirements at issue here are sufficiently stringent that they constrain our attribution of intentions to agents, in the ways sketched in the preceding paragraph. But this is enough to plug the gap in the argument to which I earlier called attention. The objection was that theoretical considerations of coherence of belief merely require you to believe that you intend to *y*, if you intend to *x* and believe that your intending to *y* is necessary to your *x*-ing; they cannot require you actually to form the intention of doing *y*. But if you can rationally believe that you intend to *y* only if you in fact intend to *y*, then rational requirements can indeed bring you to form this intention. Under the circumstances described—where you intend to do *x*, and believe that you can do *x* only if you intend to do *y*—the only rational way to

---

[54] I have in mind here the functional features of intention stressed by Bratman, in *Intention, Plans, and Practical Reason*.

bring your beliefs into coherence is to commit yourself to doing y, in the way we have seen to be characteristic of intention.

Assume, next, that there can be intentions that are not readily accessible to consciousness. I have suggested that we would have trouble making sense of intentions—commitments to realize a plan of action, as opposed to mere desires or wishes—that operate at the level of the unconscious. But suppose for the sake of argument that I am wrong about this. In the situation where this is the case, it would not seem irrational for you to have false beliefs about the content of your intentions, and my argument for instrumental rationality would consequently fail to get a grip. But equally, it seems to me doubtful that intentions that are cut off in this way from conscious belief really do introduce rational constraints on our further attitudes, of the kind represented by the instrumental principle. Someone who has an unconscious intention to (say) avenge an imagined childhood slight would not seem irrational if they fail to take the means that they (unconsciously?) believe to be necessary to that end. The postulated inaccessibility of the intention to consciousness already itself prevents the attitude from behaving in the ways characteristic of intention, and this makes it seem odd or mistaken to suppose that it introduces further rational constraints on one's attitudes. In this respect, the imagined scenario involving unconscious intentions differs markedly from the case of *akratic* intentions that has been my primary concern.

These considerations support the account of the instrumental principle that I have been developing. That account does not represent the principle merely as an application of the considerations that determine coherence and consistency relations amongst beliefs. The account additionally makes assumptions about the relations between intentions and beliefs: first, that to intend to x is to believe that it is possible that one do x; second, that one can rationally believe one intends to x only if one really does intend to do x; and third, that if one intends to x, it is rational for one to believe that one intends to x. But these further assumptions seem independently plausible, as I have endeavored to show above. Furthermore, when we try to imagine a scenario in which the further assumptions do not hold (such as the scenario involving unconscious intentions whose connections to self-awareness have been severed), we lose our grip on the basic idea that intentions introduce the constraint on our further attitudes that is expressed by the instrumental principle.

To be sure, this core requirement is not the whole of what we ordinarily think of under the rubric of instrumental rationality. The requirement corresponds roughly to the analytic principle of rational willing that Kant introduces in the second section of the *Groundwork* to explain the possibility of hypothetical imperatives: 'Whoever wills the end, wills (so far as reason has decisive influence on his actions) also the means that are *indispensably necessary* to his actions and that lie in his power.'[55] Beyond this core requirement, however, there are broader norms of

---

[55] This is from p. 417 in the pagination of the Prussian Academy edition (emphasis mine); the translation used is James Ellington, *Grounding for the Metaphysics of Morals* (Indianapolis: Hackett Publishing Co., 1981).

means-end coherence that can be brought to bear in assessment of action.[56] Practical reason does not enjoin us merely to take the means that are absolutely necessary to realize our ends, but also to take those optional means that would facilitate the realization of our overall system of plans and values. In order to produce a decent paper for the conference that is coming up in the summer, it may not strictly be necessary that one start working on it tomorrow, but that might still be a good idea, given one's overall set of aims and ambitions.

Means-end coherence of this kind, to the extent it goes beyond the core demand that one adopt those means that are necessary relative to one's ends, probably does presuppose that one endorse the ends that are in question. Thus *akratic* agents typically do not have an eye to the coherence, in this sense, between their immediate activities and their larger system of projects and values. Indeed in many typical cases what makes *akratic* activities ill-advised, from the agent's own point of view, is precisely the fact that they do not cohere well with the agent's larger system of projects and values. (One realizes that it would be best to get started on one's paper for the summer conference, and yet one goes out to a movie instead.) Practical requirements of means-end coherence may thus apply only to those ends that the agent has endorsed, as good or worth pursuing on the whole. To the extent this is the case, the theory of instrumental rationality will not be a monolithic subject, and the account I have sketched of the instrumental principle should not be interpreted as a complete account of what is customarily understood as instrumental or means-end rationality.

But we should not infer from this important insight that the instrumental principle, in the form I have discussed, is of merely minor or secondary significance. Granted, the principle applies only to cases involving means that are believed to be necessary for the attainment of our intended ends. This might seem to entail that it applies very rarely, since it is seldom the case that the means we adopt are strictly necessary to the realization of our ends—necessary, that is, in the sense of logical or physical necessity. But the principle allows for natural extensions to cases that do not involve strict necessity of these kinds.

Consider the quotidian example introduced earlier, in which I intend to get to campus by 11.00, believe that I can do so only if I set out in the car by 10.30, and believe further that I can set out in the car by 10.30 only if I intend to do so. The beliefs about necessary means involved in this example are almost certainly false if interpreted in the sense of physical or logical necessity. Thus I might hold these beliefs while lucidly conceding that it is both logically and physically possible that I will arrive at work by 11.00, even if I do not set out in the car by 10.30—a

---

[56] I borrow the expression 'means-end coherence' from Michael Bratman (see his *Intention, Plans, and Practical Reason*, 31–3). I should emphasize that nothing in Bratman's discussion of this phenomenon supports the suggestion I go on to discuss in the text, namely that means-end coherence makes sense only against a background of normative endorsement of one's ends. If one could account for this broader phenomenon in nonmoralizing terms, then a unified treatment of the whole of means-end rationality might be possible. But Bratman does little to indicate what a nonmoralizing account of means-end coherence might look like, nor does such an account seem very promising to me.

helicopter might come by at 10.50, for instance, and deposit me at my office ten minutes later. The point, however, is that nothing in my overall set of beliefs gives me any reason at all to think that this will happen.

This suggests that the notions of necessity and possibility relevant to the instrumental principle are epistemic notions, determined by our background assumptions about developments in the world and the way those developments will shape our concrete options for action. In deliberating about what to do we take many parameters as fixed, such as the fact that helicopters will not descend and whisk us off to the office; even if they are not ruled out by logical principles or the laws of physics, such occurrences seem so unlikely that we do best to proceed on the assumption that they are simply off the table. The notions of necessity and possibility at work in practical deliberation are thus notions of what is necessary and possible in the strict sense, given a host of unspoken assumptions about what is going to happen in the world.

Background assumptions of this kind may in turn have a variety of distinct sources, extending beyond purely epistemic considerations relating to the independent probability of certain events. They might, for instance, be based in prior plans or decisions made by the agent. If in addition to the commitment to get to the office by 11.00 a.m., I also have a standing intention to commute to campus with my car, then this will exclude from deliberative consideration methods of technically possible locomotion that do not involve my driving. To adopt such means would be incompatible with the belief that it is possible that I take my car to work, where that belief accompanies, in ways already canvassed, the intention to commute to campus with my car. Another source of constraints on the standpoint of deliberation are normative views that are held by the agent: thus, my assumption that I will get to work on time only if I drive my car takes it as fixed that I will not steal my neighbor's car. This is an option that is ruled out not by logic or the laws of physics but by morality, and its incompatibility with moral justification may in turn make it reasonable for me to conduct my deliberations on the assumption that the option is simply off the table. Sometimes the fundamental rationale for such assumptions will again be an epistemic one—for instance, the utter improbability of my stealing my neighbor's car. This event is of the kind that is under my intentional control, so what makes it improbable is my own view about the moral impermissibility of casual theft, together with the fact that I am appropriately responsive to considerations of this kind.[57] In other cases the rationale for the assumption that stealing the car is off the table may be more directly a normative one. In these cases, it is not the fact that I take my stealing the car to be practically improbable that renders it irrelevant to my deliberation, but the different fact that I take it to be normatively out of bounds.

These remarks only scratch the surface of a large and complex subject. But I hope that enough has been said to show how the instrumental principle, as I have interpreted it, can be extended to cover a wide range of cases involving

---

[57] Compare Bernard Williams, 'Moral Incapacity', as reprinted in his *Making Sense of Humanity* (Cambridge, England: Cambridge University Press, 1995), 46–55.

means that are not without qualification necessary for the attainment of our ends. The principle may not account for the whole of means-end rationality, but it expresses a core requirement that is both central to our deliberative experience and applicable, as I have shown, to situations in which agents are involved in the pursuit of ends that they do not themselves endorse. Furthermore, the derivation of this core requirement from theoretical principles governing belief formation helps to make intelligible its ready extension to a range of cases involving means that are not strictly necessary for the attainment of our ends, but that are necessary only relative to background epistemic and normative assumptions that shape our deliberative point of view. Our belief as agents that it is possible for us to do what we intend serves to mediate between these background assumptions and our beliefs about the strict necessity of various means, in ways that seem to accord with our deliberative experience. If by contrast we follow Broome in deriving the instrumental principle from considerations involving the internal aim of intention, it becomes harder to see how the principle could admit of natural extensions beyond the most narrow cases. The normativity of the core instrumental principle, on his account of it, stems from the idea that the pursuit of ends that it is impossible to realize would thwart the constitutive aim of intention. But the notion of possibility relevant to this account is the theorist's notion of possible truth, not the agent's understanding of what it is possible to achieve; it is accordingly obscure on Broome's account how the core instrumental principle could be extended to cases that do not involve strict logical or physical necessity, in the ways that come perfectly naturally to us when we deliberate about what we are to do.

Finally, the account I have presented seems to explain how automatically the core requirement of instrumental rationality tends to be complied with as we execute our intentions and plans. As we saw in section 2, above, there is less scope for deliberate irrationality in the sphere of belief than there seems to be in the sphere of action, and this reflects itself in the difficulty we have imagining a willful violation of the core requirement of instrumental reason.[58] When people believe that an available means is necessary relative to one of their alleged ends, but fail to adopt that means, we tend to question whether they are really committed to the end after all. The core requirement of instrumental reason thus functions more like a constraint on interpretation than do other principles of practical reason. This is one of several features of the core requirement that point toward the account of it I have developed in this section, according to which the requirement derives from basic theoretical constraints on the coherence of beliefs.

POSTSCRIPT TO CHAPTER 5

The instrumental principle, as I interpret it, instructs us to take the means that we believe to be necessary relative to our ends. My treatment of this principle

---

[58] This difficulty was brought home to me by some remarks of Brad Hooker's.

attempts to do justice to two dimensions of instrumental rationality. First, the instrumental principle applies even in cases in which we are acting in pursuit of ends that we do not ourselves fully endorse. Second, it applies in a way that involves a kind of rational pressure to revise our attitudes. We feel and respond to this pressure when we adopt necessary means to our ends, or give up our ends upon realizing that we are not willing to take the means that are necessary for their attainment. My conviction is that we can do justice to these twin features of instrumental rationality only by tracing the instrumental principle to requirements of theoretical rationality, concerning the coherence of our beliefs (including the beliefs that are bound up with the intention to pursue a given end). These are requirements whose force is familiar to us as believers, insofar as we feel and respond to a rational pressure to revise our beliefs when we recognize them to be inconsistent. Furthermore, the theoretical source of the rational pressure to revise inconsistent beliefs renders it applicable to situations in which we are acting in pursuit of ends that we do not fully endorse.

The defense of this approach in 'Normativity, Commitment, and Instrumental Reason' leaves many questions unanswered. In this postscript I wish to address a few of the objections that have recently been brought against my approach; the aim is not to offer an exhaustive treatment of the issues raised by these objections, but rather to sketch in outline the resources available within the approach for dealing with some hard cases for the theory of instrumental rationality. I shall focus on three sets of issues.

1. Revision of Belief and of Intention

The agent who fails to intend the means they believe necessary relative to an end they intend to achieve is subject to inconsistent beliefs—or so I maintain. But what is wrong with that? The set of beliefs we hold may well turn out to contain many latent inconsistencies, but this fact alone generates no particular rational pressure in the direction of making specific revisions. That our beliefs are inconsistent entails that not everything we believe can be true, but this in itself poses no special problem so long as we remain in the dark about where in our network of beliefs specific falsehoods may lie.

Of course, in the case of instrumental irrationality we can, it would seem, locate the falsehood in our beliefs. We believe the following three propositions, and know that they cannot together be true:

(a) It is possible that I do x.
(b) It is possible that I do x only if I also intend to do y.
(c) I do not intend to do y.

Joseph Raz has objected that the appeal to falsehood in this complex of beliefs fails to illuminate what is undesirable about the failure to take necessary means to one's chosen ends. In particular, he suggests, we need an explanation of the undesirability

of this false belief 'that explains why the so-called principle of instrumental rationality is one of the standards that determine well-functioning deliberative
processes'.[59] But the appeal to false beliefs does not illuminate the role of the
instrumental principle as a norm of deliberative good functioning. Thus someone
who intends to perform an action that it is in fact impossible for them to perform
might end up wasting limited resources of time and energy in an essentially fruit-
less pursuit. But if such a person happens to be instrumentally irrational, they will
spare themselves this fate. They may be subject to a false belief, but in the present
context this actually seems to be an advantage, something that is conducive to
their overall good functioning as agents.

Raz himself explains instrumental rationality by appeal to standards of effective
agency. 'If you are prone to instrumental irrationality, you are less likely to achieve
your ends, whatever they are.'[60] A certain practiced knack for taking the necessary
means to our ends is an important executive capacity, one that any successful agent
will need to acquire, and our sense that we are irrational or defective when we fail to
take the necessary means to our ends derives from the general role of this executive
capacity in relation to deliberative good functioning. I think Raz is correct to
emphasize the role of instrumental rationality as part of our good functioning as
agents.[61] But this point does not suffice to account for the full normative significance of the instrumental principle. On Raz's account, that principle serves to specify a standard of excellence in agency, defining what we might think of as a kind of
all-purpose executive virtue. But this turns the instrumental principle into an evaluative ideal, one that is not sufficiently anchored in the deliberative perspective of the
agent. Someone who believes that a given means is necessary relative to an end
that they intend to achieve will experience an immediate rational pressure to revise
their attitudes. This pressure cannot derive from the fact that they will fail to exhibit
an executive virtue if they do not revise their attitudes. For one thing, the agent may
not be aware that the principle of instrumental rationality defines a standard of executive virtue. For another, even if they think in these terms, their doing so need not
translate into any particular rational requirement to which they would feel pressure
to respond. (The *akratic* agent in particular would probably not care very much
about the fact that they are failing to exhibit excellence in agency, given that they are
not responsive to the acknowledged badness of their own immediate ends.)

My claim is that we can make sense of a kind of rational pressure to which even
akratic agents are susceptible by appealing to the apparent conflict in the beliefs to
which agents are subject when they fail to adopt means that they believe to be
necessary relative to their intended ends. But Raz apparently doubts this. He notes
that 'nothing follows about what we ought to do or believe and when we should

---

[59] See Joseph Raz, 'The Myth of Instrumental Rationality', *Journal of Ethics and Social Philosophy*,
1/1 (April 2005) 17, URL = http://www.jesp.org.   [60] Ibid.
[61] A similar view is defended by Bratman, in *Intention, Plans, and Practical Reason*, at e.g. 51—a
source upon which Raz draws.

suspend belief from the mere knowledge that a set of beliefs contains a contradiction'.[62] The fact that some subset of one's beliefs is inconsistent is no reason in itself to change the beliefs in the inconsistent set. This may be true as far as it goes, but it underestimates the extent to which awareness of localized inconsistency in belief can generate rational pressures on the believer. Even if I do not immediately know which of my inconsistent beliefs to revise, the fact that they are inconsistent is at least a *pro tanto* reason to reassess the credentials of the items in the inconsistent set. Furthermore, in the particular case at issue there is a special feature of at least one of these problematic beliefs that simplifies the process of revision in response to acknowledged local inconsistency. Thus belief (c) in the above set is a belief about my own intentions; the truth to which it is answerable is a matter that is directly subject to my volitional control. In this unusual situation, I can restore coherence to the problematic set of beliefs by adjusting my intentions regarding the necessary means, and thereby giving myself grounds for revising belief (c). If I nevertheless refuse to adjust my attitudes in this way, and retain my conviction that the means is really necessary, then I have no option but to revise belief (a), which in turn precludes me from continuing to intend the original end.

It might be thought that forming an intention to take the means in response to this kind of inconsistency fails to do justice to the nature of belief, which is answerable to independent facts of the matter about the way things are. I should revise belief (c), that I do not intend to take the means, because I have now formed such an intention; but then it seems I must have had some independent reason for adjusting my intentions in this way *before* I can revise my beliefs in the matter.[63] I agree that if belief (c) is to be revised, the only way to achieve this compatibly with the nature of belief as answerable to the truth is to revise one's intention first, by deciding or resolving to take the means. It does not follow, however, that there needs to be an independent or prior ground for forming this intention (independent, that is, from considerations about the consistency of one's beliefs). In the case at issue, where the belief in question is about a matter that is directly under my own control, the rational pressure that leads me to form an intention might well be the fact that I will *thereby* bring about coherence in a set of attitudes that includes a belief about my own intentions.

2. Questions about Possibility

The rational pressure toward revision of intentions in accordance with the instrumental principle operates not merely via beliefs, but via beliefs about the possibility of doing what one intends. Possibility is of course a vexed topic in its own right, and questions may be raised about how the notion is to be interpreted in the context of the debate about the instrumental principle.

[62] Raz, 'The Myth of Instrumental Rationality', 20.

[63] See John Brunero, 'Two Approaches to Instrumental Rationality and Belief Consistency', *Journal of Ethics and Social Philosophy*, 1/1 (April 2005), 4, **URL = http://www.jesp.org**.

Suppose that one intends to pass an examination, and believes that that in turn will happen only if one resolves to study for the examination. Suppose further that one does not intend to study, and that one knows this fact about one's intentions. In this situation, we have specific instances of belief-types (b) and (c), which together are supposed to be incompatible with a belief of type (a), to the effect that it is possible that one pass the examination. But are (b) and (c) really incompatible with (a)? There is, it would seem, a perfectly respectable sense in which it remains possible that one should pass the examination, even if one does not intend the necessary means. So long as it is possible for the agent to change their intentions regarding the means, it is possible for them to achieve the end; their doing so remains an option for choice, and something they might reasonably be held to account for failing to do. (It would hardly be an excuse for someone to plead that they were unable to pass the examination, because they failed to intend to take the necessary means.) In the generic sense of possibility as rational capacity, it is possible for us to do something even if we intend neither to do it nor to take the means that doing it requires, so long as it remains in our power to alter the intentions in question.

This generic sense of rational capacity cannot be the one that is at issue in my argument for the instrumental principle, figuring in the content of beliefs (a) and (b).[64] This raises two questions: Can we give a principled explication of an alternative notion of possibility that might figure in the content of these beliefs? And does it remain plausible to suppose that intention requires a belief in the possibility of doing what one intends, when (a) is interpreted in this way?

The conception of possibility that intuitively seems relevant to the argument of my paper is the conception of what is possible, given facts about my intentions. Something is possible in this sense if its occurrence is compatible with the rest of what we know about the world, holding fixed certain natural assumptions about the course of events, including the assumption that our own intentions will be executed.[65] Thus in thinking about the examination I assume, for instance, that I will not be struck by a sudden brainstorm in the examination room, and that the questions that are asked will not address exclusively the small segment of the syllabus that I have already mastered. For practical purposes these scenarios seem too remote and unlikely to make it sensible for me to waste any time taking them into account in my deliberations about the future. Similarly, I take it as provisionally fixed that I will execute the intentions I have formed when I am engaged in deliberative reflection. The basic function of intentions is to resolve practical questions about my own agency, taking certain questions off the immediate deliberative agenda, so that I can focus on other issues that need to be dealt with. It would defeat the purpose of deliberation, and indeed undermine our basic capacity for

---

[64] Ibid. 4–6.

[65] I say 'executed' here, to leave open the possibility that one will not succeed in achieving the end that one intends to realize. We hold it fixed that we will at least make a concerted effort to achieve what we are intending, and in that sense we assume that our intentions will be executed.

effective action, to form the intention to do x, and then proceed in our practical thinking as if it was an open question whether we were going to x.[66]

The horizon of deliberative reflection is in this way shaped by a variety of assumptions about what will happen that have their rationale in our practical point of view as agents. We can abstract from that point of view, and think about ourselves in a way that is detached from the practical problems to which deliberation is a systematic response. When we do so, we might conclude that it is possible for us to do something we have already decided not to do, insofar as we retain the basic capacity to revise our intentions. We might equally concede, in this theoretical vein, that it is possible that we will be struck by a brainstorm in the examination room even if we do not study in advance. But these assumptions are not ones that it is reasonable to make within the deliberative context of agency. From this practical point of view we assume (defeasibly) that the intentions we have formed will be executed, accepting that it is possible for us to do something only if our doing it is compatible with the assumption that our intentions will in fact be translated into action. The beliefs whose consistency is relevant to instrumental reasoning, on my account, include crucially the attitudes of acceptance within the context of practical deliberation that we have toward propositions such as (a)–(c).[67]

This explains, perhaps, why I am entitled to take it as fixed that it is not possible for me to pass the examination, when I have formed the definite intention not to study for it, and believe that I can pass only if I intend to study. But there is a different case to be considered: what if I merely fail to form an intention to study, while continuing to believe that doing so is necessary relative to my goal of passing the exam? Insofar as I have not yet formed any definite intention on the matter one way or another, I ought, even within the context of deliberative reflection, to consider it still an open matter whether I study for the examination or not. Cases of this kind bring out an indeterminacy in the content of belief (b) in the inconsistent set. This is the belief that it is possible that I do x only if I intend to do y. But we need to ask when the intention to do y needs to be formed. It might be, for instance, that the possibility of passing the examination requires only that I intend by tomorrow to devote my energy to studying. Or it might be possible to pass the examination only if I now form the intention to study for it. In the former case, the counterparts of (a) and (b) would be compatible with the belief that I do not currently have an intention to study for the exam; but they would not be compatible with that belief if the possibility claim in (b) is understood in the latter way, as requiring that I now intend to study. It follows that rational pressure to revise one's intentions will in some cases be generated by the trio of attitudes only when

---

[66] See Bratman, *Intention, Plans, and Practical Reason*, for an extended defense of this conception of the role of intention.

[67] On the notion of 'acceptance in a context', and its relevance to the practical perspective of agency, see Michael Bratman, 'Practical Reasoning and Acceptance in a Context', as reprinted in Bratman, *Faces of Intention* (Cambridge, England: Cambridge University Press, 1999), 15–34.

what is required to achieve the intended end is that one *now* intend the means. Prior to this point in time, the requirements of coherence of attitude may not yield implacable pressure to make changes in one's intentions, apart from ruling out a definite intention not to take the later means (so long as the other two attitudes remain in place). This is, it seems, as it should be—the core requirement expressed by the instrumental principle does not operate at a temporal distance, but only when we believe that steps must now be taken if we are going to realize our intended ends.

Finally, we must consider whether it remains plausible to suppose that intention requires the belief that it is possible to do what one intends, when the notion of possibility is interpreted as constrained by one's other intentions. Against this, it has been suggested that to understand intention as carrying this kind of belief in its train would rule out cases of irrationality, where we intend an end and fail to adopt the means that rationality requires of us.[68] But this objection misfires. Irrational intentions of the relevant kind are possible, on the account I favor, precisely to the extent that it is possible for the agent to hold inconsistent beliefs about the possibility (in the constrained sense) of achieving what they intend. Inconsistency of this kind is in fact rather difficult to tolerate, once it has been brought to our attention; the rational pressure we feel to revise beliefs we know to be inconsistent, in cases in which the beliefs are about matters directly under our immediate control, is ordinarily too great to resist. But this, again, accords with our ordinary understanding and practice. We are inclined to doubt whether someone really does intend the end if they don't choose the means they take to be necessary, under circumstances in which they are focused and aware and thinking clearly about their situation. It was for this reason that I suggested originally that the instrumental principle functions more like a constraint on interpretation than do other practical principles. Violations of the instrumental principle, when they occur, seem typically to involve the kind of cognitive errors in reasoning that make it possible for us to overlook easily rectifiable inconsistencies in our own beliefs, errors such as inattention and failure to put things together. This is what we should expect if the pressure to revise our intentions in accordance with the instrumental principle has its source, as I have maintained, in conflicts in our beliefs.

3. False and Incomplete Beliefs about One's Intentions

The cognitivist approach to the instrumental principle faces a different set of potential problems in the possibility that our intentions might diverge from our beliefs about our intentions. Any of the following discrepancies between intentions and beliefs about intentions seem, in principle, conceivable: I might intend to *x*, but not believe that I intend to *x*; I might intend to *x*, but believe that I intend to do *z* rather

---

[68] Brunero, 'Two Approaches to Instrumental Rationality and Belief Consistency', 5–6.

than *x*; I might have no intention to do *x*, but believe that I have such an intention; I might have no intention to *x*, but lack the belief that I have no intention to *x*. To the extent discrepancies of these kinds are possible, it would seem possible that one might exhibit failures in instrumental reasoning, without being subject to the kind of inconsistency in beliefs to which I have traced the instrumental principle.

In 'Normativity, Commitment, and Instrumental Reason' I argued that possibilities of these kinds could safely be ignored, since there are good grounds for thinking that it would independently be irrational to have mistaken beliefs about one's (consciously accessible) intentions, in the deliberative contexts to which the instrumental principle applies. This assumption might be challenged, however. Thus John Brunero writes: 'While it is plausible to claim that an agent who *intends not to Y* will believe that he does not intend to Y, it is not plausible to claim that someone who *fails to intend to Y* has the belief that he does not intend to Y. Alice may fail to intend to study and fail to notice this; it just slips her mind. But if she does not hold the belief that she does not intend to study, then there is no way on Wallace's account to convict her of instrumental irrationality.'[69]

It is of course correct that one can fail to intend to *y* without believing that one does not have this intention, and that this is a fact about one's intentions that is easier to overlook than (say) the fact that one intends not to *y*. Furthermore, there is in general nothing necessarily irrational about lacking the belief that one does not have an arbitrary intention that it would at the time have been possible for one to adopt. But the deliberative contexts to which the instrumental principle is relevant have special features, which generate rational pressure to form accurate beliefs of this kind about one's own lack of certain intentions. These are contexts in which one is reflecting about how to proceed in executing one's intention to do *x*, and one has arrived at the conclusion that it is possible that one will *x* only if one forms the intention to do *y*. I contend that a rational agent who is minimally self-aware (as I put it) will, in this special context, realize that they have not formed the very intention whose necessity relative to their larger end they have themselves explicitly affirmed. Having arrived at the conclusion that it will be possible to realize one's end only if one intends to *y*, it would be a gross lapse in deliberation to overlook the fact that one has not formed that intention.

What explains the plausible suggestion that a lapse of this kind, in the specific deliberative context at issue, would amount to a form of irrationality? We might want to say here that a tendency to form accurate beliefs about whether one has formed an intention whose necessity to one's other purposes one has explicitly affirmed is a kind of executive virtue, to be included among the traits and capacities that make us, in general, effective in the pursuit of our goals. Construed in these terms, the appeal to rationality functions to explain why it is safe to assume that minimally competent agents will be aware of their own lack of the relevant instrumental intentions in the context of the kind of deliberation that is at issue.

---

[69] Brunero, 'Two Approaches to Instrumental Rationality and Belief Consistency', 6.

Alternatively, we might say that there is reason for us to scrutinize our Intentions to this degree, insofar as doing so is a strategy that enhances our ability to realize the broader aims that are given with our nature as deliberating agents.[70] This answer might appear circular in the context of an account of the instrumental principle, presupposing that we have reason to take effective means to our ends, where the point was to explain why this is the case. But there is in fact no circularity here. In 'Normativity, Commitment, and Instrumental Reason' I distinguished between the core instrumental principle that it was my aim to offer an account of, and more wide-ranging norms of means-end coherence. The idea that we have reason to take steps that facilitate the pursuit of our broader aims is an argument that appeals to norms of the latter kind. Reliance on such norms might be an embarrassment for a theory that attempted to account for all of instrumental rationality in cognitive terms; but that was not my aim, nor do I believe it plausible to suppose that the whole field of instrumental rationality can be explained in terms of the requirements of coherence in belief that operate where the core requirement to take necessary means to one's ends gets a grip.

We have, then, two ways in which the rationality of believing that one does not intend to *y* might be accounted for, in contexts in which one has formed the intention to *x* and affirmed that it is possible for one to *x* only if one intends to *y*. At this point, however, a different and final worry might be raised. We want to say, it seems, that a failure to take the necessary means to our chosen ends is, in and of itself, a ground for rational criticism. The argument canvassed above, however, fails to do justice to this important idea. That argument establishes that agents who form beliefs (a) and (b), and who also fail to intend the necessary means *y*, are irrational if they do not also form belief (c), to the effect that they do not intend to *y*. But the argument does nothing to show that, under these circumstances, the failure either to intend the means *y*, or to revise the original intention to do *x*, is itself a form of irrationality. Rational pressure to revise one's intentions in a case of this sort emerges only after one has exhibited deliberative rationality of the prior kind, by registering the fact that one has failed to form the intention to take the necessary means. To the extent this is the case, it appears we still haven't accounted for the independent force of the instrumental principle.

To this I would respond that it is not at all clear to me that the instrumental principle really has the kind of independent rational force attributed to it in the objection. Recall that we are attempting to explain the rational pressure to revise one's attitudes in accordance with the instrumental principle that is generated by the mere fact that one has adopted the intention to achieve a given end, independently of whether the end really would be good to pursue in the circumstances, or is believed by the agent to be good. When we abstract from normative considerations about the justification for pursuing a given end, and consider merely the

[70] Michael Bratman makes this suggestion, in 'Intention, Belief, Practical, Theoretical', unpublished manuscript.

difference it makes that the agent has formed the intention so to act, it is no longer obvious at all that the failure to adopt the means that are believed necessary relative to the end is a form of irrationality. We may grant that a reason to pursue an end is *eo ipso* a reason to take other steps that would facilitate such a pursuit, so that the reason for the end transfers its rational force across the means/end relation.[71] But in the case at issue we are not assuming that there really is a good reason for the agent's pursuit of the end in the first place. Perhaps, under these circumstances, there is no rational pressure to revise one's intentions that operates independently of one's beliefs about (*inter alia*) one's own intentions.

This response could be supplemented by borrowing on Raz's executive virtue account of instrumental rationality. I have already suggested that a tendency to form accurate beliefs about the state of one's own intentions may be a rational excellence, something that contributes to one's effectiveness as an agent engaged in practical deliberation. Perhaps it is a further and distinct excellence to be disposed to revise one's intentions in accordance with the instrumental principle, as Raz maintains. This concession to Raz would not supplant the cognitivist account I have offered of the core requirement; as I argued above, the appeal to deliberative virtue fails to explain the internal rational pressure that deliberating agents register and respond to when they revise their intentions in accordance with the instrumental principle. This pressure, it seems, is present only to the extent agents are competent enough to have taken notice of the fact that they have not yet formed the intentions that they acknowledge to be necessary for the realization of their ends. But the idea that a tendency to revise our intentions in accordance with the instrumental principle is part of what it is to be an effective agent might explain the residual thought that there is something independently defective about an agent who does not make such revisions—independently, that is, of whether or not they have formed accurate beliefs about the state of their own intentions as they deliberate.[72]

---

[71] Compare Raz's discussion of what he calls facilitative reasons, in 'The Myth of Instrumental Rationality', sect. 1.

[72] It might be doubted, however, whether we can really make sense of this tendency as one that is genuinely independent of the tendency to form accurate beliefs about one's own intentions. In practice, someone will probably exhibit a knack for revising their intentions in accordance with the instrumental principle only to the extent they have a knack for registering when they lack the intentions they believe necessary relative to their ends.

PART II

RESPONSIBILITY, IDENTIFICATION, AND EMOTION

6

Reason and Responsibility

Can people ever be to blame for doing the rational thing? More broadly, what are the connections between the responsibility of moral agents and the rationality of the moral demands to which they are held accountable?

As I see matters, these questions turn on the relations between two different practical points of view. Questions about the rationality of moral conduct are in the first instance deliberative questions, arising within the first-personal perspective of an agent trying to reach a decision about how to act. The task of practical deliberation, after all, is the task of determining what one has reason to do. The claim that it is rational for a given agent to comply with moral demands can accordingly be understood as the claim that, if the agent deliberated correctly, he or she would acknowledge reason to act morally and would choose to act accordingly. To make out this claim would be to vindicate what is sometimes referred to as the authority of moral demands. As I shall understand the notion of authority, moral demands are authoritative for a given agent, in the relevant sense, if they appropriately regulate the deliberations of that agent. When this is the case, then an agent's deliberations will only count as fully rational when the agent succeeds in complying with the demands of morality.

Questions about responsibility, on the other hand, are essentially third-personal in form.[1] When we ask whether a given person is morally accountable for a given action, we are asking whether it would be fair to hold the person responsible for the action. Holding responsible is in turn an attitudinal stance that we adopt toward a person, involving a susceptibility to reactive emotions on account of what the person has done, and a disposition to respond to the person in ways that express the reactive emotions. Thus a person is blameworthy for having done

Originally published in Garrett Cullity and Berys Gaut (eds.), *Ethics and Practical Reason* (Oxford: Clarendon Press, 1997), 321–44. Reprinted by permission of Oxford University Press. Different (and variously half-baked) versions of this essay were presented at the St Andrews Conference, at the University of Pittsburgh, and at Columbia University. I am grateful to the audiences on those occasions for stimulating and helpful discussion. I owe a special debt to the members of the Mid-Atlantic Moral Theory Discussion Group, who provided an especially constructive mix of skepticism and sympathy in response to one of the earlier versions; and to Garrett Cullity and Berys Gaut, whose detailed comments on the original draft were exemplary.

[1] The ideas sketched in this paragraph are developed and defended in my book *Responsibility and the Moral Sentiments* (Cambridge, Mass.: Harvard University Press, 1994)—henceforth *RMS*. The present essay explores an issue touched on inconclusively on p. 165 of *RMS*.

something morally wrong when it would be fair to feel resentment or indignation in response to the person's conduct, and to engage in sanctioning behavior that expresses such reactive sentiments. That this is essentially a third-personal stance is not at odds with the fact that there is such a thing as holding oneself to blame. When we feel guilty for having done something morally impermissible, we are in effect standing in judgment over ourselves, viewing ourselves reflexively as appropriate targets of a certain kind of response. This stance is to be contrasted with the first-personal, deliberative standpoint we adopt when deciding what to do.

The third-personal stance of holding someone accountable defines a certain form of moral relationship. We enter into this kind of relationship to people when we hold them to moral demands, treating them as appropriate targets of reactive sentiment and sanctioning response in case they should flout those demands. The practice of holding people responsible is thus connected with the idea that moral demands can form the basis of a distinctive kind of moral community, one whose members expect each other to comply with those demands, and who hold each other to account when such compliance is not forthcoming. Furthermore, the members of such a community attain a special status when they actually succeed in fulfilling the demands of morality. Doing so equips them to enter into relationships of full accountability with people, relationships in which they are not merely held morally to account for their behavior, but in which they could actually succeed in providing such an account if asked, justifying themselves by appeal to common moral standards.

My aim in the present essay is to explore some connections between these forms of moral relationship and the question of the rationality of moral conduct—between, as it were, the accountability of moral agents and the deliberative authority of moral demands. To this end, I distinguish two different aspects of the phenomenon of deliberative authority: there is, first, the question whether a given agent has reason to comply with moral demands, or whether those demands provide the agent with reasons for action; and there is, second, the question whether the agent has *most* reason to comply with moral demands, or whether such compliance is *optimal* from the standpoint of deliberative reason. I take up the first issue, concerning reasons for action, in section 1, and then turn to the second issue, about the optimality of moral conduct, in sections 2 to 4. A primary theme of my discussion will be that the most serious and consequential issues concerning the authority of moral requirements are raised by the question of optimality, rather than by the question of reasons for action (see section 1). I shall sketch a framework for thinking about the optimality of moral conduct, which turns on the idea of congruence between the two constitutive perspectives of practical reason, the moral and the eudaimonistic (section 2). I shall then argue that the ideal of full accountability may contribute to understanding how this kind of congruence is possible (section 3). Finally, I shall explore the implications of the breakdown of convergence for relationships of minimal accountability, showing how the failure of optimality may lead to forms of diminished responsibility, and tracing the consequences of this result for our understanding of the content of moral requirements (section 4).

1. REASON AND MORAL CAPACITY

There are a number of things that I shall simply take for granted, for purposes of discussion. First among these is the idea there is a form of general competence or capacity that is a basic condition of moral accountability. This is the complex condition I have elsewhere referred to under the heading of the powers of reflective self-control.[2] It includes the capacity to grasp and apply the justifications that support moral demands, as well as the general capacity to comply with moral demands, because one grasps the justifications that support them.

The idea that these moral powers are conditions of accountability reflects the following basic assumption: Given the connection between moral demands and the justifications expressed in moral principles, it would be unfair to hold accountable those who lack the capacity to grasp such justifications and to control their behavior accordingly.[3] About these moral powers, I shall make the further assumption that they are not to be understood as all-or-nothing capacities that one either has or lacks. Rather, like other forms of general competence or capacity the powers of reflective self-control admit of degrees; they can be more or less developed, so that someone to whom these powers are ascribed may find that they are substantially impaired, either temporarily (due perhaps to local circumstances, such as unusual stress) or persistently and constitutionally (as for instance in certain cases of addiction or neurosis). Acknowledging the range of cases in which the powers of reflective self-control are impaired, I believe we should be prepared to adjust our judgments of moral responsibility accordingly. This follows from the basic idea that the moral powers to which I have referred are conditions of accountability. Granting this idea, we see that cases in which the powers of reflective self-control are substantially impaired, or in which it is extremely difficult for an agent to exercise those powers, should be treated as cases in which the agent's moral accountability is diminished. At any rate, this will be a further background assumption in the discussion that follows.

With these assumptions on the table, we are now in a position to consider the question whether accountability requires that one have reason to comply with moral demands. We may assume, to start with, that any plausible theory of reasons for action would endorse the following claim: If a certain consideration counts for a given class of agents as a reason for action, then those agents would take the consideration into account, were they to deliberate correctly.[4] This

---

[2] *RMS*, sect. 6.I.   [3] For further discussion, see *RMS*, ch. 6.

[4] I mean the idea of 'taking account' of a reason in a fairly weak sense here. In particular, it is not to be supposed that one can only take account of a reason if the reason overtly figures in the content of one's deliberation. I take account of the reasons against harming people, for instance, by structuring my deliberations in such a way that the question of harming others does not even arise, for ordinary

reflects the truistic idea that reasons for action just are considerations that have deliberative significance.[5] A further point concerns the idea of taking a normative consideration into account, for purposes of practical deliberation. I shall suppose that one who takes account of a given justification in this way is prepared to choose or decide in accordance with the justification, should other considerations not weigh more heavily, and to act on the basis of the choice or decision so arrived at. At least, one will do this in so far as one is practically rational.[6] This may be thought of as the motivational dimension of reasons for action.

Consider now a representative person who is morally accountable. Regarding the deliberative standpoint of such a person, we may say, I believe, that they must have reason to comply with the moral demands to which they are held accountable. Underlying this idea is the conception of moral accountability as a form of general capacity. We think that agents who possess the powers of reflective self-control are morally accountable, because they are competent to grasp and comply with the justifications supporting moral demands. Thus, one familiar set of conditions that deprives an agent of the powers of reflective self-control involves the impairment of the agent's capacities for practical deliberation: either these capacities are generally undeveloped (as is the case with young children), or the capacity for moral deliberation in particular is somehow undermined (as may be the case with some forms of psychopathy). When such impairments are not present, however, we often take even immoral agents to be competent to grasp and comply with moral demands, just because of their general competence as practical reasoners.[7] In order for this assumption to be warranted, however, it must be the case that there is a course of sound deliberation open to the agent in which moral justifications are acknowledged and taken into account. Only if this condition is satisfied will the general presumption of deliberative competence license the more specific conclusion that the agent is capable of grasping and complying with moral justifications. In a phrase, 'can'—the 'can', that is, of moral accountability—implies 'ought'.

But what needs to be true of people in order for it to be the case that moral justifications provide them with reasons for action in this way? Opinions notoriously divide on this point. Humeans conventionally hold that our reasons must

purposes. For a subtle taxonomy of the variety of ways in which moral considerations might impinge on one's deliberation, see Samuel Scheffler, *Human Morality* (New York: Oxford University Press, 1992), 30–4.

[5] One might contrast the claim that there is reason to act in a certain way with the claim that a given agent *has* reason to act in that way. Perhaps 'there are' reasons that a particular agent might fail to take account of, without thereby failing to deliberate correctly. But to say that the agent *has* reasons of this kind is, it seems, to make a point about what it would be for the agent to deliberate correctly.

[6] Cf. Christine Korsgaard, 'Skepticism about Practical Reason', *Journal of Philosophy*, 83 (1986), 5–25, and Michael Smith, *The Moral Problem* (Oxford: Blackwell, 1994), ch. 5.

[7] As I go on to explain later in this section, Humeans and Kantians may both agree that this presumption is warranted—though they will have different things to say about the cases in which the presumption is defeated.

somehow be based in our given desires and projects and interests [8] A little more precisely, they hold that the normative ideal of correct deliberation must be relativized to particular agents, in that what counts as correct deliberation for a given agent will be constrained by the items in that agent's 'subjective motivational set'.[9] On the other side are (for instance) Kantians, who suppose that the notion of correct deliberation need not be constrained by the antecedent items in a given agent's subjective motivational set. They typically suppose that the norms that define correct deliberation are such that anyone who reasoned in accordance with them would take moral considerations into account. If this is correct, then competence at practical deliberation carries with it the ability to appreciate the force of moral justifications, and we may accordingly say that those justifications apply to, or are reasons for, all persons, just in virtue of their status as competent practical reasoners. By contrast, Humeans such as Bernard Williams seem to think that the capacity to appreciate the force of moral justifications—and hence to take such justifications into account in one's own deliberation—is not an intrinsically rational competence. To appreciate the force of a justification is a kind of evaluative stance, and the adoption of this stance presupposes a prior orientation of the sentiments.

Construed in this way, the dispute between Humeans and Kantians about the rational basis of morality may appear to have great significance for our understanding of moral accountability. Indeed, it is natural to assume that the theory of responsibility is the domain within which this dispute will have its real substantive pay-off.[10] If, as I have suggested, accountability requires that moral justifications count for one as reasons for action, then the divergent theories of such reasons seem to determine different views about the extension of the community of morally accountable persons. Kantians may take us to be warranted in presuming that all practical reasoners may be held morally accountable, since the capacity to appreciate and act on moral justifications is somehow intrinsic to the standpoint of competent practical deliberation. Humeans, by contrast, may reject such a presumption—especially if, as in the case of Bernard Williams, they depart from the naturalism and proto-utilitarianism that Hume himself espoused, in favour of the view that the sentimental bases of ethical concern are plural, contingent, and socially and historically conditioned.[11] On this view (which we might refer to as

---

[8] In what follows I try to present the Humean idea that deliberation must begin from an agent's desires, without taking a stand on the merits of the idea. For the record I am struck by the difficulty of providing anything like an argument for this idea; compare my 'How to Argue about Practical Reason', Chapter 1 in this volume.

[9] See Bernard Williams's 'Internal and External Reasons', as reprinted in his *Moral Luck:* (Cambridge, England: Cambridge University Press, 1981), 101–13.

[10] Cf. Bernard Williams, 'Internal Reasons and the Obscurity of Blame', as reprinted in his *Making Sense of Humanity* (Cambridge, England: Cambridge University Press, 1995), 35–45.

[11] This is a leitmotiv of Williams's *Ethics and the Limits of Philosophy* (Cambridge, Mass.: Harvard University Press, 1985); see esp. chs. 2 and 9. It should be remarked that Williams himself is notably alive to the hazards of holding people responsible (cf. ibid. 36–8); he himself might not wish to endorse even a restricted presumption that people are to be treated in this way. See also 'Internal Reasons and the Obscurity of Blame'.

'neo-Humeanism'), whether a given agent is morally accountable will very much depend on the particular educational influences to which the agent has been subject, and on the kind of residue that those influences have left on the agent's continuing character.

I think it doubtful, however, that these differences are really as significant for the theory of responsibility as they initially appear to be. The main reason for skepticism on this score has to do with a phenomenon that even the Kantian will have to acknowledge, a phenomenon that we might refer to as inherent irrationality. By this I do not mean the garden variety forms of rational lapse that all of us are subject to, to one degree or another—that is, the *de facto* failure to deliberate correctly, or the different motivational failure to choose and to act in accordance with correct deliberation even when it is actually carried out. In these cases we may continue to suppose that irrational agents are capable of deliberating and choosing correctly, despite their actual failure to do so. In cases of inherent irrationality, by contrast, the assumption of continued capacity to deliberate correctly is suspended. Consider a kind of case that I have already mentioned in passing, that of psychopathy. As ordinarily understood this involves a kind of incapacity to engage in and respond to moral reasoning. Psychopaths may be incompetent to grasp and consistently apply basic moral concepts, or to see any point to those concepts when they obtain; they may thus be unable to occupy a perspective from which moral concepts appear to have genuine deliberative significance. Since Kantians maintain that the norms of correct deliberation require anyone to take moral justifications into account, they must say that psychopaths are unable or incompetent to deliberate correctly. Hence the verdict of inherent irrationality about these cases.

In cases of this sort, the connection is severed between the claim that moral justifications provide a given agent with reasons for action,[12] and the different claim that the agent is competent to appreciate the deliberative significance of the justifications. It follows that there may be practical reasoners about whom we cannot say that they are able to appreciate moral justifications, even if the Kantian is correct about the rational status of such justifications.[13] But as I mentioned above, it is the competence or capacity claim that is important for purposes of determining whether an agent can fairly be treated as a morally accountable person. This is shown by the fact that psychopathy is paradigmatically a condition that exempts

[12] I assume that the Kantian will continue to say about this case that the psychopath has reason to act morally; otherwise the contrast with the neo-Humean view will threaten to collapse.

[13] This kind of situation will be even more common on an Aristotelian conception of practical reason, according to which an elaborate course of habituation is a condition for being able to deliberate correctly. I believe this reflects important differences between the Aristotelian and Kantian conceptions of practical reason, concerning both its nature (in particular, the role of general principles in moral deliberation) and its social role. For Kant, our status as practical reasoners should provide access to a common framework of moral requirements in a way that is independent of our more particular conception of the good. Hence the idea that there should at least be a presumption that practical reasoners are capable of grasping and responding to moral principles is important for him, as it does not seem to be for Aristotle.

an agent from accountability, just in virtue of the fact that it deprives the agent of the competence to grasp and comply with moral justifications. Thus we see that a Kantian interpretation of the norms of correct deliberation would not license the conclusion that all practical reasoners are to be included within the community of morally accountable persons. It licenses, at most, a defeasible presumption that those who are capable of practical reasoning may be treated as morally accountable—a presumption that is defeated in some cases of inherent irrationality.

Now it might be thought that this still leaves room for a significant contrast between Humean and Kantian theories on the question of moral responsibility. For it seems that the neo-Humean position would not even license a defeasible presumption that agents have the capacity for reflective self-control.[14] Whether a given agent has these powers will depend on the contingent, socially conditioned dispositions to which the agent is in fact subject, and one cannot simply presume that the right kind of dispositions will generally be present. But this point of contrast seems unlikely to have any real significance in practice. Partly this is because the forms of socialization necessary to instill in people the dispositions that (on the neo-Humean view) enable them to appreciate moral justifications remain fairly widespread in our culture. We have not yet sunk to the point where it cannot generally be taken for granted that the people we interact with are competent to grasp the deliberative significance of moral justifications. So a defeasible presumption of basic moral accountability may be warranted in practice even on the neo-Humean account of practical reasons.[15]

Indeed, I am attracted to the following, stronger hypothesis: Those cases in which the neo-Humean will say that an agent is not in a position to appreciate moral justifications are very likely to be cases in which the Kantian will opt for the verdict of inherent irrationality. The plausibility of this hypothesis is connected to the fact that rational competence admits of degrees, and that its development is subject to social and educational influences. Thus the capacity to reason morally is one of the things that children acquire in the course of normal development. The cases in which this developmental process goes awry—resulting in inherent irrationality, by the Kantian's lights—are apt to be the very cases in which the neo-Humean will claim that the agent's socialization has left no psychological niche for moral deliberation to get a foothold. Of course, proponents of the two approaches will continue to say different things about such cases. But at this point the dispute between them threatens to become merely verbal, without any connection to substantive issues in moral psychology or the theory of responsibility that seemed to give the dispute its point. Perhaps it is time to put this issue aside, and focus on more consequential questions concerning the deliberative authority of moral requirements.

---

[14] Here in particular the neo-Humean view would seem to diverge in its commitments from Hume's own position, which would ground our moral powers in the sympathetic sentiments endemic to human nature.

[15] At least, the assumption is likely to be as warranted as on the Kantian view. (As I explain below, that moral considerations provide one with reasons for action is only a necessary, not a sufficient condition for accountability.)

2. RATIONAL OPTIMALITY AND THE QUESTION OF CONGRUENCE

At the start of this essay I distinguished between two different aspects of the phenomenon of deliberative authority: There is the question whether a given agent has reason to comply with moral norms, and there is the different question whether the agent has most reason to comply with such norms.[16] I turn to the second question, concerning the rational optimality of moral conduct, in this section and the ones to follow, sketching a framework for thinking about this issue, and tracing its connections with the theory of responsibility.

There is an important initial difficulty saying clearly what it means to hold that someone has most reason to comply with moral demands (the optimality thesis, as I shall henceforth refer to it). I shall start by laying out some basic assumptions that will structure my discussion. First, optimality assertions about what we have most reason to do are not to be confused with psychological assertions about what we are in fact most strongly motivated to do. This follows directly from the basic idea that practical reason is normative, together with the truism that human beings are only imperfectly rational. Second, I shall take for granted that the optimality thesis cannot be interpreted as a claim about what best advance one's nonmoral interests or maximize one's expected nonmoral utility. Moral demands function as constraints on the pursuit of individual nonmoral utility; in this sense, doing what we are morally obligated to do sometimes requires sacrifices of us. Of course, ingenious attempts have been made, in the spirit of Thomas Hobbes, to show that a strategy of constrained maximization of individual utility is actually optimal, from the standpoint of individual nonmoral advantage.[17] For purposes of discussion in this essay, however, I shall assume that compliance with moral norms cannot fully be reconciled with the effective pursuit of nonmoral advantage. Morality appears to be a source of autonomous norms, which place constraints on the pursuit of nonmoral advantage, and which are not answerable to the different norms that govern the point of view of individual well-being.

If we adopt this assumption, however, it may seem that there is no way to unpack the assertion that moral conduct is optimal from the standpoint of reason. Practical reason appears divided within itself, between a standpoint of morality and a eudaimonistic standpoint concerned with the goodness of the agent's own life, each defined by independent norms of correct deliberation.[18] We can perhaps say what it is rational to do with an eye to morality, and what it is rational to do

---

[16] The idea that compliance with moral requirements is always rationally optimal in this sense is often expressed as the claim that such requirements are 'overriding'.

[17] See David Gauthier, *Morals by Agreement* (Oxford: Clarendon Press, 1986).

[18] This contrast should not be assimilated to the different contrast between impersonal altruism on the one hand, and egoism on the other hand. The standpoint of moral deliberation may well acknowledge requirements that are essentially connected with the agent's particular situation (that grow out of personal relationships, for instance). And the standpoint of the individual good will only be egoistic if

with an eye to an individual's good, but there seems to be no common currency in terms of which to cash out claims about what it is most rational to do overall. Moreover, this will remain the case so long as we resist efforts either to reduce morality to individual well-being, construed in nonmoral terms, or to define the good life in moral terms.[19] In what follows I shall simply assume that these efforts should be resisted, that there is no single common currency of practical reason.

It does not in fact follow from this assumption, however, that we can make no sense of the optimality thesis. Though there are a number of ways one might approach this unusually difficult issue, I shall restrict myself to discussing a general strategy that has been recurrent in the tradition of philosophical ethics.[20] Any defence of the optimality thesis must try to make out the idea that moral demands, though independent from considerations of self-interest, have a kind of normative priority, so that one only deliberates correctly when one makes one's pursuit of one's nonmoral interests conditional on one's prior compliance with moral demands. The problem, of course, is to understand the appeal to correct deliberation in this assertion. This looks like a normative claim, but it cannot itself be understood either as a moral claim or as a claim about what it is in our non-moral interest to do. The moral interpretation would amount to the trivial assertion that moral demands have deliberative priority, from the moral point of view; while the alternative interpretation of the optimality thesis, as an appeal to nonmoral interest, appears to be false.

The initial difficulty concerning the optimality thesis was that practical reason seemed divided internally, leaving no single standpoint from which to formulate and assess the idea that we have most reason to act morally. If this is the problem, however, then perhaps the solution is to look for a substantive convergence between the different points of view. I do not mean by this that we should try to construct a new, overarching standpoint that is to supersede the original perspectives of morality and the individual good. The idea, rather, is to reconsider the verdicts reached from within the original perspectives, to see how far they can be brought into alignment with each other. If the conclusion that moral demands have priority over nonmoral demands could somehow be endorsed from both deliberative points of view, it will have been vindicated without prejudice to the idea that the points of view are independent from each other. The hope is that practical reason can be unified functionally, despite the plurality of its constituent perspectives, by showing that those perspectives are congruent with each other. Though we would have different standards available by which to assess the

the agent's interests and projects happen to be exclusively self-regarding. For a general discussion of the possible relations between these points of view, with helpful references to further literature, see Thomas Nagel, *The View from Nowhere* (New York: Oxford University Press, 1986), ch. 10.

[19] Cf. ibid. 195–7.

[20] For a magisterial and sophisticated presentation of this strategy—to which I am heavily indebted—see the 'congruence argument' developed by John Rawls in pt. 3 of *A Theory of Justice* (Cambridge, Mass.: Harvard University Press, 1971). Different versions of the strategy can be found in the work of Aristotle, Butler, Hume, and Kant (among others).

correctness of an agent's deliberations and decisions, these would converge substantively on the conclusion that one should pursue one's individual ends only in ways that meet the demands and constraints of morality.

This result cannot possibly be achieved, however, without modifying our understanding of the eudaimonistic point of view.[21] To this point I have spoken as if eudaimonistic rationality attends exclusively to an agent's own well-being, where this in turn is defined in terms of the agent's nonmoral interests. Interpreted in this way, however, eudaimonistic rationality does not seem to converge on the conclusion that moral demands have priority over our nonmoral interests. If congruence between the standpoints of moral and eudaimonistic rationality is to be so much as possible, we need to question the idea that the eudaimonistic standpoint is to be understood exclusively by reference to an agent's nonmoral interests.

But this idea is in fact questionable. The eudaimonistic perspective is one from which we are concerned, in the first instance, with the goodness of our own lives. In deliberating from this point of view, our aim is to answer the practical question, 'What is it for us to live well?', where living well is in turn a matter of having a variety of ends that are worth caring about, and effectively and appropriately pursuing those ends. There is nothing in the formulation of this question, however, that requires that moral ends be excluded from the set of concerns by reference to which the goodness of our lives is understood. On the contrary, for any agent subject to serious moral motivations it would only seem natural that these should have some impact on that agent's conception of living well. Of course, the concern to act rightly would play a different role in moral and eudaimonistic reasoning. From the moral point of view, our question is simply, 'What is the right thing to do?'; the deliberative field is constituted, as it were, from the perspective of our moral concern. From the eudaimonistic perspective, by contrast, we reflect on the fact that morality is one of our concerns, and ask ourselves, in light of this and other facts about our interests, what it would be for us to live well.

When the eudaimonistic perspective is interpreted in this way, however, it is no longer clear that it cannot converge on the substantive conclusion that moral demands ought to be complied with. To reach this conclusion from the eudaimonistic perspective would be to hold that our own life goes best as a whole when the pursuit of our nonmoral ends is made conditional on our compliance with the demands of morality. Indeed, for purposes of achieving convergence with the moral point of view it may be sufficient if eudaimonistic reflection yields the weaker conclusion that there is no other life that is better for us as a whole than the life in which the demands of morality are complied with. This would be sufficient to establish the conclusion that one is reasoning correctly, from the

---

[21] As Sidney Morgenbesser has reminded me, this term has potentially misleading connotations. As I shall understand it, eudaimonistic reflection must often content itself with negative conclusions, identifying activities that are parts of one's good primarily in the sense that one's own life would be impoverished if one did not engage in them. It does not follow that to engage in activities of this kind will necessarily yield 'happiness' or 'flourishing'.

eudaimonistic standpoint, in choosing to comply with one's moral obligations; and that conclusion in turn would bring the standards of eudaimonistic reflection into substantive alignment with the standards of correct deliberation that define the moral point of view.

What I would like to do now is to look at this general strategy of argument—what I shall refer to as the congruence strategy—in light of the remarks made earlier about the role of moral principles in structuring relationships of moral accountability. In introducing this topic at the start of the essay I contrasted two different points of view: the third-person standpoint of moral accountability and the first-person standpoint of practical reason. It is an assumption of the congruence strategy that the latter standpoint is subject to a further internal division, reflecting the distinction between moral and eudaimonistic deliberation, where the truth of the optimality thesis turns on the question of how far deliberation from these two constitutive standpoints of practical reason can be brought into substantive alignment. Confronted with this potential proliferation of practical standpoints, there are two salient questions that need to be addressed: first, to what extent can the standpoint of moral accountability contribute to securing congruence between the moral and eudaimonistic points of view? and what would the breakdown of congruence between these deliberative standpoints entail for relationships of moral accountability? I take up these issues in the sections to follow.

3. FULL ACCOUNTABILITY AND THE VALUE OF MORAL ACTION

An initial question concerning eudaimonistic reflection about morality is this: how are moral considerations to be registered when we reflect about what it would be for us to live well? Should we think of moral motivations in this context as simple preferences, whose potential satisfaction is to be weighed in the balance along with the potential satisfaction of our other, nonmoral preferences, in determining which courses of action would be best for us to perform?

This way of thinking about matters seems to me potentially misleading, threatening to distort our conception of moral interests by ascribing to them the wrong kind of role in eudaimonistic reflection. As I see matters, moral principles define a framework for human social life, specifying *obligations* that individuals must comply with in their interactions with each other; they rule out certain forms of behavior, as impermissible from the moral point of view, and specify other things that we are positively required to do. If cruelty and manipulation are morally wrong, for instance, then one simply must not deal with people in these ways. By specifying obligations of this kind, moral principles carve out a range of potential actions that are open to us to perform in any given situation, defining other alternatives as morally out of bounds.

Now this seems to me to have an important bearing on the question of how moral interests are to be understood within the context of eudaimonistic reflection. With respect to their content, our central moral interests are not plausibly thought of by analogy with a standard kind of positive preference regarding options and outcomes, where the satisfaction of the preference does not necessarily dictate any particular form of behavior at the time when the preference is held. My desire to see the latest Martin Scorsese movie could be satisfied by going to see the film at the next available opportunity, but it could equally be satisfied by forming and acting on a plan to see the film next week, or when it eventually appears on television. My interest in morality, by contrast, is an interest in complying with the moral principles that govern our interactions with each other, and when these principles specify strict or perfect duties, they can only be complied with successfully by continuously doing what the principles specify (avoiding cruelty and manipulation, for example): to humiliate somebody today, with the thought that one will strive to be kind tomorrow, would not really count as a way of satisfying our interest in morality.[22]

A second and more important point concerns the status of moral interests within the context of eudaimonistic reflection. It seems to me that the connection of morality with obligation has implications for the way in which moral interests are to be reflected in thinking about what it is for us to live well. If we have such interests, and if we take them seriously, then we will not be inclined to view them merely as defeasible preferences—that is, as considerations that are to be taken into account in reflecting about how it would be good to live, but that may be overridden if compliance with moral demands would render inexpedient the pursuit of our personal goals. Rather, an agent who has a serious interest in morality ought to regard compliance with moral principles as a fixed constraint on what may be counted as a good life. The task of eudaimonistic deliberation for such an agent is not merely to enter moral considerations into the balance, as factors to be weighed off against the attractions of ordinary personal projects and interests, but to discover ways of pursuing those projects and interests that also fulfill the requirements of moral principles. The appropriate metaphor for this kind of practical deliberation is not weighing things in a balance, but rather *integration*: one tries to find ways of pursuing and organizing one's activities that advance one's personal projects and interests while also fully satisfying one's moral obligations.

If this is right, then the main philosophical task for the proponent of the congruence strategy will be to show that moral interests ought to be taken into account, from the eudaimonistic point of view. That is, if it can be established that correct reflection about what makes our lives worthwhile must acknowledge the importance of our basic interest in morality, then we will already have gone a considerable distance toward securing the optimality thesis. For it seems that the

[22] Kantian imperfect duties are more like ordinary preferences in this respect; in so far as they are genuine obligations, however, they should have the indefeasible status within eudaimonistic reflection that I go on to discuss.

only sensible way to register the importance of moral considerations within eudai-monistic reflection is to take moral principles to define fixed constraints within which our personal projects and activities are to proceed. This in turn would amount to acceptance of the claim that our lives go better on the whole when the pursuit of our personal ends is made conditional on, and thereby integrated with, our compliance with moral demands. Anything short of reflection with this kind of integrative structure—such as the 'weighing in a balance' model to which I adverted above—would appear to distort our understanding of moral considerations and the interests they generate. It would represent, not an admissible way of representing the contribution of moral interests to the goodness of our lives, but rather the denial that such interests have any independent contribution to make.

The task, then, is to get moral interests on the map, for purposes of eudai-monistic reflection, showing that they are among the concerns that need to be taken seriously if we are to reason correctly about the worthwhile life. One kind of person for whom this claim might seem problematic would be the complete amoralist, someone utterly lacking in any nonderivative motivations to comply with moral principles. People of this kind would not have any interest in acting morally, and so the question might seem moot whether an interest in morality would be taken into account by them if they were to deliberate correctly about their own well-being.[23]

A different and more interesting challenge is presented by the person who is sub-ject to moral motivations, but who does not see compliance with moral principles as an intrinsic good, from the standpoint of eudaimonistic deliberation. About per-sons in this position, we might well agree that they have reason to comply with moral principles, in that they are capable of applying and acting on those principles in deliberation from a distinctively moral point of view. But when they reflect on what it is to live well, they will have trouble taking their moral motivations seriously, as important independent determinants of a good life. Perhaps they view moral principles on a loose analogy with traffic regulations: as rules that generally must be complied with in order to facilitate and enable social life, without its being the case that such compliance contributes intrinsically to making one's own life worthwhile. This sort of person need not regret having developed a motivational responsiveness to moral considerations, and a correspondingly habitual facility at adopting the moral point of view. Nor will they necessarily fail to see anything of value in acting morally, when they engage in eudaimonistic reflection. Just as com-pliance with traffic regulations is instrumentally valuable in all kinds of ways when one is out on the road (for instance, as enhancing one's own safety), so too can com-pliance with moral principles contribute instrumentally to one's own good— among other things, it helps to keep one out of trouble with the law. But the persons I am imagining will balk at admitting that acting morally is an intrinsically

---

[23] On the figure of the amoralist, see Joseph Raz, 'The Amoralist', as reprinted in his *Engaging Reason: On the Theory of Value and Action* (Oxford: Oxford University Press, 1999), 273–302.

important ingredient of the good life. In their eyes, this supposition would be akin to the rather absurd view that there is something intrinsically valuable about obeying the speed limit, even when one is on an empty road in the middle of the desert under excellent driving conditions, and the police are nowhere in sight.

If this 'traffic regulation' view of morality is correct, then it seems to me that the congruence strategy is unlikely to meet with much success. That strategy requires that compliance with moral principles should contribute directly to making the agent's own life worthwhile. But on the traffic regulation view it would simply be a mistake to suppose that compliance with moral principles should have this kind of importance, for purposes of eudaimonistic reflection. If the congruence strategy is to go forward, then, it will be necessary to challenge the traffic regulation model by showing that there is something of intrinsic value to be attained by acting morally; something, moreover, that is of sufficient importance within eudaimonistic reflection to be treated as a condition of the good life.

It is here, I believe, that attention to relationships of accountability may be of some assistance. At the start of this essay I drew a distinction between two levels of status that persons may attain within morality. There is, first, the status of being an accountable agent, someone to whom moral principles are appropriately addressed, and who may fairly be held morally responsible with reference to such principles. Someone who achieves this status is eligible for membership in a certain kind of relationship, one defined by the reciprocal stance of holding people to moral demands. But agents who are accountable in this way can attain a different and higher kind of moral status by actually exercising their powers of reflective self-determination in accordance with moral principles. To act in this way is not merely to be a person who can be held morally to account by others. It is, more strongly, to be in a position actually to give a successful account of one's doings to others, a position from which one can justify one's actions by reference to common moral principles. People who achieve this status are thereby able to enter into qualitatively superior relationships with other people. They have no need to fear or shun the gaze of their fellows, since they are capable of justifying their actions in moral terms, terms that all accountable agents should equally be able to understand and to accept.

Now, whether or not we succeed in achieving this kind of status is not a matter of indifference to most of us. On the contrary, it seems to me to be the sort of thing that is intelligible as an intrinsic contribution to our own good, something that is worth caring about for its own sake, when we think clearly about what it is to live well. The fact is that humans are deeply social creatures, and this is reflected in the urge that most people feel to be able to give an account of themselves to others—an urge that manifests itself, somewhat perversely, in the imaginative compulsion we have to rationalize when confronted with evidence of apparent wrongdoing. To put the point slightly differently, it is not a matter of indifference to most of us whether we are the objects of resentment or indignation on the part of our fellow human beings. There is a primitive desire to be thought well of by others, which is refined through socialization into a second-order interest in *justified* regard: the desire not to act in ways that could incur the well-grounded resentment or indignation of others. By enabling us to give an account of ourselves, compliance with moral principles answers to this interest, and thereby contributes to making our own lives worthwhile.

Of course, nothing I have said can be construed as a proof that attainment of the status of full accountability is an ingredient of the agent's own good. Indeed, I myself am suspicious of the very idea that philosophy could establish a thesis in the theory of value of this kind. What philosophical reflection can do is to help us to see how living morally can be a way of living well, by connecting moral behaviour to something that is recognizable to us within eudaimonistic reflection, as an important part of a good human life. This requires not merely that moral behavior be connected to something that human beings generally find intelligible, as an object of interest or concern, but that such behaviour be shown to make a direct contribution to the goodness of the agent's own life. It seems to me that the status of full accountability—being in a position to give a successful justification of oneself to other persons—is among the things that are familiar and intelligible to us in this context, as direct objects of reflexive concern about our own lives, and that by relating this status to compliance with moral principles, philosophy can help us to understand why such compliance should figure as a central constraint on eudaimonistic deliberation.

Does the argument I have sketched establish that moral behavior is an objective good, something without which no human being—including even the amoralist—could be said to have flourished or lived well? I doubt it. But for present purposes I would be content with the following, more modest conclusion: that no person who is equipped with moral motivations need regard the satisfaction of those preferences by analogy with the traffic regulation model. There is something recognizable as an appropriate object of reflexive concern about our own lives that is only attainable by complying with moral obligations, namely the achievement of a certain kind of relationship to other people. This in turn lends credence to the assumption that those persons who ascribe importance to their interest in morality, for purposes of eudaimonistic reflection, are in fact reasoning correctly about what it is for them to live well.

4. ACCOUNTABILITY AND THE STRINGENCY OF MORAL REQUIREMENTS

To say that our moral interests are important, within the standpoint of eudaimonistic reflection, is of course not to say that they are the only interests that are important in that context. Any individual with a reasonably fulfilling and balanced life is going to have all sorts of personal projects and goals and relationships that are matters of great importance, and that will need to be taken centrally into account in reflecting about how to live well. We are not merely moral agents, but also friends and lovers, philosophers and teachers, train-spotters and Mets fans, and these personal commitments provide much of the raw material for deliberation about our own good. Indeed I suspect that for most people, personal commitments of this sort are apt to be important in a way that the interest in morality almost never is. They are what Bernard Williams has referred to as 'ground projects', the sorts of things that give our lives point and meaning, and without which we would not see much reason to go on. The interest in morality, by contrast, does not seem to have this kind of significance. Even granting the intrinsic goods of moral community to which I earlier referred, these do not appear to be the kinds of goods to organize a life around: one does not live for morality the way one might be said to live for baseball or philosophy or one's children.

The fact that morality does not generally have this kind of importance can make it tempting to suppose that it could have at best a secondary contribution to make in contexts of eudaimonistic deliberation. If morality does not itself have the status of a kind of ground project, then it might seem reasonable to subordinate our interest in it whenever that interest comes into conflict with the things that fill our lives with purpose and zest. But this would be a mistake. To say that morality is not important in the way our typical ground projects are important is not to say that it is not important at all. If compliance with moral principles is an essential part of the good life, and if those principles prescribe obligations, then the person who is deliberating correctly about what it is to live well will take those obligations to define constraints or conditions on a good life. As I said earlier, the deliberative task will be one of integration: finding ways of pursuing one's projects and goals while also satisfying the requirements of morality.

The one sort of case in which this task will tend to break down is the case in which an agent's ground projects are themselves sources of obligation, and those obligations come into conflict with the obligations of morality. A schematic example is provided by any situation in which morality demands of an agent the ultimate sacrifice: if morality requires one to put one's life on the line (for instance, when the officers of a military unit have threatened to execute those soldiers who refuse to carry out their criminal order to massacre a group of innocent civilians),[24] this would naturally appear to conflict with the obligation to preserve one's own life that is grounded in one's personal and familial relationships. Here it would appear that one cannot satisfy the demands of morality while also living up to one's personal commitments, and so the integrative task of eudaimonistic deliberation would have no single solution. A different and perhaps less schematic case would be Susan Wolf's example of the parent, whose personal obligation of protection and support for her child might conflict with the moral obligation to inform the police that she has reason to suspect the child of serious criminal

---

[24] Cf. Michael Walzer, *Just and Unjust Wars* (New York: Basic Books, 1977), 313–14.

wrongdoing.[25] Here again, there seems to be no course of action available that would integrate the agent's moral obligations with the demands that are grounded in her personal projects.

Cases of this kind, in which integrative eudaimonistic reflection cannot go forward, theaten to undermine the deliberative authority of morality. Presented with a situation of this sort, it seems implausible to maintain that the agent has most reason to comply with the demands of duty. The far more natural response would be that there is no clear answer to the question what the agent has most reason to do; she is confronted with the need to decide on a course of action in a way that exceeds the capacity of practical reason to guide her toward a determinate solution. Furthermore, the forces that are arrayed against morality in this kind of situation are forces that it would be unusually difficult to resist. They represent the demands of one's identity-defining projects, requirements that one must comply with if one is to remain true to the commitments that give meaning and point to one's life. To violate these requirements, for the sake of morality, would be to betray values that are important in a way that morality generally cannot hope to be.

Now it may well be doubted how often genuine conflicts of this kind are apt to arise in life. Did Gauguin really have to leave his family in the lurch in order to remain true to his calling as a painter? Was there absolutely no deliberative solution available that would have enabled him to integrate the demands of his personal projects with his moral obligations to his wife and children? There is much room for rationalization and self-deception in cases of this kind. Nevertheless, I see no reason to deny that situations of the form I have described can sometimes come up, in which moral obligations are irreconcilably in conflict with the demands of one's important ground projects. Moreover, when such conflicts occur, and when in the face of such a conflict an agent chooses to violate her moral obligations, there is room to question whether it is reasonable to hold the agent fully to blame for this lapse. Let me explain.

At the start of this essay, I observed that the powers of reflective self-control are conditions for the reasonableness of holding people morally accountable, and also that these powers can temporarily be impaired, due to local circumstances such as extreme stress or emotional turmoil. Furthermore, when such impairments or difficulties obtain, the appropriate response would be to ascribe to an agent only a diminished level of moral accountability, and to mitigate the reactions of blame and moral sentiment that would ordinarily be called for by a moral wrong. For if the powers of reflective self-control are conditions for the fairness of these kinds of response, and we agree that those powers are severely impaired in the agent's circumstances, then we ought to adjust our reactions accordingly in recognition of this fact.

These reflections suggest a rationale for suspending ordinary relationships of moral accountability in situations in which the requirements of morality conflict

[25] Susan Wolf, 'Morality and Partiality', in J. Tomberlin (ed.), *Philosophical Perspectives*, vi. *Ethics* (Atascadero, Calif.: Ridgeview, 1992), 243–59, at 253–4.

irreconcilably with the demands of one's personal projects. Conflicts of this kind can plausibly be viewed as locally impairing an agent's capacity to comply with moral requirements, in so far as they render unusually difficult the exercise of those capacities. This is perhaps clearest in cases in which morality requires us to sacrifice our own life, since requirements of this kind would meet with powerful resistance not only from rational sources (the demands of our personal projects), but also from our primal feelings about death.[26] But the difficulty or impairment of moral power may equally be present in cases involving no primal emotions of this kind, where moral demands conflict with the requirements of one's personal relationships and commitments. To do the right thing in such a situation would mean the certain loss of one's heart's desire, the abandonment of that which invests one's life and one's activities with meaning and point. Even acknowledging the importance of morality, it would be unusually difficult to bring oneself to make a sacrifice of this kind; doing so would be powerfully opposed to forces within the structure of practical reason itself. And when reason itself is an impairment of our moral capacities, we ought to take account of that fact by moderating or mitigating our responses of blame and reactive sentiment. This is the grain of truth in the idea that it would be unfair to blame a person fully if acting morally was not the rational thing to do.

I would like in conclusion to consider briefly an issue that has received much attention in recent moral philosophy, concerning the stringency or demandingness of moral requirements. It is sometimes thought that extremely demanding theories of the content of moral requirements, such as direct utilitarianism, are inadequate because they render the deliberative authority of those requirements problematic.[27] I am inclined to agree with this verdict.[28] But I think the objection is difficult to articulate if we confine our attention to the first-person perspective of practical reason, and believe that it may be helpful to consider in this connection the role of moral principles in structuring relationships of accountability.

Suppose that moral norms gave us the first-order goal of maximizing the good, impersonally construed, so that deliberation from the moral point of view is answerable exclusively to this maximizing norm. It is a familiar thought that compliance with moral norms, construed in this way, would require a great deal of us in the way of personal sacrifice. But the more interesting point concerns the way in which sacrifice would be imposed by this kind of morality. To say that we are

---

[26] Walzer treats the case of the soldiers mentioned earlier in the text as one of diminished responsibility through duress; see *Just and Unjust Wars*, 313–14.

[27] This idea is suggested, for instance, by Nagel's argument for relaxing moral requirements in *The View from Nowhere*, 200–3, and by Scheffler's defence of 'moderation' in ch. 7 of *Human Morality*.

[28] I also think there are other, independent grounds for rejecting particular interpretations of morality as especially stringent. For instance, there is a false conception of the standpoint of moral deliberation as detached and 'impersonal' that exerts pressure in the direction of extreme stringency. Indeed, both Nagel and Scheffler betray a weakness for this conception, which makes their own defences of more moderate interpretations seem somewhat *ad hoc*. But of course these are issues for a different occasion.

always required to maximize the good, impersonally conceived, means that morality is not only demanding but peculiarly intrusive. There is a standing requirement that we contribute to the realization of a demanding positive goal, and this combination of stringency and pervasiveness—the combination Bernard Williams has pointed to under the heading of 'negative responsibility'[29]—seems likely to generate constant conflicts between the obligations of morality and the demands of our more personal projects and goals. In a world of tremendous inequality and suffering it is very doubtful that the things we are required to do, in the service of our relationships and commitments, would also happen to be the things that maximize expected overall utility, impersonally conceived—working on one's paper for the next conference or watching the Mets' home opener hardly seem to cut it when there are basic human needs and interests to be attended to. The upshot is that the requirements of morality would be in constant conflict with the demands of living an individual human life, and the integrative project of eudaimonistic reflection would be thwarted across the board. There would rarely turn out to be a solution to the problem of complying with moral obligations while also meeting the demands that stem from one's own ground projects. Moreover, given the kind of importance that attaches to such personal projects, the breakdown of eudaimonistic reflection would threaten to permanently impair our moral capacities, creating a standing impediment within practical reason to the regulation of conduct by the light of moral principles. As a result, it would never be reasonable to hold people fully accountable by the standards of a moral theory of this kind.

This, I believe, is a sufficient reason for rejecting direct utilitarianism. It is not just that this theory would be extremely demanding, but that it is demanding in a way that would systematically thwart the project of integrative eudaimonistic reflection, and thereby undermine the practice of moral accountability. The concern that we have on this score is a reflection of our conception of morality as defining a common set of standards for a moral community, by appeal to which the conduct of each person can be justified and criticized in terms that all are able to understand and to abide by. This conception commits us to the view that moral demands must be capable of serving as the basis for reciprocal relations of moral accountability, and that constraint would be violated by an interpretation of moral requirements which necessarily resulted, under the familiar circumstances of human life, in a fundamental breakdown of the integrative project of eudaimonistic reflection.

Of course, not everyone accepts the conception of morality to which I have just adverted. Proponents of some religious conceptions of ethics, for instance, tend to see moral standards not as bases of reciprocal relations between persons, but in the

[29] Bernard Williams, 'A Critique of Utilitarianism', in J. J. C. Smart and Bernard Williams, *Utilitarianism: For and Against* (Cambridge, England: Cambridge University Press, 1973), 75–150, sect. 3.

context of nonreciprocal relations between the individual believer and god. Someone attracted to this approach will not find the objection to highly demanding interpretations of morality that I have tried to articulate persuasive.[30] Direct utilitarians, who often resemble the proponents of religious interpretations of morality in their view of the stringency of moral requirements, are also notoriously skeptical of our existing practice of moral responsibility.[31] They tend to view this as a residue of primitive retributivist systems of thought, which ought to be replaced, so far as possible, by more therapeutic and constructive forms of moral relationship. If this helps to explain the failure of utilitarians to grasp the force of the objection I have tried to articulate, however, it does not necessarily undermine that objection. The inability of utilitarians to make sense of the practice of holding people responsible as anything other than a relict of primitive retributivism is itself one of the things many of us find problematic about the utilitarian conception of the moral life.[32]

A different line of response would call attention to the fact that the authority of morality, on the account of it I have sketched, is a contingent matter. It has become a commonplace in discussions of the relation between morality and the individual good to observe that this relation is liable to be affected by the social conditions in which an individual lives.[33] The authority of morality can thus be seen as a political achievement. In a more egalitarian social world, for instance, the demands that generalized beneficence would make on the currently affluent would presumably be far less stringent than they are at present. Direct utilitarians might insist that moral requirements, on their account of them, can indeed serve as the basis of reciprocal relations of moral accountability—not in the actual world of extreme inequality, perhaps, but in a social world in which such inequalities had been substantially reduced.

There are two difficulties with this response. The first is that it is unclear whether the reduced stringency of direct utilitarianism in a different social world would alone be enough to remove completely the kind of problem I have identified. That problem stems not just from the fact that utilitarian morality imposes stringent demands, but rather from the way those demands are articulated,

---

[30] It seems to me that the ideal of morality as a form of self-transcendence (discussed for instance by Scheffler in *Human Morality*, 120–1) is naturally at home in this kind of context. Note too that one might subscribe to this kind of ideal in the guise of a 'personal morality', without thinking that it should also structure one's relations with other agents. In my view, this is the right way to interpret the form of 'moral perfectionism' discussed by Stanley Cavell, in *Conditions Handsome and Unhandsome: The Constitution of Emersonian Perfectionism* (Chicago: Chicago University Press, 1990).

[31] This shows itself, for instance, in the familiar utilitarian distinction between the question of the wrongness of an action, and the question whether the consequences of blaming the agent for it would be optimific; see e.g. J. J. C. Smart, 'An Outline of a System of Utilitarian Ethics', in Smart and Williams, *Utilitarianism: For and Against*, 3–74, at sect. 7.   [32] Cf. *RMS*, sect. 3.1.

[33] See e.g. Nagel, *The View from Nowhere*, 204–7; Shelly Kagan, *The Limits of Morality* (Oxford: Clarendon Press, 1989), 393–9; Scheffler, *Human Morality*, ch. 8; and Peter Railton, 'Alienation, Consequentialism, and the Demands of Morality', as reprinted in Samuel Scheffler (ed.), *Consequentialism and its Critics* (Oxford: Oxford University Press, 1988), 93–133, at 122–5.

namely, in the form of a standing first-order goal, by reference to which one is to justify each of one's choices and activities. The achievement of more egalitarian social conditions might bring about a formal reduction in the conflicts between moral and personal obligations, making it more frequently the case that the things one is required to do in the name of one's projects and commitments are also things that satisfy the moral demand that one always seek to maximize the impersonal good. But the intrusiveness of morality remains, on this conception of it, imposing a demand that one justify each of one's actions as a direct contribution to a standing and positive moral objective, and this requirement seems likely to distort one's eudaemonistic reflection in other disturbing ways. One of the things that follows from the special kind of importance we ascribe to our ground projects and relationships is that we take them to make demands on us that are independent of our other moral and nonmoral commitments, and this way of thinking about them would be threatened by a requirement that we act on our personal projects and commitments only when doing so coincides contingently with the first-order moral goal of maximizing the impersonal good. A kind of alienation would set in.

The second difficulty is simply that we need moral standards to structure our relations with other persons in the imperfect world in which we actually live. Even if direct utilitarianism could provide a reasonable basis for responsibility relations in a substantially egalitarian social world, it does not follow that it provides a reasonable basis for responsibility relations in the actual circumstances of modern social life. We need to know what is permissible and obligatory under these circumstances, where such judgments can serve in justification and moral criticism of our own conduct and the conduct of others. Theories that violate this desideratum, in virtue of their overly stringent interpretations of the demands of morality, are difficult for us to take seriously as theories of anything we could recognize as morality— even if they could be taken seriously in a social world utterly unlike our own.

7

Moral Responsibility and the Practical Point of View

1. INTRODUCTION

Moral responsibility, on the approach I favor, is a matter of normative competence. To be a morally accountable agent is to possess certain general capacities for moral reasoning, which we might refer to as powers of reflective self-control. These general powers include above all the capacity to grasp and apply moral principles, and the capacity to control one's behavior by the light of such principles.[1] Indeed, I would hope that proponents of many different views might agree with these abstract pronouncements. Disagreements, I believe, center not so much on the importance of the powers of reflective self-control as on their interpretation, in particular, whether and in what forms those powers presuppose freedom of the will.

If this is right, there will be two salient points at which ontological issues intrude on the theory of responsibility. First, there is the question whether the powers of reflective self-control that make us accountable persons have a real object. Those powers are forms of normative competence, involving the ability to reason correctly about moral issues and to respond appropriately to the moral reasons one grasps. But if there are no moral reasons or values, such powers would come to nought—there would be nothing for them to be about, as it were. We might refer to this as the normative side of responsibility. On the other side—the personal side, as we might put it—there are equally ontological issues to be addressed. These center around the question of whether persons are in fact equipped with the powers of reflective self-control. If we call those who possess

Originally published in Ton van den Beld (ed.), *Moral Responsibility and Ontology* (Dordrecht: Kluwer Academic Publishers, 2000), 25–47. Copyright © 2000 Kluwer Academic Publishers. Reprinted with kind permission of Springer Science and Business Media. Many thanks to the other participants at the Utrecht conference on Moral Responsibility and Ontology for very helpful comments and criticisms. I owe a special debt to the following people, who provided extensive and invaluable oral and written feedback on earlier versions of this contribution: Christopher Grau, Jimmy Lenman, Sally Sedgwick, Angela Smith, and Ton van den Beld.

[1] For a defense and development of these claims, see my book, *Responsibility and the Moral Sentiments* (Cambridge, Mass.: Harvard University Press, 1994).

such powers moral agents, the question is whether we can or should accept an ontology that leaves room for moral agents in this sense.

It seems to me important to bear in mind that the theory of moral responsibility raises ontological issues of both kinds. Philosophers working on these problems have traditionally focused their attention primarily on the personal side of matters. The central issue has been the following: Can the forms of freedom and capacity important to responsibility be reconciled with our standing as natural beings? But if moral agency is understood in terms of normative competence, there will also be ontological issues to be addressed that touch on the normative side of the question, centering on the existence or reality of moral reasons and values.

This is important, because it helps to bring into clear focus the range of approaches that may be taken to the ontological issues. On the normative side, I would single out four options as especially significant. There is, first, the position we might call eliminative naturalism. Proponents of this position operate with a theoretical criterion of reality, according to which only those entities and properties exist that contribute to explaining our observations and our practices. Applying this criterion to the case of moral values and reasons, eliminative naturalists conclude that these entities do not exist, because they are not needed to account for our moral activities—they are essentially superfluous from the theoretical point of view.[2] Opposed to this position are two forms of moral realism that share the theoretical criterion of reality, but contend that moral reasons and values are after all needed to explain central aspects of our moral practices. These positions are reductive naturalism and nonreductive (or Platonist) realism. The former holds that moral entities and properties can satisfy the explanatory criterion, because they are identical with (clusters of) natural entities and properties, while the latter would insist that the explanatory criterion can be satisfied even in the absence of a satisfying reduction of this kind.[3] Finally, there is what might be called the practical reason approach. Defenders of this approach concede that moral reasons and values may be otiose when it comes to explaining and predicting what people do. But they reject the theoretical criterion of reality, affirming the autonomy of practical reason and the independent legitimacy of the entities postulated for purposes of practical deliberation.[4] On this approach, the test for

[2] See Gilbert Harman, *The Nature of Morality* (New York: Oxford University Press, 1977), chs. 1 and 2, and J. L. Mackie, *Ethics: Inventing Right and Wrong* (Harmondsworth: Penguin Books, 1977), ch. 1.

[3] For a clear example of the reductionist strategy, see Peter Railton, 'Moral Realism', as reprinted in Stephen Darwall, Allan Gibbard, and Peter Railton (eds.), *Moral Discourse and Practice* (New York: Oxford University Press, 1997), 137–63. Other prominent contemporary versions of moral realism— such as those defended by David Brink, in *Moral Realism and the Foundations of Ethics* (Cambridge, England: Cambridge University Press, 1989) and Richard Boyd, in 'How To Be a Moral Realist', as reprinted in Darwall et al. (eds.), *Moral Discourse and Practice*, 105 35—are harder to classify in terms of my rough schema; these theories, though nonreductionistic, are at the same time clearly naturalist in their inspiration. Platonist versions of nonreductionistic realism figure in contemporary discussions primarily as a foil for the presentation of anti-realist positions; see e.g. Mackie, *Ethics*, ch. 1.

[4] A good example of this approach is Christine M. Korsgaard, *The Sources of Normativity* (Cambridge, England: Cambridge University Press, 1996). Korsgaard represents her position as a

the existence of moral reasons and values is not whether such entities are needed to explain and predict human behavior and experience, but whether moral claims stand up to distinctively normative reflection about what there is reason for us to do.[5]

Roughly analogous positions can be identified on the personal side of the debate. Corresponding to the two forms of naturalism about moral reasons and values is the view that persons are to be attributed only those psychological states and capacities that are necessary to explain the actions they perform, where explanation in turn proceeds in essentially scientific terms. This view finds expression in the characteristically empiricist assumption that human action is causally determined by states of belief and desire to which persons are subject, and with respect to which they are basically passive—an assumption we might refer to as psychological determinism. Some who are attracted to this position are incompatibilists. They maintain that genuine responsibility would require a kind of freedom at odds with the assumption of psychological determinism, and conclude that such responsibility is impossible.[6] In this respect, their position resembles that of the eliminative naturalists about moral reasons and values. Corresponding to reductive naturalism in the normative debate, on the other hand, is the position of traditional compatibilists. They hold that our status as accountable agents can be reconstructed fully in terms of the conceptual resources delivered by psychological determinism, drawing on a conditionalist interpretation of freedom to distinguish between those forms of causal determination that undermine responsibility and those that do not.[7] The hallmark of this broadly naturalist approach, in both its compatibilist and incompatibilist versions, is the idea that the explanatory standpoint of theoretical reason, as interpreted in the sciences, is decisive when it comes to questions of ontology.

Opposed to this kind of naturalism is a position in some ways analogous to nonreductive realism in respect to moral reasons and values, the theory of agent-causation. Proponents of this position agree with the incompatibilist naturalists

form of constructivism rather than 'dogmatic' realism; but, as she admits, it does enable us to say that there are moral reasons and values, and these seem to me appropriately viewed as ontological commitments of a kind. Different, less constructivist versions of the practical reason approach might be Thomas Nagel, *The View from Nowhere* (New York: Oxford University Press, 1986), ch. 8, and T. M. Scanlon, *What We Owe to Each Other* (Cambridge, Mass.: Harvard University Press, 1999), chs. 1–2.

[5] As should be evident from this paragraph, I construe the theoretical perspective (here and in the remainder of this contribution) as the perspective of scientific reason, defined by the aims of explanation and prediction. It is not to be confused with the more general perspective of belief. The latter is, like the standpoint of practical reason, a first-person, deliberative point of view that is constitutively concerned with reasons. (It differs from the standpoint of practical reason, however, in not presupposing the kinds of volitional capacity that I shall be discussing later in this paper.) For some suggestive remarks on the perspective of belief as a first-person, deliberative point of view, see Richard Moran, 'Self-Knowledge: Discovery, Resolution, and Undoing', *European Journal of Philosophy*, 5 (1997), 141–61.

[6] Compare J. J. C. Smart, 'Freewill, Praise, and Blame', *Mind*, 57 (1948), 291–306.

[7] For the classic modern statement of this position, see Moritz Schlick, *Problems of Ethics*, trans. David Rynam (New York: Dover Publications, 1962), ch. 7.

that genuine moral agency cannot be reconstructed in terms of psychological determinism. They agree, further, in accepting that ontological commitments must in general satisfy a criterion of explanatory significance. But they disagree with the naturalists in their interpretation of this criterion. According to the theory of agent-causation, there will be moral agents just in case there are some events that cannot be explained in scientific terms, but that can be explained by appealing directly to an agent, construed as a kind of unmoved mover.[8] The resulting theory differs from both forms of naturalism, then, in denying that human actions can be explained in a way that is continuous with the explanations offered in the sciences for other events in the world.

Finally, there is in the theory of moral agency an analogue of the practical reason approach. Characteristic of this approach is the rejection of the explanatory criterion in ontology, and a corresponding insistence on the autonomy and independence of practical reason vis-à-vis theoretical reason. Applied to the personal dimension of responsibility, this approach results in a position reminiscent of Kant's.[9] The powers that distinguish us as moral agents do not meet the explanatory criterion; we would not need to postulate them in order to satisfy our interest in explaining and predicting the things people do. But this does not entail that those powers are not real. Their point and rationale lie rather in their significance for practical reason. The capacities for reflective self-control and self-determination are automatically presupposed when we ourselves engage in first-person deliberation about what to do, and we project these same capacities onto other persons, insofar as we assume them to be appropriate targets of moral address and potential subjects of joint deliberation.

This hasty sketch already suffices to illustrate the immense complexity of the ontological issues raised by the theory of responsibility. Simplifying greatly, we might make the following generalizations. Proponents of the two kinds of naturalist approach operate with an antecedent, explanatory criterion of what there is, provided by scientific practice, and argue that responsibility is legitimate only to the extent it can be made sense of in terms of this ontological scheme. Those who favor positions in the third and fourth groups, by contrast, start with our distinctively moral practice of holding persons responsible, and urge that our ontology should be enlarged, as necessary, to accommodate the commitments of that practice. Differences between the approaches in these final two groups turn on the question of whether and how the expanded ontology is answerable to explanatory constraints. Proponents of nonreductive realism and the theory of agent-causation share with the naturalists an explanatory criterion of what there is, but suggest that moral values and moral agents contribute to patterns of explanation that go beyond the

---

[8] A concise presentation of this position is Roderick M. Chisholm, 'Human Freedom and the Self', as reprinted in Gary Watson (ed.), *Free Will* (Oxford: Oxford University Press, 1982), 24–35.

[9] See e.g. the last section of the 'Analytic' of the *Critique of Practical Reason*, the 'Critical Elucidation of the Analytic of Pure Practical Reason', 89–106. (References to Kant, here and elsewhere, use the pagination of the Akademie edition.)

explanations prevalent in the sciences. Defenders of the practical reason approach, on the other hand, reject the idea that our ontological assumptions must be dictated by explanatory considerations, asserting the independence and autonomy of the practical point of view and of the ontological commitments peculiar to it.

My own sympathies lie with the last of these positions. I believe that we should be willing to expand our ontology to accommodate the commitments of our moral practices, and that the practical reason approach provides the best conceptual underpinning for this attitude. At the same time, it has to be conceded that the approach is not without its difficulties, especially when it comes to the theory of the moral agent. Most pressing, to my mind, is the question of whether the ontological commitments of moral practice are constrained in any way at all by the naturalistic perspective of science. Offhand, it seems plausible that the project of understanding our moral practices might require us to make assumptions about what there is that go beyond the ontological commitments of the sciences. But it seems equally plausible to suppose that these further assumptions should at least be *compatible* with the explanatory claims made in the sciences. Thus, if moral practice presupposed that there are (say) witches, it would not follow that we should simply expand our ontology to accommodate beings of this kind. Their postulation would simply not hang together with prevailing scientific accounts of what goes on in the natural world;[10] the autonomy of the practical point of view does not entail that absolutely anything goes. Yet on some interpretations, the practical reason approach entitles us to grant that there are moral agents, even if the following two theses are also true: that moral agency requires absolute freedom of will, and that our best scientific explanations are completely deterministic. Why should this be thought any less objectionable than the expansion of our ontology to include witches?

In the remainder of my contribution I shall sketch an interpretation of the practical reason approach that speaks to this concern, addressing the question of the standing of persons as moral agents. I begin (section 2) by isolating an aspect of moral agency that is difficult to make sense of in naturalist terms, namely the capacity for choice. This volitionalist capacity is part of the powers of reflective self-control, as I understand them, and the difficulty of accounting for it in naturalist terms has made the theory of agent-causation seem attractive to some philosophers. I suggest, however, that the practical reason approach might yield a superior interpretation of this dimension of moral agency. This suggestion is first criticized and then refined in section 3, which attempts to explain clearly just what it means to locate agency in relation to the standpoint of practical reason. A particular aim of this section is to give a sense to the idea that agency is a phenomenon of the

---

[10] I do not mean that the postulation of witches is merely something that cannot be motivated by scientific considerations alone, since this kind of independence from scientific reason is already allowed for by the thesis of the autonomy of the practical point of view. The idea, rather, is that the existence of witches would in some way *conflict* with the scientific point of view, alleged witches being equipped with causal powers that (for instance) are disallowed by the laws of nature.

practical point of view, while also doing justice to the fact that the concepts of agency and choice have an explanatory dimension. In section 4 I explore the limitations of the practical reason approach, arguing that there are some patterns of naturalistic explanation of human behavior, including above all the theory of psychological determinism, that cannot be reconciled with the assumption that we possess the capacity for choice. At the same time, I suggest, the practical reason approach can help us to see why other patterns of naturalistic explanation— including deterministic explanations—need not threaten the assumption that there are moral agents, in the sense of persons who can fairly be held accountable.

2. CHOICE AND DESIRE

The powers of reflective self-control are forms of general competence or capacity. They involve the capacity to grasp and apply the reasons expressed in moral principles, and to control what one does by the light of one's moral understanding. My first question is the following: what does this capacity for control imply about the structure of the will?

The answer, I would suggest, is that the capacity for control is best understood in what might be called volitionalist terms. According to the volitionalist position I have in mind, the will is not merely a susceptibility to motivating states of desire, but a capacity for active self-determination. Underlying this interpretation is the assumption that our motivations divide fundamentally into states of two different kinds. There are, first, motivations with respect to which we are basically passive, such as conscious desires, inclinations, yearnings, and various longer-term dispositions. I shall call such motivations given desires. Second, there are motivations that are not merely given, but that directly express our activity as agents, such as choices, decisions, and intentions to act. The power of self-determination relevant to moral responsibility, I maintain, is a capacity for motivations of this second, volitionalist kind.[11]

Let us take a closer look at this contrast between different kinds of motivating state, starting with given desires. These motivations are rather like sensations, in that they are presented to us in experience rather than being things that we ourselves *do*. Of course, desires and sensations differ in a number of respects. Most importantly, desires are conceptually structured in a way sensations are not; they have propositional objects, for instance, and are typically accompanied by evaluative thoughts. The conceptual structure of given desires makes it possible for them to respond to our deliberated judgments about what we have reason to do, much as Aristotle thought that the appetitive and other desires of the virtuous would obediently fall in line with their rational verdicts about the good.[12] But as

---

[11] See my *Responsibility and the Moral Sentiments*, sect. 5.2.

[12] This aspect of desires is emphasized by Angela M. Smith, in 'Identification and Responsibility', in Ton van den Beld, (ed.), *Moral Responsibility and Ontology* (Dordrecht: Kluwer Academic Publishers, 2000), 233–46.

Aristotle would be the first to admit, given desires are not *necessarily* sensitive to judgments about the good in this way.¹³ Furthermore, even when our given desires respond to our reasoned verdicts about action, their doing so is not something that is directly under our control. In this respect, given desires are not to be classified as voluntary phenomena.

Generalizing, we may say that the class of given desires encompasses all those motivating states that are potential objects of self-awareness in the processes of reflection leading up to a determination to act. The 'given-ness' or 'passivity' of such desires can thus be traced to the structure of reflective consciousness.¹⁴ Given desires are states we take account of in deliberating about what we have reason to do (such as being attracted to the prospect of going to a party tonight), and they are also states we find ourselves in after we have reached a settled verdict through such reflection (such as remaining attracted to the party option even after one has concluded that it would be better to put in an appearance at the philosophy convention). But they are not the only kinds of motivation of which we are capable. There are, in addition to the sorts of desires that we can reflect on in deliberation, the distinctively active states of intention, choice, or decision, which characteristically bring deliberation to a final conclusion.

The volitionalist approach that I favor thus turns on the distinction between these active motivations and the given desires to which we are subject. In saying this, I do not mean to imply that all of the motivations conventionally referred to as desires are—like given desires—states with respect to which we are basically passive, objects that are presented to reflective consciousness. In philosophical practice it is customary to operate with an extended concept of desire as pro-attitude, encompassing not only the phenomenologically significant states of attraction I have called given desires, but also such volitional states as intentions and choices, as well as evaluative and normative judgments.¹⁵ I have no quarrel with this extended usage, as long as it is kept in mind that the various motivating states collected under the term desire have different roles to play in the processes of deliberative agency.

In particular, it is important to be clear that volitional motivations are *independent* from our given desires, in the following sense. What an agent chooses or intends to do is not a function of the given desires to which the agent is subject at the time. Indeed, because our given desires as a class are not necessarily responsive to deliberative reflection, we need a capacity for motivation that is independent of those desires if we are to possess the powers of reflective self-control necessary to moral responsibility. The potential unresponsiveness of given desires shows itself in the fact that they are the kinds of psychological states that present us with temptations to violate the requirements of reason. We will be in a position to act rationally in the face of temptation, then, only if we are equipped with a basic capacity for

¹³ See Watson, 'Free Agency', as reprinted in Watson (ed.), *Free Will*, 96–110.
¹⁴ On this point, compare Korsgaard, *The Sources of Normativity*, lecture 3, esp. 92–4.
¹⁵ Compare G. F. Schueler, *Desire* (Cambridge, Mass.: MIT Press, 1995), ch. 1.

self-determination in the face of competing desire, as it were. A general capacity for choice of this kind, for instance, is what we implicitly impute to blameworthy agents when we assume that they have the power to resist the immoral desires to which in fact they give in. That persons possess this form of competence is thus a necessary condition for their being directly subject to moral requirements that they flout.[16]

This same assumption is reflected in our deliberative practice as agents. In thinking about what to do, we take it for granted that we have a capacity for self-determination that outstrips the desires that are objects of deliberative reflection. The discovery that one is strongly attracted to the option of staying in bed, for instance, does not yet answer the practical question of whether that is what one is going to do. Indeed, it seems a discovery of this kind cannot answer the practical question if our activity as practical reasoners is to be fully intelligible. In deliberation, we try to determine what to do by reflecting on the question of what there is reason for us to do. This whole process makes sense, however, only on the assumption that we are capable of determining ourselves to act in ways that align with our deliberated verdicts about what we ought to do. But as we have seen, it is in the nature of our given desires that they are not automatically in alignment with our verdicts about our reasons. It follows that our competence to comply with the conclusions of moral deliberation involves the power to choose what we shall do in ways not laid down by the desires to which we are passively subject.[17]

My next question is this: given that moral agency requires the capacity for volitionalist motivation, how should we regard the various approaches to the ontological issues that I sketched at the start of this contribution? Let us take the naturalist approaches first. Clear examples of this kind of approach are theories that accept what I earlier referred to as psychological determinism, the thesis that our actions are causally determined by our beliefs together with our given desires.[18] If this thesis is accepted, it seems to me, then we shall have to conclude that there are no moral agents in the sense I have been talking about. Such agents are distinguished by, among other things, the capacity for volitionalist motivation, and this cannot be reconciled with the thesis of psychological determinism. Accepting this thesis, naturalists would seem to have two options: either they may deny altogether the distinction between given desires and volitions that I have maintained is central to our understanding of ourselves and others as accountable agents. Or, they may admit some surface distinction between these two classes of

[16] It is not alone sufficient, of course: in addition, the person must have the capacities for moral understanding and reasoning that are also included under the powers of reflective self-control.

[17] For persons whose given desires were always automatically in alignment with their deliberated verdicts, the volitionalist power of choice might not be a condition of moral agency and accountability in this way. But we are not such persons.

[18] Strictly speaking, psychological determinism would require that there be exceptionless laws linking these psychological states with the intentional actions and bodily movements they cause. For further discussion of psychological determinism, see Christopher Mark Grau, 'Moral Responsibility and Wolf's Ability', in van den Beld (ed.), *Moral Responsibility and Ontology*, 129–42.

motivation, but then offer a reductionistic account of volitionalist motivations, analysing these as combinations of beliefs and given desires, or insisting that they are themselves determined causally by such beliefs and desires.[19]

These characteristically empiricist strategies seem to leave no room for the genuine capacity for self-determining agency. Understood in volitionalist terms, this capacity involves the power to choose what one does independently of the given desires to which one is subject; but psychological determinism in the forms just mentioned amounts to the denial that persons are equipped with such a power. Defenders of the naturalist approach traditionally insist that persons could have done otherwise, even in a world in which their actions are determined by their given desires, insofar as they would have acted otherwise, had they been subject to different configurations of desire.[20] But conditionalist analyses of this variety do not capture the distinctive kind of capacity that seems to be required for moral agency, which is a capacity for choosing in ways that are independent from the given desires to which one is *actually* subject.

Considerations of this kind have led some philosophers to reject naturalist accounts in favor of the third kind of approach I sketched at the start of this paper, the theory of agent-causation. This theory begins from the thought, which I have endorsed, that the capacity for choice is an active power of persons to determine what they shall do independently of the desires to which they are subject. In exercising this capacity, it seems, we ourselves fix an answer to the question of what we are going to do, in a way that cannot be traced back to the operation of psychological states and forces in us. Proponents of agent-causation conclude that persons are equipped with a special causal power different in kind from the ordinary form of causality linking events in the natural world, a power that is effective precisely at those points at which such ordinary causal relations break down. The hallmark of this approach is thus the contention that our ontology can accommodate moral agents only if and to the extent that we need to postulate such agents in order to explain events that cannot be accounted for in ordinary scientific terms.

Now I share the sense of many critics that this way of thinking about moral agency is incredible. The theory of agent-causation is problematic, because it interprets the capacity for choice as a causal power of persons whose rationale lies in its direct contribution to explaining what goes on in the natural world. The theory holds that agency is possible only on the condition that there are natural events (such as firings of neurons in a person's brain[21]) that cannot be explained causally in terms of other events, but that instead must be accounted for by appeal to persons. This is to understand the human capacity for choice as part of an

[19] Even those who reject psychological determinism can maintain, of course, that such volitional states as intention and choice in some sense cause the actions we perform (see the following section for further discussion of this point). What they deny is that these volitional states can be either reduced to, or causally explained by, combinations of beliefs and given desires.

[20] See e.g. Donald Davidson, 'Freedom to Act', as reprinted in his *Essays on Actions and Events* (Oxford: Clarendon Press, 1980), 62–81.

[21] Compare Chisholm, 'Human Freedom and the Self', 29.

explanatory theory of the world, something we are led to postulate by our interest in causal explanation and prediction—an interest that is definitive of what might be called the theoretical point of view. But this is not the only way to see matters. On the practical reason approach sketched at the start of this paper, the power of choice has its natural home in the context of the practical point of view, a distinctively first-personal perspective defined by our interest in the deliberative question of what we ought to do.

Understood in this way, the practical point of view is the standpoint of practical reason, a standpoint we adopt when we reflect about what we have reason to do. To say that the power of choice has its natural home in the context of this perspective is to say that it is our preoccupation with deliberative questions of practical reason, and not our interest in explanation and prediction, that leads us to postulate that agents are equipped with this power.[22] We inevitably assume that we ourselves have this capacity when we undertake to deliberate about what we should do. As I said above, the idea that we have it in our power to determine what we shall do in ways independent of our given desires provides the natural context for our own deliberative activity. In this sense, the power of choice is primarily a first-personal, deliberative phenomenon.[23]

The proponents of agent-causation correctly grasp that moral agency cannot be rendered fully intelligible unless we abandon the thesis of psychological determinism. What they fail to see is that the phenomenon of moral agency also cannot be rendered fully intelligible without articulating an alternative to the theoretical standpoint of explanation and prediction. Theorists of agent-causation interpret the insight that persons have the capacity for active choice as a thesis about their causal powers, where causal powers are in turn understood as items whose significance is primarily explanatory. In effect, it is assumed that agency will be possible only if it contributes positively to the explanation and prediction of events that fall within the purview of scientific theorizing, but are inexplicable in terms of such theorizing. Agent-causation theorists thus maintain that the activity of persons presupposes that the chains of causation linking ordinary events are inherently gappy, the gaps marking points at which explanation requires an irreducible reference to an agent, construed as a kind of unmoved mover.[24] The resulting picture extracts from the familiar phenomenon of self-determination an ontological

---

[22] For a different but complementary justification of the capacity for decision by reference to its role in the context of practical deliberation, see Michael E. Bratman, *Intention, Plans and Practical Reason* (Cambridge, Mass.: Harvard University Press, 1987).

[23] This is not to say that it is an essentially private activity—there is, for one thing, the utterly familiar activity of collective deliberation, conducted from the perspective not of 'I' but of 'we'. For another, I assume that our reasons must be capable of being made intelligible to other persons whose deliberative problems are very different from our own. This is the role of advice, which involves a kind of hypothetical deliberation, detached from the corresponding capacity for self-determination that accompanies practical reflection in the first person. One asks what a given person in a given situation would have reason to do, where the person in question is not oneself, and the situation described is not one's own.   [24] See Chisholm, 'Human Freedom and the Self', 32.

commitment that is hard to take seriously, suggesting that our status as agents confers on us a divine prerogative of intervention in the causal order of nature from a position mysteriously outside it.

Difficulties of this sort seem likely to persist so long as we continue to interpret agency as an essentially explanatory phenomenon. To avoid them, we could follow the naturalist route sketched above, which would mean abandoning the volitionalist conception of motivation. Alternatively, we could attempt to rescue the volitionalist conception by removing it from the context of theoretical reason and placing it within the normative framework of practical reason. Viewed in this new light, the power of choice is not understood as a causal force in competition with other forms of causality, something for which a space would need to be cleared in the order of nature. Rather it speaks to the normative interests regulative of the practical point of view, a standpoint into which we project ourselves when we deliberate about what we ought to do. Deliberation requires us to assume that the question as to what we are going to do is not settled by our given desires, but that we have it in our power to determine the answer to that question for ourselves. And the fact that the capacity for self-determination is presupposed by practical reason in this way is the point and rationale of the volitionalist conception.

3. REFINEMENTS

The suggestion just made is that moral agency should be understood as a phenomenon of the practical point of view, where this in turn is a standpoint that is defined and shaped by our interest in the normative question of what there is reason to do. But this suggestion cannot be accepted, just as it stands. One might be prepared to concede that reasons and values are essentially normative phenomena, whose reality and significance are in no way called in question if it turns out that they are not needed to explain and predict what people do. But with agency things appear otherwise. Talk of agency seems implicitly and essentially explanatory in its aspirations—the grammar of the concept, one is tempted to insist, is explanatory and not normative. To say that agent A has the capacity for self-determining choice, for instance, is to ascribe to A a kind of causal power to bring things about; and when A in fact does something—say, x—it seems we can explain x by adverting to this causal power, noting that A chose to do x. This suggests that the standpoint from which we ascribe to persons the capacity for choice is not free from explanatory aspirations, raising a serious doubt about the distinction I have drawn between the theoretical and the practical points of view.

The important truth in this line of objection is that moral agency is part of a network of concepts that collectively have explanatory significance. The capacity for self-determination may be thought of as a power to bring things about; in particular, it is a power to make choices or decisions about what one is going to do—a distinctively *active* power. Choices in their turn are items that play a direct role in accounts of human action. The paradigmatic context for explanations that employ the volitional concepts of intention and choice is one in which we see that someone is moving in complicated, goal-directed ways, without being able to figure out what they are up to. Noticing that A is bustling about at an uncharacteristically early hour, we might be moved to ask, 'Why is A doing that?' The natural way of answering this type of question is to cite information that brings to light the intention or plan underlying A's behavior, such as: 'She has a lecture to give in Havana this afternoon and needs to get to the airport to catch her flight.' Here we draw on information about A's intentions to explain what A is doing, in a perfectly familiar way.

This suggests that the aspect of moral agency that I focused on in the preceding section of this paper—namely, the capacity for choice—cannot simply be extracted from all contexts in which explanation is at issue. Indeed, I would contend that there are facts of the matter about persons' possession and exercise of this distinctive capacity, and that such facts are accessible to theoretical reason. After all, it is not through deliberation that one determines whether or not another agent A is equipped with the capacity for choice, still less is this the normal way of figuring out the content of the choices that A has made. Practical deliberation is the method whereby one tries to establish what one has reason to do; it is not by itself a technique for establishing what another person has already done or is capable of doing. If this is correct, however, it seems the practical reason approach to moral agency cannot be sound. Unlike reasons and values, moral agency is not well thought of as a phenomenon of the practical point of view.

But this wholesale rejection of the practical reason approach is too swift. The points I have just drawn attention to do not, I believe, require us to abandon this approach. Rather they call on us to formulate its central insight more carefully, explaining precisely what it means to situate the phenomenon of agency within the context of deliberative reason. To this end I would emphasize the following four points; together they suggest that the explanatory network to which our concepts of moral agency and choice belong is subordinate to the interests of practical reason.

(i) First, there is an important and elementary distinction to be drawn between choices themselves, and the capacity for choice. In the preceding discussion it was observed that such volitional items as choices and decisions have a direct explanatory contribution to make in relation to the actions that people perform. It is far from obvious, however, that the *capacity* for choice, which is one of the defining elements in our conception of moral agency, has an analogous explanatory contribution to make. The capacities of persons are not in general to be thought of as causally sufficient triggering conditions for the performances that count as exercises of those capacities. That one is able to speak Dutch, for instance, is a causally enabling condition for one's engaging with understanding in a Dutch conversation, but the linguistic capacity alone cannot be cited to explain why one conducted a particular Dutch conversation when and as one did. Similarly, one's capacity for choice is what makes it possible for one to choose in ways that are independent from one's given desires. By itself, however, that capacity cannot explain why or how one makes the particular choices one does. The concept of a human capacity simply does not play this kind of explanatory role.

Failure to grasp this point is an underlying flaw in the theory of agent-causation. Proponents of this theory suppose that our status as agents will be secure only if it can contribute to explaining our actions in a way analogous to the way ordinary events explain the further events they give rise to—namely, as causally triggering conditions. But if agency is primarily a matter of our capacities, it is a kind of category mistake to expect it to make this kind of contribution to explanations of what people do. This becomes clear if we think about what it adds to our understanding of a choice to do *x* to learn that it was A who made the choice. Information of this kind does not by itself help to explain the choice to do *x*; it does not, for instance, tell us anything that would make it intelligible why *x* was chosen instead of, say, *y*. In the libertarian tradition it is customary to concede that freedom of the will entails that what the agent does cannot ultimately be explained, so that there is an ineliminable element of arbitrariness or inscrutability involved in human agency. There is an insight here, namely that appeals to the agent do not suffice to render action fully intelligible. Construed as part of an explanation, then, such appeals entail that action is essentially inscrutable, and this is the conclusion that the libertarian accordingly draws. But the correct conclusion is that agency is a matter of general capacity, and capacities are not well understood on the model of causally triggering conditions:[25]

(ii) What then is the relation between moral agents and the particular decisions and choices they make? There are, I would suggest, two sides to this issue, corresponding to the distinction between the third-person and the first-person points of view. From the former standpoint, the primary relation between agents and the choices and decisions they make is *ascriptive*. To say that the choice to do *x* is due to A is not a way of answering the question of why the choice was made; it speaks to a different kind of question, *viz.*, to whom is the choice to be ascribed?[26] In the different context of first-personal deliberation, however, things are otherwise. Here we are not in the business of ascribing actions to ourselves, for the simple but

[25] Granted, there are a variety of ways of explaining action by appealing to aspects of agents other than their capacities, such as the fact that agent A has a set of character traits that are typically reflected in choices to do things such as *x*. But this further information is extraneous to the claim that is centrally at issue here, the claim, namely, that the choice to do *x* is due to A. *This* claim, I have suggested, entails that A was equipped with a power to choose what to do in ways not determined by the given desires to which A is subject, including A's enduring character traits. Two things follow from this. First, reference to an agent's character cannot be understood as explaining the agent's actions deterministically, if we are to hold onto the idea that the agent is a practical reasoner. Second, to the extent we gain some explanatory insight into a person's actions by appeal to the person's character, the *explanans* is not the agent, but the agent's character traits; on this point, see Chisholm, 'Human Freedom and the Self'.

[26] Compare Donald Davidson, 'Agency,' as reprinted in his *Essays on Actions and Events*, 43–61, at 52.

important reason that there is not yet any action to be ascribed. Our task, rather, is to decide which action is to be performed, and in this context agency is above all a matter of identity, of who and what we are. To be an agent is to be a person for whom it makes sense to grapple with the question of what one ought to do, and this in turn requires, for reasons already canvassed, that we think of ourselves as having the power of self-determining choice. It is precisely from the perspective of one equipped with this power of choice that we deliberate about what we are to do.

Suppose, then, that we exercise this power by choosing to do *x*. From the first-personal, deliberative perspective, it certainly *seems* as if we had brought something about in doing so. And understood in the proper way, this feeling is veridical: we did bring something about, namely the choice or decision to *x*. Moreover, we did this in a way that directly implicates our identity as agents, by exercising our power of choice.[27] There are reciprocal links, of a conceptual nature, between agency and choice, such that we cannot understand either of these phenomena without reference to the other. To be a moral agent, I have suggested, is precisely to be equipped with the capacity for self-determining choice; choices, on the other hand, are items that require an agent as their bearer, somebody whose identity as an agent is expressed in the act of choice. From the perspective of agency, we are wont to think of ourselves as having the causal power to initiate choices, independently of the psychological states to which we are subject, and this way of thinking is in order so long as the notions of causation, power, and bringing about are supplied with a first-personal, deliberative interpretation. The mistake is to interpret these notions in retrospective, explanatory terms.

(iii) The preceding remarks suggest that, from the third-personal, explanatory perspective, agency does not contribute to explaining the particular choices people make. Its explanatory contribution is different: citing the capacities characteristic of agency can help to render intelligible, and thereby to explain, the status of persons as practical reasoners. Thus, we ascribe the power of choice to other persons as a way of making sense of their standing as moral agents; moral agency in this sense is the condition under which it is possible for persons to be subject to moral norms, regardless of whether or not they manage to comply with those norms. Furthermore, when we ourselves succeed in doing what is right in the face of temptation, we thereby confirm that we are equipped with the volitional capacity I have been talking about. Postulating that capacity may not explain exactly why we did what we did, but it helps to explain how it was possible for us to act in accordance with moral reasons.

Explanations of this kind, however, are in an important sense subordinate to the normative interests of practical reason. Most basically, the explanandum in these contexts is the status of persons as practical reasoners, a phenomenon that would not exist to be explained if we did not take for granted the independence of

---

[27] I do not mean that considerations pertaining to their identity are taken into account by agents in the course of deliberation that culminates in choice. The idea, rather, is that our identity as agents is in part constituted by our having the power of choice, in the ways I go on to discuss in the text.

the practical point of view, construed as the standpoint from which we consider questions about what we ought to do. The power of choice is postulated to render intelligible a person's capacity to engage in reflection of this distinctively practical variety, and this phenomenon presupposes the autonomy and legitimacy of the questions that define the standpoint of practical reason.

These are questions about our reasons for action, considerations that count for and against potential courses of action that people might perform, and that provide the subject matter for deliberative reflection. If we gave up thinking that there were reasons for action, there would be nothing that would require to be made sense of by postulating that persons are equipped with the capacity for volitionalist choice. Creatures who cannot engage in genuine practical deliberation, because for instance there is nothing for such deliberation to be about, do not require the capacity to choose in ways that are independent from their given desires. Their behavior might be rendered explicable by attributing to them intentional states of some kind, but we would not need to ascribe to them the volitional and cognitive capacities that are distinctive of deliberators. These are the capacities that enable one to adopt the standpoint of practical reason, posing for oneself the question of what one ought to do, assessing potential answers to that question so that one can arrive at a reasonable verdict, and choosing in compliance with the verdict thus arrived at. It is our capacity to adopt this standpoint ourselves that renders us confident that there are genuine questions to be answered through deliberation, and our treatment of other persons as subject to moral norms betrays the assumption that they are capable of adopting this standpoint too.[28]

(iv) The practical point of view is thus presupposed by explanations that appeal to the concepts of agency, choice, rationality, and the like. We might say that this standpoint raises distinctive explanatory issues, even though it is not itself concerned directly with explanation and prediction, insofar as it introduces phenomena that would not require to be explained if there were no activity of deliberative reflection in the first place. The network of concepts to which agency belongs is explanatory in relation to these essentially deliberative phenomena, and in this sense agency itself may be considered a deliberative phenomenon.

This brings out a further point of difference between the practical reason approach and the theory of agent-causation. According to the latter theory, the credentials of agency are secured by showing that it contributes to filling gaps in the explanations offered by the natural sciences. There are occurrences in the natural world—firings of neurons in the brain and the like—about which the following three sorts of claim can be made. First, these occurrences fall within the scope

---

[28] There are large issues, that I cannot go into now, about whether the capacity to adopt the deliberative perspective and to comply with its verdicts suffices for moral accountability. These issues turn in part on the question of whether moral reasons for action are conditioned by the antecedent motivations to which a given agent is subject (as Bernard Williams maintains, in 'Internal and External Reasons', as reprinted in his *Moral Luck* (Cambridge, England: Cambridge University Press, 1981), 101–13). For present purposes, what matters is that the general capacity for deliberation is at least a necessary condition of moral accountability.

of scientific explanation; ontologically they are the sorts of item to which scientific laws apply. Second, scientific theory is unable to explain these events by appeal to other events that equally fall within the scope of the theory's laws. Third, these very same occurrences can be explained causally by reference to an agent, where agents are presumably not the sort of items that fall within the scope of ordinary scientific theorizing. It is this combination of claims that makes agency appear ontologically peculiar, a phenomenon that is at once not of the natural world, but mysteriously capable of impinging on it.

The practical reason approach offers a different and more satisfactory picture of these matters. Agency is construed as part of a network of concepts that have explanatory work to do. But the items to be explained are not identical with the items to which scientific theory applies; at any rate, they are not characterized in the same way the explananda of the natural sciences are described. The capacity for choice, for instance, is postulated to account for the status of persons as practical reasoners, and this is not a phenomenon to which the explanatory ambitions of natural science extend. The explanatory context introduced by the standpoint of practical deliberation is in this way discontinuous with the context of natural scientific theorizing. There is accordingly no reason to expect that the explanations developed within the two contexts, and the ontological commitments that distinguish those explanations, will stand in any very simple relation to each other.[29]

4. THE INSULATION STRATEGY

The practical reason approach rests on a basic distinction between the theoretical and practical points of view. This distinction traditionally figures prominently in Kantian treatments of practical reason and the will, but Kantians typically go beyond the points I have made so far. Not only do they deny, as I have also done, that the standpoint of practical reason is concerned with explanation and prediction. They maintain in addition that no pattern of explanation to which we might be committed for theoretical purposes could possibly conflict with the commitments of the practical point of view.[30] The underlying idea seems to be that the theoretical and practical points of view amount to different and nonoverlapping frames of discourse. In order for two claims that we might make to be in conflict with each other, the argument would go, they must be claims that we endorse within a single frame of discourse. Assuming that the theoretical and practical

---

[29] For some subtle reflections about the differences between explanations couched in 'personal' and 'impersonal' terms, see Jennifer Hornsby, 'Agency and Causal Explanation', as reprinted in her *Simple Mindedness* (Cambridge, Mass.: Harvard University Press, 1997), 129–53.

[30] See Christine M. Korsgaard, 'Creating the Kingdom of Ends: Reciprocity and Responsibility in Personal Relations', as reprinted in her *Creating the Kingdom of Ends* (Cambridge, England: Cambridge University Press, 1996), 188–221, sect. 3; 'Morality as Freedom', as reprinted in her *Creating the Kingdom of Ends*, 159–87, esp. 174–6; and *The Sources of Normativity*, sect. 3.2.2.

standpoints represent different frames of discourse, it follows that the claims made within each of them cannot be in conflict; there is, in effect, no single, common standpoint from which such claims are jointly endorsed.

This line of thought, which we might dub the the insulation strategy, is undeniably attractive; but the considerations canvassed in the preceding section suggest that it cannot be correct. For purposes of argument we may begin by agreeing that the theoretical and practical points of view represent different frames of discourse, insofar as they subserve the divergent aims of explanation and justification. We may agree, further, that two claims may only be in conflict if they can both be endorsed within what is in some sense a single frame of discourse. It is unclear, however, that the distinction between the aims of theoretical and practical reason entails that the claims made in pursuit of these aims cannot possibly be in conflict.

I have contended that we can only make sense of persons as subject to moral demands if we suppose that they are equipped with a volitionalist power of choice. I have also contended that one can have this kind of active power only if what one does is not determined by the psychological states to which one is passively subject, including above all one's given desires. If this is correct, however, then it would appear that we cannot really be moral agents if what I earlier referred to as psychological determinism is true. That is, there is a certain schema for the *explanation* of human behavior, according to which such behavior is caused by the beliefs and given desires to which persons are subject, that cannot be reconciled with the practical point of view.

How is this possible, if, as I have supposed, the practical and theoretical standpoints are defined by divergent aims? Conflict of this kind is possible, it seems to me, because a standpoint can have explanatory *implications* even if it is not itself directed to the resolution of explanatory questions. As we saw in the preceding section, the standpoint of practical deliberation introduces a distinctive set of phenomena that pose a problem for theoretical reason, calling for explanation. It is in connection with this theoretical problem that the explanatory significance of such concepts as agency and choice is to be understood. In particular, it turns out that we can make good sense of the status of persons as practical reasoners only if we assume that they are capable of choosing what to do in ways not determined by their beliefs and given desires. The insulation strategy thus appears to fail. In order to protect the claims of practical reason from the very possibility of conflict with theoretical reason, it is not enough to characterize the two standpoints as distinct frames of discourse, organized around divergent intellectual aims. It is necessary in addition to ensure that the standpoint of practical reason cannot have theoretical implications, and this additional thesis is implausible.

This is the reason, it seems to me, why Kant's own version of the insulation strategy does not succeed. In a notorious passage from the *Critique of Practical Reason* Kant alleges that from the practical point of view we can make sense of a person's actions as transcendentally free, and so imputable, even if the same actions, theoretically conceived, admit of a deterministic explanation in terms of the agent's character traits.[31] The difficulty with this suggestion does not lie with Kant's basic distinction between the standpoints of theoretical and practical reason by reference to their aims. It lies rather with the details of the explanation that is proposed from the theoretical point of view. If, as I suppose, transcendental freedom in Kant's sense involves the power of self-determining choice—the capacity, in his terms, to take an incentive into one's maxim[32]—then it seems that we cannot have that power at all if the version of psychological determinism Kant himself embraces for theoretical purposes is correct. We possess the capacity for choosing independently of our desires only if it is not the case that what we do is determined by those desires.

Once the insulation strategy has been challenged in this way, however, more general deterministic threats may seem to loom. In particular, it begins to seem as if any form of theoretical determinism would equally pose a challenge to our practical understanding of ourselves as agents. Agency, I have suggested, involves the capacity to determine what we do in ways independent of the desires that are presented to us as potential objects of deliberative reflection. One rationale for this claim seems to be that given desires are states with respect to which we are merely passive; if our actions were caused by desires of this kind, the result would be that agency itself drops out of view. But if we are passive with respect to our desires, we are equally passive with respect to the physical states of our bodies and the world around us—these states too are objects of theoretical observation, and not as such subject to our direct control. It appears to follow that any form of deterministic explanation, even one couched in exclusively physical terms, would challenge our understanding of ourselves for practical purposes. There seems to be no room for agency in a deterministic world, regardless of whether the determinism at issue is of a psychological or nonpsychological variety.

But this response is premature. The question at issue concerns the precise nature of the theoretical commitments raised by the standpoint of practical reason itself. Once this question is kept clearly in focus, it will emerge that there are grounds for distinguishing between psychological and nonpsychological forms of determinism. Though psychological determinism would undermine our status as moral agents, the same cannot be said of nonpsychological versions.

To see this, we need to return to the question, touched on in section 2, above, of why moral agency requires that we are equipped with the capacity for self-determination independently of our given desires. Here three points regarding the nature of such desires deserve particular emphasis. First, there is the theme discussed in section 2, above, namely, that given desires do not align automatically

---

[31] See the last section of the 'Analytic' of the *Critique of Practical Reason*, esp. 94–100. But compare the 'Introduction' to Kant's *Metaphysics of Morals*, 213–14, 226, where he characterizes the human power of choice negatively as independence from determination by sensible impulses; for the reasons I explain in this section, it is hard to see how a power of choice understood in these terms could be reconciled with the kind of psychological determinism Kant himself flirts with in the passage from the second *Critique*.

[32] See, above all, Kant's *Religion within the Limits of Reason Alone*, bk. 1.

with our own verdicts about what there is reason for us to do. Nothing is more familiar to us than the experience of being attracted to a possible action that we ourselves believe should not be performed.[33] Second, given desires are inherently motivating states. They are springs of action, providing a potential basis for intentional action regardless of whether we think their objects are genuinely worthy of pursuit.[34] Third, given desires are conditions to which we are subject personally, states that are predicated of us as persons—one says, for instance, that A wants to *x*, or came to desire to *x* at time *t*. The result is that given desires have a distinctive kind of significance for reflection from the standpoint of practical deliberation; we register them as states to which we are subject, which present us with potential temptations to transgress against what we ourselves understand to be the requirements of reason.

It is because given desires have this kind of significance for deliberation that our standing as moral agents requires that we have the capacity for self-determination independently of such desires. To be a moral agent is to have the power to act by the light of one's conception of what one ought to do. In light of what I have said about the deliberative significance of given desires, however, it seems that one can have this power only if one is capable of choosing what one shall do in ways not laid down by states of that kind. This is why the thesis of psychological determinism poses a challenge to our understanding of ourselves in practical deliberation.

Once we are clear about these matters, it also becomes clear that other forms of determinism would not pose a similar challenge to our conception of ourselves as moral agents. A challenge of this kind is presented only if the items that figure in deterministic explanations—that is, the states or events that combine with deterministic laws to account for other states and events—possess the significance for deliberation that distinctively attaches to given desires. But this condition is not satisfied by nonpsychological versions of determinism. Thus, the various states of our brain and our body, described in purely physical terms, do not have the status of potential temptations to transgress what we take to be the requirements of reason. They are not, as such, motivational states, capable of expressing themselves directly in intentional action; indeed, they are not even predicated of us personally— they are states of our brains and bodies, not of *ours*. So in practical reflection the question cannot even be broached whether such physical states do or do not align with our verdicts about what we ought to do. But if this question does not arise, the physical states at issue cannot be invested with the kind of significance characteristic of desires. Consequently a determinism couched in physical terms would

[33] On this point, see (again) Watson, 'Free Agency'.

[34] There is a question about how desires can 'give rise' to intentional action if they do not cause it in the way described by psychological determinism. Here is a possibility: having the desire makes a certain action appear attractive from the agent's point of view, and the agent decides to perform that action because it is attractive in this way, without being caused to do so by the desire. I discuss this suggestion at greater length in my paper 'Addiction as Defect of the Will: Some Philosophical Reflections', Chapter 8 in this volume.

pose no direct threat to our standing as persons who are equipped with the power to comply with norms of reason.

This discussion can be summarized by recalling that the powers relevant to our standing as moral agents are matters of general capacity or competence. Moral agents are competent to do what they judge they ought, even in the face of circumstances that they are aware of, from the deliberative perspective, as potential obstacles to rational action. For reasons we have seen, psychological determinism would entail that persons do not possess this kind of general competence. Physical determinism, by contrast, would not clash with our understanding of the general capacities that distinguish persons as moral agents. It entails, perhaps, that we could never have done otherwise, holding fixed the facts about prior physical states of the world and the laws of nature. But the physical impossibility of doing otherwise, in this sense, must not be mistaken for a claim about our general psychological powers as agents. In a sense, the terms in which physical determinism is couched are too remote from the deliberative categories of power, competence, temptation, choice, intentional action, and the like to pose a challenge to those categories.[35] Thus, we could retain the competence to choose in ways independent from the given desires to which we are subject, even if the laws of physics are deterministic in nature; by contrast, our competence in this respect would be called in question directly by the thesis that our actions are determined psychologically by the very forces that present themselves to us as temptations to do what we should not. This is why psychological determinism, in the sense I have isolated, poses a special threat to our standing as moral agents, subject to moral demands regardless of whether we succeed in complying with them.

Now, as a practical matter we might have no option but to go on deliberating as we always have even if psychological determinism were true. This is the insight on which defenders of the insulation strategy build when they argue that no thesis about human action adopted for purposes of explanation and prediction would threaten our continued activity as practical reasoners.[36] The problem, however, is that our activity as practical reasoners goes together with a certain way of understanding ourselves, as equipped with the power to choose what we shall do independently of the given desires that are objects of reflective consciousness. It is by virtue of this implicit self-understanding that the practical point of view has implications regarding the explanation of action, implications that cannot be reconciled with the thesis I have called psychological determinism.

I cannot now go into the question of whether this thesis is true. By way of polemical conclusion, however, I shall simply report that the thesis does not strike me as very plausible. Psychological determinism exemplifies in a striking way the tendency to interpret folk psychology as a mechanistic or 'quasi-hydraulic' theory

---

[35] For further discussion of these claims, see my *Responsibility and the Moral Sentiments*, chs. 6 and 7. See also Hornsby, 'Agency and Causal Explanation'.

[36] Compare Korsgaard, *The Sources of Normativity*, 94–5.

of the causal operations of the human mind.[37] But this interpretation does not correspond very well with our actual practice in regard to folk-psychological attribution. We do not assume that the states that move us to act are either themselves given desires, or the causal products of such desires, nor are there compelling theoretical considerations that would recommend this way of seeing things. Indeed, if the argument of this contribution is on the right track, it is no accident that we do not deploy folk-psychological vocabulary as if it were a deterministic theory. The phenomena that are accounted for by appealing to agents and their choices are conditioned by our understanding of such agents as practical reasoners, and this introduces constraints on the shape such accounts may assume. The psychological explanations that interest us are explanations that shed light on the activities of persons, understood as creatures who adopt and act from a deliberative point of view of their own, and for reasons we have seen this rules out the assumption that such explanations are deterministic.

If psychological determinism can safely be rejected, however, then I see no general obstacle in the way of expanding our ontology to accommodate the commitments of moral practice, including above all the idea that at least some of us are moral agents.

[37] I borrow this suggestive expression from John McDowell; see his 'Non-Cognitivism and Rule-Following', in Steven Holzman and Christopher Leich (eds.), *Wittgenstein: To Follow a Rule* (London: Routledge and Kegan Paul, 1981), 141–62, at 155.

8

Addiction as Defect of the Will: Some Philosophical Reflections

It is both common and natural to think of addiction as a kind of defect of the will. Addicts, we tend to suppose, are subject to impulses or cravings that are peculiarly unresponsive to their evaluative reflection about what there is reason for them to do. As a result of this unresponsiveness, we further suppose, addicts are typically impaired in their ability to act in accordance with their own deliberative conclusions. My question in this paper is whether we can make adequate sense of this conception of addiction as a volitional defect. In particular, I want to focus on some philosophical assumptions, from the theory of action, that bear directly on the very idea that addiction might impair the agent's volitional capacities. Understanding this idea, I shall argue, requires that we start out with an adequate conception of the human will. Only if we appreciate the kinds of volitional capacities characteristic of normal agents can we conceptualize properly the impairment of those capacities represented by addiction, and assess the implications of such impairment for questions of responsibility.

It might be thought that there is no particular problem understanding how the impulses of an addict could constitute forms of volitional defect. Such impulses are often depicted in the philosophical literature as literally irresistible, and irresistible impulses impair our volitional capacities by artificially restricting the class of actions that it is open to us to perform. Alternatively, addictive conditions are sometimes pictured as bypassing the will altogether, causing us to do things that do not even satisfy the minimal conditions of voluntariness. But neither of these suggestions can be taken very seriously. Addicts typically behave in ways that are at least minimally voluntary, doing things that they themselves intend to do, with basic knowledge of the consequences and so on. Nor is there any sound reason to suppose that the impulses underlying such intentional behavior are, in the vast

Originally published in *Law and Philosophy* 18 (1999), 621–54. Copyright © 1999 Kluwer Academic Publishers. Reprinted with kind permission of Springer Science and Business Media. I received much helpful feedback on earlier versions of this paper from the other participants in the Carolina Workshop in Law and Philosophy in September 1998, as well as from audiences at the Universities of Oxford and Reading in March 1999. I own a special debt to Karin Boxer, Kirsten Petzold, and Angela Smith for detailed and probing comments; and to my 'Hilfskräfte' Ninja Kaiser and Jacob Klingner for excellent research support.

majority of cases of addiction, literally irresistible. If there were, it would be an utter mystery how people ever succeed in overcoming their addictive conditions by exercising strength of will, and yet this seems to happen all the time.

The question that will concern me in this paper is whether addiction can appropriately be thought of as a volitional defect, once we have departed from the simplifying assumptions that addictive behavior is nonvoluntary and that the impulses generated by addiction are irresistible. What is it about such impulses that makes it fitting to speak of them as impairments of our volitional capacities, if they neither bypass the will altogether, nor constitute forces that it is impossible for us to resist? Some theorists have voiced a healthy skepticism about the very idea that addiction could be a volitional defect, if it does not function in one of the two ways just mentioned.[1] I hope to show that there may still be some sense to this idea, even after we have rejected the false pictures about how the impulses of the addict operate. To see why this is the case, however, we shall need to consider the more basic issues of how desires in general provide motivations to action, and of the relation of such motivations to our choices and intentions.

An influential approach to these issues in motivational psychology is what I shall call the hydraulic conception of desire. On this conception, desires are thought of as vectors of causal force to which we as agents are subject, and which determine the actions we end up performing. The leitmotiv of this approach is the idea that agents always do what they most want to do, where the concepts of desire and strength of desire are construed in substantial terms, with genuine explanatory work to do. I shall argue that this approach should not be accepted as it stands. It goes wrong in basically depriving agents of the capacity for self-determination, turning all cases of action on wayward desires into cases in which the agent was subject to forces that were irresistible under the actual (psychological) circumstances. This yields a false understanding of our powers of deliberative agency, collapsing the important distinction between those states of desire to which we are merely subject, on the one hand, and motivational states that are under our immediate control on the other.

I contend that these difficulties can be avoided by adopting in their place a volitionalist motivational psychology. The leading idea of this approach is that motivations divide into two fundamentally different kinds. Some motivations are states with respect to which we are passive, conditions that we more or less find ourselves in. These given desires, as they might be called, are to be contrasted with other motivations that are directly up to us, such as choices and decisions. By acknowledging this fundamental distinction, we can avoid the problems that confront the hydraulic model of desire, arriving at a more satisfactory account of the volitional capacities of normal agents. This in turn will pave the way for an improved understanding of how addiction could constitute a form of volitional impairment. That, at any rate, is what I hope to establish in my discussion.

---

[1] See e.g. Stephen J. Morse, 'Causation, Compulsion, and Involuntariness', *Bulletin of the American Academy of Psychiatry and the Law*, 22 (1994), 159–80.

The paper divides into five sections. The first offers some general reflections about the concept of addiction. In the second, I consider different ways of modelling the volitional capacities of ordinary agents, defending the volitionalist approach over the hydraulic model. In section 3 I address questions about the nature of desires and about their contribution to reflective agency, once such agency is conceived in terms of the volitionalist model. The fourth section brings these abstract considerations to bear on the specific problem of understanding addiction as a form of volitional defect, while the conclusion briefly explores some implications of the favored volitionalist model for questions of moral and legal responsibility.

1. THE CONCEPT OF ADDICTION

What is addiction? What distinguishes the impulses that are due to addiction from other kinds of desire to which we are subject? These are vexed questions, and I am far from competent to give a complete answer to them.[2] But I should like to begin my discussion with a few general remarks about the concept of addiction.

In the popular understanding addiction is typically pictured as a long-term, dispositional condition, characterized by a susceptibility to distinctive kinds of impulse to action, which we might refer to as A-impulses or A-desires. Such desires seem to be distinctive in at least the following respects.[3] First, A-impulses are unusually resilient; they persist or assail us periodically during periods when they are left unsatisfied, in a way that seems detached from our own deliberative verdicts about the value to be gained by satisfying them. Second, they are experienced as unusually intense, leading us to speak of addicts' *cravings* for the substances to which they are addicted.[4] Third, A-desires are linked in various ways with our conceptions of pleasure and pain. Satisfying A-impulses can be a source of often visceral satisfaction, while the failure to satisfy them is in turn painful and unpleasant (producing withdrawal symptoms and the like). Finally, the susceptibility to A-impulses typically has a physiological basis; it can be connected, for instance, with transformations induced by repeated consumption of a particular substance in the reward system of the person's brain.[5]

---

[2] For a helpful overview of current approaches, see Jerome H. Jaffe, 'Current Concepts of Addiction', in Charles P. O'Brien and Jerome H. Jaffe (eds.), *Addictive States* (New York: Raven Press, 1992), 1–22.

[3] My conclusions here are broadly in agreement with the characterization of addiction as an acquired appetite offered by Gary Watson, in 'Disordered Appetites: Addiction, Compulsion, and Dependence', as reprinted in his *Agency and Answerability: Selected Essays* (Oxford: Clarendon Press, 2004), 59–87.

[4] I use the word craving here in a nontechnical sense, to designate desires of particular intensity; I do not mean the technical use sometimes found in discussions of addiction, according to which cravings are literally irresistible impulses that overwhelm all ordinary capacities for deliberate self-control. For criticism of the technical use, see Herbert Fingarette, *Heavy Drinking: The Myth of Alcoholism as a Disease* (Berkeley and Los Angeles: University of California Press, 1988), 41–3.

[5] Compare George Ainslie, 'A Research-Based Theory of Addictive Motivation', *Law and Philosophy*, 19 (2000), 77–115.

These characteristics clearly cannot be understood as specifying strict criteria for addiction. This seems true even if we leave aside the cases in which social scientists and others speak of addictive personality traits in an extended or metaphorical sense, as in talk about addiction to shopping or internet surfing as characteristically modern phenomena. Thus, I myself seem to be subject to a mild addiction to caffeine, yet prolonged periods without coffee do not induce in me anything aptly characterized as a genuine craving for the substance, only feelings of drowsiness, mild discomfort, light headache, and the like. So urgency cannot be construed as a strictly necessary condition for the status of an impulse or desire as addictive. Still, in the philosophically most interesting cases, A-impulses tend to be experienced as especially intense—this is one of the features, after all, that makes it attractive to think of addiction as impairing our volitional capacities in some way. We might perhaps best respond to this point by thinking of the four characteristics I have identified as defining an ideal type of the A-impulse, while allowing that there are individual examples of A-desires that do not display all the mentioned features.

A further interesting question is raised by the fourth condition, that A-impulses are typically based in physiological transformations induced by (prolonged) ingestion of a chemical substance of some kind, such as ethynol, nicotine, cocaine, amphetamine, or opium. That this is the case is of course an immensely important fact when it comes to understanding the etiology of addiction. It also seems to be reflected in common understanding of what addiction is. Thus, the line between literal and extended or metaphorical cases of addiction (such as the aforementioned cases of addiction to shopping and surfing the web), in ordinary thinking about these matters, would seem to correspond roughly to whether or not the A-impulses an agent experiences are grounded in a physiological condition or not. In cases that do not involve ingestion of a chemical substance, we are (perhaps mistakenly) inclined to suppose that the nonstandard behavior patterns will not be correlated systematically with identifiable kinds of neurophysiological transformation, and we therefore tend to regard those behavior patterns as at best analogous to genuine cases of addiction.

Nevertheless, for my immediate philosophical purposes it does not seem to matter all that much whether or not A-impulses actually have a physiological basis. Perhaps there are other, nonphysiological conditions that dispose a person to experience impulses otherwise just like the impulses of the literal addict, impulses, that is, that are resilient, urgent, and connected with the person's conception of pleasure and pain. If so, those conditions will raise precisely the same issues concerning potential volitional impairment that are raised by strict cases of addiction. In making this claim, I am assuming that it is not possible for a physiological condition to interfere with our volitional capacities if it is not constitutively linked to impulses that exhibit the characteristics of urgency, resilience, and connection with pleasure and pain. Perhaps volitional impairment by a strictly neurophysiological condition would be possible, if we thought of such impairment as a completely nonvoluntary phenomenon or symptom. But I have already expressed doubts about whether this is the right way to conceive addictive behavior, which typically seems to exhibit the kinds of focus and goal-directedness characteristic of much garden-variety intentional action.

Granted, there is probably a lot of simple automatism—the unthinking, habitual performance of ritualized executive tasks—in the daily activities of somebody subject to addiction: think in this connection of the routine lighting-up of a cigarette by the ordinary smoker.[6] But automatism of this variety would be hard to make sense of as a direct effect of neurophysiological conditions that were completely unconnected from the kinds of desires, emotions, and sensations that are phenomenologically accessible to us. Such automatic routines as the addict exhibits presumably develop through habituation, as adjustments to one's state of dependency, ways of staving off the unpleasant effects of continued substance deprivation. It is difficult to imagine how such routines might become established if the neurophysiological condition of dependency was not directly linked with the kinds of conscious psychological phenomena I have spoken of. In any case, automatism itself, though perhaps a kind of bypassing of the will, does not seem to me to represent necessarily an impairment of the agent's volitional capacities. Thus, it is far from obvious that persons who perform certain executive tasks automatically are in any way *unable* to control their behavior through reflection; from the fact that one did not engage in a particular activity deliberately, it clearly does not follow that one lacked the power to exercise deliberate control over what one was doing at the time. For these various reasons, it seems to me that the physiological side of addiction can safely be ignored, for purposes of my discussion of volitional impairment. What is at issue is whether and how addiction might constitute a defect of the will, and in this context the aspects of the phenomenon that are of interest are the ones capable of registering phenomenologically within the agent's point of view.

The questions I have been discussing to this point concern the adequacy of the characteristics identified above as necessary conditions of addiction. It has emerged that we may regard the three features of resilience, urgency, and connection with pleasure and pain to be necessarily exhibited by those A-impulses that represent potential defects of the will, even if they are not strictly necessary conditions for addiction in all its forms. Further questions can be raised, however, about whether the features I have mentioned, when jointly present, are sufficient conditions of addiction. Consider, for instance, the large class of bodily human appetites, including the elemental impulses associated with food, drink, elimination, sexual gratification, and basic physical comfort. These impulses seem to exhibit all of the characteristics I have proposed. To proceed in reverse order: the bodily appetites have a (neuro)physiological grounding; they are plainly connected with our most primitive experiences of pleasure and pain; they display the

---

[6] Compare Rogers Albritton's discussion of alcoholism, in 'Freedom of Will and Freedom of Action', *Proceedings of the American Philosophical Association*, 59 (1985–6), 239–51.

kind of urgency typical of cravings, especially when gratification is delayed for a prolonged period of time; and they seem resiliently independent of our own deliberative reflection. In all these respects natural appetites appear to resemble the paradigm cases of A-impulses I have been focusing on, and yet we do not ordinarily think of ourselves as being (say) addicted to food or water or sex.

Underlying this verdict is presumably the assumption that it is a good (or acceptable) thing to indulge one's bodily appetites, at least when this is done in moderation, with due regard to moral norms, prevailing social conventions, and the like. This brings out a normative element in ordinary thinking about addiction. We label an impulse addictive only if its satisfaction is something that we tend to disapprove of—as being, for instance, difficult to reconcile with a worthwhile, dignified human life—and this does not seem to be the view we take of the bodily appetites. This point about common classification, however, is not of much philosophical depth. For one thing, the negative normative judgments associated with classifications of desires as addictive amount to very rough generalizations at best. Even if satisfaction of bodily appetites is generally good or acceptable, this is far from being the case in every individual situation in which such appetites are felt, as cursory reflection on virtually everyone's experience with hunger and sexual longing will confirm. Furthermore, there are equally cases in which consumption of chemical substances ordinarily classified as addictive must be counted, under the circumstances, highly desirable. Consider an elderly patient suffering from debilitating pain that can only be relieved significantly by an addictive drug, such as morphine, where the risks of treatment with the drug are otherwise no worse than those of the alternative and less effective medications that are available.[7] It would be a kind of narrow dogmatism to insist that prescription of the addictive drug to the patient under these circumstances could not possibly be a good thing to do, simply because consumption of the drug will dispose the patient to the kind of resilient, urgent impulses I have been talking about.

This suggests that the normative presumptions reflected in our classification of impulses as cases of addiction are not by themselves terribly significant. In particular, they do not seem significant when it comes to the question of whether A-impulses can constitute impairments of our volitional capacities. What is significant for this latter question is a different normative dimension of both A-impulses and bodily appetites, namely the condition I have referred to under the heading of resilience. Desires are resilient, in this sense, when they are unresponsive to the agent's own deliberative reflection. Whether a given desire exhibits this kind of responsiveness is not, it should be stressed, simply a matter of its being in actual alignment with the agent's reflective verdict about what they ought to do. At least since Harry Frankfurt's influential discussion of the willing addict,[8] philosophers have been

---

[7] For a sensible discussion of some actual cases of this kind, see Graham Oddie, 'Addiction and the Value of Freedom', *Bioethics*, 7 (1993), 373–401.

[8] In 'Freedom of the Will and the Concept of a Person', as reprinted in Harry G. Frankfurt, *The Importance of What We Care About* (Cambridge, England: Cambridge University Press, 1988), 11–25.

accustomed to the idea that the status of a desire as an A-impulse need not preclude its being one that the agent also endorses, from the standpoint of evaluative reflection. What distinguishes A-impulses of this variety as products of addiction is, above all, a counterfactual property that they possess: A-impulses that are actually endorsed by their agent are desires that would continue to assail the agent—and would retain much of their urgency—even if the agent did not view their objects as good or worthwhile. It is the fact that A-impulses are unresponsive to deliberative reflection in this way that makes them resilient, and resilience in turn is perhaps the philosophically most interesting and salient feature of A-impulses.

In respect of resilience, however, A-impulses and bodily appetites are largely on all fours. The normative dimension discussed above would lead us to expect, perhaps, that bodily appetites would more often be in actual alignment with the agent's deliberative reflection than is the case with A-impulses. But desires of both kinds seem to be resilient in the sense just specified. This is the case, even if we accept the Aristotelian view that our bodily appetites are susceptible to a degree of habituation, which brings it about that our conception of the pleasant is directly responsive to our views about the good. (Persons who are virtuous by Aristotle's lights would ordinarily not take pleasure in a meal or a sexual act if they did not think that such activities were right to engage in, under the circumstances, and to this extent even their bodily appetites will exhibit a degree of counterfactual responsiveness to reasoned reflection.) There are, after all, fairly clear limits beyond which bodily appetites are no longer subject to domestication—sexual longing that has gone unsatisfied for a prolonged period, for want of a fitting occasion or partner, generally does not just go away by itself. This becomes even more apparent when we expand our view to consider persons who are not virtuous in Aristotle's sense.

Resilience thus does not seem characteristic of A-impulses alone, but is also exhibited to a certain extent by the natural bodily appetites. Moreover, it is the feature of A-impulses that is of greatest importance for the idea that such impulses can be defects of the will. A defect of the will, I suppose, should be understood as a condition that impairs our ability to act well, without necessarily depriving us of the capacity to think clearly and rationally about what we are to do. That is, agents subject to such a defect may succeed in deliberating correctly about what they ought to do, but will nevertheless be impeded in their capacity to translate their deliberated verdicts into action. It is the resilience of A-impulses that makes them candidates for being volitional defects of this kind, and it is presumably the case that their urgency and connection with pleasure and pain further contribute to their playing this role. In all these respects, however, A-impulses often resemble our natural bodily appetites. I conclude that an adequate explanation of addiction as a volitional impairment will have a degree of generality, applying potentially not merely to cases of addiction in the strict sense, but also to other desires that exhibit the combined features of resilience, urgency, and connection to pleasure and pain.

2. MODELS OF THE WILL

The remarks of the preceding section suggest that we must focus on the transition from deliberation to action if we are to make sense of the idea that A-desires represent potential defects of the will. Offhand, it would seem that the urgency of wayward A-impulses must somehow impair our capacity to act in accordance with our own deliberated conclusions, if such impulses are to be counted as volitional defects. To understand whether and how such impairment might be possible, we need to look at the phenomenon of deliberative agency more generally. What goes on when agents succeed in translating their deliberated conclusions into action, and what are the potential contributions of desire both to facilitating and to thwarting this process?

It will assist the discussion of these questions to begin by considering an influential way of thinking about the role of desire in deliberative agency. This model, which I shall dub the hydraulic conception, pictures desires as vectors of force to which persons are subject, where the force of such desires in turn determines causally the actions the persons perform. This approach may be thought of as offering a particular and contentious interpretation of the more or less truistic dictum that persons always do what they most want to do. That dictum is truistic so long as the notion of desire is construed liberally enough to include any of the so-called 'pro-attitudes' ordinarily thought to play a role in the etiology of action, including such states as intention, decision, and choice. The latter states can themselves often be identified, more or less, with the actions we perform; what exactly I am doing in executing a certain course of boldly movements is thus typically a matter of the intention in action with which those movements are made. In such cases, the idea that the desires on which one acts are the desires that are strongest says merely that they are the intentions with which one acts. There is nothing in this idea to rule out the possibility that the agent who does x could have chosen to do y instead, even holding fixed the other intentional states to which the agent was subject at the time. To say that we always do what we most want, where 'want' can be interpreted in this sense of intention in action, is thus to say nothing more interesting than that human action is an intentional or goal-directed phenomenon.[9]

The hydraulic conception extracts from the dictum a more interesting and controversial thesis by assuming a different and more restrictive notion of desire. According to this more restrictive notion, desires are conceptually and empirically distinct from our intentions in action, in the sense that one can want to do something without necessarily intending or choosing to do it. They are given to us, states that we find ourselves in rather than themselves being primitive examples of

---

[9] Compare G. F. Schueler's discussion of the 'pro-attitude' conception of desire, in his *Desire* (Cambridge, Mass.: MIT Press, 1995), ch. 1.

agency, things that we ourselves do or determine. The hydraulic conception maintains, furthermore, that desires that are given in this way have a substantive explanatory role to play in the etiology of intentional action. They determine which action we perform by causing the bodily movements that we make in acting, the assumption being that the strength of a given desire is a matter of its causal force in comparison to the other given desires to which we are subject.

The hydraulic conception thus goes beyond the truistic thesis that all actions are intentional, by postulating a causal explanation of such actions in terms of states of given desire with which the actions themselves are not to be identified. Distinctive of the conception is the answer it gives to the question of whether the agent who does *x* could have chosen to do *y* instead, holding fixed all the agent's desires, beliefs, and intentional states other than those that are partially constitutive of the action of *x*-ing itself. The hydraulic model conceives of strength of desire in such a way that this is not possible. The claim that we always do what we most want to do is taken to entail that the agent who does *x* could not have chosen to do *y* instead, given the full configuration of intentional states to which that agent was subject immediately prior to action. The desire that leads agent S to do *x* is postulated to be stronger causally than the other motivations to which S was subject, and from this it follows that no other action was strictly possible for S so long as the attitudes to which S was subject at the time are held fixed.

The hydraulic model is in fact rarely endorsed explicitly in this bald form. More typically, philosophers accept the truistic dictum I articulated above, and then proceed to interpret it in terms that only make sense if the hydraulic conception is implicitly taken for granted.[10] A good test for whether the dictum has been developed in this way is a philosopher's account of *akrasia*, in which agents fail to comply with their deliberated verdicts in the face of temptation. A characteristic assumption in discussions of this phenomenon is that the wayward desire that leads the agent to act *akratically* must have been the desire that was causally strongest, at the time of action—it was, after all, the desire that actually won out. But if this is the case, the question naturally arises as to why cases of ordinary weakness do not simply collapse into cases of psychological compulsion or addiction. The comparative causal strength of the *akratic* desire renders it impossible to resist, under the postulated psychological circumstances, and this apparently traces weakness to the kind of volitional incapacity represented by compulsion and addiction.

The response to this problem favored by those to whom I attribute the hydraulic model is couched in counterfactual terms. Take a case of ordinary *akrasia*, in which I conclude that finishing work on the paper for the conference is the action I ought to perform, but I end up going shopping at the mall instead. About this case, we may suppose that the comparative strength of my desires to work on the paper and

---

[10] Compare the formulation and interpretation of the 'motivational perspective' on action offered by Philip Pettit and Michael Smith, in 'Backgrounding Desire', *Philosophical Review*, 99 (1990), 565–92, and 'Practical Unreason', *Mind*, 102 (1993), 53–79; see also Alfred R. Mele, *Autonomous Agents* (New York: Oxford University Press, 1995), ch. 2.

to go shopping would have been sufficiently altered to bring it about that the former prevails, if a certain thought had only occurred to me at the time (such as the thought that Mike Corrado will be very angry if the paper is not finished soon).[11] Or we may point to a third desire, (say) to exercise control, which is sufficiently strong that it could have motivated a distinct course of action—for example, issuing a self-command—even in the face of the powerful temptation to shop; this distinct action, it is suggested, would in turn eventually have altered the overall balance of desire, causing me to work on the paper after all.[12] In cases of psychological compulsion or addiction, by contrast, we may suppose that the counterfactual postulation of similar thoughts and desires would not have altered the balance of motivation sufficiently to bring it about that I do what I believe best.

Accounts of *akrasia* that are developed in these terms are, I maintain, implicitly committed to the hydraulic model. Desires are conceived as vectors of force, independent of the actions performed, that motivate actions by their exertion of causal influence. There is a kind of psychological determinism at work in this approach, which reveals itself in the suggestion that the only scenarios in which *akratic* agents would have succeeded in complying with their deliberated verdicts are scenarios in which they are subject to a different configuration of desires and beliefs. *Given* the causal force of the various desires to which they are actually subject, together with their actual beliefs, it turns out that *akratic* agents simply lack the capacity to do what they judge best.

This kind of psychological determinism is in my view the underlying philosophical commitment of the hydraulic model; but it is also its undoing. The problem, in broad terms, is that the model leaves no real room for genuine deliberative agency. Action is traced to the operation of forces within us, with respect to which we as agents are ultimately passive, and in a picture of this kind real agency seems to drop out of view.[13] Reasoned action requires the capacity to determine what one shall do in ways independent from the desires that one merely finds oneself with, and an explanatory framework that fails to leave room for this kind of self-determination cannot be adequate to the phenomenon it is meant to explain. In this respect, the hydraulic model falls short.[14]

[11] Compare Philip Pettit and Michael Smith, 'Freedom in Belief and Desire', *Journal of Philosophy*, 93 (1996), 429–49. See also Jeanette Kennett and Michael Smith, 'Frog and Toad Lose Control', *Analysis*, 56 (1996), 63–73.

[12] See Alfred R. Mele, *Irrationality: An Essay on Akrasia, Self-Deception, and Self-Control* (New York: Oxford University Press, 1987); see also his *Autonomous Agents*, ch. 3.

[13] On this point, see J. David Velleman, 'What Happens When Someone Acts?', as reprinted in his *The Possibility of Practical Reason* (Oxford: Clarendon Press, 2000), 123–43. (Velleman's presentation of this problem is exemplary, though I do not agree with the reductionist solution he proposes.)

[14] These remarks may seem to have a libertarian cast that fits poorly with my other published views about responsibility and agency (in *Responsibility and the Moral Sentiments* (Cambridge, Mass.: Harvard University Press, 1994)). So to set the record straight: I take the emphasis on the capacity to rise above one's given desires to be an appealing feature of libertarian and agent-causation theories, something that they get right. Unlike the proponents of such theories, however, I do not believe that this important capacity must be incompatible with determinism in every form (though it is

The hydraulic model does offer a strategy for distinguishing between ordinary weakness and cases of addiction and compulsion, in the counterfactual terms sketched above. A-impulses are treated as distinctive, insofar as their causal strength is sufficiently great that they would still have prevailed, even if (contrary to fact) the agent had been equipped with the sorts of beliefs and desires ordinarily implicated in self-control. At the same time, A-impulses can be distinguished from strictly irresistible desires insofar as there are counterfactual conditions, involving the application of *extraordinary* techniques (12-step programs and the like), under which they would be defeated. But this merely enables us to classify A-desires appropriately, as distinct both from the wayward desires ordinarily involved in *akrasia* and desires (if indeed there are such) that are literally irresistible. Lost in this classificatory scheme is the important idea that *akratic*, addicted, and compelled agents retain a capacity to initiate a regime of self-control that cannot itself plausibly be reconstructed in terms of responses under various contrary-to-fact conditions. We think of such agents as possessing the power to struggle against their wayward impulses, not merely in counterfactual circumstances in which the desires and beliefs to which they happen to be subject are different, but in the psychological circumstances in which they actually find themselves. Holding those circumstances fixed, the hydraulic model places *akratic*, addicted, and compelled agents in what is essentially the same boat: the causal forces of the desires to which they are actually subject leave them with no real alternative to the wayward actions that they all end up performing.

These considerations make the hydraulic conception ultimately unacceptable, as an interpretation of the motivating role of desires within deliberative agency. The alternative I would favor is the one referred to earlier as the volitionalist model; its distinctive features can best be introduced by contrasting them with those of the hydraulic conception. The latter approach pictures deliberative agency as consisting, essentially, in two distinct moments. There is, first, the agent's practical or evaluative judgment about what there is most reason to do, or what it would be best to do on the whole; and there is, second, the agent's motivational state, which is a function of the causal strength of the desires to which the agent is subject.[15] If the agent is lucky, these two states will be in alignment with each other, so that the agent is most strongly motivated to perform the action that the agent believes, at the time, to be best.[16] But whether

---

irreconcilable with the kind of psychological determinism I have attributed to the hydraulic conception). For more on these matters, see my 'Moral Responsibility and the Practical Point of View', Chapter 7 in this volume.

[15] Some versions of the hydraulic model tend to collapse this distinction, treating practical judgments in noncognitivist terms, as themselves expressions of our given desires. This variant gives us a nonaccidental connection between practical judgment and motivation, but at the considerable cost of depriving practical judgment of its potential autonomy from given desire.

[16] Compare the ideal of orthonomy advocated by Pettit and Smith in 'Practical Unreason', 77: 'The important thing is not to assume control . . . [but] to be someone in whom desires are neither too strong nor too weak.'

this kind of alignment is achieved is not really something that is up to the agent to determine.[17]

True, the hydraulic model makes available a notion of self-control, which we ordinarily think of as a matter of bringing it about that one does what one believes best in the face of temptation. This is interpreted according to what might be called the 'cold shower' paradigm: we achieve control by devising strategies to influence causally the motivational strength of the desires to which we are subject, such as exposing ourselves to a cold shower, or thinking of the queen, when an access of inappropriate sexual appetite overcomes us. Now I do not doubt that strategies of this kind can sometimes be effective ways of bringing our wayward desires into line, thereby helping us to translate our deliberated verdicts into action. But to suppose that self-control must always conform to the cold shower paradigm turns us into passive bystanders at the scene of our own actions. We don't really determine which actions we perform directly, rather we attempt to manipulate the psychological influences to which we are subject, in the hope that *they* will eventually bring it about that we do what we judge to be best. Agency, to the extent it survives at all, seems restricted to the initiation of such strategies of indirect self-manipulation. But consistent development of the hydraulic approach banishes it from the scene even there. Either the exercise of control gets traced to the occurrence of a psychological event—such as the agent's thinking a certain thought—that is not an intentional action at all. Or room is left for the deliberate initiation of a strategy of control, but this in turn is conceived as the result of further causal forces operative within the agent's psychological economy at the time when the exercise of control began.[18]

To avoid these problems, we need in my view to expand our conception of the basic elements involved in reflective agency, acknowledging a third moment irreducible to either deliberative judgment or merely given desire. This is the moment of what I shall call volition. By 'volition' here, I mean a kind of motivating state that, by contrast with the given desires that figure in the hydraulic conception, is directly under the control of the agent. Familiar examples of volitional states in this sense are intentions, choices, and decisions. It is distinctive of states of these kinds that we do not think of them as belonging to the class of mere events in our psychological lives, along with sensations, moods, passing thoughts, and such ordinary states of desire as being very attracted to the chocolate cake in front of one at the café. Rather intentions, decisions, and choices are things we do, primitive examples of the phenomenon of agency itself. It is one thing to find that

---

[17] There are more sophisticated versions of the hydraulic approach that better capture our sense of ourselves as agents, though they remain inadequate in other respects; Velleman's favored reductionist account of agency in 'What Happens When Someone Acts?' might be an example. For discussion, see the remarks about 'meta-internalism' in my paper 'Three Conceptions of Rational Agency', Chapter 2 in this volume.

[18] For these two options, see the following debate: Alfred R. Mele, 'Understanding Self-Control: Kennett and Smith on Frog and Toad', *Analysis*, 57 (1997), 119–23, and Jeanette Kennett and Michael Smith, 'Synchronic Self-Control is Always Non-Actional', *Analysis*, 57 (1997), 123–31.

one wants some chocolate cake very much, or that its odor reminds one of one's childhood in Detroit, quite another to resolve to eat a piece. The difference, I would suggest, marks a line of fundamental importance, the line between the passive and the active in our psychological lives.[19] Agency is not merely a matter of subjection to motivational states, understood as vectors of force. It is manifested in our exercising the capacity to choose for ourselves what we are to do. An adequate conceptualization of reflective agency must do justice to this point, postulating a distinctively volitional moment in addition to the moments of deliberative judgment and merely given desire.

The volitionalist model just sketched is not meant as a detailed contribution to the philosophy of action. It is offered instead as a schematic framework for thinking about the kind of agency distinctive of those creatures capable of practical reason. From the first-personal standpoint of practical deliberation we take it that we are both subject to and capable of complying with rational requirements, and the volitionalist approach enables us to make sense of this deliberative self-image. Persons who are equipped with the power of self-determining choice retain the basic capacity to comply with their judgments about their reasons, even when their merely given desires are feeble or rebellious. Their actions are not merely the causal products of psychological states that they happen to find themselves in at the time, rather they have the power to determine for themselves what they are going to do. By exercising this power, such persons can bring about a kind of rational action that is not merely due to the fortuitous coincidence of rational judgment and given desire, but that is a manifestation of the very capacities that make them, distinctively, *agents*.[20]

3. DESIRES AND REFLECTIVE AGENCY

The volitionalist model accounts for rational agency in terms of motivating states with respect to which we are distinctively active. Action is an expression of choice or decision, not the result of psychological forces operating on us. This raises an important question, however. If ordinary, given desires are not needed to account for the capacity of persons to comply with their deliberated verdicts about action, what role is left for them to play in the etiology of reflective agency? Don't they become fifth wheels, spinning pointlessly in relation to the processes responsible for human action? I do not think that this is the case, and seeing why it is not will be important if we are to make sense of the idea that A-impulses can be forms of volitional incapacity.

[19] I should stress here that many motivational states seem to straddle this distinction in ways that make them difficult to classify. Most salient among these are states of being attracted to a course of action precisely because one judges that it would be good to perform. The involvement of evaluative judgment in these states makes it misleading to describe them as states with respect to which we are merely passive (as Angela Smith has helped me to see). And yet, being attracted to a course of action is not under our direct control in the way our intentions, choices, and decisions seem to be.

[20] For further development of these points, see my 'Three Conceptions of Rational Agency', Chapter 2 in this volume.

Let us start with the context of practical deliberation that leads to the formation of a judgment about what one has reason to do. One way in which given desires could contribute to the processes of reflective agency is by providing data to be taken account of in such practical deliberation. There are influential theories according to which the normative reasons for action that provide the subject matter for this kind of deliberation are exclusively a function of our desires. These theories hold that one can have a reason to do, say, x only if one has some antecedent desire that could lead one to be motivated to do x.[21] For the record, such theories do not seem to me very plausible. Indeed, the volitionalist model sketched in the preceding section undermines the most serious consideration advanced in favor of them, namely the alleged need to postulate a connection between normative reasons and antecedent desires in order to explain the motivational effects of reflection about our reasons. But I don't want to get into that right now. The more important point for the present is that even those who reject the thesis that all reasons for action are grounded in desires should concede that our given states of desire are often relevant to normative reflection about our reasons. This is one important contribution they have to make to the processes of reflective agency.

Granted, it is easy to be misled about the precise nature of their contribution in this context.[22] One natural way of picturing this contribution is to suppose that agent S's reason for doing x will consist, in many cases, simply in the fact that x-ing would satisfy one of S's given desires. But this picture, however natural, seems to me distorted. In the normal cases in which our reasons are conditional on our given desires, it is not simply the fact that those desires would be satisfied by a given course of action x that gives us reason to choose to do x. At least it is not, so long as we avoid equivocating on the notion of satisying a desire. In the most general sense, satisfaction is a purely formal concept. To say that a desire is satisfied, in this formal sense, is merely to say that the state of affairs that is desired has come to pass; with many desires, this can be the case independently of the subjective facts about the original bearer of the desire, including that person's knowledge of whether or not the desire has been satisfied.[23]

In another sense, however, satisfaction is precisely a subjective condition, a sensation or complex of sensations that is initiated by, or itself consists in, the satisfaction in the purely formal sense of some desire that a person has. Thus, if all goes well and the case is otherwise normal, S's desire to eat a crab cake will actually give way to satisfaction in this second sense—to an experience of culinary pleasure—when the desire is formally satisfied. Clearly, satisfaction or pleasure of this kind

[21] See, most influentially, Bernard Williams, 'Internal and External Reasons', as reprinted in Williams, *Moral Luck* (Cambridge, England: Cambridge University Press, 1981), 101–13.

[22] I am indebted here to Warren Quinn, 'Putting Rationality in its Place', as reprinted in Quinn, *Morality and Action* (Cambridge, England: Cambridge University Press, 1993), 228–55.

[23] Thus my preference that a long-lost friend should be thriving may be satisfied, in this sense of formal fulfillment, even if I never find out what has become of him.

can be a normative reason for acting, one moreover that is conditioned by our desires, since what one takes pleasure in at a given time is at least in part a function of one's desires at that time: what one feels attracted to, is in the mood for, is crazy about, and so on.[24] This is not the only way in which given desires can contribute to determining what we have normative reason to do, but it is a basic and important way; one, moreover, that is especially relevant to the operation of A-impulses. I shall return to this point below.

The contribution of desire to reflective agency just discussed may be considered a positive contribution, part of the successful translation of practical reason into autonomous, reasoned behavior. But desire can exert an influence on the processes in which such agency consists that is negative rather than positive, inhibiting the orderly progression from deliberative reflection through to corresponding action. What makes this possible is, in the first instance, the unruliness of desire, the fact that many desires are not responsive to our practical reasoning about how we ought to act. To take a banal example: I may believe that I ought not to go for a second piece of cake, but find that I continue to desire to eat some more all the same. Here we may suppose that the fact that I want another piece of cake has already been taken into account in arriving at the verdict that I ought not to have one; reflecting on this fact in light of the other considerations that speak against having a second piece, I correctly conclude that the desire by itself is not sufficient to override or outweigh those considerations. And yet the desire persists all the same. When this sort of thing happens, our desires can present obstacles to the processes in which deliberative agency consists. Indeed this is precisely what must happen in the case of A-desires, the resilience of which expresses itself in their unresponsiveness to deliberative reflection. The question is how exactly such resilient desires can interfere with deliberative agency, and whether the form of interference they provide is well thought of as a defect of the will. Before we can answer this question, we need to look more closely at the nature of desires. I shall concentrate primarily on examples that share the characteristic features of A-impulses: resilience, urgency, and connection with pleasure and pain.

The first thing to note is that there are various ways of thinking about the link between such desires and pleasure and pain.

One might, for instance, treat the desire itself as an intrinsically dysphoric condition; in these terms, the pleasure or satisfaction associated with the fulfillment of the desire would be (or at least be related to) the cessation of this dysphoric sensation, while the pain attendant on nonfulfillment would simply represent the continued and increasingly intense experience of desire itself. Now I am not convinced that this is the best way to think about all impulses related to pleasure and pain. While there are no doubt some desires and appetites that are themselves dysphoric—extreme hunger is perhaps the best example—in many other cases it seems that we can have desires for the pleasant that are not accurately thought of

---

[24] Our reasons in these cases have what T. M. Scanlon calls 'subjective conditions'; see his *What We Owe to Each Other* (Cambridge, Mass.: Harvard University Press, 1998), ch. 1.

on the model of intrinsically painful sensations. Furthermore, the dysphoria picture threatens to generate a vicious regress. It suggests that the motivating power of desire is connected with its experiential painfulness; but this suggestion can only be made sense of on the assumption that we have a basic desire to avoid painful sensations, and the obvious question arises as to how the motivating power of *that* background desire is to be accounted for. Sooner or later, it seems, we shall have to postulate a primitive disposition to avoid pain and go for pleasure that is not construed on the model of a dysphoric state. In that event, however, we may as well admit that there are first-order desires relating to prospective pleasure and pain that are not themselves literally painful.

An alternative and to my mind more satisfactory approach to such desires is to think of them on the model of perceptions rather than sensations.[25] Desires to obtain some prospective pleasure or to avoid a prospective pain may be conceived as quasi-perceptual modes of presentation of these anticipated sensations. They are like perceptions in exhibiting conceptual structure, without necessarily being or resting on full-blown judgments. Thus, in cases that are distinctly irrational one can desire an experience under the aspect of the pleasant, while judging on reflection that the experience in question would probably not be all that pleasant after all, on the whole; an example might be a case of commodity fetishism, where one finds oneself wanting to possess, say, a new toaster oven or lawn mower that one doesn't really need, while knowing from experience that fulfillment of such free-standing consumerist desires is generally a source of disappointment and mild depression rather than satisfaction. In such a case, the desire consists in part in one's thinking about the potential course of action or experience in terms of some evaluative category, its persistently presenting itself to one as, say, pleasant.

Furthermore, like other forms of perception (optical illusions, for example), the presentation of a potential course of action under an evaluative category of this kind is not necessarily something that is fully under one's voluntary control. This is what makes possible the kind of divergence of desire and considered judgment just mentioned, where one continues to desire something as pleasant, while not really believing that it would be all that pleasant on the whole. This in turn is connected with a third and still more distinctive feature of the class of desires we are considering, *viz.*, the way one's attention is focused on the possibility for action that strikes one as pleasant.[26] It is part of the mode of presentation characteristic

---

[25] For some suggestive remarks in a similar vein, see Dennis W. Stampe, 'The Authority of Desire', *Philosophical Review*, 96 (1987), 341–81. (I would reject, however, the conclusions Stampe draws from the perceptual analogy concerning the role of desire in practical reasoning.) I should also stress in this context that the points I shall make about desires for pleasure are not meant to apply to all states that are referred to as desires in philosophical parlance (which include, among other things, the distinctive kind of 'pro-attitudes' I have referred to as volitions). The phenomenological account I shall develop is an account of that subclass of desires, of which A-desires are an example, that can present an agent with temptations in contexts of deliberation and decision.

[26] Compare Scanlon's remarks about desire in the 'directed attention' sense, in *What We Owe to Each Other*, ch. 1, and Watson's discussion of the ways in which desires can be *compelling*, in 'Disordered Appetites', sect. 3.

of appetitive desire that the prospective action or experience one thinks of under an evaluative category should tend to dominate one's conscious experience. Gleaming images of the toaster oven from the advertisements keep appearing before one's mind's eye, and one's thoughts turn repeatedly to questions related to the acquisition of such an item. The focusing of one's attention in a certain direction is one of the most salient characteristics of A-desires, and it helps to explain their resilience in the face of conflicting judgment, especially when temporal distinctions are taken into account. Someone in the grip of an intense impulse to smoke some crack cocaine, for instance, will find their thoughts focused very relentlessly on the immediate pleasure associated with that course of action, even if they judge that there is more pleasure and less agony to be gained in the long term from desisting.

Desires for pleasure, then, may be thought of as quasi-perceptual modes of presentation of a course of action under the aspect of the pleasant, which are not under one's voluntary control, and which manifest themselves consciously in the direction of one's attention onto the desired activity or experience. To say that a desire of this kind is strong or urgent, something approaching a craving, is accordingly to say that it is a state in which one's thoughts and attention are directed onto the desired activity or experience with particular force or intensity. We have, in other words, a *phenomenological* conception of strength of desire. Desires are not urgent in virtue of their causal force; that approach, as we have seen, renders exercises of strength of will in the face of strong temptation something close to a conceptual impossibility. What makes some desires particularly urgent is rather the way things seem experientially to the person who is in their grip. Urgent desires can seem to take over the course of one's thoughts, presenting one with highly vivid candidates for action, colored in an evaluative light, that one is unable simply to ignore. In many cases urgency may be manifested further in the experience of dysphoric sensations and other emotions, including anxiety, fear, and excitement. As I argued above, dysphoric and emotional elements of this sort do not seem to be present in all cases of desire for the pleasant, but when such desires become particularly intense they are doubtless often accompanied by discomfort and other dysphoric sensations and feelings.

Once the urgency of A-impulses is understood in these phenomenological terms, however, we can begin to gain a realistic appreciation of the ways in which those impulses can impede reflective agency. It is to this issue that I now turn.

4. A-IMPULSES AND THE IMPAIRMENT OF REFLECTIVE AGENCY

In considering the obstacles posed by A-desires to reflective agency I want to put to the side the following possibilities: that individual acts of drug consumption might be justifiable, in moral and prudential terms, and that addiction itself might operate as a kind of excuse. Obviously, many A-impulses, construed as quasi-perceptual representations of a prospective course of action or experience as pleasant, are veridical. The reason why it strikes one vividly that ingesting some more of a certain drug would be very pleasant is that it would in fact be so, whereas the failure to take the drug is likely to be quite unpleasant, involving eventually the various painful symptoms customarily referred to under the heading of withdrawal. When this is the case, the comparative pleasure to be gained by consumption could be such as to render that option justified, especially if such conditions as the following are also satisfied: the drug is readily available, in plentiful supply, at reasonable cost; its use would not interfere with one's other important life pursuits; the side-effects of consumption for one's health are otherwise negligible; its use would not require one to breach one's responsibilities to friends, family, and others; and so on.

Even when these conditions of ordinary justification are not satisfied, however, addiction might function to excuse the addicted agent from blame for the act of consumption.[27] This possibility is raised by cases in which the painful withdrawal effects of abstention are unusually great. In such cases, it could become permissible for the agent to embark on a course of action that would ordinarily be prohibited (morally and otherwise), in order to avoid the painful effects of abstaining from consuming the drug to which they are addicted. This scenario, in which it is assumed that addiction functions much like ordinary coercion or duress to excuse the agent from blame for a deed that would otherwise be impermissible, clearly cannnot be extended to cover very many of the offenses of interest to the law. Rudeness and incivility, and such minor offenses as littering and jaywalking, might conceivably be excusable in this way, if they were sincerely believed by the agent to be necessary to avoid the anticipated and severe distress of withdrawal; but the strategy would not apply to more serious violations of legal and moral norms. The reason for this is that a duress defense is generally recognized under the law only when the agent is plausibly threatened with death or grievous bodily harm, and the discomfort of withdrawal from a substance to which one is addicted can hardly be compared with such effects.[28] In any case, I shall simply bracket such issues, assuming that we are dealing with situations in which the anticipated painful effects of abstention would not constitute an excuse analogous to coercion or duress, and in which the balance of risks and benefits is not such as to justify consumption in ordinary moral and prudential terms.

Consider, then, a person addicted to a drug such as heroin, who is considering whether to obtain some more of the drug for another fix. The issue, just to be clear, is not the effect of actual consumption of the drug on the person's capacities for deliberative agency, but rather the effects on those capacities of the urgent

---

[27] For a general account of the conditions that excuse persons from blame, see my *Responsibility and the Moral Sentiments*, ch. 5.

[28] Compare Morse, 'Causation, Compulsion, and Involuntariness', and Herbert Fingarette, 'Addiction and Criminal Responsibility', *Yale Law Journal*, 84 (1975), 413–44, at 437–8. See also Gary Watson, 'Excusing Addiction', as reprinted in his *Agency and Answerability*, 318–50.

A-desires to which the addiction disposes the person. We may suppose, to begin with, that such desires might interfere with the person's capacity to deliberate rationally about the normative considerations that speak for and against the act of shooting up. To be sure, even the most intense A-desire would presumably not deprive one altogether of the ability to appreciate the most fundamental moral, legal, and factual parameters of one's situation. Supposing that the case really is one in which consumption is not justifiable in terms the agent would accept, these parameters might include such facts as the following: that possession of heroin is subject to legal sanctions; that its purchase therefore involves certain prudential dangers; that use of the drug poses significant risks to one's longer-term health; that such use interferes in still more significant ways with activities and relationships one values, and so on. What may be impaired by an intense A-impulse, however, is one's capacity to weigh these normative factors accurately and judiciously, in reflection leading to a verdict about what one has most reason to do on the whole.

On the phenomenological account I have offered, A-desires involve the intense focusing of one's attention onto the anticipated pleasures of (say) drug consumption, perhaps accompanied by other painful sensations and emotions. But someone subject to such a quasi-perceptual state will presumably find it difficult to think clearly about the overall balance of reasons bearing on the decision to consume or abstain from consuming the drug. Let us suppose that the anticipated pleasure and release from discomfort is of little normative significance in comparison to the clear prudential and moral disadvantages of continued heroin consumption, and that the agent in question would agree that this is the case when reflecting calmly about the issue in circumstances that do not involve the presence of intense A-desires. Adding such a desire to the mix, it seems, would make it much harder for the agent to reach this conclusion and to keep it firmly in view. The focusing of one's attention onto the pleasures of consumption that is brought about by A-desires is apt to encourage one to overestimate the value and importance of those pleasures, in reflecting about what one is to do, and this distorting effect can be considered an impairment of the agent's capacities for practical rationality.[29]

In saying this, I do not suppose that such an impairment should be thought of on the model of total incapacitation. The urgent A-desire is not itself a belief or judgment to the effect that the desired state or action is good on the whole, but merely a presentation of that state or action that is colored in evaluative terms; in this respect, it is unlike the delusional false beliefs to which some forms of mental illness may dispose those whom they affect. Furthermore, I see no reason to conclude that such quasi-perceptual presentations of an alternative for action should render an agent altogether unable to think clearly about the normative considerations that actually bear on the decision to perform the action. Reaching the conclusion that short-term pleasure does not justify the decision to consume a given drug, in light of the other

---

[29] The effects of strong A-desires on the rationality of the agent subject to them are emphasized in Stephen Morse, 'Hooked on Hype', *Law and Philosophy*, 19 (2000), 3–49.

factors that need to be taken into account, is not altogether beyond the psychological powers of persons who are subject to intense A-impulses. It is merely difficult to do, something that requires effort, concentration, strength of will, and so on; moreover that this is the case is perfectly intelligible once we are operating with the phenomenological conception of strength of desire. My claim is that this effect of A-impulses on the processes of deliberation deserves to be thought of as at least a partial impairment of our capacities for reflective agency.

It does not yet amount to a defect of the will, however. The forms of interference with reflective agency just discussed represent impairments of our capacities for rational thought about the normative issues bearing on action. A defect of the will, by contrast, would be a form of interference with the processes of reflective agency that goes beyond, and is independent from, deficiencies in respect to rationality alone. To home in on the question of whether addiction can constitute such a defect of the will, we need to imagine a case in which an agent correctly arrives at the conclusion that abstention would be the best course of action on the whole, while nevertheless remaining subject to urgent A-impulses to shoot up. That such a scenario is possible follows from the point that A-impulses are resilient, since, as we have seen, resilience precisely consists in the unresponsiveness of desires to evaluative reflection.[30] So our imagined agent is one who judges that abstention would be best, but retains an especially intense desire to consume some more of the drug. Should we think of this condition as a potential defect of the will?

We should not, if such a defect is understood as a complete incapacitation of our volitional powers. The power to choose in accordance with one's deliberative judgments would be completely obliterated by A-desires only on the assumption that those desires are literally irresistible, and I have already rejected that assumption (along with the related causal interpretation of strength of desire). But I see no reason to think that a defect of the will must amount to a form of total incapacitation of the will. We saw above that it can be appropriate to speak of impairment of our powers of practical reasoning even in cases in which such impairment is partial rather than complete. Similarly, I believe we should be prepared to grant that there are impairments of our volitional powers that do not amount to cases of complete incapacity to act in ways we ourselves deem best. Moreover, the phenomenological conception of strength of desire I have been developing makes it fairly clear why urgent A-impulses should amount to volitional defects of this kind. To be in the grip of such an impulse is to be made vividly aware of a concrete alternative for action, presented in terms that appear highly attractive. Even if one succeeds, in the face of such a desire, in reasoning correctly to the conclusion that it should not be acted on, its continued presence and urgency will make it comparatively difficult to choose to comply with the deliberated verdict one has arrived at. The A-impulse that persists in a situation of this kind is the extreme case of the phenomenon of

[30] That is, from reflection about what one has most reason to do. It is compatible with resilience in this sense that A-desires are connected to thoughts about the prospective pleasure to be gained through action, in the ways outlined in sect. 3, above.

temptation, a psychological condition that facilitates the choice of an action the agent believes ill-advised, by directing the agent's thoughts onto the alleged attractions to be gained through that action. An intense and systemic temptation of this variety, I submit, is appropriately thought of as a kind of volitional defect.

Consider as an analogy a different kind of temptation, in which A-desires are not at issue. Suppose that after consultation with my doctor I have reached the conclusion that it would be best on the whole to reduce substantially my cholesterol level. Suppose further that, without being in any way addicted to the things, I am very fond of certain high-fat foods (Belgian chocolates and premium Vermont ice cream, let us say) that I need to avoid if I am to attain my goal of reducing my cholesterol level. It seems obvious that it will be far easier for me to comply with my deliberated judgment about what to do if there are not large supplies of chocolate and ice cream lying about in my cupboards and refrigerator. The physical presence of such items presents me vividly with concrete possibilities for action that are undeniably attractive in a certain respect, even if they are not the alternatives I favor on the whole. My reflective judgment about what to do represents one option for the will, but the vivid awareness of a very pleasant alternative, prompted by my literal perception of chocolate and ice cream in my environment, represents a different possibility, one whose rewards would be immediate and visceral.

This is an understandable effect of the perception of the forbidden foodstuffs on what might be called the phenomenological field of agency—one's immediate awareness of a set of options as concrete and appealing alternatives for action. It seems clear that an alteration of this kind in the field of agency would make it more difficult for me to act well by my own lights —and not merely by interfering with my capacity to think clearly about the pros and cons of a rich diet. Even if I remain convinced that it would be best on the whole to stay away from ice cream and chocolates, the vivid presentation of these items as dietary alternatives may impair my capacity to choose in accordance with this verdict, by making the act of choice itself much harder than it otherwise would be. If this is correct, however, then it should be equally clear that urgent A-impulses can also represent impairments of our powers of choice. On the phenomenological conception of them I have sketched, such impulses are to be understood as involuntary, quasi-perceptual presentations of experiences and actions as unusually pleasant. But the effects of such conceptualized presentations of concrete options on the field of agency are in the relevant respects just like the effects of my literal perception of chocolates and ice cream in the case described above.[31] By making one vividly aware of

---

[31] In fact, the two scenarios I have described here are really two instances of the same basic kind of case. In the first scenario, we must suppose that the literal presence of the forbidden foodstuffs incites in us a desire to consume them, since chocolate and ice cream would not make us 'vividly aware' of pleasant possibilities for action if they did not give rise to such a desire. The difference between the scenarios is simply that in the first, an intense desire is caused by the literal perception of the substance that is to be consumed, while this is not so in the second case. On the general role of situational cues in giving rise to A-desires, see George Loewenstein, 'Willpower: A Decision-Theorist's Perspective', *Law and Philosophy*, 19 (2000), 51–76.

alternatives for action that promise an immediate and visceral pleasure, A-impulses bring it about that compliance with one's settled better judgment would require effort, concentration, strength of will. In these ways, A-impulses represent potential impairments not only of our capacities for rational deliberation, but also of our volitional power to comply with the verdicts of such deliberation.

Against this, it might be urged that my account of volitional defects due to addiction does not succeed in distinguishing them adequately from impairments of an agent's rationality. The account builds on the effects of A-desires on the phenomenological field of agency; but, the reply would go, any agent who is subject to these effects is also necessarily subject to an impairment of rationality. Such an agent may succeed in judging (correctly, as I have been supposing) that it would be best on the whole not to satisfy their intense A-desire. But the continued presence of the desire will necessarily distract their attention from the practical judgment they have arrived at. Much in the way of Aristotle's *akrates*, they will find themselves unable to focus with full concentration on the normative conclusions that they accept. Doesn't this mean that the threat posed by addiction to deliberative agency is at bottom a threat to our rationality, and not a defect of the will?

In answer to this question, I would offer the following observations. First, facts about the direction of one's attention occupy a curiously liminal position in respect to the divide between the rational and the nonrational in our psychological lives. In themselves, attention, interest, vivid presence to consciousness and the like would seem to be features of our emotional and desiderative biographies.[32] According to the phenomenological account of A-desires I have endorsed, for instance, to be subject to such a desire is (*inter alia*) to have one's attention directed onto certain possibilities for action, conceived of as pleasant in some way. This is, in part, a cognitive phenomenon, involving a susceptibility to thoughts of distinctive kinds, but it is not on that account unequivocally a defect of rationality. The focusing of attention that is constitutive of desire becomes a clear defect of rationality only to the extent that it impinges on our ability to form true beliefs and to draw correct inferences from them; but in the sorts of cases I have been considering we were to suppose that A-desires do not cause impairments of these kinds.

To be sure, the failure to choose in accordance with one's correct practical judgment about what one ought to do may be counted a failure of rational inference in the broadest sense. This will be the case on the plausible assumption that it is a requirement of rationality that we choose in accordance with our conclusive practical judgments about what we have reason to do.[33] Note again, however, that a failure in this respect does not license the conclusion that the agent was altogether incapable of choosing correctly. It is attractive, but misleading, to picture our

---

[32] They are treated this way, for instance, by Michael Stocker, in *Valuing Emotions* (Cambridge, England: Cambridge University Press, 1996), ch. 1.

[33] This is one version of the thesis referred to as internalism in discussions of normative reasons for action; see e.g. Christine M. Korsgaard, 'Skepticism about Practical Reason', as reprinted in her *Creating the Kingdom of Ends* (Cambridge, England: Cambridge University Press, 1996), 311–34.

motivational psychology in terms of standing dispositions to action that are triggered causally if (and only if) the agent's attention is focused sufficiently on the possibilities for action that are to be chosen. This picture is really just a variant of what I earlier referred to as the hydraulic conception. On the volitionalist alternative I have recommended as superior to the hydraulic model, the capacity for self-determination is not something that can be reconstructed in terms of a deterministic theory of the operations of the mind. This means, in particular, that the basic capacity to choose in accordance with our evaluative beliefs can survive even in the presence of psychological conditions that tend to direct our attention away from the objects of those beliefs. Intense A-desires may make the exercise of reflective self-control difficult, but they do not render it impossible.

In the end, the admission that there are norms of rationality governing volition as well as belief deprives the distinction between defects of rationality and defects of the will of its theoretical interest. The relevant distinction to draw in this area is within the class of defects of rationality, between impairments of our capacity for practical judgment and impairments of our capacity to choose in accordance with our practical judgments. The kinds of volitional impairments I have tried to characterize in this section represent ways in which A-desires can lead us astray even when we succeed in judging correctly what we should do. If choice in accordance with one's practical judgments is itself a requirement of reason, however, then such volitional impairments will also be defects of rationality, in an extended sense.

For this reason (among others), I am uncertain whether the position I have defended in this paper provides support for the jurisprudential thesis that the law should acknowledge the category of volitional defect in addition to that of defect of rationality. I strongly suspect that a legal code that only allows for the latter form of impairment of deliberative agency can reach the same verdicts about particular cases of addiction as a code that acknowledges both rational and volitional forms of impairment. For purposes of philosophical self-understanding, however, it is important to be clear that a phenomenon such as addiction can present different kinds of obstacles in the way of our acting well. Doing so helps us to appreciate not only the variety of things that can go wrong when we try to translate our values into action, but also the complexity of our capacities for deliberative agency even when they are functioning well.

5. CONCLUSION

The main themes of my discussion can be summarized very succinctly. I have defended a volitionalist conception of the will as against the hydraulic conception of the contribution of desire to action. In terms of the volitionalist theory, I have tried to explain how addiction might impair our capacity to choose in accordance with our deliberated verdicts about what we ought to do. What are the implications of this position for questions about the moral responsibility of addicts for their actions?

I would like to make three brief, concluding observations by way of answering this question. The first is that dichotomizing approaches to the responsibility of the addict are not very helpful, and should be avoided. Discussions of this issue sometimes convey the impression that there are basically only two options: either the behavior of the addict is viewed as fully voluntary, or it is treated as the completely involuntary symptom of a disease. But moral accountability is not in general an all or nothing matter.[34] The capacities for deliberative agency that render us accountable are not only complex, they are also liable to various degrees of development or defect. The specific kinds of defect that I have traced to addiction are best understood as impairing our powers of reflective self-control, without depriving us of those powers altogether. Agents who are subject to urgent A-impulses are not thereby rendered unable to deliberate well about action, or to choose in accordance with their deliberated verdicts; it is rather that the correct exercise of their powers of deliberative agency is considerably more difficult in the presence of persistent A-impulses than it would otherwise be. Addiction, in other words, should be thought of as producing a condition of potentially diminished accountability. It moves an agent into that grey area in which the powers that make us accountable, though still present, are present only in a reduced degree. This may be frustrating to our desire for clear-cut, yes/no answers to questions about the accountability of addicts for their behavior, but it seems to reflect well the inherent difficulty both of the phenomenon and of the normative problems it raises.

Even if we make due allowances for this kind of intractability, however, it seems to me that the range of behaviors from which addiction might plausibly be thought to exempt an agent from accountability is rather restricted; this is the second of my concluding observations. Consider, in particular, the kinds of 'other-regarding' criminal behavior often associated with addiction to controlled substances, such as theft, assault and battery, homicide, and so on. A person subject to urgent A-desires might find that their satisfaction would be facilitated by a criminal action of one of these kinds, and so we may suppose that refraining from such an action might be somewhat more difficult for the addict than for a person not subject to similar impulses. It would be incredible, however, to claim that the difficulty involved here is sufficiently great to constitute an exemption from accountability for such criminal behavior.[35] That is, we reasonably expect and demand that people refrain from theft, assault, homicide, and the like, even when doing so means that they must forgo the intense satisfactions to which their attention is directed by the A-impulses to which they are subject. In this respect, the situation of the addict seems little different from that of other agents who have strong personal motives, apart from literal self-defense, for engaging in such criminal activity (such as financial exigency or an intense desire for revenge).

---

[34] Compare my *Responsibility and the Moral Sentiments*, chs. 6–8.
[35] Compare Morse, 'Causation, Compulsion, and Involuntariness'.

The forms of behavior to which the status of diminished accountability would seem primarily relevant are the self-regarding activities directly associated with satisfaction of A-desires themselves: purchase and consumption of a controlled substance, for instance. Understanding addiction as a partial impairment of one's capacities for reflective self-control, we may be led to view it as diminishing the agent's moral accountability with respect to such questionable self-regarding activities. (I bracket here, of course, the difficult issues of whether consumption of addictive substances ought to be morally and legally sanctioned, and of the responsibility of the addict for becoming addicted in the first place.[36]) My final observation is that this result is likely to be most significant when it comes to our personal interactions with those who suffer from addiction. The acknowledgment that addiction impairs one's capacities for reflective agency can encourage understanding for the addict's plight, helping us to move away from cartoonish, 'just-say-no' approaches to the problem, and to appreciate the contribution that sophisticated techniques of self-control and social support can make in overcoming urgent A-impulses. At the same time, the volitionalist conception that I have defended should discourage the equally cartoonish image of the addict as a mere victim, someone helpless in the presence of a force that is beyond the human capacity to resist. Addicts are not rendered completely powerless by the A-impulses to which they are subject. By acknowledging this fact in our interactions with those who are addicted—treating them as moral persons, equipped in a basic degree with the powers of reflective self-control—we may encourage in them a more empowering self-conception, thereby enhancing the chances that they shall succeed in overcoming the obstacles placed by their condition in the way of acting well.

---

[36] Questions about the justifiability of legislation proscribing addictive drugs, and their connection with the issue of whether addiction can function as a defense under the criminal law, are explored by Douglas Husak in 'Addiction and Criminal Liability', *Law and Philosophy*, 18 (1999), 655–840.

9

Caring, Reflexivity, and the Structure of Volition

Among the significant legacies of Harry Frankfurt's work on agency and personhood is the attention he has drawn to fascinating but neglected complexities in the structure of the will. Personhood is not exhausted by the capacity for intentional action, but involves additional resources of interest and concern that help to define who we are. Thus not everything that a person does intentionally is something that the person fully identifies with. Some of the actions we perform are ones that we are estranged from in a certain sense, insofar as they do not reflect our values, priorities, and sense of what is really important in life. It thus emerges that there can be internal as well as external obstacles to the autonomous realization of our ends.

A second and distinct legacy of Frankfurt's work has been to offer a particular way of conceptualizing these complexities of human agency. The central and most influential feature of Frankfurt's interpretation of these phenomena is the distinction between orders of desire. Frankfurt begins with an essentially Hobbesian conception of the will, as effective first-order desire.[1] According to this conception, the will of an agent is simply that desire that is causally effective in moving the agent to action; it is thus something that can be ascribed to any creature to whom it makes sense to attribute desires. The distinctive features of those agents who are *persons* emerge only with the introduction of desires of higher-order, which in Frankfurt's account define the person's characteristic point of view, and enable us to decide whether agents are estranged from or identified with their effective motivating attitudes. The significance of higher-order attitudes for questions of identification derives in large measure from their peculiarly reflexive character. They are responses to the person's own states of desire and preference, and hence

Originally published in Monika Betzler and Barbara Guckes (eds.), *Autonomes Handeln* (Berlin: Akademie Verlag, 2000), 213–34. Reprinted by permission. Many thanks for helpful feedback to audiences at the Australian National University, Macquarie University, Monash University, and to participants in the 'Pfingstkurs' on Frankfurt's work at the University of Bielefeld.

[1] See 'Freedom of the Will and the Concept of a Person', as reprinted in Harry G. Frankfurt, *The Importance of What We Care About* (Cambridge, England: Cambridge University Press, 1988), 11–25, at 14.

they exhibit the kind of reflective self-consciousness that seems to distinguish persons from other creatures capable of rudimentary agency.[2] When these higher-order desires are wholehearted, they fix the person's distinctive standpoint on the world, defining what Frankfurt in his later writings refers to as the person's sense of what is important.

Frankfurt himself never puts the matter this way, but I believe that many philosophers have been attracted to his interpretation of human agency because of its latent noncognitivism. The distinction between orders of desire apparently enables us to do justice to the complexities of human agency to which Frankfurt has drawn attention, without departing from the basic assumption that the attitudes essentially constitutive of our standpoint as persons are in the way of nonrational commitments rather than genuine judgments as to what is or is not the case. If this accounts for the appeal of Frankfurt's position for many of his readers, however, it also represents the weakness of that position, for I believe that noncognitivist interpretations of human agency are ultimately unacceptable. An 'authentic and perspicuous'[3] model of the volitional structures characteristic of persons must build on the assumption that the attitudes definitive of the real self are evaluative judgments, and not merely motivational pushes and pulls (of whatever hierarchical order).

One aim of the present essay is to collect some considerations that support the assertion I have just made. In particular, I explain why the apparatus of a hierarchy of desires does not seem to me a helpful way of conceptualizing the volitional structure of persons. I also offer some observations about the essential reflexivity of human agency. Frankfurt seems to me right to stress that our volitional capacities are distinctively reflexive or self-conscious; the challenge is to accommodate this dimension of personhood without falling back on the unhelpful apparatus of a hierarchy of desires. Throughout I attend primarily to Frankfurt's more recent writings, in which the phenomenon of caring about something is used to bring into focus the peculiar complexities of human volition. At issue is the question of what it is to identify with one's actions, where identification is understood as a condition of authentic and autonomous agency, and not as a condition of freedom or moral responsibility.[4]

---

[2] The emphasis on reflexiveness is particularly pronounced in Frankfurt's papers 'Identification and Wholeheartedness', as reprinted in *The Importance of What We Care About*, 159–76, and 'The Faintest Passion', as reprinted in Harry G. Frankfurt, *Necessity, Volition, and Love* (Cambridge, England: Cambridge University Press, 1999), 95–107.

[3] This is from 'Identification and Wholeheartedness', 164. The phrase 'the real self' that appears later in this sentence is an allusion to Susan Wolf's illuminating discussion of Frankfurt's position in her book *Freedom within Reason* (New York: Oxford University Press, 1990).

[4] I offer some critical remarks about Frankfurt's account of responsibility in my book *Responsibility and the Moral Sentiments* (Cambridge, Mass.: Harvard University Press, 1994), 171–5, 256–65. In general, it seems to me of the utmost importance to distinguish issues of responsibility from issues of autonomous or authentic agency, for I doubt that there is a single notion of identification that is sufficient for both responsibility and autonomy. In Frankfurt's recent writings on caring, the notion of autonomy seems to be primarily (and appropriately) in the foreground (I return to the distinction between responsibility and autonomy in sect. 2 below).

1. REFLEXIVITY AND DESIRE

In 'Identification and Wholeheartedness' Frankfurt writes: 'The notion of reflexivity seems to me much more fundamental and indispensable, in dealing with the phenomena at hand, than that of a hierarchy.'[5] This remark strikes me as deeply correct. In the present section I explain why the notion of a hierarchy of desire distorts rather than enhances our understanding of the complexities of human agency, and suggest a different way of conceptualizing the reflexivity characteristic of such agency.

Consider a typical if trivial occasion for practical reflection, about (say) how one is to spend the coming evening. Such reflection often takes as its starting point some desire or inclination of the agent's. I may find that I am positively disposed toward the prospect of going out to a film tonight, and proceed to deliberate about this desire. Deliberation of this kind presupposes a kind of reflexivity. It is possible only if we are able to step back from our motivating attitudes, and to make those attitudes themselves objects of reflection. If we did not exhibit this kind of self-consciousness, we would not be capable of the kind of autonomous self-determination characteristic of human agency; our reflection would be restricted to questions concerning the attainment of ends that are simply given to us, by whichever of our first-order desires are momentarily the strongest.[6]

To this extent, I agree with Frankfurt that reflexivity is essential to personhood. The question is whether the kind of reflexivity that is important in this connection is well thought of in terms of the notion of a hierarchy of desires. I do not believe that it is; to see why not, it will be helpful to compare two different ways of developing the trivial example of practical reflection introduced above, in which my desire to go to a film provides an occasion for deliberation.

According to the first interpretation of this process—what I shall call the hierarchical model—the reflection that is induced by the desire to go to the movies culminates in the formation of what are literally second-order desires. In stepping back from my initial inclination, I treat it as an episode in my own psychological biography, one which figures as the object of my attention as I deliberate. My thought is directed, in other words, onto the fact that I have a desire to go to the movies, rather than onto the propositional content of that first-order desire, or any evaluative judgments that may be associated with it. Abstracting from these matters of content, we are left with a notion of desire that is congenial to noncognitivism, as a brute pro-attitude or positive tendency of some kind in regard to my seeing a film tonight. Furthermore, the process of deliberating about such psychological

---

  [5] 'Identification and Wholeheartedness', 165 n.
  [6] The importance of reflexivity to human agency is also emphasized by Christine Korsgaard in *The Sources of Normativity* (Cambridge, England: Cambridge University Press, 1996), esp. lecture 3. My remarks about the proper interpretation of reflexivity apply to a certain extent to Korsgaard's use of the notion, which exhibits some of the same unclarity that affects Frankfurt's.

data will be complete when I have acquired a further psychological item of the same basic type at the level of second-order reflection: for instance, a whole-hearted pro-attitude or positive tendency in regard to my both having and acting on the original first-order desire to see a film.[7] The fact that I form higher-order attitudes of this kind is what sets me apart from mere wantons, who are completely indifferent as to the constitution of their will, and may be said not really to care about what they end up doing one way or another. And the fact that these attitudes are literally reflexive both distinguishes my deliberation as that of a person, and imbues the results of my deliberation with authority vis-à-vis my initial first-order attitudes.

The hierarchical model of personhood and identification is strongly suggested by Frankfurt's talk of a hierarchy of desires; it is, in fact, the most straightforward and literal way of understanding his account of personhood and reflective agency. But the interpretation is not compelling. Many of the difficulties with it have been articulated ably before, so I shall offer only a brief discussion of them, concentrating on two main points.[8] First, in ordinary contexts of deliberation it is not the case that deliberating agents think primarily about their first-order desires themselves, considered as episodes in their psychological biography. When I am prompted by my desire to see a movie to engage in practical reflection, it is not the desire itself—for instance, the state of being attracted in some way by the prospect of seeing a film—that I will tend to focus on, but rather the concrete merits of the activity that I find myself attracted to. Construed as a general account of the kind of reflection through which we constitute ourselves as agents, identifying with or distancing ourselves from particular inclinations to which we are subject, Frankfurt's hierarchical model thus seems distorted. It does not do justice to the outward focus that is characteristic of such deliberation.

Furthermore, when questions arise about the status of our first-order desires, it is obscure how they can be resolved simply through the generation of further desires of higher order. I take it that ordinary first-order desires provide potential material for practical deliberation, because the fact that we are inclined to engage in some activity does not by itself resolve the question of whether the activity would be good in any way, something we really have reason to go in for.[9] The task of practical deliberation is ordinarily to settle evaluative or normative issues of this

---

[7] In 'Identification and Wholeheartedness' Frankfurt seems to endorse the suggestion that the higher-order attitudes relevant to identification are not of the same basic type as the first-order desires upon which we reflect, but are to be construed rather as *decisions*. In his more recent paper 'The Faintest Passion', however, he returns to speaking of the relevant higher-order attitudes as desires regarding the constitution of one's will (that is, as higher-order 'volitions', in the special language of 'Freedom of the Will and the Concept of a Person'). The condition that the higher-order desires of this kind be *wholehearted* is developed in 'The Faintest Passion' in terms of the notion of satisfaction, which is a matter of the *absence* of restlessness or uncertainty with regard to one's higher-order desires; see 'The Faintest Passion', sect. 7.

[8] See esp. Gary Watson, 'Free Agency', as reprinted in Watson (ed.), *Free Will* (Oxford: Oxford University Press, 1982), 96–110.   [9] Compare Korsgaard, *The Sources of Normativity*, 92–4.

kind, issues that are left open by psychological facts about the state of our first-order inclinations and dispositions. If this is correct, however, then it must be obscure how the generation of further psychological items of the same general type, at the level of second-order reflection, could possibly suffice to bring practical deliberation to a satisfactory conclusion.

The point is not that it is necessarily arbitrary to identify persons with their higher-order desires, or that we cannot make sense of wholehearted identification without postulating a potentially unending system of nested attitudes of higher and higher orders. Frankfurt may be correct in holding that the reflexivity of second-order desires sets them essentially apart from desires of other kinds, and that wholeheartedness is a negative condition, so that the potential regress of identifying attitudes can be blocked.[10] But the real problem remains. This is that desires are the wrong kinds of entities through which to bring practical deliberation to a satisfactory resolution. The very features of first-order desires that present a problem for practical deliberation, namely their potential independence from normative judgment, render second-order desires essentially ill-suited to resolve that deliberative problem. If I can find myself attracted by the idea of going to a movie regardless of whether doing so would really be a good thing, I can equally find myself with a higher-order attraction to acting on such a desire when doing so would not be a good idea. Given the evaluative terms of the question we pose to ourselves in practical deliberation, it is a kind of category mistake to think that a satisfying answer can be provided in terms of facts about the state of our psychological inclinations at any level. An evaluative question calls for an evaluative response—some claim about what we have reason to do, or what action it would be good to perform—not a descriptive report about the current state of our subjective leanings.

To this it will be replied that Frankfurt does not envisage reflection culminating in a descriptive report of the agent's higher-order desires. Deliberating agents do not proceed by ascending to the level of third-order reflection, and trying to ascertain whether there is factual alignment between their wholehearted second-order desires and their effective first-order motivations. Rather they engage in second-order reflection on their first-order desires, which (if all goes well) culminates in the formation of wholehearted second-order desires. This is correct, but it will succeed in disarming the objection at hand only if the formation of the second-order desire can be equated with the endorsement of an evaluative judgment, suited by virtue of its normative content to answer the question from which deliberation begins. But (a) this evaluative interpretation of desire strains against the apparent noncognitivism of the hierarchical model, the assumption that the desires important to identification are nonjudgmental matters of brute psychological inclination, attraction, and repulsion. And (b) if we are allowed to help ourselves to evaluative judgments at the level of second-order reflection, the question arises why we cannot also appeal to them at the level of first-order thought about what to do.

---

[10] This is Frankfurt's latest response to the mentioned objections, in 'The Faintest Passion'.

As I noted above, deliberation typically has an outward focus and phenomenology, and in accordance with this we should expect it to be brought to a conclusion by a first-order evaluative judgment about the goodness of concrete alternatives for action, not by an evaluative verdict about our psychological states themselves.

Frankfurt's response to the latter point is his repeated insistence on the reflexivity or self-consciousness of human agency. He evidently takes reflexivity to be the hallmark of personhood, and believes this is most perspicuously accounted for in terms of the hierarchical model. But if the points made above are correct, the hierarchical model does not really provide a perspicuous conceptualization of ordinary practical deliberation. Moreover it is possible to do justice to the reflexivity characteristic of human agency, while also accommodating the distinctively evaluative terms in which practical deliberation is typically conducted. Returning to the simple example of deliberation introduced earlier, I shall now sketch a second interpretation of reflection, the substantive model, which avoids the problems that plague the hierarchical account.

The substantive model agrees with the hierarchical model in holding that reflexivity is necessary for the kind of deliberation characteristic of human agency. Only if I can step back from my desire to go to the movies can I engage in the kind of reflection that sets me apart as a person. Where the substantive model departs from the hierarchical interpretation is in its account of the process of reflection that is set in motion when we step back in this way from our desires. According to the hierarchical interpretation, such reflection abstracts from the content of our desires, focusing instead on the brute psychological fact of our being inclined one way or another in regard to a concrete possibility for action (such as going to see a film). By contrast, the substantive interpretation holds that desires are not fully intelligible when construed noncognitively, as matters of brute psychological inclination, and that reflection about them can accordingly be conducted only in substantive evaluative terms. Let me elaborate a bit on both points.

Noncognitivist approaches must assume the availability of descriptions of human psychological motivation from which all evaluative vocabulary has been expunged. At some fundamental level, our actions and motivations can be explained in terms of the operation of brute psychological forces; evaluative vocabulary comes on the scene only later, and serves essentially to express these nonnormative psychological pushes and pulls.[11] But it may be doubted whether we can really make sense of psychological explanations that are fundamentally purged of evaluative concepts in this way. The paradigmatic experience of wanting something, at any rate, is one that is essentially evaluatively colored.[12] When I am

[11] Compare Simon Blackburn, *Ruling Passions* (Oxford: Oxford University Press, 1998), ch. 3.

[12] I expand on the conception of desire sketched here in my paper 'Addiction as Defect of the Will: Some Philosophical Reflections', Chapter 8 in this volume. Related conceptions of desire are defended by T. M. Scanlon, in *What We Owe to Each Other* (Cambridge, Mass.: Harvard University Press, 1998), 39–41, and by Joseph Raz, in 'When We are Ourselves: The Active and the Passive', as reprinted in his *Engaging Reason: On the Theory of Value and Action* (Oxford: Oxford University Press, 1999), 5–21.

aware of a desire to go to a film this evening, I find my thoughts turning to the prospect of seeing the movie in question, and this prospect presents itself to me as attractive. The latter aspect, of attraction to the desired activity, is theoretically elusive. Noncognitivists may insist that there is an irreducible noncognitive *affect* of attraction. Even if we make room for such an affect, however, it cannot be the whole story about phenomenal desire, and it is certainly not the aspect of such desires that is relevant to practical reflection. A brute affect of attraction to the prospect of going to a movie would hardly be intelligible to us as a desire. Unless we can articulate what it is about the course of action that seems desirable, the affect directed toward it will appear essentially inscrutable, more like an itch or a sensation than a real desire. Phenomenal desire resembles perception in presenting cognitions about how things are. In the case of desire, these thoughts are structured evaluatively, through concepts that represent potential courses of action as good along some dimension—in the example introduced above, its appearing to me that it would be *pleasant* to see a particular movie.

Moreover, it is only in virtue of having this kind of evaluative content that desires provide raw material for deliberative reflection. My reflexive conscious-ness of my desires involves essentially the capacity to stand back from the evaluative cognitions through which they present concrete courses of action to me, as eligible candidates for choice. Wanting to go to the movie, I am aware that this option seems to me to be good, insofar as it would be pleasant in some way or other; but my reflexive distance from this attitude enables me to refrain from endorsing the evaluative thought associated with the desire, to ask whether it really would be good to go to the movie after all. This is the evaluative ques-tion that reflexivity poses for practical deliberation, and it calls for first-order evaluative thought about the concrete merits of the course of action to which I find myself attracted. The hierarchical model pictures such reflection as abstracting from the content of first-order desires, and focusing on the fact of one's attraction itself. According to the substantive model, however, if we abstract completely from the content of our first-order desires, we will no longer be able to reflect on them at all—they reduce to inarticulate affects. The task of deliberative thought is accordingly a first-order one, of assessing the evalua-tive cognition that is constitutively associated with the original desire. I must decide, for instance, whether and in what ways it really would be pleasant to go to the film, and whether and in what ways cinematic pleasure provides a sound reason to go out to a movie this evening (given my other alternatives and commitments).[13]

Suppose I reach a positive verdict as a result of this kind of deliberation, concluding that it would indeed be good to see a movie tonight, in the way it seems to me to be while in the grip of my first-order desire. Arriving at this conclusion is a matter of accepting, through the exercise of my critical and

---

[13] Compare Scanlon, *What We Owe to Each Other*, 65–6, to which I am indebted here.

deliberative faculties, the evaluative cognition presented to me by my desire to go to a movie. When this condition is satisfied, we may speak of my identification with my original first-order desire. But such identification is achieved without the formation of a reflexive attitude that is literally of higher-order.[14] Identification is brought about not by taking a stand on the fact of my desiring to go to a movie, but by endorsing the content of that desire, accepting that it really would be good to do what, in virtue of my having the desire, it seems to me that it would be good to do. In these respects, the substantive model improves on the hierarchical interpretation presented earlier. Deliberation is represented as having an outward focus and phenomenology, insofar as it addresses the concrete merits of the actions one is attracted to performing, and it is brought to conclusion through the formation of an evaluative judgment that is appropriate to the concerns from which deliberation in the first place begins. These virtues can be purchased, however, only at the cost of abandoning the apparent noncognitivism that, if I am right, has attracted many philosophers to Frankfurt's account of the structure of volition.

2. CARING AND THE GOOD

Now it is not initially clear that Frankfurt himself would necessarily object to interpreting his account of human agency along the lines of the substantive model. On the one hand, his reliance on the notion of higher-order attitudes to explicate the reflexivity of such agency strongly suggests the hierarchical model sketched in section 1; and there is at least one point at which he explicitly distances himself from interpretations of reflexivity that are couched in evaluative terms.[15] On the other hand, Frankfurt is sufficiently vague about such central concepts as desire and deliberation as to leave it open whether these could be unpacked in terms of the substantive model.[16] Thus we might be tempted to identify the endorsing higher-order desires of which he speaks with the kinds of

---

[14] Here I disagree with the interesting account of identification advanced by Michael E. Bratman in 'Identification, Decision, and Treating as a Reason', as reprinted in his *Faces of Intention* (Cambridge, England: Cambridge University Press 1999), 185–206. Bratman construes our identifying attitudes as reflexive decisions to treat our desires as reason-giving. But if the account of desire I have sketched is on the right lines, then (a) desires themselves rarely provide reasons for action, and (b) the attitudes through which we identify with our desires concern the contents of those desires rather than the fact of our having the desires. That is, they are first-order evaluative judgments about what there is reason for us to do, and not decisions to treat our first-order desires in some way or other.

[15] 'Identification and Wholeheartedness', 166 n., where Frankfurt writes that the alternatives to the hierarchical model strike him as 'worse: more obscure, no less fanciful, and (I suspect) requiring a resort to hierarchy in the end themselves'.

[16] In 'Autonomy, Necessity, and Love', as reprinted in Frankfurt, *Necessity, Volition, and Love*, 129–141, at 137, Frankfurt seems for instance to favor a noncognitivist understanding of the passions, writing that the motivational effectiveness of these states 'is entirely a matter of *sheer brute force*. There is nothing in them other than the magnitude of this force that requires us, or even encourages us, to act as they command.' In the same article, however, he explicitly contrasts passions of this kind with love, which is among the higher-order attitudes important for identification. And in

evaluative judgments through which the substantive model envisages deliberation being brought to a conclusion.

In his more recent writings, however, Frankfurt seems to foreclose this interpretative possibility. His reflections on the themes of caring and importance, in particular, suggest that the attitudes definitive of our essential standpoint as persons cannot be understood simply as evaluative judgments. Those attitudes are most fundamentally a matter of what we care about wholeheartedly. But, Frankfurt contends, first-order evaluative endorsement is neither necessary nor sufficient for caring about something in the way that defines who we really are. In this section, I shall look at some of the arguments Frankfurt advances in favor of this conclusion, with the aim of defending the substantive interpretation against them.

Perhaps Frankfurt's most basic complaint is that evaluative endorsement is not sufficient for caring or identification. The intuitive thought here is that one can perfectly well accept that something is good or valuable without caring about it very much, indeed without really caring about it at all. In this kind of context it would be at best misleading to use evaluative judgment as a criterion for identification. Thus Frankfurt writes: 'Each of us can surely identify a considerable number of things that we think would be worth doing or worth having for their own sakes, but to which we ourselves are not especially drawn and at which we quite reasonably prefer not to aim.'[17]

This point initially seems to have a good deal of force, and yet on closer examination it becomes quite unclear whether it really tells against the substantive model. Frankfurt is doubtless correct to contend that we can judge something to be valuable without really caring about it, and so without its being among the commitments that define our identity as persons. I may regard the lives of a bourgeois banker or a social activist to be worthy and admirable in their different ways, and yet it may mean nothing to me that I fail to exhibit what is admirable in these modes of living, and that I am not especially drawn towards them. But the evaluative judgments at issue in this kind of case are not the ones with which the substantive model would identify the standpoint of personal reflection. What is important for the substantive model are the evaluative judgments an agent endorses within the context of practical reasoning about concrete alternatives for choice and decision, such as the judgment that it would be best to embark on a particular course of action, in the sense that the action in question is one that the agent has a good and sufficient reason to go in for. The evaluative judgments I endorse about the banker and the social activist, however, are not judgments of

---

'The Importance of What We Care About', as reprinted in 80–94, at 85. Frankfurt writes that such higher-order attitudes are 'constituted by a complex set of cognitive, affective, and volitional dispositions and states', a statement that at least leaves room for the kind of interpretation of identifying attitudes favored by the substantive model.

[17] 'On Caring', in Frankfurt, *Necessity, Volition, and Love*, 155–80, at 158. Compare 'The Importance of What We Care About', 83, and 'The Faintest Passion', 106.

this kind. That I take these lives to be worthy and admirable may perhaps be necessary for my concluding that I myself have good reason to emulate them, but it is hardly sufficient. In the context of reflection about what line of work to pursue, all manner of factors enter in that go beyond one's assessment of the basic worthiness and decency of a particular career option, including such factors as one's own interests and abilities, one's prospects for employment and success, and the likelihood that the demands of the career will leave room for one to pursue one's other basic interests and relationships.

Suppose, then, that after taking all such factors into account, I conclude that it would be best (say) to remain in philosophy rather than starting over as an investment banker or a social activist. The substantive model would hold that this judgment partially defines my distinctive point of view, articulating my reflected verdict on the deliberative question of what I have reason to do in this domain. Can I really be alienated from an evaluative commitment of this kind, failing to care about whether or not I comply with it? There seem to be two possible scenarios to consider here. First I may find—'when the chips are down', as Frankfurt likes to say—that I simply cannot work up much enthusiasm for philosophy, despite its being the line of occupation that I myself regard as best for me to be involved with.[18] It would perhaps be natural to say about this scenario that I find I do not really care about the occupation I take myself to have most reason to pursue. Furthermore, this fact about the state of my interests might well call in question the authority of my evaluative judgment about which career I should opt for. It does this, however, not by undermining in general the standpoint of evaluative reflection, but by raising a doubt about the truth of the particular evaluative judgment I have endorsed.

As I suggested above, facts about the interests and enthusiasms of a person are among the factors that are normatively relevant to determining which among the many worthy and admirable professions a person has most reason to make their own. Someone who discovers that they cannot work up any enthusiasm for the career they have chosen therefore may have reason to revise their judgment that the career in question is best for them, or to suspect that their original judgment was a matter of false consciousness or self-deception of some kind (reflecting, for instance, an unconscious wish to please a disapproving parent). To accommodate cases of this kind, the substantive model may require some refinement. We might want to say, for example, that the evaluative judgments a person endorses within practical deliberation are properly authoritative, when it comes to questions of identification and autonomy, only when the person's deliberative and rational

---

[18] See 'The Importance of What We Care About', 84–5 (discussing Sartre's famous example of the resistance fighter). Further references to what we discover about our volitional and affective nature 'when the chips are down' may be found in the following texts by Frankfurt: 'Alternate Possibilities and Moral Responsibility', as reprinted in Frankfurt, *The Importance of What We Care About*, 1–10, at 3; 'Freedom of the Will and the Concept of a Person', 16; 'Identification and Wholeheartedness', 174; 'The Faintest Passion', 101; and 'On the Necessity of Ideals', as reprinted in Frankfurt, *Necessity, Volition, and Love*, 108–116, at 111.

faculties are functioning well, and the person is correctly weighing and assessing the evidence and other considerations that are available.[19] But these modifications would not alter the basic thrust of the substantive model; its claim that the stand-point of reflective agency is the point of view of evaluative judgment, and not that of nonjudgmental affect or volition, would remain essentially intact.

In a second possible scenario, I would remain notably unenthusiastic about the career choice I have decided would be the best under the circumstances. By con-trast with the first scenario, however, we may suppose in the second that I have correctly taken my own lack of enthusiasm into account in arriving at the verdict that it would be best for me to remain in that line of work. It might be the case, for instance, that none of the things I am genuinely enthusiastic about represent real-istic career options, so that the question of what I am to do to make a living must be based on other kinds of consideration altogether. Two observations seem to be in order about this kind of situation. First, it is unclear to me that we should really say about it that I do not *care* about my chosen career path. Intuitions on this point seem essentially divided. On the one hand, the fact that I am genuinely uninterested in (say) philosophy is one that we might be tempted to express with the claim that I do not really care about the subject. On the other hand, the further fact that I have correctly concluded that this is the line of work I should be involved in makes that very same claim ring rather false. If, for instance, I dili-gently apply myself to the subject despite my lack of enthusiasm, in the conviction that doing so is the best course open to me under the circumstances, I would thereby seem to demonstrate that I care about doing well in it, despite my under-lying lack of interest in the subject itself.[20] Divided intuitions of this kind suggest that the phenomenon of caring may not be sufficiently well defined to admit of uniform philosophical treatment.[21]

Whatever we end up saying about caring in this scenario, the more basic question is whether the lack of enthusiasm there postulated calls in question the identification of the person with the conclusions of evaluative reflection. My sec-ond observation about the scenario is that this does not appear to be the case. That I find myself unenthusiastic about the career option I have determined it would be best for me to pursue is regrettable, but in the unhappy scenario under considera-tion it does not entail that I am estranged from my practical judgment concerning the merits of the available alternatives. It is a fact of life that enthusiasm, keen interest, and caring in the affective sense cannot always be mustered in regard to

---

[19] This would bring the substantive model close to the 'reason view' defended by Susan Wolf, in *Freedom within Reason*. It should be noted, however, that the issues about moral responsibility and freedom that primarily concern Wolf do not align exactly with the questions about identification, authenticity, and autonomy to which the substantive model is addressed.

[20] Compare Frankfurt, 'The Importance of What We Care About', 85.

[21] In 'Comments on Frankfurt', *Synthese*, 53 (1982), 291–4, Alasdair MacIntyre raises the inter-esting question whether caring represents 'a residual category, the name for a ragbag in which is to be found a set of assorted items whose resemblance to each other lies chiefly in this, that they are no longer studied by moral philosophers' (p. 294).

the courses of action that we take ourselves to have most reason to engage in; this is among the factors that tempt us to act *akratically*, and that must be fought against if we are to succeed in translating our values into action.[22] (Another factor, of course, is our *excess* enthusiasm for alternatives that we have determined we should not go in for.) It would perhaps be pleasant if our interests and enthusiasms aligned perfectly and automatically with the conclusions of evaluative reflection. The fact that they do not, however, gives us no reason to question the claims of evaluative reflection to articulate our authentic and authoritative point of view on the world, as persons.

Independently from reflection on such cases, there may be some residual tendency to suppose that alienation from one's values must be possible.[23] Can't I find myself appalled by my own materialism and selfishness, and wouldn't this amount to a kind of estrangement from my own evaluative commitments and priorities? Certainly it sometimes seems natural to say things like this; the question is whether they really undermine the substantive model. I do not think they do. We need to be very clear about what exactly we are estranged from when we claim to be estranged from our own values. In the examples cited, the most plausible candidate, I would maintain, are patterns of action over time that reflect our own emotions and desires, where these in turn are essentially associated with evaluative thoughts, in the way sketched in section 1, above. When I reject my own materialism, for instance, I am rejecting my tendency to place inordinate importance on matters of material consumption and acquisition: the way conspicuous consumption presents itself to me as attractive, and the way in which this tendency influences my own choices and actions. Rejection of these tendencies must itself be motivated, however, and the standpoint which gives such rejection its authority is precisely the standpoint of evaluative reflection emphasized by the substantive model. Thus if I am appalled by my own materialism it must be the case that I question the evaluative thoughts latent in my own actions and feelings, and this

---

[22] What should be said about cases in which we give in to such temptations, and do what we ourselves agree would be wrong or ill-advised, on the whole? Intuitions about identification may seem to break down in such cases. Gary Watson, for instance, who in 'Free Agency' defends what I take to be a version of the substantive model, has more recently contended that cases of weakness pose a problem for that model. In his paper 'Free Agency and Free Will', *Mind*, 96 (1987), 145–72, at 149–50, Watson contends that agents who act 'perversely' by their own lights may nevertheless be fully identified with what they do. Here it is vital to recall the distinction between the issues of autonomy and responsibility drawn above. To the extent weak-willed or perverse agents fail to translate their own values successfully into action, we may say that they are estranged from what they do; they do not identify with their actions, in the way important to issues of authenticity and autonomy. On the other hand, they may still be identified with their actions in the different sense that they act freely, committing themselves to what they do in the way that could potentially open them to moral censure and blame. I develop a motivational psychology capable of doing justice to identification in this second sense in my paper 'Normativity, Commitment, and Instrumental Reason', Chapter 5 in this volume; see also my *Responsibility and the Moral Sentiments*, chs. 5–6. In the present paper however my focus, like Frankfurt's, is on identification in the first sense.

[23] See David Velleman, 'What Happens When Someone Acts?', as reprinted in his *The Possibility of Practical Reason* (Oxford: Clarendon Press, 2000), 123–43 at 134.

is itself a matter of first-order evaluative reflection (leading to the judgment, for instance, that conspicuous consumption is at best a source of hollow and ephemeral pleasures).[24] Far from undermining the substantive model, cases of estrangement from one's own values thus seem to presuppose it.

There is a different kind of example that might seem to raise doubts about the authority of evaluative reflection. This involves situations in which an agent reaches a clear verdict about what it would be best to do in contexts of decision that are themselves fairly trivial. Frankfurt himself offers the example of preferences regarding ice cream. If I like the flavor of (say) vanilla ice cream, it will probably be correct to say of me that I have reason to choose this flavor, and that the (moderate) consumption of vanilla ice cream is for me an intrinsically worthwhile activity. But it is equally likely that satisfaction of my ice cream preference is a matter of little or no real importance to me, something I do not really care about at all in the way that is significant for questions of identification. 'There is no incoherence in appraising something as intrinsically valuable, and pursuing it actively as a final end that is worth having in itself, and yet not caring about it.'[25]

Examples of this kind do not really tell against the substantive model, however. Here it is important to bear in mind that evaluative judgments represent responses to concrete contexts of decision. Thus the judgment that I have reason to choose vanilla ice cream is not a free-floating commitment that must compete with all my other commitments (to family, friends, projects, and the like). It is much more likely to be a response to a particular and constrained deliberative problem, such as the question of what to fix for dessert after a light summer meal. Within the deliberative context defined by this problem, my preference for vanilla ice cream might in fact be the most important consideration there is, so that the judgment that it would be best to have vanilla ice cream for dessert is that attitude with which I am most authentically identified. Of course, the deliberative context within which this judgment is arrived at is itself comparatively insignificant. It would be a mistake, however, to infer from the triviality of the deliberative context that the evaluative conclusion I draw within that context is one from which I am estranged in any way. There is a sense in which it seems right to say that considerations such as my preference for vanilla ice cream are matters of no real importance to me, in the grand scheme of things, and I shall discuss this kind of verdict in section 3, below. The present point is that the unimportance in this sense of my preferences regarding dessert is no basis for questioning the authority of evaluative judgments based on such preferences within their proper deliberative context. Often life presents us with deliberative problems that are in themselves comparatively trivial, and when this is the case, the sincere evaluative responses we devise

---

[24] A different possibility—to which Frankfurt is especially alert—is that one might be essentially ambivalent at the level of deliberative reflection. Whereas Frankfurt would construe such ambivalence in terms of conflicting highest-order attitudes, I would contend that it involves a tendency to endorse conflicting evaluative judgments.   [25] Frankfurt, 'On Caring', 159.

to these problems have as good a claim as any attitudes to represent our distinctive point of view.

The objections I have discussed to this point have all questioned the sufficiency of evaluative judgment for caring and identification. But Frankfurt seems to doubt the necessity of evaluation for caring as well. Thus it is a leitmotiv of his recent work that the persons and things we care most about, the objects of our love, do not engage our interest and attention because of our judgments regarding their antecedent value and importance.[26] We do not decide to care about a lover or a child (say), on grounds of a judgment about the independent worth of these persons or of the activity of caring about them. Rather we find that we care about particular persons and things, in a way that is both contingent and not subject to our own volitional control. And affective contingencies of this kind in turn determine what as a matter of fact is important to us. If we take caring to be the stance that is significant for questions of identification and authenticity, this suggests a basic doubt about the adequacy of accounts of the phenomenon in terms of the notion of evaluative judgment.

Again, however, it is important to keep clearly in focus the kind of evaluative judgments that figure in the substantive model, as well as the context of deliberation to which those judgments represent responses. Frankfurt is surely correct to remark that unwilled contingency plays a large role in determining whom and what we love. But it does not follow from this that our standpoint as agents cannot be identified with the point of view of evaluative reflection about what we have reason to do.

It is rarely (if ever) the case that we determine whom and what we love by deliberating about the question; rather we more or less fall into our loves, in processes that elude complete deliberative planning.[27] Contingencies of affection and interest of this kind are clearly of immense importance in determining the shape and direction of our lives, and among the more significant ways they affect us is by giving us *reason* to do things that we would not otherwise have reason to do. To take a very elementary example, if I happen to love *x*, then the fact that I do becomes highly relevant when I think about how I should organize my life. Depending on the circumstances, it may for instance provide a sufficient reason for engaging in any number of activities together with *x* (going to a film or to a bar on Tuesday, or moving in together for the summer). Contingencies of love and affection are in this way directly and highly relevant to deliberative reflection about action, even if these contingencies themselves escape our deliberative control. In holding that evaluative judgment is authoritative for questions of identification and personhood, the substantive model need not contend that the

---

[26] This theme seems implicit in many of the essays collected in the second half of *Necessity, Volition, and Love*. See e.g. 'On Caring', pt. 2, sect. 5.

[27] That love is contingent in this way does not mean that it is disconnected from evaluative thoughts about the value of the person who is loved. For a highly suggestive discussion of the evaluative commitments of love, see David Velleman, 'Love as a Moral Emotion', *Ethics* 109 (1999), 338–74.

reasons on which we base our conclusions about what it would be best to do are themselves matters that we have it in our power to influence directly. In can thus do full justice to the role of non-reasoned contingency in giving substance to our emotional lives.

It is possible that Frankfurt would object that this account casts the deliberations of the lover in an overly self-conscious and scheming light. There is an interesting passage in his paper 'On Caring' that contrasts the deliberations of a lover of x with those of a person acting out of duty, in situations in which each acts with the intention of helping x.[28] Frankfurt remarks that the dutiful and the loving agents both have the same reason for (say) giving money to x: 'namely, that the money will be helpful to him'.[29] The differences between them emerge when it comes to explaining why they regard the fact that giving the money would help x as a reason. The dutiful person takes this fact to be a reason, because they both believe that duty requires one to help x, and want to fulfill their moral obligations. With the lover, by contrast, the conception of the same fact as a reason can be explained solely by reference to the circumstance that they love x. There is no need to appeal in addition to the further circumstance that they want to do what love requires, since this is built into the circumstance that has already been appealed to; taking benefits to x to be reasons is in part *constitutive* of loving x in the first place.

This passage suggests a challenge to my account of the deliberative relevance of contingencies of love and affection. I proposed that lovers properly regard such contingencies as sufficient reasons for engaging in joint activities with those they love, in concrete contexts of practical deliberation. But Frankfurt might object that this assimilates actions done from love too closely to the paradigm of action out of duty. Just as the dutiful agent reflects on the fact that helping would be right from the perspective of the desire to act rightly, so I seem to have represented lovers as reflecting on the fact of their love itself, from the perspective of the desire to be good lovers (or something of that sort). This distorts the essential immediacy of the motivational structures of love and affection, and turns action out of love into something altogether too self-conscious and intellectualized.[30]

I would respond by saying that Frankfurt's account of the motivational structure of love strikes me as altogether too sentimentalized. The problems begin with the contention that the dutiful and loving donors both give money to x for the same reason, *viz.*, that doing so will help x. This contention confuses the agents' reasons with their immediate intentions; what the two donors have in common is the latter, not the former. Each donor *aims* to give x money, as a way of helping him, but

---

[28] Frankfurt, 'On Caring', 174–6.   [29] Ibid. 175.

[30] Frankfurt does not voice this complaint in so many words, but it seems strongly suggested by the things he does say. For instance: 'it is merely a tautology that a lover takes the fact that a certain action would be helpful to his beloved as a reason for performing the action. His taking it as a reason for performing the action is not the outcome of an inference. That it provides him with this reason is not a conclusion that the lover reaches by reasoning from the premise that he loves his beloved' (ibid. 176).

their *reasons* for performing this action are different. For the dutiful donor, the considerations that speak in favor of helping *x* might include the fact that *x* is in serious need, and that it would be wrong to refrain from helping people in serious need when one can do so at little cost to oneself. For the loving donor, by contrast, the considerations that recommend helping *x* include essentially the fact that *x* is someone they love. Nor does the emotional immediacy of love exclude self-conscious awareness of this fact on the part of the lover. On the contrary, only by incorporating this fact in the deliberations of the lover can we capture the exclusivity of the reasons that love provides. After all, from the perspective of the lover it is not the case that the considerations that recommend helping *x* also recommend helping any other needy agent who might happen to come along. Clear-thinking lovers will acknowledge that their emotional entanglement with particular persons gives them reason to attend to the needs of those persons that do not generalize to cases in which the emotional basis of love is lacking.[31] To think otherwise is to suppose that love is not merely immediate and spontaneous, but literally stupid.

I can only speculate as to why Frankfurt should have been tempted to deny this point. There is a kind of noncognitivism latent in his discussion of the motives of love and duty that seems to expunge from the conclusions of deliberative reflection the kind of content I have ascribed to them. Both the lover and the dutiful agent are represented as responding to the same 'reason', which is the plain fact that giving money will help *x*. They differ in the considerations that lead them to 'regard' this fact as a reason, where these considerations must account for their being actively motivated to provide monetary assistance. If we suppose that the additional motivating factor can only be something on the order of an essentially noncognitive pro-attitude, we will have cause to deny that the crucial difference between the dutiful and loving agents is a matter of the content of the reasons that they acknowledge and act on.[32] That difference must rather be located on the side of the brute psychic forces that incline the two agents to perform the single kind of action to which they both find themselves attracted.

---

[31] Two points of clarification are in order here. First I do not mean to deny that the reasons of the lover are implicitly general in form. In fact they are (though the lover will probably not focus on this dimension in the heat of action). Thus the clear-thinking lover would acknowledge that any other lover as well has reasons to attend to the needs of those they love that do not apply to nonbeloved persons whose needs are similarly acute. Second, it should be stressed that I am not claiming that the lover's reasons are primarily reasons of moral duty. Like Frankfurt, I agree both that there are special moral duties pertaining to those with whom we are involved in close relationships, and that lovers nevertheless typically act out of love rather than out of a sense of these special duties (ibid. 175; compare 'Autonomy, Necessity, and Love', 140). I also believe, however, that a sharper appreciation of the cognitive and normative commitments of ordinary loving action can help to soften the artificial dichotomy between the motives of love and duty; on this point, compare Velleman, 'Love as a Moral Emotion'.

[32] Actually, even on Frankfurt's own account there must be some differences in the content of the reasons on which the two agents act. The dutiful agent conceives their situation as one in which the helping act is commanded by duty, whereas the lover sees the situation as one in which their beloved would be assisted; otherwise the different motivational structures attributed to the two types of agent would not get a grip, as it were.

For reasons sketched in section 1, however, I do not find this noncognitive conception of desire plausible, and without it the way is open for a more perspicuous and compelling account of the different motivational structures of love and duty. In particular, we can acknowledge that emotional contingencies profoundly affect the deliberative reflections of lovers, providing them with reasons for action that they would not otherwise have, and appropriately altering thereby their conception of what it would be best to do.

3. REFLEXIVITY REDUX: THE CASE OF EUDAIMONISTIC DELIBERATION

To this point I have been primarily concerned to challenge Frankfurt's account of identification and personhood in terms of higher-order desires. Reflexivity may be the condition that makes possible identifying practical deliberation, but I have contended that such deliberation is normally an attempt to reach first-order conclusions about our reasons for acting in particular ways. In ordinary contexts, our well-grounded verdicts about what we have most reason to do define our authoritative standpoint as agents, and we are autonomous when we succeed in acting in a way that is guided by and in accordance with such evaluative verdicts.[33]

Having made these points, however, I now want to glean a more positive message from Frankfurt's reflections on caring and the structure of volition. In particular, I shall try to identify a basic if rather specialized context of practical deliberation that exhibits the kind of directly reflexive structure familiar from Frankfurt's writings, and that is closely connected to the issues of caring and importance that have figured so prominently in his recent work. This is the context of what I should like to call eudaimonistic reflection.

In reflection of this kind, we step back from the large patterns of concern that shape our deliberations about concrete problems, and think about those concerns themselves. By concerns here I mean the kinds of commitment and activity that most fundamentally color our personality as agents—what Christine M. Korsgaard refers to as aspects of our 'practical identity', and Bernard Williams calls our 'projects'.[34] Concerns of this kind serve to structure our ordinary deliberations about what to do in quotidian contexts, providing us with first-order reasons for

---

[33] I discuss the idea of guidance by one's conception of what there is reason to do in my paper. 'Three Conceptions of Rational Agency', Chapter 2 in this volume.

[34] See Korsgaard, *The Sources of Normativity*, 100–2; and Williams, 'Persons, Character and Morality', as reprinted in his *Moral Luck* (Cambridge, England: Cambridge University Press, 1981), 1–19. Korsgaard and Williams construe practical identities and projects as items that can successfully survive the kind of eudaimonistic reflection I am attempting to characterize; Korsgaard writes, for instance, that a practical identity is 'a description under which you find your life to be worth living and your actions to be worth undertaking' (*The Sources of Normativity*, 101). I shall construe projects and practical identities more broadly, as basic structural features of our character and personality that are open to assessment in eudaimonistic reflection.

choosing or rejecting particular alternatives that are open to us, in the ways already illustrated in section 2, above. In eudaimonistic reflection, however, we abstract from this dimension of our basic concerns, and think about those patterns of concern themselves, focusing on the contribution they make to our own lives.

The question we ask in this kind of context, I would suggest, is not in the first instance whether we are made happy or well-off by virtue of having the kinds of projects we do. Happiness and well-being do not seem to me to be necessary touchstones for eudaimonistic reflection, and particular projects can reasonably be affirmed through such reflection without making positive contributions along these dimensions of assessment. Thus, a devoted scientist or artist may endure great hardship and sacrifice in the interests of their grounding professional projects, and nevertheless affirm the contribution that these projects make to their own lives. In doing so, they would be asserting that their lives are made better by containing and being shaped by artistic and scientific activity—not happier or pleasanter, to be sure, but more worthwhile and meaningful.[35] For this reason it seems appropriate to refer to the reflection in question as 'eudaimonistic', since *eudaimonia* is properly construed not as a matter of happiness or well-being, but of living well as a human being.

Eudaimonistic reflection in this sense exhibits many of the features that Frankfurt takes to be important for identification and personhood. It is, in the first place, literally reflexive in a way ordinary practical deliberation is not. Take, for example, the kinds of projects or concerns that are most readily affirmed in contexts of this kind, namely significant work and personal relationships. Friendships and work provide us with all manner of first-order reasons for engaging in particular activities that promote the interests of our friends and the goals given by our professional projects. In eudaimonistic reflection, however, we abstract from these particular contexts of decision, and think about our friendships and professional projects themselves, focusing on the contribution they make to the meaningfulness of our own lives. This, I would submit, is a kind of deliberation that is appropriately characterized as reflexive.[36] Perhaps it would be misleading to say that deliberation of this sort is a matter of reflection on our first-order *desires*; certainly it does not proceed by focusing on first-order tendencies to action, construed in noncognitive terms as brute psychic pushes and pulls. Rather in eudaimonistic reflection we think about the emotional bases of our grounding projects (where these involve a significant cognitive dimension, as I argued in

[35] Frankfurt himself emphasizes questions of meaning in 'On the Usefulness of Final Ends', as reprinted in *Necessity, Volition and Love*, 82–94. Compare Susan Wolf, 'Happiness and Meaning: Two Aspects of the Good Life', in Ellen Frankel Paul, Fred D. Miller, Jr., and Jeffrey Paul (eds.), *Self-Interest* (Cambridge, England: Cambridge University Press, 1997) 207–25.

[36] It presupposes, for instance, the general ability to imagine alternatives 'of oneself' emphasized in Jan Bransen, 'Identification and the Idea of an Alternative of Oneself', *European Journal of Philosophy*, 4 (1996), 1–16. Note, however, that in some cases the projects on which eudaimonistic reflection focuses may be so fundamental to one's identity that one might not be able to imagine a concrete 'alternative of oneself' without them.

section 1, above), together with the activities that give expression to such emotions and commitments.

Second, the projects and concerns we affirm through eudaimonistic reasoning seem correctly describable as matters of importance to us, things we care about in an especially significant way. When we say, for instance, that the pleasures of vanilla ice cream (discussed in section 2, above) are of no real importance, we can plausibly be taken to mean that those pleasures are not among the items that register within the context of eudaimonistic deliberation, as making our lives meaningful or worthwhile. Frankfurt seems to me wrong to suggest that importance in this sense is necessary for identification—as I suggested above, in trivial contexts of decision our evaluative verdicts may be based on unimportant criteria of this kind, without that calling in question our identification with them for the purposes at hand. It is also worth bearing in mind that ephemeral bodily pleasures might well be among the things that do matter to a person, when thinking about what makes their life meaningful or worthwhile. There is nothing necessarily absurd or appalling about the view that at least part of what renders one's life worthwhile, from one's own point of view, is precisely the availability within it of a range of basic bodily satisfactions.[37] On the other hand, most of us would probably not contend that minor culinary pleasures (say) can really compete with the kinds of concern that centrally shape our deliberations as agents; we do not care about them in the same way, and this can be construed as a verdict reached in eudaimonistic reflection about the things that make our lives meaningful or worth living.

Third, endorsement of our projects and concerns in eudaimonistic reflection exhibits characteristic structural features that Frankfurt has drawn attention to in his recent work, involving relationships between means and ends. The kinds of projects that are most obviously important to us, such as close friendships and significant work, can be regarded as sources of final ends. Thus we have reason to help those with whom we are befriended for their own sake, regardless of the adventitious consequences of helping (within, for instance, our own hedonic economy). And yet, when we reflect on the contribution of friendship to our own lives, the fact that it provides us with final ends of this kind may be among the features that enable us to endorse it. Being the sort of person who has reason to help certain others for their own sake, in the way characteristic of friendship, may make our own lives more meaningful, insofar as it expands our horizon of concern and opens us to intense and otherwise inaccessible experiences.[38] On the other hand, certain activities that have instrumental value, because (for instance) they are useful or productive in some way, can also be inherently valuable to us precisely on account of their exhibiting this kind of instrumental value.[39] What makes it good

[37] Here a quotation from Gary Watson ('Free Agency', 104 n. 8) seems appropriate: 'It is reported that H. G. Wells regarded the most important themes of his life to have been (1) the attainment of a World Society, and (2) sex'.   [38] See 'On Caring', 172–4.

[39] Frankfurt, 'On the Usefulness of Final Ends', esp. 90–1; 'On Caring', 176–8.

for us to be committed to such activities for their own sake may in part be the fact that they represent forms of constructive work that are appropriate to our interests and talents. If we wish to emphasize the apparent air of paradox surrounding this, we could say that our projects are instrumentally valuable to us on account of the fact that they are sources of intrinsic or noninstrumental ends, and they are inherently valuable precisely insofar as they are instrumentally good in various ways.[40] Frankfurt goes on to suggest that traditional Aristotelian accounts of the relation between ends and means have neglected these complex reciprocal structures of justification[41]—a questionable assertion, in my view, but not one that it is necessary to go into here.

The example of Aristotle raises two further issues about eudaimonistic reflection that I should like briefly to touch on in conclusion. The first of these concerns the critical dimension of eudaimonistic deliberation. Aristotle himself appears to assume that reflection about questions of flourishing and the human good has critical potential. It is not merely the attempt to clarify what the deliberating agent happens, as a matter of contingent psychological fact, to care about, but raises questions about the worthiness of potential objects of care and concern. Moreover it seems to me that any plausible account of eudaimonistic reasoning should hold onto this critical dimension.[42] Without it, reflexive contemplation of our first-order projects and concerns threatens to degenerate into an exercise in getting in touch with one's feelings, rather than being a genuine example of reasoning or deliberation.

In saying this, I do not mean to suggest that perfectly objective answers are available to the question of what makes human life, in general, meaningful or worthwhile. Eudaimonistic reflection is distinctively conducted from the agent's own point of view. In asking whether a candidate project contributes to the meaningfulness of our lives, we do not want to know whether it is meaningful or significant for other people, or from the point of view of the universe, but whether it is meaningful for us, and this will in part be a matter of whether we can find meaning in the project, or see it as making our lives worthwhile.[43] We might concede that a given project is of a sort that can perfectly well contribute to the meaningfulness of a life, but not take our own lives to be meaningful in virtue of containing such a project. To this extent, eudaimonistic reflection will irreducibly be shaped by the personal sensibilities of the agent who is reflecting. On the other hand—and this

---

40 Compare Frankfurt, 'On Caring', 178.

41 See esp. 'On the Usefulness of Final Ends', 82–4.

42 Frankfurt would not necessarily disagree with this: see 'The Importance of What We Care About', sect. 6. He proposes one concrete criterion for critical assessment, namely that it be possible for the agent to care about a candidate project that is up for assessment (p. 94); but this clearly doesn't take us very far, since it is all too obviously possible for people to care about things that do not merit this attitude. Indeed, as I go on to argue in the text, eudaimonistic reflection typically begins from projects that an agent already cares about to some extent; in this deliberative context the question of the *possibility* of caring about the project up for assessment will already have been settled, and so be useless as a criterion that guides our critical reflection.

43 Compare Frankfurt, 'On the Usefulness of Final Ends', 85.

is where the critical dimension comes in—it should not be thought that absolutely anything goes, or that the question of whether our own lives are meaningful is sufficiently answered by appealing to the psychological fact that we happen to find them meaningful.

Earlier I suggested that the desires from which ordinary practical deliberation often begins can be viewed (in part) as cognitions of what we have reason to do, which are up for first-order assessment through the deliberation they provoke. In a somewhat analogous way, eudaimonistic reflection will typically take as its starting point some actual pattern of commitment or concern that already structures the deliberations and character of the agent; that a project plays this structuring role makes it the kind of thing that the agent is inclined to care about, as making their life worthwhile, and the question to be answered in reflexive deliberation about the project in question is whether this is a reasonable or appropriate attitude to adopt. What is called for in such critical reflection, I would suggest, is above all a matter of normative *articulation*. Eudaimonistic reflection is brought to a successful conclusion when agents are able to characterize their projects accurately as making a genuine contribution to the goodness of their own lives.

Consider the kinds of cases that seem paradigmatically able to survive eudaimonistic scrutiny: namely, close personal relationships and significant work. It seems fairly obvious that these sorts of projects admit of true descriptions under which they can be seen to make important contributions to the goodness of the agent's own life. Friends, for instance, not only have first-order reasons for helping those with whom they are befriended and engaging with them in joint activities, they also are open to a range of enriching experiences and possibilities of emotional support in virtue of their friendships, and these can correctly be viewed as contributions to the goodness of their own lives. In other cases, however, we may find ourselves unable to arrive at a plausible account of how our ongoing projects and relationships contribute to the goodness of our own lives. We may be working exhausting hours on projects that are both intrinsically and subjectively uninteresting, fetishistically pursuing a certain conventional image of success, when alternative ways of making a reasonable living are open to us. Or perhaps certain of the relationships we are involved in turn out on reflection to be exploitative, parasitic, or otherwise self-destructive and debasing.[44] In cases of this kind it seems plausible to say that the things we find ourselves caring about do not really merit this attitude, that they are not intelligible as positive contributions to the meaningfulness of our own lives, and the possibility of this kind of verdict is what gives eudaimonistic reflection its critical edge.

This brings me to morality, and to a final observation about eudaimonistic deliberation. I believe—though there is not the space to defend the claim here—that

---

[44] For a helpful discussion of the possibilities for critical reflection of this kind, see Annette Baier, 'Caring about Caring: A Reply to Frankfurt', as reprinted in her *Postures of the Mind* (Minneapolis: University of Minnesota Press, 1985), 93–108.

getting clear about the distinctively reflexive context of eudaimonistic deliberation can help us to understand better a traditional and important worry about the authority of moral requirements. The worry, forcefully expressed in certain writings of Bernard Williams,[45] is that morality has little chance of being important to us in the way our grounding projects and commitments are, and that it consequently cannot hope to compete when its demands threaten to constrain our pursuit of those projects and commitments. There is a strong echo of this worry in Frankfurt's papers on caring, the suggestion that morality is not the sort of thing that it makes sense to care about.[46] In the terms I have been developing, the idea would be that when we step back from our first-order reasons to comply with moral demands, and ask about the ways in which morality affects our own lives, it may be difficult to see it as making the kind of direct contribution that (say) close friendships and significant work can make. Complying with moral requirements may keep us out of trouble, and encourage others to cooperate with us in our projects, but these are at best indirect contributions, not things that in their own right make our lives worthwhile and meaningful.

This seems to me to be an important challenge, one that it is both necessary and illuminating to grapple with. At the same time, I would contend that traditional moral philosophy provides resources for thinking about this challenge that have hitherto been rather poorly understood. Thus, part of the appeal of such theories as utilitarianism, Kantianism, and contractualism in ethics is that they provide at least implicit articulations of the contribution that morality is capable of making to the goodness of the agent's own life. The role of autonomy in Kant's ethics, for instance, can be understood in these terms, as an account of the way in which our own lives are made more worthwhile by our compliance with the apparently austere demands of morality. Similarly, utilitarianism seems to rest on a personal ideal of transcendence, according to which our lives acquire meaning and significance through our contribution to the good of all sentient creatures;[47] while contractualism suggests a motivating ideal of free and open relationship to our fellows.[48] Much work remains to be done to characterize precisely the potential challenge to morality posed by personal projects and concerns, and the resources that moral philosophy can offer for responding to that challenge. But we should begin by situating both the challenge and the possible responses within the distinctive context of eudaimonistic reflection to which Frankfurt's work on the phenomenon of caring seems to point.

[45] See e.g. 'Persons, Character and Morality'.
[46] See e.g. 'The Importance of What We Care About', 80–2; also the preface to *Necessity, Volition, and Love*, p. x.
[47] Compare the ideal of transcendence discussed (though not endorsed) by Samuel Scheffler in *Human Morality* (New York: Oxford University Press, 1992), 120–1. The utilitarian vision of meaning through contribution to a cause that is larger than oneself finds especially clear expression in Peter Singer, *How Are We to Live? Ethics in an Age of Self-Interest* (Oxford: Oxford University Press, 1997).
[48] Compare Scanlon, *What We Owe to Each Other*, ch. 4.

10

Ressentiment, Value, and Self-Vindication: Making Sense of Nietzsche's Slave Revolt

In its broad outlines the account of the origin of modern morality that Nietzsche offers in the first essay of his *Genealogy* is reasonably clear. The account begins with the postulation of two different schemes of value, organized around the pairs of opposites good/bad and good/evil, which are associated respectively with the contrasting personality types of the noble and the slave. Characteristic of the slavish personality structure are the negative affects of hatred and *ressentiment*, which, deprived of a natural outlet, become pent up and fester within the psyche of the powerless until reaching 'monstrous and uncanny proportions' (GM, I. 7).[1] The slave revolt begins when these sentiments 'become creative and give birth to values' (GM, I. 10), initiating a historical process through which the universalistic, Christianized values of good and evil largely come to supplant the aristocratic values of good and bad.

Though this story is clear enough in its general outlines, however, it is not at all clear how exactly the psychological processes the story describes are really supposed to work. The crux is the causal relation that is posited between the *ressentiment* of the powerless slaves and the new table of values to which that psychic force allegedly gives rise. There is a natural way of thinking about this causal nexus—the strategic interpretation, as I shall call it—that makes sense of the basic idea that *ressentiment* should give rise to the erection of a new table of values, in an event that might accurately be described as a revolt. But I shall argue that the

Forthcoming in Brain Leiter and Neil Sinhababu (eds.), *Nietzsche and Morality* (Oxford: Oxford University Press); reprinted by permission. I received much stimulating feedback on earlier versions of this paper from audiences at the Humboldt University in Berlin, the University of Vienna, and the University of Canterbury in Christchurch. Brain Leiter provided helpful comments on the penultimate draft. I owe a special debt to Bernard Reginster for extensive and constructive suggestions about an early version of the paper, and in general for many stimulating discussions over the years about Nietzsche's moral psychology. Work on this project was conducted with the generous support of a Research Award from the Alexander von Humboldt Foundation.

[1] Parenthetical references in the text will be to sections of Nietzsche's *On the Genealogy of Morals*; other references to texts by Nietzsche will be given in notes. Quotations from the *Genealogy* will follow the Kaufmann and Hollingdale translation: Friedrich Nietzsche, *On the Genealogy of Morals*, trans. Walter Kaufmann and R. J. Hollingdale, ed. Walter Kaufmannn (New York: Vintage, 1989).

causal links postulated by this interpretation are ultimately untenable, yielding a narrative that is riddled with paradox at the level of both psychic mechanism and social process. We need a different, nonstrategic way of understanding how *ressentiment* could eventuate in Nietzsche's slave revolt, and the main aim of my paper will be to develop such an interpretation. To do so, it will be necessary to think systematically about the nature of *ressentiment*, and about the psychological situation of those who are subject to this emotion in a conceptual landscape defined by the aristocratic values of good and bad. The key to understanding how a new table of values might emerge under these conditions, I shall argue, is to acknowledge the profound human need for a distinctive kind of self-conception, one that I shall refer to as vindicatory. The *ressentiment* of the powerless leads them to internalize a new evaluative scheme that makes sense of their basic emotional orientation to the world. This expressive relation between emotion and value, I shall argue, is the crux for understanding Nietzsche's striking claim that the *ressentiment* of the weak is one of the main sources of modern moral consciousness.

Nietzsche's writings are among the most important documents in our philosophical tradition that grapple with issues in what we now call moral psychology. But not all of his reflections in this vein seem to me to be of equal value. His exploration of asceticism in modern moral consciousness, for instance, has less relevance today than in Nietzsche's own time, as social morality in the western world has moved away from the Victorian emphasis on instinctual self-denial as an end in itself. Some have celebrated Nietzsche's reflections on the will as examples of a laudably minimalistic or naturalistic approach to understanding the psychological preconditions of morality.[2] But this part of Nietzsche's ethical writing strikes me as overrated: there are ways of interpreting rational agency and volition that avoid his objections, and that seem superior to the mixture of epiphenomenalism and psychological determinism that he appears to recommend.[3] The real strength of Nietzschean moral psychology lies in his insight into the pathological deformations of personality associated with modern moral consciousness, especially where they involve the interplay of emotional forces and evaluative ideals. The account of the emergence of the good/evil table of value out of the *ressentiment* of the powerless is a brilliant example of this tendency in Nietzsche's polemical critique of modern morality, one that should repay the effort at critical reconstruction that it is my aim in this essay to provide.

1. THE STRATEGIC INTERPRETATION

I want to begin by sketching an interpretation of the psychic mechanisms involved in the slave revolt that seems to me to be implicit in much work on this

---

[2] See Bernard Williams, 'Nietzsche's Minimalist Moral Psychology', as reprinted in his *Making Sense of Humanity* (Cambridge, England: Cambridge University Press, 1995), 65–76.

[3] See e.g. my *Responsibility and the Moral Sentiments* (Cambridge, Mass.: Harvard University Press, 1994). Nietzsche flirts with epiphenomenalism at *Twilight of the Idols*, VI. 3, e.g., while characterological determinism is evident in GM, Preface, sect. 2, and throughout *Ecce Homo*.

topic. I am tempted to say that the account I shall describe is the default interpretation of the slave revolt, in part because it gives a clear sense to Nietzsche's characterization of this episode in cultural history as a 'revolt', in part because it captures at least some aspects of the complex historical process that Nietzsche is concerned to understand. But the default interpretation cannot be the whole truth about the slave revolt, for reasons that I shall also try to explain.

The psychological force that drives the slave revolt, on any account of it, is the *ressentiment* of the slaves. The strategic interpretation understands this emotional orientation primarily in terms of its aim. *Ressentiment* is a negative affect of hatred on the part of the powerless toward their oppressors, involving the desire to strike out against them, in ways that will harm them and deprive them of their cultural and social advantages. The slave revolt may then be thought of strategically in relation to this fundamental aim, as an undertaking that is precisely calculated to harm the powerful. The inferior position of the powerless means that they are unable to pursue this goal directly, through actions that are immediately damaging to the interests of the powerful. So they resort to a more indirect strategy, erecting a new table of values as a devious way of undermining the position and advantages of the people they despise.

There are several considerations that speak in favor of this strategic reading of the slave revolt. For one thing, Nietzsche himself often writes about the events involved in the slave revolt in strategic terms. He describes the invention of the Christian ethic of love, for instance, as part of a 'truly grand politics of revenge' on the part of the Jewish people (GM, I. 8), suggesting that it was a calculated effort to strike a blow against the oppressors of Israel. To the extent this political characterization is accurate, the slave revolt must involve activities on the part of at least some of its proponents that are conceived of strategically in relation to the goal of harming the powerful masters. The strategic interpretation takes this political dimension of Nietzsche's account to capture the defining moment of the slave revolt, which consists essentially in activities undertaken with the aim of subverting the power and position of those whom the powerless hate.

Furthermore, understanding the slave revolt in these strategic terms fits with other things that Nietzsche prominently says about it. Thus *ressentiment* plausibly involves the desire to inflict harm on those at whom it is directed, so the aim that is central to the strategic interpretation is one that *ressentiment* may be understood to supply. According to the strategic interpretation, *ressentiment* becomes 'creative' when the desire to achieve that aim finally becomes insistent enough to lead to action. And insofar as the actions in question are undertaken with the aim of inflicting harm on the powerful, they can be characterized accurately as a form of revolt. They are attacks on the politically and socially powerful, which are expressly calculated to undermine their position and to harm their central interests.

In these respects, then, the strategic interpretation would seem to recommend itself, as a natural way of understanding the processes that Nietzsche is describing in the first essay of the *Genealogy*. But the interpretation cannot ultimately be sustained; I want to identify three insuperable difficulties that arise when we think about the slave revolt in the terms that it suggests. First, there is a basic problem that is encountered when we try to make sense of the intentions with which the new table of values was erected. The strategic account interprets this as an activity whose goal is to land a blow against the strong and powerful. It is very hard to understand, however, why anyone would choose to pursue this goal by a strategy so feckless and obscure as the erection of a new table of values. This strategy is reasonable only if the new evaluative scheme is something whose articulation and propagation is likely to damage the interests of the politically and socially powerful. But why should the weak believe that the evaluative activities in which the slave revolt consists would have this effect? If the powerful are truly powerful, they could be expected simply to ignore the evaluative scheme that is proposed as an alternative to their own, or perhaps to suppress attempts on the part of the weak to advocate in its defense. The strategic interpretation requires that the weak understand the erection of a new table of values in the logic of instrumental rationality, as a course of action that is effective relative to the goal of revenge against the powerful. But unless they are massively deluded, it seems highly unlikely that they would be able to think of their actions in these terms. Doing so simply does not seem to make much sense.

For similar reasons, the strategic interpretation renders mysterious the historical effects of the slave revolt, as Nietzsche describes them. At the end of the seventh section of the first essay in the *Genealogy*, Nietzsche famously remarks that the slave revolt in morality has a history of two thousand years, which we are no longer able to see clearly precisely because it has been victorious. If we think about the revolt in the terms which the strategic interpretation provides, then its victory or success should consist in revenge, where this in turn involves harm or damage to the powerful, of a kind that perhaps eventually leads to their virtual elimination. But why should the erection of a new table of values have had this effect? One would think the truly powerful would simply brush aside the new evaluative rhetoric of the slaves, or crush politically the weak and slavish people who resort to such rhetoric in daily life. In short, the considerations that make it mysterious why the weak would think of their actions as effective means of revenge against the powerful equally render mysterious the postulated success of those actions over the centuries.[4]

There is a third difficulty, however, that is even more serious than the first two problems I have described. This is that the slave revolt becomes a self-undermining process if we conceptualize it in the terms that the strategic interpretation proposes. To this point I have spoken of the slave revolt as involving the erection

[4] For a clear statement of this problem, see Mark Migotti, 'Slave Morality, Socrates, and the Bushmen: A Reading of the First Essay of the *Genealogy of Morals*', *Philosophy and Phenomenological Research*, 58 (1998), 745–79. In sect. 2, below, I shall offer a different response to the problem from the one Migotti favors.

of a new table of values, as if this were a mere act of rhetoric or transparent propagandizing. But it is clear that Nietzsche does not understand the revolt in such superficial terms as these. It occurs, he says, when *ressentiment* becomes creative and gives birth to values, and this process involves more than merely the invention of a new discourse or set of evaluative terms. Values come into existence only to the extent a new discourse of value is internalized and taken seriously, as a framework for organizing life and experience. An evaluative framework of this kind leads one to prefer some things to others, shaping one's deliberations about action, and providing a basis for criticizing social institutions and individual behavior. But the erection of a new table of values, to the extent it is undertaken with the aim of exacting revenge against the powerful, would precisely fail to give rise to values in this sense.

To see this, we need only note that the new values are supposed to take root in precisely the population whose members are subject to pent-up hatred and *ressentiment*. The strategic interpretation takes these emotions to supply the powerless with a goal—the destruction of the noble class—that the invention of new values is calculated to bring about. But the strategic understanding of the revolt on the part of the slaves undermines the very processes that the revolt itself is supposed to consist in. We can speak of the invention of new values only insofar as the scheme organized around the opposition between good and evil comes to be internalized by the slaves, as a comprehensive framework of the sort described above. A scheme that the slaves themselves understand in strategic terms, however, cannot really play this role in their lives. To the extent the scheme is viewed strategically, as an instrument of revenge, it cannot function as a fundamental framework for preference, deliberation, and criticism. And to the extent it plays these roles, it cannot be viewed by the agent whose experience it fundamentally shapes as a device that is calculated to bring about revenge.[5]

It might be thought that these difficulties can be avoided if we postulate—as Nietzsche's text would seem to allow—that the strategic calculation involved in the slave revolt occurs at the level of unconscious psychic processes. Perhaps the slaves are not really aware that they embrace the evaluative scheme of good and evil as a way of achieving revenge against the powerful. In that event they might fully internalize those values while remaining ignorant of the strategic goals that the process of internalization was originally calculated to achieve. I would agree that Nietzschean *ressentiment* operates beneath the radar of consciousness in the slave revolt, and also that there are conflicts and tensions between the unconscious forces that sustain modern morality and the content of the values in which that

---

[5] Similar questions about the slave revolt are raised by Rüdiger Bittner, '*Ressentiment*', in Richard Schacht (ed.), *Nietzsche, Genealogy, Morality: Essays on Nietzsche's 'Genealogy of Morals'* (Berkeley and Los Angeles: University of California Press, 1994), 127–38. Bittner develops his objection in the language of agency, suggesting that it undermines the idea that the slave revolt is the result of a creative act on the part of the slaves (cf. pp. 133–4). I agree with him about this (understanding action to be behavior undertaken through the logic of strategic rationality), but disagree that it tells against Nietzsche's story (rather than a common interpretation of that story).

morality consists. But these facts do not suffice to remove the problem I have been attributing to the strategic interpretation. For one thing, the unconscious motives at work on the strategic interpretation still involve the aim of achieving revenge against the powerful, and it remains obscure why the slavish should believe at any level, conscious or unconscious, that their invention of a new table of values is likely to advance this aim. (This is a further application of the first objection canvassed above.)

Moreover, it seems implausible to suppose that the unconscious processes at work in Nietzsche's account of the slave revolt follow the linear logic of instrumental rationality that is central to the strategic interpretation. Those in the grip of *ressentiment* and hatred may well have desires to harm and thwart the powerful that they are not fully aware of, at the level of conscious reflection. But it would be peculiar if unconscious forces of this kind operated to sustain the values of modern morality through calculations centered on the relation between means and ends. Unconscious processes tend to follow more primitive logics of association, expression, and symbolic representation. The question is, how exactly might such unconscious processes be involved in the Nietzschean narrative of the origins of modern morality?

2. THE EXPRESSIVE INTERPRETATION

The strategic interpretation sees the meaning of the slave revolt as lying in its instrumental relation to an end that is given by *ressentiment*. The aim it attributes to *ressentiment*, namely to inflict harm on the hated masters, seems one that genuinely belongs to it. But *ressentiment* is more than merely a desire to inflict harm or suffering on someone. How exactly *ressentiment* goes beyond a mere desire to harm is not something that Nietzsche himself spells out very explicitly.[6] To make sense of the role Nietzsche ascribes to this emotion, we need to supplement the letter of his texts with an independent examination of the phenomenon to which he is drawing attention, situating *ressentiment* more precisely in relation to other social sentiments and reactions. By attending systematically to the circumstances that plausibly nurture this complex emotional phenomenon, I shall argue that we can arrive at a more satisfactory understanding of the causal role of *ressentiment* in generating and sustaining the new evaluative framework of good and evil.

---

[6] In GM, I. 10, where the concept is first explicitly introduced, Nietzsche characterizes *ressentiment* as a reaction against a hostile external world, and he contrasts the 'reactive' mode of evaluation to which to *ressentiment* gives rise with the self-affirmation involved in aristocratic evaluation. Drawing on these passages, Brian Leiter suggests that the 'core elements' of *ressentiment* include 'a negative, evaluative reaction to an external state of affairs that is unpleasant but which one cannot address through physical action'; see his *Nietzsche on Morality* (London: Routledge, 2002), 204. But this characterization is at once obscure (what is an 'evaluative reaction'?) and underdescribed. Not every negative reaction to an unpleasant and unyielding stimulus counts as *ressentiment*. To arrive at an illuminating account of the moral psychology of *ressentiment*, we need to think more systematically about the distinctive features of the emotion and the circumstances in which it emerges, drawing on Nietzsche's texts, but going beyond them to arrive at a fuller picture.

Ressentiment can be understood as a general emotional orientation of the person. It emerges under conditions in which people find themselves systematically deprived of things that they want very much to possess, without any prospects for improvement in this respect. But systematic deprivation is not sufficient for the emergence of *ressentiment*. If everyone was equally subject to a condition in which they are denied coveted goods—as for instance in a natural emergency, such as a devastating famine or earthquake—the result might be a tendency to feelings of rage, frustration, and depression in the populace at large, but not the kind of focused hatred characteristic of *ressentiment*. For the latter emotions to emerge, there need to be some people who are singled out from the rest in not being deprived of the coveted goods, and who are publicly known not to be deprived. The Ur-context of *ressentiment* is one in which some people have things that you very much desire, but that you lack and feel yourself unable ever to obtain. Thus Nietzsche's slaves are systematically excluded from enjoying many of the desirable things that the masters in their society have in abundance, including status, material possessions, and above all political power and influence.[7] *Ressentiment* is fundamentally occasioned by invidious comparisons of this kind.

In the circumstances that give rise to it *ressentiment* bears some similarity to envy, which is also about a person's lack of access to goods that others are conspicuously able to enjoy. But envy does not have the quality of intense and focused malice that distinguishes *ressentiment*. It seems perfectly possible to envy someone their wealth or professional good fortune, say, without wishing them ill or feeling any particularly negative affect toward them personally. Envy of this variety might be structured by the thought, 'I'm just as good or deserving as he is', and one can entertain this thought without believing that the target of envy is unworthy or undeserving in any way; nor does this emotion require one to feel hostility or hatred toward the person who is envied. These latter forms of focused negative affect, which seem very much characteristic of Nietzschean *ressentiment*, emerge under circumstances that structurally prevent a person from ever coming to enjoy the desired goods that the more fortunate have access to in abundance.[8] Ordinary envy might well be assuaged by one's coming into possession of the desirable items

---

[7] I take it here that one of the most important desiderata for an account of *ressentiment* is the fact that Nietzsche associates it paradigmatically with the outlook of the slavish. We should therefore expect that its origin and structure would reflect features that are distinctive of the position of slaves within a culture, and comparative structural deprivation seems highly salient in this connection.

[8] Compare Bernard Reginster, 'Nietzsche On *Ressentiment* and Valuation', *Philosophy and Phenomenological Research*, 57 (1997), 281–305, at 286. A more extensive treatment, which also emphasizes the structural conditions that give rise to *ressentiment*, is Max Scheler, *Das Ressentiment im Aufbau der Moralen* (Frankfurt am Main: Vittorio Klostermann, 1978), ch. 1. In GM, I. 10, Nietzsche entertains tentatively the possibility that noble types might occasionally be subject to feelings of *ressentiment*, remarking that such feelings will immediately be discharged by the noble person who is subject to them, and so fail to fester and grow. This might appear to be at odds with the suggestion that *ressentiment* grows out of structural deprivation. But we can imagine that the masters Nietzsche is here thinking of are only selectively deprived of things that they desire (e.g. a given sexual partner or political office), in ways that are compatible with lack of deprivation in many other domains of their life and experience.

that one formerly lacked, as when a person finally wins the raise or the profes-sional standing that they took themselves all along to deserve. Envy grows into *ressentiment* when ordinary rectification of this kind is (believed to be) impossible, because one is systematically prevented by one's nature or one's circumstances from acquiring the things that one so covetously desires.

Nietzsche shows great psychological insight in his assumptions about the trans-formation that envy undergoes under conditions that involve structural deprivation of this kind. The intensification of hatred into which envy grows becomes focused specifically on the persons who are comparatively privileged; though it is occa-sioned by relative disadvantage, it is no longer really about the fact of relative dis-advantage, but about the individuals who are advantaged, whom the unfortunate come to despise. But why should envy come to assume this quality of personal hatred under conditions of this kind? What explains its transformation into an affect that is essentially focused and personal in the way I have described? This question may not have any very deep or illuminating answer. The process through which ordinary envy turns into the kind of personal animus involved in *ressenti-ment* cannot plausibly be traced to any further emotion or complex of ideas. It seems to me a primitive mechanism, one that can perhaps be understood to reflect our deeply social nature, our nearly obsessive concern for our relative standing within local and less local communities. Under conditions of structural depriva-tion, in which we permanently lack access to what Rawls calls the social bases of self-respect, the ordinary tendency to envy may be transformed into something quite different: an intensely personal loathing of those who are more fortunate than we are.

This focused emotional orientation toward the fortunate involves the desire to lash out at them that was discussed in the preceding section of this paper. The strategic interpretation correctly attributes desires of this kind to the slavish types in whom *ressentiment* flourishes. But it goes wrong in its account of the relation between such desires and the new table of values to which *ressentiment* gives rise. The fundamental emotional dynamic of the slave revolt is not the selection of means to an end that is set by one's desires. It is the *expression* of one's negative emotional orientation toward the powerful, in the embrace of an evaluative framework that makes sense of that basic orientation.[9]

To understand this emotional dynamic, we need to reflect on the situation of the powerless in the period immediately preceding the invention of the new table of values. *Ressentiment* has festered within these people for years, building up to the point where it becomes the dominant emotional orientation of their lives.

---

[9] Similar ideas are sometimes vaguely hinted at in the secondary literature. For example, in *Nietzsche on Morality*, 202–4, Brian Leiter describes the slave revolt as a 'projection' of the *ressentiment* of the slaves. See also Bittner, '*Ressentiment*', 133–4, who remarks that suffering and *ressentiment* might give rise to new moral convictions in something like the way a disease gives rise to symptoms. But neither Leiter nor Bittner offers any detail about how exactly the new table of values might be understood as the projection or symptom of an emotion such as *ressentiment*. It is the burden of my paper to try to work out in clear terms this central Nietzschean idea.

This involves a concentration of hatred and hostility directed toward the people in their society who are powerful, successful, and outwardly flourishing. At the same time, the evaluative framework that is available under these cultural conditions characterizes the objects of this concentrated negative affect as precisely good in a superlative degree. In the terms of the evaluative schema of good and bad, it is the aristocratic masters who are paradigms of positive value, and the characteristics that distinguish them from the rabble—their superior discernment, independence, confidence, and so on—are singled out for praise and celebration. So the powerless find themselves in a conceptual situation in which the negative affect that dominates their emotional lives is directed at individuals whom they themselves seem compelled to regard as exemplars of value and worthy of admiration. This is a highly unstable combination of attitudes, one which is antithetical to the slaves' ability to make sense of their own deepest emotional experience.

In my view, the slave revolt should be understood as a response on the part of the slavish to this psychic tension.[10] The weak are subject to attitudes that color their experience of the social world, in ways that cannot be reconciled with the dominant ethical ideology that they themselves have so far accepted. So they come to embrace a new and more congenial scheme of values. This new evaluative scheme is the expression of their underlying *ressentiment*, insofar as its adoption can be explained in terms of that emotional orientation, which is postulated to be prior to it in the order of causation. *Ressentiment* becomes creative and gives birth to values when the tensions that attend it lead the powerless to adopt and internalize a wholly new evaluative framework. The causal nexus linking *ressentiment* to this new framework does not follow the logic of means/end rationality, but the more archaic pattern of emotional self-interpretation. The slaves adopt the scheme of values organized around good and evil, because doing so enables them to make sense of their experience of the world, which is mediated by the sentiments of hatred and *ressentiment*. If the masters are evil, then hatred of them becomes a response that is merited by its object, and the latent tensions in the world view of the slaves are thereby resolved.

This way of understanding the causal role of *ressentiment* in the slave revolt—the expressive interpretation, as I shall call it—has several immediate advantages. For one thing, it makes very good sense of some of the more prominent strands in Nietzsche's reflections about the slave revolt. Nietzsche emphasizes repeatedly, for instance, that the negative pole is basic in the morality of good and evil, and he contrasts the resulting scheme in this respect with the more affirmative morality of

---

[10] In *Das Ressentiment im Aufbau der Moralen* Scheler also treats the slave revolt as a response to psychic tensions in the self; see e.g. 32–4. A similar approach is developed by Reginster in 'Nietzsche on *Ressentiment* and Valuation', who emphasizes the tension between the repressed desire for power of the aristocratic priests and their inability to satisfy that desire overtly, a tension that is crystallized in their experience of shame; see e.g. Reginster, 'Nietzsche on *Ressentiment* and Valuation', 286–7, 296–7. But Scheler and Reginster give an account very different from mine of how tension is released through the slave revolt, one that remains wedded to the structures of instrumental rationality, and that ultimately treats the new values as pieces of false consciousness.

good and bad. The concept of evil, Nietzsche says, is 'the original thing, the beginning, the distinctive *deed* in the conception of a slave morality' (GM, I. 11, p. 40; cf. GM, I. 10). This fits well with the idea that the slavish scheme has its origin in the need to make sense of the essentially hostile affect of *ressentiment*. The problem to which the new morality is a response is the fact that this hostile orientation is directed at objects that have heretofore been regarded as superlatively good. What is required, in light of this problem, is a different way of conceptualizing the landscape of value, one that represents the objects of *ressentiment* as worthy of this kind of negative orientation. By coming to see them as evil, one can experience one's own deep hostility as something that is appropriate to its object, and to the extent this is the case the category of evil is indeed the 'original thing . . . in the conception of a slave morality'. It is the original thing in the sense that the invention of this category is what most basically resolves the psychic tension to which the slave revolt is a response.

Furthermore, the expressive interpretation attributes a plausible causal role to the unconscious forces of hatred and *ressentiment*. These are pictured as combining with the prevailing ethical framework of good and bad to create a situation of acute psychic tension and instability. The powerless might not be fully aware that they are in the grip of *ressentiment*, but the focused and intense hatred it involves will inevitably color their experience profoundly, in ways that sit very uneasily with the dominant ethical ideology of good and bad. Under these circumstances their whole emotional orientation toward the social world will be fraught with latent tension and conflict; it will not cohere with the values that they themselves accept and attempt to live by, and this tension and conflict will be experienced as forms of anxiety, discomfort, and alienation. The contribution that the new table of values makes is essentially to resolve this acute psychic discomfort, something that is likely to be experienced by the weak as profoundly satisfying. This is the primitive dynamic of self-interpretation to which I earlier referred, and the supposition that unconscious processes might operate in accordance with this dynamic has the ring of truth to it.[11]

This is one respect in which the account I have proposed seems clearly superior to the strategic interpretation, with its postulation of unconscious calculation about means and ends. But Nietzsche clearly does use the language of strategic agency in his discussions of the slave revolt. To take just one example, the 'revaluation of

[11] To the extent the internalization of new values relieves the anxiety and discomfort of the slavish masses, it might be described as a means to that end. It does not follow from this, however, that the expressive processes I have postulated operate through the logic of instrumental *rationality*. A process implicates this form of rationality when its operation requires the agent to conceptualize their actions in terms of the relation between means and ends (either consciously or unconsciously). The expressive processes I have described, however, do not require the agent to think about them in this way. The slaves adopt new values because doing so helps them to make sense of their emotional experience, thereby relieving a condition of psychic distress; but they do not need to be aware, at any level, that the adoption of new values will bring about this effect. (I am indebted to Herlinde Pauer-Studer for pressing me to be clearer about this point.)

values' in which the slave revolt consists is characterized by him as 'an act of the most spiritual revenge' (GM, I. 7, p. 34), a characterization that suggests calculation with the aim of striking out against the masters. How is this tendency in Nietzsche's theory to be reconciled with the expressive interpretation, which understands the slave revolt in fundamentally nonstrategic terms?

To answer this question, we need first to think about Nietzsche's suggestion that the erection of a new table of values amounts to a revolt. This political language acquires a straightforward meaning on the strategic interpretation, which represents the powerless as engaged in a course of action whose avowed aim is to strike a blow at the masters, and hence as a kind of uprising. The expressive interpretation, by contrast, treats the erection of new moral values in nonstrategic terms, as in the first instance a response to psychic tensions internal to the outlook of the slavish. A psychological process of this kind would not seem to be political in its overt meaning or in the intentions with which it is carried out. But it might nevertheless inadvertently be a process of great political significance, carrying political meanings in its effects if not in its intent, and this is the way I would suggest we think about Nietzsche's talk of revolt. The response to the pent-up tension that the powerless experience is their invention of a new ethical vocabulary, where this is to be understood not as a cynical rhetorical display, but as the acceptance and internalization of a new evaluative framework for organizing their responses to the world. To take this step, under the conditions that prevail at the time of the slave revolt, is in effect to challenge the authority of the masters to be the final arbiters in questions of value. Their verdicts about what is good and bad are no longer taken as valid or regulative for the responses of everyone, and to the extent this is the case their superior standing in normative questions will have been called into question. By challenging the normative authority of the masters in this way, the slaves may be thought of as having initiated a revolt, even if it was not their conscious or implicit aim to do so.

In the preceding section, I raised the question of how the slave revolt could possibly have succeeded over time, in the way Nietzsche clearly believes that it has. If the revolt is the attempt to strike out directly against the masters by erecting a new evaluative scheme, it is hard to understand how it might have been successful on its own terms; the superior position of the masters should have ensured their immunity to the effect the slaves were—however obscurely—aiming to achieve. On the alternative interpretation I have proposed, the central moment of revolt is not the immediate attempt to inflict physical or psychic harm on those who are powerful, but rather the challenge to their normative authority that is implicit in the acceptance of a radically new evaluative framework. If this is what the revolt essentially consists in, however, then we get a very different and more intelligible account of its eventual success. The challenge to the authority of the masters will have been successful when they are no longer taken to be the final arbiters in questions of value. For this condition to be achieved, it is only necessary that more and more people come over time to internalize the new table of values organized around the concepts of good and evil. How this might occur is not at all difficult to understand. Supposing that the new values really do fit well with the psychic structures characteristic of pent-up *ressentiment*, it is only natural that they would take firm root among the oppressed and frustrated masses in urbanized European culture, coming eventually to be the dominant evaluative schema for individual deliberation and social criticism.

In thinking about this historical process, there is no need to suppose, initially at any rate, that the strong types should themselves accept the new values of the slavish masses, in a process akin to religious conversion. This would represent a direct capitulation to slave morality, something that would indeed be hard to make sense of as the deliberate act of a genuinely higher nature. Nevertheless the cultural authority of the strong will effectively be undermined, and their broader interests thereby damaged, when the alternative value system they espouse has been eclipsed and marginalized through the dominance in the population at large of modern, Christianized morality.[12] Moreover, once this process has been set in motion, we may suppose that it will have further, indirect effects over time on the ability of those with the native capacity for distinction to realize their true potential. Thus Nietzsche suggests that the ideological parameters of modern life, in which a large majority have taken to heart a system of values that supports leveling, democratic, egalitarian policies and practices, are inimical to the emergence and development of higher individuals.[13] Under these social conditions, there will be fewer and fewer truly distinguished specimens of humanity, the natural successors to the aristocratic nobles of an earlier era. Furthermore, such higher types as are able to emerge will lack the confidence of their predecessors; their thinking will inevitably be corrupted by the ethical orthodoxy under which they came to maturity, which will leave traces in their own evaluative outlook.[14] These outcomes are for Nietzsche a potential source of nihilistic despair about modern culture, and at least one basis for his multifaceted criticism of the slave morality that is prevalent in that culture (cf. GM, I. 11, I. 12).[15]

---

[12] The slave revolt does, then, eventually inflict harm on the masters, as the strategic interpretation maintains, insofar as it undermines their cultural authority. But the expressive interpretation supplies the mechanism whereby this kind of harm is gradually inflicted, a mechanism that is missing when the revolt is thought of exclusively in terms of strategic rationality. This mechanism operates without our needing to suppose that the masses deliberately aim to inflict harm on the masters through their adoption of the new value scheme.

[13] Nietzsche clearly assumes that modern European culture has a leveling and egalitarian tendency that is inimical to the development of higher specimens of humanity; see GM, I. 12, on 'the diminution and leveling of man' (p. 44), also the 'Anmerkung' at the end of the first essay of the *Genealogy*, with its discussion of the effects of an evaluative scheme on 'producing a stronger type' of human being (p. 56). It is not perhaps entirely clear why the democratizing values of modernity should have had this effect; one could imagine that a hereditary aristocracy would lead the rulers over time to become decadent and effete, while a culture that gives opportunities to everyone might tend to encourage genuine innovation and continual renewal (in spiritual and intellectual domains, at any rate, if not necessarily on the battlefield).

[14] See e.g. GM, III. 14, where the masses are described as having 'poison[ed] the consciences of the fortunate with their misery' (p. 124), making them ashamed of their good fortune; also GM, I. 16, where it is said to be the decisive mark of the higher natures in contemporary culture to be 'divided in this sense and a genuine battleground of these opposed values' (p. 52).

[15] For a persuasive and comprehensive treatment of this important theme in Nietzsche's philosophy, see Bernard Reginster, *The Affirmation of Life: Nietzsche on Overcoming Nihilism* (Cambridge Mass.: Harvard University Press, forthcoming).

With this account of the slave revolt in hand, let us now return to the issue of Nietzsche's strategic descriptions of the processes in which the revolt consists. The most important thing to note about this issue is that Nietzsche distinguishes clearly between the masses of *ressentiment*-filled slaves, and a smaller group, the so-called priestly aristocracy, whose relation to the slavish masses is complicated. On the one hand, the priests are described as having an emotional orientation to the social world that has much in common with the powerless masses. It is in them, for instance, that hatred is said to have grown to 'monstrous and uncanny proportions' (GM, I. 7, p. 33), a hatred that stems primarily from their impotence vis-à-vis the noble warrior class. In this respect, then, the aristocratic priests would seem to share with the masses the kind of *ressentiment* that is rooted in a situation of irremediable structural deprivation. On the other hand, the priests are precisely unlike the powerless masses in constituting an aristocracy of their own. They are a group apart from the masses, being superior to them in qualities of mind and character, in ways that make it fitting to speak of them in the language of nobility.

Now it is striking that Nietzsche's strategic descriptions of the slave revolt apply primarily to the activities of the priestly aristocracy. Thus it is the Jewish priestly class that is said to have practiced a 'secret black art of truly grand politics of revenge, of a farseeing, subterranean, slowly advancing, and premeditated revenge' in advancing the new table of values (GM, I. 8, p. 35; cf. GM, I. 7). This can be reconciled with my expressive interpretation of the slave revolt in the following way. We may suppose that it is a reflection of the superiority of the priestly aristocracy that its members take a clear-eyed, strategic attitude toward the processes in which the slave revolt basically consists. Those processes involve the acceptance and internalization of a new set of values, on the part of a populace whose deepest emotional experience is thereby rendered intelligible. I have argued that this emotional dynamic would not succeed if the powerless masses viewed the new table of values in strategic terms, as something to be advocated solely as a way of striking a blow against the master class. The aristocratic priests, I now want to suggest, grasp the susceptibility of the masses to this dynamic, and exploit it expressly for the purpose of undermining the power and position of the warrior class. That is, without really accepting the new table of values themselves, they cynically advocate on its behalf, in the expectation that the values will catch on over time among the masses who join with them in resenting the power of the political aristocracy.[16] There is, in other words, a strategic dimension to the slave revolt, but strategic rationality does not capture the primary psychological dynamic in which that revolt consists. It is rather a secondary or parasitic

[16] Contrast Reginster, 'Nietzsche on *Ressentiment* and Valuation'. Reginster takes the psyche of the priests to be the primary site at which the slave revolt takes place, and he supposes that it leads the priests to be deeply self-deceived about the nature of their own real values; see pp. 289, 291, 297. By contrast, I take the priests to be initiators and facilitators of a process that takes place elsewhere, in the psyches of the slavish, and to be free from self-deception about their values and aims as they play this role. This interpretation fits better the overt strategic language Nietzsche deploys in talking about the role of the aristocratic priests.

phenomenon, which characterizes the thinking not of the masses in whose psyches the revolt takes place, but only of an elite group, the priestly aristocracy.

In at least one respect, however, it may be misleading to characterize the strategic calculations of the priestly class as a secondary phenomenon in relation to the slave revolt. Nietzsche often represents the priestly nobility as the driving force behind the revolt. In section I. 7 of the *Genealogy*, for instance, he says that it was the Jews ('that priestly people') 'who, with awe-inspiring consistency, dared to invert the aristocratic value-equation' (p. 34), a statement that suggests that the priests played the leading role in the revaluation of values. Similarly, in *Beyond Good and Evil* (sect. 261) Nietzsche apparently denies that the slaves have it in them to create values, suggesting that this is uniquely the prerogative of those who are by nature masters. But this strand too can be reconciled with my interpretation. We may suppose that it was the priests who originally thought to invert the noble values of good and bad, articulating for the first time a different way of conceptualizing the landscape of value. To the extent this is the case, we may say that they created the new values, and that their act of creation is temporally prior in the chain of events in which the slave revolt consists. At the same time, however, this act of creation would not have succeeded in bringing new *values* into existence unless there were other people in the world who were emotionally primed to internalize the new evaluative vocabulary that the priests had invented. It is for this reason that I described the role of the priests as secondary. Their genius can be said to consist in the invention of an ideology that is precisely calculated by them to mesh with the emotional orientation of the oppressed masses. They thus deliberately set in motion and nurture the expressive processes through which the slaves come to embrace a new evaluative scheme, processes that constitute, strictly speaking, the true birth of new values.[17]

This account of the role of the ascetic priests attributes to them a devious plan to achieve genuine revenge against the masters whom they hate, a revenge that involves harming the masters, and undermining their comparative cultural authority and political and social advantages. At times, however, Nietzsche appears to describe the revenge that is involved in the slave revolt in less literal terms. Of the psychic force that becomes creative and gives birth to new values, for instance, he says that it is 'the *ressentiment* of natures that are denied the true reaction, that of deeds, and compensate themselves with an imaginary revenge' (GM, I. 10, p. 36). Here he seems to be talking about the very force that is at work in the expressive dynamic I have been discussing in this section, the *ressentiment* of the masses that leads them to embrace the new values of good and evil. In what sense can their doing this be characterized as compensation for their literal impotence, through a revenge that is merely imaginary?

---

[17] To the extent the aristocratic priests are engaged in this strategy of premeditated revenge, their activities can straightforwardly be characterized as a revolt, insofar as they are aimed at undermining the power of the masters. Thus the multifarious processes in which the revolt consists will involve both overt and covert political meanings.

There is nothing particularly mysterious about the idea that thoughts and fantasies can provide psychic gratification for a person whose options for action are in reality limited. Gratifications of this kind belong to the archaic logic of unconscious processes, which operate in accordance with assumptions about the 'omnipotence of thought' that are characteristic of infantile mental life. We all experience pleasures that reflect the continuing latent operation of these patterns of thinking in adult life, as for instance when we indulge in sadistic fantasizing about someone who has done us wrong, or daydream about the victory of the political party that we have been working in vain to support all these years. It would be no surprise if the unconscious *ressentiment* of the masses provided a source for archaic satisfactions of this kind, involving an imaginary revenge against the powerful who are the objects of this focused negative affect.[18]

The more interesting question is why the internalization of the new table of values should provide an occasion for the operation of this kind of mental process. To do so, it would need to involve a representation of the powerful in thought, as suffering the kind of harm or comeuppance that might be imagined as revenge. But it is not at all clear why Nietzsche might have thought that the slave revolt itself involves representations of this sort. As a result of the revolt the slaves come to think of the powerful masters as supremely evil, but to think of them in these terms is not to represent them (either consciously or unconsciously) as having been harmed or undermined in any way.[19] Perhaps Nietzsche supposes that the powerless are dimly aware of their new moral scheme as a challenge to the authority of the masters; building on this dim awareness, they might imagine themselves to be striking out against the masters in doing something that eventually will undermine their superior position. This is reminiscent of the strategic interpretation, with the difference that the act of harming the masters is not part of a postulated unconscious calculation, but rather something that is fantasized about by the slaves.[20]

A different and more likely possibility is that the element of fantasized revenge is not so directly connected to the acceptance of new values in which the slave revolt consists. After all, in the passage quoted above Nietzsche does not strictly say that the slave revolt itself is a form of imaginary revenge, only that it is the result of the kind of *ressentiment* that compensates for impotence through such revenge. Perhaps Nietzsche is merely noting that the same psychic force that

---

[18] Contrast Bittner, '*Ressentiment*', 132–3. Bittner suggests that this kind of fantasizing can provide psychic gratification only if the agent is (temporarily) unaware that they are fantasizing. But this seems to me to be untrue to experience, perhaps underestimating the extent to which infantile patterns of mental activity leave traces in adult life.

[19] A person can be evil and still, by all outward measures, flourishing.

[20] This way of understanding Nietzsche's talk about imaginary revenge would entail that elements of strategic thinking infect the outlook of the slavish masses themselves (at least at the level of fantasy), not merely that of the priestly aristocracy. It would not follow, however, that the expressive interpretation would thereby have been supplanted. On the contrary, the mechanism whereby the fantasized revenge is enacted precisely presupposes the susceptibility of the masses to the expressive processes I have described.

becomes creative in the slave revolt also finds expression in other forms of modern Christianized thought, ones that involve fantasies in which the powerful are brought low and made to suffer. The most obvious example would be Christian stories about damnation and the last judgment, such as the remarkable passage from Tertullian that Nietzsche quotes extensively toward the end of the first essay of the *Genealogy* (GM, I. 15). On this reading, which I myself would favor, the element of imaginary revenge is not really integral to the slave revolt itself, but rather a by-product of the unconscious psychic forces that are primarily at work in the creation of new values, and further evidence of their pervasive presence and operation.

3. VALUE AND EMOTION

The expressive interpretation seems to me to make good sense of the central processes that Nietzsche is describing in the first essay of the *Genealogy*. But there are large philosophical questions that the interpretation raises, questions that need to be grappled with before we can really take seriously the account Nietzsche is offering of the role of *ressentiment* in giving birth to new moral values. In this section I shall address four sets of issues.

A first question concerns the primacy of *ressentiment* vis-à-vis value. Nietzsche's genetic story assumes that the powerless are subject to *ressentiment* before they embrace the values that are organized around the pair of opposites good and evil. This emotional orientation becomes pent up in the psyches of the weak, growing ever more intense until it finally gives birth to new values in the slave revolt. It is the priority of *ressentiment*, its temporal precedence and logical independence from modern values, that enables us to explain the acceptance of those values by appeal to this emotional state. But it is not clear that we can really make sense of *ressentiment* as an emotional condition that is independent of an evaluative framework or point of view.

There are in fact two aspects to this potential difficulty. One is the general concern that *ressentiment*, like many emotional states or conditions, makes sense only against the background of an evaluative commitment of some kind or other. Pride, for instance, presupposes that one takes oneself to have done or produced something that is good and worthy of admiration, while shame is an emotional response to an aspect of oneself that one views with dismay, as vicious, or disfigured, or base. If *ressentiment* is like these emotions in presupposing an evaluative framework, then it may be doubted whether we can appeal to it to account for the adoption by the slaves of the values through which they view the world. A second and related aspect of this problem is that some of the specific values potentially associated with *ressentiment* seem at odds with the new values that the emotion is said to give rise to. Thus it seems that we experience *ressentiment* toward people when they are in a conspicuously good way in comparison to ourselves, and when we feel that we are prevented from realizing the goods that they exhibit or manifest in a striking degree. This suggests that the target of *ressentiment* must be conceptualized in positive terms, as possessing things or properties that are worthy of admiration and pursuit. But this positive evaluation of the targets of *ressentiment* is precisely at odds with the negative assessment of them that is integral to the morality of good and evil. To express the problem as a paradox, *ressentiment* appears to presuppose the very values that are repudiated in the slave revolt; but then the new table of values that is internalized by the slaves would preclude them from feeling the very sentiment that is supposed to find expression in their act of revolt.[21]

These problems can be illustrated by looking at two emotions that are superficially similar to Nietzschean *ressentiment*, namely resentment and envy. Resentment is a reactive sentiment that is bound up with our tendency to hold people morally accountable for their actions. Its distinctive feature—at least this is what I have elsewhere argued[22]—is its connection to moral demands. In the paradigm cases, one resents another person when one believes that they have wronged one, doing something that violates a moral obligation to which one holds them in one's interpersonal relations. If this is right, however, then resentment is an essentially moral sentiment, presupposing the acceptance of moral standards on the part of the agent who is subject to the emotion. An emotion with this structure clearly cannot be called on to explain the agent's fundamental moral outlook, since an outlook of that kind is implicated in the emotion itself. Similarly, many episodes of common envy seem to be occasioned by one's awareness of the person envied as good or admirable in some way or other. One envies the person who is supremely confident in social situations (when one is not oneself), or who is sharp or clever or successful or unusually attractive. Here the danger is that the emotion is bound up with a positive evaluative assessment of its target, in a way that is at odds with the superlatively negative evaluation in which the emotion finds expression in the slave revolt.

But Nietzschean *ressentiment* is precisely unlike both resentment and ordinary envy in these respects. As interpreted in the preceding section, it is a kind of focused hatred that grows out of a situation of structural comparative deprivation, and its essential features are psychically primitive by comparison with both moralized resentment and common envy. To be subject to this sentiment, one needs to

---

[21] Reginster, in 'Nietzsche on *Ressentiment* and Valuation', takes the opposite response to the paradox from the one I would favor. He affirms that noble-valuation is built into the experience of *ressentiment*, and denies that the new values are genuinely accepted by the priests in whom the slave revolt takes place, who are said to be deceived about what they really value (see e.g. pp. 296–7). By contrast, I deny that *ressentiment* really presupposes the acceptance of the aristocratic values repudiated in the slave revolt.

[22] See *Responsibility and the Moral Sentiments*, ch. 2. The distinctions between Nietzschean *ressentiment* and moralized resentment appear to be overlooked in Robert C. Solomon, 'One Hundred Years of *Ressentiment*: Nietzsche's *Genealogy of Morals*', in Schacht, (ed.), *Nietzsche, Genealogy, Morality*, 95–126, esp. 103, 115–18.

conceptualize oneself as lacking access to things that other people in one's social world conspicuously possess, where this is experienced as a kind of deprivation. Deprivation might in turn appear to be an evaluatively laden concept, implying that the things one lacks access to are good or valuable along some dimension. But it does not need to be evaluatively colored in this way. To experience oneself as deprived by comparison to others it is enough that there are things that one simply desires to possess, things that other people have and that are unattainable for oneself. In these terms, the psychic structure of Nietzschean *ressentiment* might involve a susceptibility to elemental desire or longing, the kind of brute urge observable in young children when they strike out at their siblings or make off with their playmates' toys. If it makes sense to attribute such primitive desires to adult human beings, then a conceptual framework will be in place that will make possible the kinds of experiences that give rise to Nietzschean *ressentiment*. There is no need to postulate that the slavish evaluate the powerful as genuinely good, still less need we assume that they take themselves to have been wronged by those whom they come to hate, in the style characteristic of moralized resentment.[23]

The crux, then, is the idea that the powerless masses are subject to a kind of longing or desire to possess things that is intelligible independently of evaluative concepts and attitudes. If this idea is plausible, then we can make sense of their *ressentiment* as a phenomenon that is primary vis-à-vis the value system that the emotion is invoked to explain. Now I myself do not believe that ordinary, conscious desire really is intelligible apart from an evaluative point of view.[24] But we should recall that Nietzschean *ressentiment* is not among the surface phenomena of mental life; it is rather an unconscious state of mind, which colors the agent's experience of the world without reaching to the level of full conscious awareness. It seems to me quite likely that the desiderative states operative at this unconscious level of psychic functioning are states of archaic bare striving to possess, states that do not imply the acceptance or application of evaluative concepts on the part of the agent in their grip. If this right, however, then psychic structures would seem to be in place that render intelligible the kind of *ressentiment* that Nietzsche's explanatory narrative requires. The experience of structural deprivation that is essential to *ressentiment* can be made sense of in terms of the frustration of archaic

[23] A different possibility is that those in the grip of *ressentiment* view the powerful as *possessing* things of value, without necessarily *being* good or admirable themselves (for instance, in the dimension of ethical assessment of character). This kind of evaluative framework would seem compatible with, and so leave room for, the extreme negative assessment of the masters that is involved in the new table of values to which *ressentiment* eventually gives rise. I doubt, however, that the tensions within the evaluative outlook of the slaves would entirely be eliminated by this way of understanding *ressentiment*. In terms of the new table of values, among the things that make the powerful evil are precisely their possession of traits and qualities that the weak presumably covet themselves (including, above all, power and strength); cf. GM, I. 7, also the parable of the lambs and the birds of prey in GM, I. 13. So if *ressentiment* involves essentially a positive evaluation of those traits and qualities, it will be at odds with the new forms of assessment to which it itself is supposed to give rise.

[24] See my 'Addiction as Defect of the Will: Some Philosophical Reflections', Chapter 8 of this volume. See also T. M. Scanlon, *What We Owe to Each Other* (Cambridge, Mass.: Harvard University Press, 1998), ch. 1.

desire, and the priority of *ressentiment* vis-à-vis evaluation that Nietzsche assumes can thus be maintained.

A second set of questions about Nietzsche's account concerns the gratification that I have suggested would be occasioned by the acceptance and internalization of new values on the part of those in the grip of *ressentiment*. The idea is that these values would speak to an unconscious need to which the powerless are subject, enabling them to make sense of their basic emotional orientation to the social world, as one that is appropriate to its immediate object. But this idea may seem to sit uneasily with a different strand in Nietzsche's account of modern morality, his depiction of it as a kind of pathology. It seems clear that Nietzsche views the Christian morality of good and evil, especially in its asceticized form, as a fundamentally unhealthy psychic formation, one that is inimical to the forces necessary to sustain life itself, and a cause of exquisite suffering and torment. The evaluative framework of good and evil allows the powerless to characterize their hated enemies in superlatively negative terms. But its requirements, especially in the 'moralized' and 'ascetic' guise they assume over time, also become instruments for rechanneling aggressive energies back against the self who is their original subject (GM, II. 21, III. 15). These energies, which first come on the scene as responses to suffering (GM, III. 15, p. 127), thus become co-opted into a psychic economy that intensifies the suffering to which they originally were a response, leading Nietzsche to describe asceticized Christian morality as 'the true calamity in the history of European health' (GM, III. 21, p. 143, cf. GM, II. 19).[25]

This interpretation of modern moral consciousness as a profound pathology, a device for the internalization of aggressive instincts that intensifies the suffering of those who are in its grip, may seem hard to reconcile with the idea that the same evaluative framework originally served to gratify a psychic need on the part of the slaves. But in fact these aspects of modern morality are not really incompatible with the expressive account I have been developing. Nietzsche himself is always alert to the ways in which a single phenomenon can bear multiple meanings, having causal consequences (for instance) that are multifaceted, and that ultimately work at cross-purposes. In the case at hand the supposition would be that a phenomenon that originates in the satisfaction of a psychic need might at the same time, through an instantiation of the law of unintended consequences, be disadvantageous in relation to other psychic processes, and hence a source of both gratification and suffering. Thus modern moral values might be adopted because they enable the weak to make sense of their emotional experience of the world, even though those same values become co-opted into a system for intensifying the torment of the agent who is in their grip.

---

[25] These processes are unhealthy, I take it, for the masses who accept the ideology of ascetic morality, increasing their suffering and inhibiting in them the very instincts necessary to sustain life itself. To characterize modern morality in these terms, as a form of psychic pathology, is of course not to say that the masses could realistically do any better.

Given the deleterious consequences Nietzsche attributes to the Christianized morality of modernity, it would in fact be highly peculiar if it did not gratify some psychic need on the part of the masses who have embraced it, and the drive to make sense of one's emotional situation seems well suited to play this role. Nietzsche invokes a similar drive at the end of the third essay of the *Genealogy*, noting that the incorporation of ascetic ideals into Christian morality enables the suffering to make sense of their condition, presumably as one that is deserved on account of their inherently sinful nature (GM, III. 28).[26] On my interpretation, essentially the same drive (or 'will') to understand and to attach meaning to one's situation is at work in the original transformation of *ressentiment* into a new evaluative scheme.

In both contexts in which it appears to play a role, the need for meaning operates in a distinctive way. In particular, it does not give rise to a clear-eyed or scientific understanding of the psychic forces actually at work in the people who seek to make sense of their situation in the world; their internalized aggression and *ressentiment* remain, to a large extent, beneath the surface of consciousness. What happens, instead, is that the powerless masses are led to think about themselves in terms that are essentially evaluative, and that therefore provide a kind of vindication of their most fundamental ways of experiencing the world. Thus suffering acquires a meaning under the ascetic interpretation of morality, becoming a cosmically just condition, one that is peculiarly fitting for the profoundly sinful natures we take ourselves to be.[27] Similarly, the interpretation of the powerful masters as embodiments of evil enables the slavish masses to make sense of their emotional experience, insofar as the immediate object of their *ressentiment* can be thought of in terms that render this powerful sentiment peculiarly appropriate. The evaluative self-conception that is made possible by these forms of moral consciousness I shall call vindicatory, since its point is to provide a kind of justification for the conditions of life that are characteristic of the suffering masses.

This aspect of Nietzsche's position, however, raises a third set of questions. For one thing, there is something puzzling about the claim that the evaluative scheme of good and evil provides a vindication of the slaves' emotional experience. For the new values to which the slave revolt gives rise have a content that condemns the very emotion that originally motivated them and that continues to sustain them over time. This is the aspect of Nietzsche's narrative that has led some to see it as delivering the materials for a kind of internal critique of modern moral consciousness. Thus from the standpoint of one committed to such Christian values as patience, humility, pacifism, and justice, it would presumably be an embarrassment

[26] See also *Thus Spoke Zarathustra*, I. 15, and *The Gay Science*, sect. 1.

[27] Here it is perhaps misleading to speak of self-vindication, insofar as ascetic morality precisely serves to characterize the person who accepts it as pervasively sinful. This moral outlook nevertheless provides a value-laden vindication of some aspect of the situation of the self in the world, in this case the experience of suffering. It is in this broader sense that the notion of 'self-vindication' should be construed.

to learn that the psychic forces that sustain these very commitments amount to forms of personal hatred and *ressentiment*. Far from vindicating the slave's emotions, the new table of values actually appears to undermine their moral legitimacy.

This is correct as far as it goes, but it is not grounds for rejecting the expressive account. The inconsistency it reveals is not a feature of my interpretation of the slave revolt, but of the outlook of the slaves in whom the expressive processes take place. Thus it is a matter of surface paradox rather than psychic impossibility that the values embraced in the slave revolt should provide a basis for criticizing the very emotions that gave rise to those values in the first place.[28] The emotional experience of the slaves is vindicated through the adoption of values that brand the hated masters as evil. But those same values, if consistently applied in an exercise of honest self-assessment, would lead the slaves to lament their original susceptibility to the feelings of *ressentiment* that so deeply color their experience.[29] That the evaluative and emotional structure they inhabit is unstable in this way is part of what makes their predicament so highly problematic, on Nietzsche's account of it. There is no way for them to satisfy completely their desire for self-vindication while confronting the whole truth about their own emotional situation.

But why is it that human beings need self-vindication of this kind? What accounts for the drive to make sense of one's condition and orientation in evaluative terms, as one that is appropriate, or just, or fitting? I am not certain that there is a good Nietzschean answer to this question, at the end of the day. It might simply be a contingent psychological fact that many people need to understand themselves in this way, as subject to conditions that can be made sense of through the lens of an evaluative framework. As an empirical generalization this would seem to be a plausible hypothesis, which receives some confirmation from such common phenomena as psychological rationalization. The alacrity with which people grasp at specious justifications for their political preferences and personal behavior is remarkable, and suggests the operation of a deep need to think of oneself in terms that provide vindication for one's attitudes and behavior.

But is this psychic need really so prevalent a feature of human life? Consider the outlook of the priestly aristocracy. I have suggested that the members of this class should be understood as taking an essentially cynical attitude toward the slave revolt that they foment in the masses. Without themselves accepting the new values of good and evil, they encourage the powerless to accept and internalize those values, seeing this as part of a strategy to undermine the masters over time. This strategic orientation of the priests to the slave revolt seems to assume that they are able to accept their hatred of the masters for what it is, without needing to accept

---

[28] Nietzsche's account of ascetic ideals in the third essay of the *Genealogy* exhibits this same kind of complexity. There the need that is gratified in ascetic morality, namely the need to inflict harm, serves only to increase the suffering of the agent to which that need itself originally was a response.

[29] This is presumably part of what keeps the psychic forces of *ressentiment* and hatred beneath the radar of consciousness.

the vindicatory self-narrative to which the ordinary masses cling. They are simply people who despise the powerful masters, for no other and no better reason than that the masters are in possession of things that they too would like to possess, but that they have no access to. And so they strike out against the masters, acting strategically with the aim of inflicting harm on them and eventually undermining their superior position entirely.

Indeed, it seems plausible to assume that the ability to understand and accept their true emotional orientation on its own terms, without seeing it as justified by or appropriate to its circumstances, may be a sign of the higher nature of the priests in comparison to the powerless masses. They form a kind of aristocracy precisely insofar as they are not driven to internalize an evaluative rationalization of their essentially hostile emotional experience of the world. It would not be quite accurate, however, to conclude from this that the priests feel no need whatsoever to accept a vindicatory interpretation of themselves. Nietzsche in fact writes as if the need for this kind of self-conception were a fairly universal feature of human psychology, treating it as perhaps the most fundamental manifestation of the will to power that he virtually identifies with life itself. Thus even the original valuations of the aristocratic warrior class, through which the scheme of values good/bad is articulated, are described as serving as instruments of self-glorification.[30] Similarly, insofar as the priests are able to see themselves as striking a strategic blow against the hated masters, they will be able to make sense of their experience in terms of the aristocratic values that they continue to accept. Their hatred might not ultimately be justified by intrinsic features of its object, but because they take positive action against the masters, they can understand themselves as exhibiting the kind of self-assertion and strength that the noble table of values precisely celebrates. Their good fortune by comparison with the slaves consists in part in their ability to construct a vindicatory narrative of their own situation in the world while retaining a kind of clarity about their own psychic needs and emotions that is missing in the benighted masses.

A final set of questions I want to touch on concerns the metaphysics of value that Nietzsche's account of the creative dimension of *ressentiment* requires. Nietzsche's immediate interest, it seems clear, is in the relation of evaluative structures to the emotions and experiences of the person who accepts them. Values are not thought of as systems of propositions that might be considered true or false representations of an independent domain of evaluative fact; rather they are interpreted as expressions of distinctive personality types, and assessed by reference to their effects on the persons who accept and internalize them. This general way of

---

[30] See *Beyond Good and Evil*, sect. 260. Nietzsche here (and also in sect. 261) contrasts the active mode of valuation of the masters with the passive or receptive mode that is characteristic of the slaves, a contrast that might appear to suggest that the slavish mode of valuing things is heteronymous, and entirely indifferent to any need for self-vindication. But the later sections of the third essay of the *Genealogy* make clear that the will for meaning is equally at work in the valuations of the masses in modern culture, however passive or perverted those valuations might be in other respects.

approaching questions about value is suggestive of a kind of anti-realism, which denies that there are any independent facts of the matter about values or norms. And Nietzsche has in fact been interpreted along these lines, as (for instance) an anti-realist about (nonprudential) value, who holds that there are no objective facts about good and evil, because such facts are not needed to explain the psychological phenomena that Nietzsche is primarily interested in.[31] Raymond Geuss offers a pithy statement of this outlook in the following summary of Nietzsche's metaethical position: 'In the final analysis there is just the mass of human individuals and groups exercising power or being dominated, succeeding or failing at various projects, and, at a slightly eccentric angle to this world of direct action, a flux of admiration of various things by various people and of disgust at various things by various people who have or have not tried and have or have not succeeded in influencing their own reactions of admiration and disgust.'[32]

There are numerous passages in Nietzsche's writings that hint at a metaethical position of this kind. But I am not convinced that these passages should be taken completely at face value. It is not obvious to me that Nietzsche was really interested in offering a consistent theory of the metaphysics of value, a worked-out position that might be assigned a precise position on the landscape of metaethical views. His dismissive remarks about objectivity in the realm of value can often be read as polemical invitations to attend to the role of evaluative outlooks within the economy of human drives and purposes. When he writes, for instance, that 'nature is always valueless, but has been *given* value at some time',[33] he is, strictly speaking, saying that there are no mind-independent facts about value; but his *aim* in saying this is to get us to think about the psychological process of investing things with value.

Furthermore, this interest in the moral psychology of value is in the service of a more comprehensive critique of modern morality, and it is hard to reconcile these critical purposes of Nietzsche's with a literal anti-realism about reasons and values. At least part of his critique of modern morality focuses on its deleterious consequences for the emergence and development of genuinely higher types of humanity, people who can inspire confidence in the species, and counteract thereby the

---

[31] See Leiter, *Nietzsche on Morality*, 146–55.

[32] Raymond Geuss, 'Nietzsche and Morality', 191. Geuss goes on to suggest that the flux of admiration and disgust 'gives rise to a wide variety of different "oughts"' (ibid.). But the acknowledgment of local and contingent 'Verbindlichkeiten' of this kind is actually at tension with the metaethical picture that Geuss ascribes to Nietzsche. Either there is, in the 'final analysis', just a flow of attitudes such as admiration and disgust, or there is in addition to such natural psychological facts a set of distinctively normative or evaluative claims about what variously situated individuals have reason to do. The fact that 'Verbindlichkeiten' are local and contingent rather than universal does not make them part of the natural flux of human attitudes and reactions. (The difference here is that between an anti-realist position that holds that there are no true claims about what anyone has reason to do, and an 'internalist' position that allows for such truths, but holds that reasons are conditioned by the desires and attitudes of the agent who has them.)   [33] *The Gay Science*, sect. 301.

tendency to nihilism in contemporary culture. This critical argument becomes completely banal, however, if we attribute to Nietzsche himself an anti-realist conception of the evaluative and normative domains. According to this kind of metaethical position, there is nothing that is genuinely and independently valuable, or worthy of choice, admiration, and pursuit; there are merely the preferences and desires that different people happen to have at different times and for different things. We might be able to say that contemporary morality is bad *for* the higher specimens of humanity, insofar as it is deleterious to their interests and their flourishing. But we cannot say either that these 'higher' types really are superior examples of human nature in themselves, or that it is an objectively good thing that they should come into being and flourish. Nietzsche himself simply happens to admire the kinds of people he refers to as higher types, and so his criticism of modern morality comes down to the charge that it frustrates the satisfaction of his own preferences concerning the development of the species (preferences that he presumably hopes his readers will share).[34] If this is what his critique amounts to, however, then an appropriate response would be, 'So what?' Why should anyone care whether modernity is hospitable to the contingent preferences and desires of Nietzsche and his targeted readers (as opposed, say, to the preferences of the masses)? The whole critical animus of his account seems to make sense only if we take the distinction between higher and lower types objectively, as marking a genuine distinction of rank in regard to the development of human nature and potential, and only if we take it to be an objectively good thing that genuinely higher natures should be able to come into existence and flourish.[35]

For these reasons, I think it is difficult to attribute to Nietzsche himself a straightforwardly anti-realist conception of (nonprudential) value and reasons for action. How exactly his critique of modern morality can be reconciled with his occasional anti-realist pronouncements is a problem, to which I do not have a

[34] Leiter pretty much embraces an interpretation of Nietzsche's critical project in just these terms, in *Nietzsche on Morality*, 149–50. He recognizes that this reading may not seem to comport with Nietzsche's unqualified critical conclusions, but dismisses this tendency in Nietzsche as rhetorical excess; see *Nietzsche on Morality*, 153–5.

[35] Against this, it might be said that it overlooks the distinction between metaethical reflection about moral discourse and its metaphysical commitments, and the first-order 'moralizing' that goes on when we deploy moral discourse in practice. Nietzsche's critical animadversions on modern morality serve to express his strong attitudes about the development of the human species, and there is nothing in an anti-realist view that would preclude such moralizing discourse from being as vigorous as one might please. (Compare Simon Blackburn, *Ruling Passions* (Oxford: Oxford University Press, 1999)—though Blackburn is a 'quasi-realist', not an unvarnished anti-realist about morality.) But I think the question remains as to why the rest of us should take Nietzsche's vigorous moralizing seriously, if it really functions as the anti-realist presumes. Furthermore, Nietzsche himself does not distinguish hermetically between first-order moralizing and metaethical reflection. His apparently anti-objectivist pronouncements are sprinkled throughout the works in which he is conducting his critical examination of the value of moral values, and this makes it seem very artificial to ignore them for purposes of thinking about that critical project. Given the integral relation of those pronouncements to Nietzsche's critical project, we cannot take them as straightforward statements of an anti-realist metaethical view, for the integration of such statements into his polemic would seem at cross-purposes to his critical intentions.

worked out solution (beyond suggesting that these pronouncements can be read as polemical invitations to think about value as a psychological phenomenon). Leaving aside the issue of Nietzsche's own metaethical views, however, it seems plain that Nietzsche does not think that people in general hold an anti-realist conception of the good. His own account of our evaluative practice and our emotional experience suggests that we take values to be objective in the way that anti-realism denies, so that if he is an anti-realist about this domain, his view will amount to a kind of error theory. This can be seen very clearly by reflecting on his account of the slave revolt, as I have reconstructed it in this paper.

Consider the role of values in relation to the *ressentiment* of the slavish masses. I have characterized this relation as one of expression, and the language of expression might seem to comport well with a noncognitivist interpretation of evaluative discourse. But the details of the expressive account I have developed in fact preclude such an interpretation. *Ressentiment* finds expression in the slave revolt through the postulated need for vindicatory self-understanding. The adoption of a new table of values satisfies this need, however, only on the assumption that the new values capture independent facts of the matter about genuine distinctions of merit. The emotional orientation of the slaves is vindicated in the relevant sense when it can be experienced by the slaves as one that is uniquely appropriate to its object, insofar as the object is taken to be evil. The sense of vindication thus operates on the supposition that the values that are affirmed in the revolt are prior to and independent of the emotional stances that they are taken to validate. We might put this by saying that the expressive dynamic at work in the slave revolt requires that the slaves themselves do not understand the values they embrace in expressive terms.

Of course it is possible that people are mistaken to view their values in this objective way. Nietzsche could himself favor an anti-realist position, even while granting that values are generally *taken* by people to be objective; in that event, as I noted above, his position would have the shape of an error theory. But it is an interesting consequence of this that Nietzsche's account of the creative aspect of *ressentiment* can to some extent be detached from larger issues in metaethics about the objectivity of value. As long as one is prepared to concede that evaluative discourse carries a claim to objective validity, one will be in a position to take seriously Nietzsche's story about the way in which *ressentiment* gives rise to new values. This means that even those of us who are not attracted to an anti-realist account of value might be able to take on Nietzsche's central insights about the role of the emotions in relation to evaluative consciousness.

In the contemporary world, those insights seem likely to have their primary relevance not in relation to the universalistic morality of the Enlightenment, but in connection with such phenomena as religious fundamentalism and nationalistic self-assertion. Countless people live today under conditions of structural comparative deprivation of the kind that gives rise to Nietzschean *ressentiment*, and the inarticulate hatred that builds up under these conditions makes them easily susceptible to evaluative ideologies of a distinctive sort. These ideologies—conservative fundamentalism in the United States, militant Islamism in the Middle East and Asia, revanchist nationalism in parts of the old Soviet empire—may be inimical to the true interests of the people who embrace them. But they nevertheless speak to a need that Nietzsche identified, the need for a vindicatory interpretation of one's own basic emotional situation and experience.[36] The contemporary successors to Nietzsche's ascetic priests, it seems to me, are the populist politicians, preachers, and imams of revenge, who exploit the *ressentiment* of the masses for their own transparently cynical purposes. And Nietzsche's account of the slave revolt can help us to understand the psychic forces that render so many people vulnerable to the ministrations of this new priestly class.

[36] The expressive function of these contemporary ideologies is, in fact, more obvious than is the case with the more generalized morality of modernity that Nietzsche was considering. Hatred is closer to the surface in these ideologies, and they do not shrink from calling explicitly for revenge against those who are condemned as evil infidels, historical enemies of our people, liberal elitists, etc. This makes them less interesting from a psychological point of view—less complex, paradoxical, self-undermining, and so on—but perhaps even more dangerous.

PART III

MORALITY AND OTHER NORMATIVE DOMAINS

11

Virtue, Reason, and Principle

A common strategy unites much that philosophers have written about the virtues. The strategy can be traced back at least to Aristotle, who suggested that human beings have a characteristic function or activity (rational activity of soul), and that the virtues are traits of character which enable humans to perform this kind of activity excellently or well.[1] The defining feature of this approach is that it treats the virtues as functional concepts, to be both identified and justified by reference to some independent goal or end which they enable people to attain (human flourishing, rational perfection, participation in practices, 'narrative unity' in a life). Some recent philosophers seem to have hoped that by following this perfectionist strategy, we might attain a more convincing account of our moral practices than rule-based theories of ethics have been able to provide.[2]

But the hopes are not well founded. The perfectionist strategy requires us to specify an independent goal or end which the virtues best enable us to attain, and if the strategy is to succeed the goal or end that it specifies must constitute an objectively good state for humans to be in—otherwise the claim that the virtues enable us to achieve this end or goal will not serve to justify or support them. The prospects for identifying an independent goal or aim which is objectively good in this way, however, do not look very good. Those ends which are genuinely good states for humans tend to be too vaguely characterized to support the claim that the virtues best enable us to attain them (consider 'flourishing', or 'rational excellence' in this connection); while those ends which are more determinate tend to be poor candidates for an objective human good (consider 'the narrative unity of a life spent searching for the human good', proposed by Alasdair MacIntyre).[3]

Originally published in *Canadian Journal of Philosophy*, 21 (December 1991), 469–95. Reprinted by permission. Conversations with Samuel Freeman, Michael Smith, and especially Wolfgang Mann were helpful in clarifying the ideas developed in this paper. I have also benefited from the very useful comments of two anonymous referees for the *Canadian Journal of Philosophy*. Work on the paper was supported by a grant from the Research Foundation of the University of Pennsylvania.

[1] See esp. the *Nicomachean Ethics*, Bk. I, ch. 7.
[2] See e.g. Alasdair MacIntyre, *After Virtue* (Notre Dame: University of Notre Dame Press, 1981); and James Wallace, *Virtues and Vices* (Ithaca: Cornell University Press, 1978).
[3] *After Virtue*, ch. 15.

If we abandon the perfectionist strategy, however, the question arises whether a philosophical study of the virtues has anything distinctive to contribute to our understanding of morality. In my view, the most promising way to return a positive answer to this question is to focus on the issues of practical reason and practical rationality. Thus it has seemed to many philosophers that an Aristotelian approach to the virtues yields a conception of practical reason and its corresponding excellence (*phronesis*, or practical wisdom) which does not fit readily into the Humean and Kantian categories that have become conventional in contemporary discussions. Among the most prominent of these philosophers is John McDowell. His suggestive recent work on the virtues aims in part to defend and develop a broadly Aristotelian account of practical reason and practical rationality as an alternative to the now-standard Humean and Kantian accounts.[4] At the same time McDowell is explicit in rejecting the perfectionist strategy sketched above— indeed, he goes so far as to question whether Aristotle himself ever meant to follow that strategy.[5] If McDowell is right about this, then the study of the virtues can contribute a distinctive perspective to our understanding of practical reason, even if we give up the unpromising perfectionist strategy.

I shall take McDowell's work on practical reason to provide my starting point in this essay—both because McDowell has gone further than other philosophers in trying to explain and defend an Aristotelian conception of practical reason, as a live option in contemporary discussions; and because the account he provides is difficult enough to benefit, in my view, from critical reconstruction and analysis. But my aim in the essay is not simply to scrutinize McDowell's views. By looking in detail at his position, I think we can learn something more generally about the problems and the prospects of a broadly Aristotelian approach to practical reason.

My discussion of these issues in what follows divides into three sections. In section 1, I set out the conventional Kantian and Humean positions on practical reason, and consider the arguments that McDowell brings to bear against these accounts. Here I maintain that Humean and Kantian accounts share a common commitment to the idea that the requirements of virtue can be formulated in terms of general principles or procedures for practical reflection, and I suggest that McDowell's alternative account is distinctive in rejecting this idea; but I conclude

---

[4] McDowell's views are developed in the following series of papers (which I shall henceforth refer to by abbreviations of their titles): 'Are Moral Requirements Hypothetical Imperatives?', *Aristotelian Society*, supp. vol. 52 (1978), 13–29; 'Virtue and Reason', *The Monist*, 62 (1979), 331–50; 'The Role of *Eudaimonia* in Aristotle's Ethics', reprinted in Amélie Rorty (ed.), *Essays on Aristotle's Ethics* (Berkeley and Los Angeles: University of California Press, 1980), 359–76; 'Non-Cognitivism and Rule-Following', in Steven Holtzman and Christopher Leich (eds.), *Wittgenstein: To Follow a Rule* (London: Routledge and Kegan Paul, 1981), 141–62; 'Values and Secondary Qualities', in Ted Honderich (ed.), *Morality and Objectivity* (London: Routledge and Kegan Paul, 1985), 110–29; and 'Might There Be External Reasons?', in J. E. J. Altham and Ross Harrison (eds.), *World, Mind, and Ethics: Essays on the Ethical Philosophy of Bernard Williams* (Cambridge, England: Cambridge University Press, 1995), 68–85.   [5] See 'The Role of *Eudaimonia*'.

that McDowell's stated objections to principle-dependent accounts of practical reason are not compelling. Even if McDowell's specific arguments against Kantian and Humean approaches are unsuccessful, however, it may still be the case that his Aristotelian alternative is superior, and this is the possibility I turn to in section 2 of the essay. I contend that there are two ways to develop McDowell's alternative account, one of which yields a version of rational intuitionism, while the other pictures practical reason as a form of connoisseurship; and I argue that the connoisseurship interpretation is the more promising one. In section 3, however, I try to show that the connoisseurship interpretation encounters two potential problems, when applied in the conditions that govern modern moral life; and I urge that it is too early to give up on principle-dependent accounts, in favor of McDowell's Aristotelian alternative.

1. REASON, DESIRE, AND THE CONCEPTION OF HOW TO LIVE

Kantian and Humean positions in ethics traditionally differ on the question of whether reason can give rise to a motivation to act. The Kantian answers this question affirmatively, holding that pure reason can be practical in its issue, and that it is possible to explain motivation and action in terms of the grasping of reasons or justifications for action. The Humean, by contrast, returns a negative answer to the question. On this view, rational reflection cannot by itself give rise to motivation; rather, motivation has its source in the agent's prior desires, and practical reasoning (to the extent it exists) must always begin *from* those desires.[6]

It is important to bear in mind that both parties to this debate can and should acknowledge that desires always have a role to play in the explanation of motivation and action. That is, the Kantian no less than the Humean should maintain that motivation requires the presence of desires.[7] Once this point is admitted, however, the Kantian will want to attach great significance to a distinction

---

[6] I follow McDowell in distinguishing between practical reason and practical reasoning (see 'Virtue and Reason', 349 n. 22): the former refers to the broader class of cases in which motivation and action are explained in terms of reasons; the latter, to the subset of these cases in which motivation and action are preceded by an episode of reasoning or deliberation. I assume that the Kantian and the Humean take divergent positions on the broader issue of practical reason, which determine correspondingly divergent positions on the question of practical reasoning.

Note also that the Humean claim that practical reasoning has its source in an agent's desires needn't entail that such reasoning is instrumental or maximizing. On this point see Bernard Williams, 'Internal and External Reasons', as reprinted in his *Moral Luck* (Cambridge, England: Cambridge University Press, 1981), 101–13—discussed by McDowell in 'Might There Be External Reasons?'

[7] The reason for this, in brief, is that motivation and intentional action are goal-directed phenomena, where such goal-directedness in turn requires the presence of desire; cf. Thomas Nagel, *The Possibility of Altruism* (Princeton: Princeton University Press, 1978), ch. 5. McDowell accepts this point: see e.g. his 'Are Moral Requirements', 14–15.

between two different kinds of desires. Some desires—what Thomas Nagel has called the 'motivated' ones[8]—are such that they can appropriately be explained in terms of other propositional attitudes of the agent's. This form of explanation is distinctive in that the propositional content of the states which explain the motivated desire also rationalize or justify the desire; and we may accordingly say that the defining mark of motivated desires is that they admit of a *rationalizing explanation*. Unmotivated desires, on the other hand, are simply desires that do not admit of such a rationalizing explanation.[9]

In these terms, a crucial point at issue between the Humean and the Kantian concerns the form taken by the rationalizing explanations of motivated desires. For their part, Humeans maintain that such explanations always terminate with the citation of a basic evaluative premise, which cannot be explained or justified in rational terms, but which is fixed, rather, by some intrinsic or unmotivated desire. This is what the Humean means in saying that motivation always has desire at its source, and that practical reasoning necessarily begins *from* the agent's prior or given desires. Kantians, by contrast, deny these claims. They insist that pure reasoning or reflection—processes of thought that do not begin from the agent's prior desires—are sometimes sufficient both to produce motivation, and to explain rationally the motivated desires involved in such motivation.

The conventional debate about practical reason, then, does not concern the presence of desires, on occasions of motivation and action; rather, it concerns the form taken by rationalizing explanations of desires. Kantians, however, characteristically make a further claim as well. This is that distinctively moral motivations and actions are requirements of rationality, so that a person who reasoned correctly should be motivated to act *morally*. For instance, Kant himself took the categorical imperative to represent a kind of norm of reason, which if applied correctly would lead one to perform all the actions that are morally required, and only actions that are permissible from the moral point of view. If this is right, it evidently follows that persons who do not act morally must be guilty of a kind of irrationality, a failure to bring their thought and action into conformity with the requirements of reason. On a Humean position, by contrast, this will not necessarily be the case. The Humean represents practical reason as having its source in antecedent desires, and a person who lacks moral motivations might fail to have any other antecedent desires that could be advanced by becoming morally virtuous. Of course, the desires at the basis of moral reasoning night be extremely entrenched and widely distributed in human populations, as a matter of empirical fact. For his part, Hume seemed to think that an instinct to benevolence is knitted

---

[8] *The Possibility of Altruism*, 29. McDowell refers to such desires as 'consequential' or 'consequentially-ascribed' desires: see 'Are Moral Requirements', 15, 25.

[9] For a more detailed discussion of the distinction between motivated and unmotivated desires, and its significance for the dispute between Kantians and Humeans, see my paper, 'How to Argue about Practical Reason', Chapter 1 in this volume.

into the fabric of the human mind. More recently, T. M. Scanlon has represented moral reasoning as responding to a powerful and widespread desire that people have to justify their actions and policies to others, on grounds that no one could reasonably reject.[10] Neither of these accounts, however, provides resources for saying that the agent who lacks moral motivations altogether is on that account irrational. On this point Humean and Kantian approaches diverge, even if—as in the case of Scanlon's contractualism—the basic pattern of moral reasoning that the Humean describes has a Kantian flavor.

In the terms of this conventional debate, McDowell's broadly Aristotelian position does not fit comfortably into either of the received Kantian or Humean categories. He rejects the Humean position on the issue of practical reason and motivation, but he does so without endorsing the Kantian claim about the rationality of morality.

Take first the issue of the rationality of ethics. In his paper 'Are Moral Requirements Hypothetical Imperatives?', McDowell avers that the person who does not act virtuously need not on that account be irrational.[11] I take this claim to be the denial of the characteristically Kantian position that moral action is a requirement of reason, such that the person who reasoned or deliberated properly would be led to act morally. For if that Kantian position were correct, then the person who is not morally virtuous would be guilty of a kind of irrationality. In a different paper,[12] McDowell supports and develops this position with an interpretation of the *ergon* or function argument found in Book I of Aristotle's *Nicomachean Ethics*. On this interpretation—which McDowell recommends as an appealing alternative to contemporary (Kantian) views—the point of the *ergon* argument is not to cite considerations which will rationally convince the amoralist to go over to the life of moral virtue. The thought that it must be possible to cite some such consideration, if morality is not to be revealed as a sham, is a Kantian prejudice, one that McDowell urges us to give up. What the amoralist needs is not rational argument, but a change in *character*, of the sort that can best be achieved through a program of moral training or habituation such as Aristotle describes in the *Nicomachean Ethics*.[13]

[10] 'Contractualism and Utilitarianism', in Amartya Sen and Bernard Williams (eds.), *Utilitarianism and Beyond* (Cambridge, England: Cambridge University Press, 1982), 103–28.

[11] 'Are Moral Requirements', 13, 24. Cf. 'Might There Be External Reasons?', §5, where McDowell represents the claim that the amoralist is necessarily irrational as 'bluff'. In the same section of this paper he allows that there might be a sense in which an amoral person could be considered irrational, associated with the normative claim that a virtuous agent is seeing matters 'correctly' or 'aright'; but he concludes that it would be best not to describe the amoralist in these terms, as the description encourages the mistaken inference that there is a process of reasoning or deliberation that could lead the amoralist to become virtuous.   [12] 'The Role of *Eudaimonia*', esp. §§10–14.

[13] Cf. 'Might There Be External Reasons?' (esp. §4), where McDowell says that if a person has not been brought up to be virtuous, then it will generally be too late to reason with the person; what is required, to make such a person virtuous, is rather something like 'conversion'.

Now, it is plausible to suppose that the character one acquires, as a result of this kind of training or habituation, will largely be defined by a certain class of 'unmotivated' desires. These are the long-term or standing desires, the dispositional states that determine an agent's basic aims and goals, values and projects. They are 'unmotivated', because they are not rationally explicable in terms of other propositional attitudes of the agent's. We do not account for their origin by adverting to any process of reasoning or deliberation that the agent goes through; rather, standing desires emerge gradually in the process of education and training, resulting from repeated performance of actions of certain general types.[14]

If this is right, however, then a natural view to take would be that these 'unmotivated' standing desires are the source of the agent's motivations, fixing the ends that practical reasoning and deliberation will aim at. That is, McDowell's rejection of the Kantian claim about the rationality of morality would appear to commit him to a Humean position on the question of practical reason and motivation. McDowell himself does not draw this inference, however. On the contrary, he offers a highly disparaging picture of the Humean approach to motivational psychology. In one especially memorable passage, for instance,[15] he says that Humean accounts are wedded to a 'quasi-hydraulic' conception of the mind, which represents the will as the source of the forces that issue in behavior. The language here might seem to suggest that what is wrong with the Humean view is its (alleged) commitment to a mechanistic or causal account of the mind.[16] But the suggestion is most likely inadvertent. McDowell's central complaint, repeated and developed in his other writings on ethics, is with the broader and more basic Humean claim that desires are the *source* of motivations: the idea that unmotivated intrinsic desires fix the necessary starting points for practical reasoning and deliberation.

The question is, how does McDowell support this complaint? What exactly is meant to be wrong with the Humean approach to practical reason; and can McDowell reject this approach, without being led back to a Kantian position on the rationality of morality? McDowell's answer to these questions is strongly influenced by his reading of Aristotle.[17] He argues, in particular, that there is a distinctive feature of virtuous motivations, emphasized by Aristotle, which cannot be accounted for within the framework of Humean and Kantian approaches.

---

[14] A good account of this process can be found in Myles Burnyeat's paper 'Aristotle on Learning to be Good', in Rorty (ed.), *Essays on Aristotle's Ethics*, 69–92.

[15] 'Non-Cognitivism and Rule-Following', 155.

[16] Michael Smith interprets McDowell's complaint this way (and deftly deflates the complaint so interpreted) in his paper, 'The Humean Theory of Motivation', *Mind*, 96 (1987), 36–61, at 43–4. In 'Might There Be External Reasons?', §6, McDowell states more clearly than in his earlier papers that he does not object to the claim that reason-giving explanations are causal, only to the rigid schema into which the Humean attempts to force all such explanations.

[17] My exposition in the remainder of this section relies mainly on 'Virtue and Reason', which I take to contain the most developed statement of McDowell's objection to the Humean approach.

Consider an ordinary case of virtuous action—say, stopping on one's way home from work to help a stranger push his car out of a snow bank. McDowell, as I understand him, admits that we can give a 'core explanation' of such an action that conforms to the Humean schema for explaining motivations.[18] The question at issue is not whether there will be a desire present on this occasion of motivation—for reasons mentioned above, we must say that in intentionally stopping to assist the stranger the virtuous agent had a desire to help the stranger get his car out of the snow. The question is how we are to explain this motivated desire, and on this question McDowell admits that our original or core explanation will turn out to satisfy the Humean strictures. Thus we can account for the motivated desire to help the stranger by invoking (say) the agent's belief that the stranger needed assistance, plus a general or standing benevolent desire or concern[19] to help people when they are in need of assistance (where this general disposition to benevolence is a result of the training or habituation of the agent's sentiments from youth).

Core explanations of virtuous action, then, conform to the Humean pattern. But McDowell contends that we cannot attain a complete explanation of virtuous action by attending to such core explanations alone, because of the *unity* of the virtues.[20] The standing concerns or desires that mark the termini of core explanations correspond to individual virtuous traits. But virtue is not just an unorganized collection of such virtuous traits; rather, individual virtuous traits can only count as virtuous at all if they are copresent with other virtuous traits, and if the whole collection of such traits is appropriately structured and organized. To return to our example, suppose that the person who stops to help the stranger in the snow had not been driving home from work at the time, but instead transporting a badly injured friend to the hospital. We could, it seems, give precisely the same 'core' explanation of the action of pushing the stranger's car, with a standing benevolent desire fixing the immediate end of the agent's action. But it would be an error to suppose that the action so explained is virtuous in this context, because the agent's obligation to help the friend ought to have taken precedence. Virtue requires a plurality of concerns or desires, structured in a certain way, and we will only comprehend why an individual action was virtuous if we can see the action in the context of the agent's other standing concerns, and appreciate why one concern rather than another was effective in motivating the agent to act.

It is at this point, McDowell suggests, that we need to go beyond the Humean approach to practical reason. He argues that we can only attain a complete understanding of virtuous action by appealing to the virtuous person's overall *conception of how to live*; for it is this conception that governs the relations among the agent's individual standing concerns, and renders intelligible why one such concern

---

[18] 'Virtue and Reason', 342–3.
[19] McDowell himself uses the expression 'concern'; I take it he means by this the kind of long-term or standing desire I characterized above.   [20] 'Virtue and Reason', 332–3, 342–6.

rather than another was effective on a given occasion, in motivating the agent to act.[21] What finally explains virtuous action, it seems, is not the standing desire cited by a 'core' explanation, but the overall conception of how to live that structures and organizes the virtuous agent's individual concerns.

Of course, Humean and Kantian approaches to practical reason will have their own way of accounting for the virtuous agent's guiding conception of how to live. On a Humean approach, for instance, the conception of how to live would most naturally be interpreted as an unmotivated higher-order desire, which plays an executive or regulative role in rational reflection about what to do.[22] Thus on a utilitarian account the higher-order desire that is meant to regulate the virtuous agent's practical reflection is a form of generalized benevolence, whereas a contractualist account would postulate a higher-order desire to act in ways that can be justified to others, on grounds that no one could reasonably reject. On both of these accounts the higher-order desire regulates practical reflection by specifying a general procedure or pattern of reasoning that guides the virtuous agent's decisions about what to do. Kantian accounts share this tendency to construe the virtuous agent's conception of how to live in terms of a general procedure or regulative pattern of practical reflection; only there is no need, on a strictly Kantian account, to postulate an unmotivated higher-order desire corresponding to the cited procedure. Kant's own categorical imperative procedure, for instance, is meant to have rational authority in regulating our decisions about what to do, quite independently of whether we happen to have a higher-order desire to submit to that procedure.

Clearly, McDowell needs to reject these interpretations of the conception of how to live, if he is to succeed in staking out an alternative to Humean and Kantian approaches; but his objections to them, and his own alternative interpretation, require careful reconstruction. With apparent reference to the Humean interpretation, McDowell concedes that the conception of how to live is what he calls an 'orectic' psychological state,[23] which presumably means that it is desire-like in some respects. But he nevertheless does not think the conception of how to live can be construed as an 'over-arching' or higher-order desire, as the Humean would try to interpret it, because the desires involved in virtuous action are not 'independently intelligible'.[24] Now it is not always clear what exactly McDowell has in mind when he objects that Humean accounts postulate an independently intelligible desire at the source of the virtuous agent's motivation

---

[21] 'Virtue and Reason', 343–6.

[22] A different Humean position would say simply that the agent should act on whichever first-order desire happens to be strongest, at the time of action. But I take it this would amount to a denial that there is anything like a conception of how to live that could guide or regulate the virtuous agent's choices.   [23] 'Virtue and Reason', 345, 346.

[24] Ibid. 345–6; 'Are Moral Requirements', 18–20, 22–3; 'The Role of *Eudaimonia*', 372–3. McDowell attacks the idea of an 'over-arching' desire at the root of virtuous action, in place of the conception of how to live, in 'Virtue and Reason', 343.

and action. McDowell sometimes seems to have taken the Humean to be claiming that all motivation has the *same* desires at its source, so that it would be a sufficient refutation of the Humean to show that the virtuous person's higher-order desires are simply not shared by the nonvirtuous agent.[25] But this claim is not sufficient to refute a minimally sophisticated version of the Humean position; the basic Humean thesis is that motivation has its source in desire, and this is distinct from, and weaker than, the claim that all motivation has the *same* desires at its source.

At other points, and more subtly, McDowell attributes to the Humean the view that the higher-order desires which originate motivation must at least be externally intelligible—intelligible, that is, to those who do not share the desires themselves.[26] But it is not obvious what the force of this claim is meant to be, as a criticism of the Humean view. Presumably a desire will be intelligible to a person just in case that person can anticipate the objects and activities that the desire would lead one to pursue, and understand sympathetically why those objects and activities might be found desirable. Now McDowell seems correct to suppose that the desires that turn up in Humean accounts of moral reasoning are not likely to be externally unintelligible, in this sense. Humeans tend to select desires such as generalized benevolence, or the contractualist desire to act in ways that can be justified to others, in part precisely because they are fairly widely distributed, and because they pick out ends that people tend naturally to respond to under normal educational circumstances. But if McDowell finds this aspect of Humean accounts implausible, he needs to explain more specifically why the postulated desires do not provide an adequate basis for moral reasoning; it is not enough simply to observe that Humean accounts tend to represent the moral motives as widespread and accessible. And even if such an explanation should be forthcoming, so that the higher-order desires that regulate moral behavior are shown to be neither widely distributed nor intelligible to those who lack them, this would not undermine the more basic Humean strategy of accounting for moral reasoning in terms of such higher-order desires. Higher-order desires might remain the regulative starting-points for moral deliberation, even if they are neither widely distributed nor easily intelligible to those who are not themselves virtuous already.

There is, however, one further way we might interpret the notion of independent intelligibility, which suggests a more reliable contrast with Humean and Kantian interpretations of the conception of how to live. Thus both Humeans and Kantians maintain that the virtuous agent's conception of how to live is independently intelligible, in the sense that it can be formulated as a general procedure or principle for practical reflection, independently of and prior to particular circumstances of action and decision. Take the categorical imperative procedure, for instance, or the contractualist appeal to justification on the basis of hypothetical

---

[25] See e.g. 'Virtue and Reason', 346; 'Are Moral Requirements', 19–20, 23, 25–6.
[26] See, again, 'Virtue and Reason', 345–6.

agreement: these forms of practical argument mark out the kinds of reasons that should regulate the virtuous agent's decisions quite independently of the details of any particular situation that might confront a virtuous agent. To say that the conception of how to live is independently intelligible, in this sense, is just to say that it is specifiable in terms of general principles or procedures; and practical reasoning which is regulated or governed by such a conception of how to live will therefore be reasoning in accordance with such general principles or procedures. We may put this by saying that, on Humean and Kantian accounts, moral reasoning on the basis of a conception of how to live is *principle-dependent*.

Here, I think, we have a genuine point of contrast with McDowell's understanding of the conception of how to live; for on McDowell's interpretation the virtuous agent's conception cannot be captured in terms of general principles or procedures, capable of being specified in advance of the circumstances of action. Rather, McDowell follows Aristotle in supposing that the requirements of virtue resist codification in any exhaustive and exceptionless set of rules or principles.[27] Moral reasoning in accordance with the conception of how to live, on McDowell's conception, therefore cannot be construed as principle-dependent reasoning. This raises two questions: why does McDowell reject the idea that the requirements of virtue can be given an adequate specification in terms of general principles or procedures? And how are we to understand the alternative that he offers to principle-dependent conceptions of moral reasoning? I shall address the first of these questions in the remainder of this section; the second question will be taken up in the section to follow.

Perhaps McDowell's most frequently stated objection to principle-dependent accounts of the conception of how to live is that they are committed to a simplistically mechanistic picture of moral reasoning. Thus he complains that the general principles or procedures which figure in Humean and Kantian accounts would be 'mechanically' applicable to cases, in a way inadequate to the complexity of a 'reasonably adult moral outlook'.[28] Hence, McDowell seems to suggest, a tolerably sophisticated conception of how to live cannot be formulated in terms of such antecedent principles or procedures. Taken at face value, however, this objection rests on something of a caricature of Kantian and Humean approaches; for there is no reason to think that antecedent moral principles or procedures of justification would need to be mechanically applicable to cases in the objectionable way McDowell describes. For example, the more sophisticated recent interpreters of Kant agree in emphasizing the complexity of the processes whereby the categorical

---

[27] 'Virtue and Reason', 340–2; cf. 'The Role of *Eudaimonia*', 12, 14; 'Values and Secondary Qualities', 122. In these passages McDowell is echoing Aristotle's famous claim that generalizations in practical philosophy hold only for the most part; see e.g. *Nicomachean Ethics*, 1097b12 ff.

[28] 'Virtue and Reason', 336; cf. the reference to 'the inexorable workings of a machine', on 339. Indeed, mechanistic images and terminology recur frequently in McDowell's characterization of the views in moral psychology that he opposes: for two other examples, see 'Non-Cognitivism and Rule-Following', 155; and 'Values and Secondary Qualities', 122.

imperative procedure is brought to bear in the moral life.[29] Thus, the identification of an agent's maxim is anything but a mechanical procedure; and the implementation of a universalizable maxim, in specific historical and cultural circumstances, requires extensive reliance on forms of perception and intelligence that cannot in their turn be understood as involving the mechanical application of antecedent procedures and principles. The categorical imperative procedure may tell you that you ought to be kind or helpful; but this will not take you very far if you lack the powers of judgment and imagination to determine what would be the truly kind or helpful action, in a given situation and culture.[30]

The literal charge of mechanical applicability thus does not seem to hold against the more interesting variants of Kantian and Humean strategies. But perhaps, in making this charge, McDowell has something different in mind. His complaint might be an expression of skepticism about the whole idea that general principles or procedures could ever be adequate to the task of determining all of our particular duties or requirements in life. If such skepticism is justified, then the role of judgment and perception in moral decision cannot be restricted to the application of general principles, or to the implementation of general procedures of reflection and justification; judgment and perception must be more fundamentally or extensively implicated in determining what we are to do.

The problem, however, is that McDowell has given us no reason to accept such general skepticism about the adequacy of principle-dependent conceptions to determine our particular moral duties and requirements. General skepticism of this sort might seem reasonable, if one thought that the conception of how to live should amount to a comprehensive individual conception of the good, capable of filling out in detail one's view of the valuable or desirable life; for it is indeed questionable that one's comprehensive conception of the good might be specifiable, even in outline, by reference to any general principle or procedure of reasoning. But it would be a mistake—one perhaps encouraged by talk about the 'conception of how to live'—to think that the principles or procedures which figure in Kantian and Humean accounts are meant to play this role. On their most plausible construal, such principles or procedures are not ways of giving content to a comprehensive individual conception of the good, but function as moral *constraints* on individuals in the conduct of their lives—they represent what Kant called 'supreme limiting conditions' on one's pursuit of ends. There is no general reason

---

[29] See e.g. John Rawls, 'Themes in Kant's Moral Philosophy', in Eckart Förster (ed.), *Kant's Transcendental Deductions* (Stanford: Stanford University Press, 1989), 81–113 (esp. §1); Otfried Höffe, 'Kants kategorischer Imperativ als Kriterium des Sittlichen', as reprinted in his *Ethik und Politik* (Frankfurt am Main: Suhrkamp, 1979), 84–119; and Onora O'Neill, 'Consistency in Action', as reprinted in her *Constructions of Reason* (Cambridge, England: Cambridge University Press, 1989), 81–104.

[30] Similar remarks apply, I think, to the version of contractualism proposed by Scanlon in 'Contractualism and Utilitarianism', which I have presented as a version of the Humean position. The charge of mechanical applicability might have more force against utilitarian versions of the Humean position, though even here I think the objection requires careful handling.

to suppose that even a thoroughly 'adult' conception of such moral constraints could not be spelled out in terms of general principles or procedures.

Beyond the specific objection on grounds of mechanical applicability, there is a more general tendency in McDowell's work to associate Kantian and Humean strategies with discredited foundationalist approaches in philosophy. Thus he suggests at one point that principle-dependent conceptions of practical reasoning rest on a broader philosophical prejudice, to the effect that rational processes must be capable of being exhibited as 'automatically compelling, without dependence on our partially shared "whirl of organism".'[31] McDowell is apparently assuming here that the attempt to characterize moral reasoning in terms of general principles or procedures represents an effort to step outside our actual moral practices, and to legitimate them by constructing a rational justification for morality from the ground up, as it were. Indeed, this interpretation of Kantian and Humean approaches may explain why McDowell's criticism of them slides so easily between the idea that moral reasoning is principle-dependent and the different idea that it must be externally intelligible. For if the motivation of principle-dependent accounts is the desire to provide a foundationalist justification of moral practices, the principles appealed to would have to be ones that those external to moral practices understand and respond to. At any rate, McDowell finds this foundationalist motivation deeply suspect, and suggests that once we have weaned ourselves from it (with the help of Wittgenstein's reflections on rule-following), there will no longer be any temptation to adopt a principle-dependent conception of moral reasoning.

Here again, however, McDowell's argument against principle-dependent interpretations of moral reasoning rests on something of a misconception. Take Scanlon's version of contractualism, on which moral reasoning is represented as appealing to a higher-order desire to act in ways that can be justified to others, on grounds no one could reasonably reject. What motivates this account, I think, is not a wish to provide an external justification of moral practices, but the desire to *interpret* those practices in a way that displays the nature and appeal of moral reasons. To challenge that account it would be necessary to find fault with the details of Scanlon's interpretation, and to offer a better interpretation in its place; but the invocation of general anti-foundationalist considerations will not by itself tell against the account. Even strictly Kantian approaches do not necessarily seem vulnerable to such anti-foundationalist considerations. Granted, the Kantian position, as I have represented it, does attempt to show that moral requirements are requirements of reason, and that they in some sense make claims on all of us.

---

[31] 'Virtue and Reason', 340. On the point at issue see, more generally, the whole of §4 of that paper: though there are many things going on there, at least one of them is an attack on the idea that philosophical thought about our moral practices 'should be undertaken at some external standpoint, outside our immersion in our familiar forms of life' (p. 341). As an objection to the kinds of principle-dependent accounts I have sketched, this complaint assumes that those accounts have foundationalist aspirations, and that is the assumption I am challenging.

But this attempt need not take the form of going altogether outside moral practices, by (say) reducing moral motivations to considerations of enlightened self-interest. Rather, in its more sophisticated versions the Kantian position can be seen as offering its own interpretation of our moral practices, an interpretation on which *sui generis* moral motivations are revealed to be patterns of reflection to which we are all potentially responsive.[32] This is an ambitious undertaking, perhaps even an unpromising one, but it does not necessarily rest on a dubious desire to provide an external foundation or justification for moral practices.

I hope I have now said enough to raise some doubts about the cogency of McDowell's stated objections to principle-dependent accounts of moral reasoning. To represent moral reasoning in terms of the following of general principles or procedures is not necessarily to characterize it as a mechanical or mindless process. Nor is it necessarily to suppose that our moral practices require an external foundation or justification. Rather, I have suggested that Humean and Kantian appeals to principle-dependent conceptions of practical reasoning should be seen as interpretations of our moral practices, which aim to illuminate the nature and appeal of distinctively moral reasons. Even if McDowell's conception of these accounts is something of a caricature, however, it might still be the case that his own understanding of the virtuous agent's conception of how to live represents a superior interpretation of our moral practices. This is the possibility that we now need to assess; but to do so it will first be necessary to get clearer about what McDowell's alternative is.

2. INTUITION AND CONNOISSEURSHIP

To this point I have represented McDowell's account of the conception of how to live in negative terms, as resting on a rejection of principle-dependent conceptions of the requirements of virtue. McDowell does not seem to think that the practical reasoning of the virtuous agent can be represented accurately as an appeal to general principles or procedures, capable of being formulated independently of particular situations of virtuous action. At the same time he evidently believes that the virtuous agent's individual decisions about what to do are deliverances of practical reason. This leaves open the question of how we are to understand, more positively, the distinctively rational processes that lead to and support the virtuous agent's decisions.

---

[32] In this connection, see Nagel's remarks about the 'method of interpretation', in *The Possibility of Altruism*, 4, 18–23. Cf. 'Might There Be External Reasons?', §5, where McDowell attributes to moral philosophers the desire to discover a 'knockdown' argument which would enable them to 'force' those indifferent to morality into caring about ethical ends. My point is that this characterization simply does not apply to sophisticated proponents of the Kantian approach, such as Nagel, who are under no illusions about the efficacy of their interpretations as instruments of moral reform or persuasion.

McDowell himself does not give us much help in answering this question. His account clearly requires that reason have a positive role to play in leading a virtuous life; but like Aristotle before him, McDowell tells us very little about what this form of practical reasoning is like, beyond saying that it does not involve the application of general principles or procedures. To give the account some definite contours, and to see more precisely how it differs from Humean and Kantian strategies, it will therefore be necessary to go somewhat beyond the literal text of McDowell's various papers. In what follows, I want to suggest that there are two different ways in which McDowell's broadly Aristotelian account of practical reason might be developed: one of these yields a kind of rational intuitionism, and I shall contend that this way of developing the account is not very plausible. A second and more promising possibility delivers a conception of moral reasoning as a form of connoisseurship; after sketching this interpretation, I shall return, in the final section of the paper, to consider its merits as against the principle-dependent interpretations of moral reasoning offered by Humeans and Kantians.

To begin, note that principle-dependent accounts of moral reasoning provide terms for justifying individual virtuous decisions. Faced with a decision about what to do, the virtuous agent appeals to the antecedent principles or procedures, and deliberating in accordance with these principles or procedures yields a reason for choosing one alternative over the others that are available. Now one way to develop an alternative to such accounts would be to deny that the virtuous agent has *any* reason or justification for her individual virtuous decisions and choices. Rather, it might be that the virtuous agent, when faced with a decision, immediately sees or grasps what would be the right thing to do, without needing to offer any further reason or justification for her decision. Of course, it will always be open to the virtuous agent to defend her decisions about what to do by saying (for instance) that she has chosen to do the right thing, or that she has done what is for the best, on the whole. But these locutions do not need to be taken as providing an independent justification or rationale for her decisions. Rather, they may simply reflect the fact that the virtuous agent has direct insight into the requirements of virtue, occasion by occasion, where this insight does not admit of discursive justification.

To develop McDowell's account in this way would be to turn it into a kind of rational intuitionism: moral reasoning would be construed as involving an element of quasi-perceptual intuition, where the virtuous agent's intuitive responses are taken to be constitutively rational ones.[33] And there is much in McDowell's writings that could be taken to support this interpretation. Thus, it is a prominent refrain in McDowell's work on ethics that the experience of the virtuous life is

---

[33] I have in mind here a form of intuitionism which holds that virtuous agents have a direct, noninferential, quasi-perceptual grasp of the right or correct thing to do in particular circumstances of action (i.e. what Sidgwick called the 'perceptional' phase of intuitionism: see *The Methods of Ethics*, 7th edn. (Indianapolis: Hackett Publishing Co., 1981), Bk. 1, ch. 8).

marked by certain distinctive ways of perceiving one's circumstances of action. He writes: 'a conception of how to live shows itself, when more than one concern might issue in action, in one's seeing, or being able to be brought to see, one fact rather than another as salient'.[34] This perception of certain features of situations as salient is in turn explained as follows: when the virtuous agent determines that a certain concern is to be acted on, in a given situation, the claims made by competing concerns are ordinarily *silenced*, in the sense that they are not taken to provide the agent with *any* reason for action.[35] To have the conception of how to live characteristic of virtue, then, is to have a special perceptual sensitivity to the features of situations that present us with concrete moral requirements. This element in McDowell's account echoes Aristotle's tendency to resort to perceptual terminology when talking about practical wisdom, and suggests that it is indeed appropriate to construe his account of moral reasoning along intuitionist lines.[36]

If this perceptual component is to be integrated into an account of practical reason, however, then it needs to be maintained that the virtuous agent's capacity for immediate intuition is a distinctively rational capacity. How are we to construe this further claim? The most appealing way to do so, I should think, would be to say that the virtuous agents' intuitive responses about what it is right to do are constitutively rational responses. That is, McDowell might deny that rational processes are exclusively processes that are controlled by or justifiable in terms of further reasons or justifications; rather, rationality might be said to consist in part in a disposition to offer certain direct, intuitive responses to practical situations, where these responses do not admit of any further justification. This would give to the intuitive responses of virtuous agents a role perhaps analogous to that which Wittgenstein assigns to agreement in judgments, as a condition of communication by means of language.[37] The community of the virtuous would be construed as sharing a Wittgensteinian *Lebensform*; and the immediate judgments of the virtuous about what it is right or good to do would be constitutively rational, because they are among the conditions that make moral discourse within such communities possible.

Having sketched this intuitionist reading of McDowell's account, however, I think it has to be admitted that it does not represent the most promising way of developing his ideas about practical reason. This is not to say that McDowell

---

[34] 'Virtue and Reason', 344.

[35] See ibid. 345–6, also 334–5; and compare 'Are Moral Requirements', 26–9; 'The Role of *Eudaimonia*', 372–3.

[36] Cf. the references to *aisthesis* in Aristotle's discussion of *phronesis* in Book VI of the *Nicomachean Ethics*. The dimension of informed perception in a broadly Aristotelian approach to practical reason is also stressed in David Wiggins, 'Deliberation and Practical Reason', in Rorty (ed.), *Essays on Aristotle's Ethics*, 221–40. Whether Aristotle himself took practical reason to include a dimension of perceptual intuition is a more complicated question, whose resolution requires (at least) an interpretation of Aristotle's notoriously obscure remarks about *nous* in Book VI of the *Nicomachean Ethics*

[37] See e.g. Ludwig Wittgenstein, *Philosophical Investigations*, ed. G. E. M. Anscombe and R. Rhees, trans. G. E. M. Anscombe (Oxford: Blackwell, 1953), §§241–2.

would not want to treat the community of the virtuous as sharing a kind of Wittgensteinian *Lebensform* (whatever that might involve); nor is it to deny that rational moral discourse must rest on something like agreement in judgments. The problem is that, on the intuitionist interpretation just sketched, the appeal to agreement in judgments that are not themselves rationally justifiable occurs altogether too swiftly. The intuitionist interpretation says that the virtuous agent simply and immediately perceives what is the right thing to do, in each of the circumstances that confront her, without being able to offer any rational support or justification for these intuitive judgments. But in complicated normative questions about the conduct of life we reasonably expect people to have *something* to say in defense of their beliefs about the moral correctness, or rightness, of acting in certain ways. Thus, in the case sketched earlier we expect the virtuous driver to be able to give some account or justification as to *why* it is right to help someone out of a snow bank if one is on one's way home to watch the news, but not the right thing to do if it means breaking an engagement to drive a friend to the hospital— even if she cannot appeal to a general procedure or principle, equally applicable in other cases that might arise.[38] At the least, she ought to be able to point to some morally significant distinction between the two cases which justifies their differential treatment. Her inability to provide any account of this kind would impugn her pretension to have a conception of how to live capable of guiding her conduct rationally through the complexities of life.[39]

Now I suspect that McDowell himself would not want to resist this conclusion. Virtue, he would say, involves a perceptual sensitivity to the morally relevant features of situations; but this perceptual sensitivity should not be construed as a constitutively rational capacity for unerring insight into the right or the good. Nor should the possession of this perceptual sensitivity be taken to preclude the provision of reasons or justifications for the virtuous agent's individual decisions about what to do.[40] On the contrary, it would be natural to suppose that the perceptual

---

[38] It is of course not required that the virtuous agent actually have this justification running through her head at the time when she acts, only that she be able to provide it if asked. Thus we may suppose that in the heat of action, the virtuous agent will often be able to perceive immediately what it is that she is required to do. This would support McDowell's account of the phenomenology of salience and silencing, without requiring us to give these phenomena an intuitionist interpretation.

[39] Cf. McDowell's remarks about danger, in 'Values and Secondary Qualities', 119. There McDowell suggests that the normative aspect of our responses to danger—the idea that those responses are *merited* by the things we take to be dangerous—shows itself in our ability to give an account of what makes certain sorts of situations dangerous (what he refers to as an 'explanatory theory of fear'). At the end of the same article, however, McDowell denies that the account provided need take the form of a set of general principles (pp. 122–3). This lends support to the connoisseurship interpretation of his views on practical reason, which I shall develop below.

[40] Thus there are several points at which McDowell commits himself to the availability of arguments or justifications for the virtuous agent's decisions: see e.g. 'Are Moral Requirements', 21–2; 'Virtue and Reason', 342; 'Might There Be External Reasons?', §4. These passages suggest that the arguments available to the virtuous agent have a 'rhetorical' character, and so fall short of 'rationally necessitating' their conclusions; I take it the import of such remarks is to reiterate McDowell's view that moral argument and justification cannot be reconstructed as an appeal to antecedent principles.

sensitivity precisely discloses to the virtuous agent the particular reasons or justifications in favor of doing what virtue requires, occasion by occasion. What is distinctively rational about this perceptual sensitivity, one might even say, is that it enables the virtuous to discern such reasons or justifications in the particular situations that confront them. At the same time the emphasis on perception in this account serves to underline the fact that moral reasons or justifications are not grasped by appeal to any antecedent procedure or set of principles, as principle-dependent accounts of moral reasoning would require. Rather, practical reason enables the virtuous agent to see what her reasons or justifications are in a way that is *essentially* bound up with perception of the particular features of the situations in which those reasons or justifications obtain.

Interpreting McDowell's account along these lines yields a picture of practical reason as a form of connoisseurship. For connoisseurship is precisely the ability to appreciate heterogeneous, case-specific reasons for choice or preference by means of informed judgment or perception rather than the application of general principles or procedures. Thus a connoisseur (of wine, for example) is able to make discriminations which have normative force, between better and worse wines. But these discriminations cannot be understood as involving the application of general principles or procedures, for there is no such procedure or set of principles which explains what makes for a good wine, in all cases. Nor would it be accurate to describe the connoisseur's discriminations as the deliverances of intuition, since the connoisseur can provide, in every case, a justification as to what makes a particular wine good or bad. Furthermore, it is plausible to regard the capacity to make these discriminations, and to provide the corresponding case-specific justifications, as a kind of rational capacity, insofar as it represents a refinement of critical discernment and intelligence.

Applying this connoisseurship model to the case of virtue seems to me to provide the most promising way of working out McDowell's conception of the role of practical reason in the virtuous life. The model itself offers a legitimate paradigm of one kind of rational capacity, whose application to the understanding of virtue results in a conception of practical reason that differs interestingly from both Humean and Kantian approaches. Moreover, this conception of practical reason preserves and explains several claims that have often been taken to distinguish an Aristotelian account of the moral life. It represents practical wisdom as a kind of refinement of judgment, involving a capacity to discern the particular features of situations that provide case-specific reasons for action—just as the wine connoisseur has an especially refined capacity to identify the qualities which make particular wines good or bad. Second, and perhaps more important, a connoisseur is someone whose judgments and discriminations set the final standards for deciding normative questions in his area of expertise.

Thus there is no independent set of rules or procedures which could be applied by anyone to determine the quality of an arbitrary bottle of wine; rather, a good wine simply is a wine that connoisseurs agree in finding case-specific reasons to approve of. This echoes Aristotle's own tendency to characterize virtuous actions by reference to the ideal of the virtuous agent, as those actions that the *phronimos* would choose, performed as the *phronimos* would perform them.[41] Such passages suggest very strongly that the concept of the virtuous agent is *basic*, in the context of an Aristotelian approach to ethics; and the connoisseurship interpretation of practical reason helps us to understand why an Aristotelian might take the concept of the virtuous agent to be basic in this way. Given the absence of a principled specification of the requirements of virtue, it is not possible to characterize virtuous action except by reference to what the person of practical wisdom would do in particular situations.[42]

3. CONCLUSION

The connoisseurship interpretation thus captures many distinctively Aristotelian claims, and it does so in a way which allows us to make sense of McDowell's contention that the Aristotelian account of practical reason is distinct from both Kantian and Humean approaches. The question remains, however, whether the connoisseurship model offers a more plausible interpretation of the role of reason in the moral life than principle-dependent accounts can provide. This is not a question that I can hope to settle in the space of the present essay. But in conclusion I would like at least to identify two potential problems for the connoisseurship interpretation of practical reason. One problem concerns the applicability of the connoisseurship model in contemporary circumstances of moral discourse; the other concerns the sufficiency of the connoisseurship model even in those circumstances where it can be said to apply. I do not see these problems as decisive objections to McDowell's neo-Aristotelian conception of moral reasoning; they challenge neither its intelligibility, nor its legitimacy as a model or interpretation of one kind of rational process. My aim, rather, is to locate two respects in which the model of connoisseurship seems potentially inadequate to the predicament of morality in our culture, in the hope that doing so will help to make clear the continuing appeal of the principle-dependent conceptions of moral reasoning that McDowell rejects.

The first problem stems from disagreement. It seems to me that the connoisseurship model will plausibly be construed as a model of rational processes only in conditions in which there is a high degree of agreement among the connoisseurs.

---

[41] Cf. 'Virtue and Reason', 331, 347.

[42] McDowell is of course not the only philosopher to have emphasized the elements of non-principle-dependent, case-specific judgments in Aristotle's account of *phronesis*; for another recent example, see Charles Larmore, *Patterns of Moral Complexity* (Cambridge, England: Cambridge University Press, 1987), ch. 1. There are also clear affinities between this approach to the requirements of virtue and the holistic particularism about reasons defended by Jonathan Dancy, in *Ethics without Principles* (Oxford: Clarendon Press, 2004).

Of course this is not to say that there can never be disagreement among connoisseurs which does not impugn the rational status of their judgments or preferences.
But such disagreement must be distinctly limited: if there were extensive lack of
convergence among connoisseurs of wine as to which wines are good and which
bad, then it would be correspondingly implausible to suppose that their judgments are rationally well supported, or that they represent a normative ideal of
correct discrimination. If this is right, however, it suggests that the connoisseurship model will only yield a compelling account of practical reason in cultural
conditions in which there is widespread agreement among the virtuous as to what
virtue requires, in particular situations of action.[43]

Perhaps such conditions obtained in the historical communities in which
Aristotle himself lived and wrote, but they are notably absent today. Confronted
with a great diversity of cultural influences, in a context of vast discrepancies of
wealth both within and between political communities, we seem to live in an era
in which virtue itself has become problematized, and which is correspondingly
open to competing interpretations of what morality requires of us. In conditions
such as these, the connoisseurship model seems an unpromising way to make out
the claim that questions about what to do are susceptible of rational resolution.
Individuals may take themselves to have case-specific moral reasons for the
particular actions they perform (such as commitment to a certain kind and level of
charitable activity, or a decision to make a professional sacrifice in order to help a
friend), and discerning these reasons will require various rational capacities for
intelligence, imagination, reflection, and so on. But other connoisseurs of the
moral life are apt to be moved by case-specific reasons for acting in quite different
and incompatible ways, and this will undermine the normative dimension of
practical reason: the idea that the exercise of judgment enables its possessor to discern the uniquely *correct* or *right* thing to do, in particular circumstances of action.
The connoisseurship model, in short, does not seem to be applicable to the case of
practical reason in conditions of extensive disagreement among the virtuous.

Perhaps McDowell could respond to this difficulty by acknowledging a plurality of moral subcommunities, constituted by agents who largely agree as to what
virtue requires of them.[44] The connoisseurship model might then account for the
reasoned identification of correct action within these subcommunities, even if it
cannot provide a means for resolving disagreements between members of different
such communities. Developing his account along these lines, however, will only
make more acute a second difficulty which McDowell's approach faces, stemming

[43] I am not suggesting here that correctness of judgment is *constituted* by convergence or
agreement in judgment, on the connoisseurship model; but that a degree of convergence among the
connoisseurs is at least a condition for the truth of the claim that their powers of judgment enable
them to see matters correctly, or aright.

[44] Cf. 'Values and Secondary Qualities', 127 n. 35, where he suggests that the requirement of
convergence or agreement in an account of correct judgment should be 'radically relativized to a
point of view'.

from its apparent elitism. Restricted in its applicability in this way, the connoisseurship interpretation implies that virtue is *esoteric*, in the sense that the rational capacities to grasp and appreciate the virtuous agent's decision are the exclusive possession of those have themselves been inducted into a particular subcommunity of virtue.[45] Thus an agent who is not already a member of such a subcommunity will lack the qualities of refined judgment that are necessary in order to grasp the case-specific reasons in favor of the actions that virtue is taken to require, within the subcommunity—just as a person inexperienced in wine will be unable to appreciate what makes a particular claret distinguished.

About such an esoteric interpretation of virtue, however, the question arises as to whether virtue so interpreted has any relevance at all to the lives of those who are not themselves virtuous already. Especially if we acknowledge a plurality of subcommunities of virtue, it will look as if the powers of practical reason internal to those subcommunities are particular refinements of human ability that have no more claim on people generally than (say) the capacity to appreciate wines, or twelve-tone music, or good darting matches on British television.[46] And yet it is a familiar and reasonable aspiration of morality to provide a more comprehensive framework for regulating human behavior, imposing requirements even on those who are not already virtuous. Aristotle's own moral theory seems to speak to this aspiration. In particular, the perfectionist strategy which I discussed at the start of this paper helps to explain how a conception of virtue which would otherwise be esoteric makes claims on all (male, nonslave) humans. It does so, Aristotle suggests, because the refinement of judgment of the *phronimos* represents the unique realization or perfection of our essential rational nature. But as I noted earlier, McDowell explicitly rejects this perfectionist strategy, and denies that Aristotle himself meant to adopt it. Without it, however, the connoisseurship interpretation is apt to seem a rather pale vindication of the role of reason in the moral life. It avoids the instrumental implications often associated with the Humean conception of practical reason, but it does not do enough to avoid the subjectivism and relativism that are frequent corollaries of such a conception.

---

[45] In this connection see again McDowell's remarks about the 'external intelligibility' of the virtuous agent's conception of how to live (discussed in sect. I, above).

[46] In 'Might There Be External Reasons?', McDowell contends that an amoral agent may have an 'external' reason for acting as the virtuous agent does. As he develops this point, however (see esp. §6), it turns out to involve an extremely weak notion of an external reason. On McDowell's view, the claim that the amoral agent has an external reason to act virtuously is simply a reflection of the virtuous agent's confidence in her own ethical outlook, a confidence which is supported by distinctively ethical arguments. This sort of confidence, however, might equally be sustained by members of a number of different moral subcommunities (or by the aficionado of music of the second Viennese school, to take McDowell's own example of a nonethical case). To say that one has an external reason, in this sense, is to say no more than that there is a way of acting or judging which is in conformity with the (possibly esoteric) standards of some community. Even if we allow McDowell this way of speaking, however, the question remains as to the authority of an esoteric conception of morality to govern the lives of those who are not themselves virtuous already. This is the question I am raising in the text.

This suggests that the question we need to ask about the connoisseurship model is not so much whether it applies to the case of virtue, but whether it is by itself a sufficient substitute for principle-dependent conceptions of practical reason. Recall that even on a principle-dependent account, there will be room to acknowledge the powers of refined judgment that are central to the connoisseurship interpretation. This is in effect the point I made in section I, above, when I argued that general principles or procedures would not necessarily be mechanically applicable to cases. Principle-dependent interpretations hold that the basic patterns of moral reasoning can be formulated in general terms; but the application of general principles or procedures in particular cases will require a capacity for discerning the case-specific features of situations that make some ways of acting in accordance with the procedures or principles better than others. An account of virtue should take this into account, by making room for connoisseurship in its ideal conception of the morally admirable agent, and by holding that moral education has as part of its task the cultivation of these powers of connoisseurship. But this does not exclude the possibility that we can formulate general principles or procedures which provide the governing framework for all moral reasoning and deliberation.

The issue, in these terms, is whether we should rest content with a conception of moral reasoning as connoisseurship, or whether we should seek to supplement it with a principle-dependent interpretation of the basic patterns of moral reflection. Once the question is put in this way, however, I think the continued attractions of principle-dependent accounts will be apparent. First, the construction or formulation of principles or procedures of rational justification in the ethical life seems well suited to the conditions of fragmentation and disagreement that so characterize the contemporary ethical world. The primary task of practical reason in such conditions, one should have thought, is to provide a framework or context within which disagreements can be pursued and, as far as possible, rationally resolved; and the search for general principles or procedures of moral reasoning, if it could be completed, would deliver precisely such a framework.[47] The identification of general principles or procedures of moral reasoning should also go some way toward addressing the problem of the authority of morality to govern or regulate our lives. Following the Humean strategy, we might try to show that the principles speak to some basic concern or desire—such as the desire to be able to justify oneself to others on grounds no one could reasonably reject—that is widely distributed and deeply entrenched in human psychology, as a matter of empirical fact.[48] And it could potentially be interpreted in Kantian terms, as an extension or development of forms of reasoning to which we are all susceptible, whatever our antecedent desires. In this case moral reasoning, far from being

---

[47] This is, I take it, one source of the continuing appeal that utilitarianism has for many people, though I myself find Kantian strategies, or Scanlon's quasi-Humean contractualism, to be much more promising.   [48] This is Scanlon's suggestion, in 'Contractualism and Utilitarianism'.

esoteric, would represent a kind of justification which anyone is capable of grasping and responding to.[49]

Whether accounts of this kind can be made plausible is of course not a question that I can answer in this paper. It is enough to observe that principle-dependent strategies have some attraction, as against the Aristotelian alternative that I have extracted from McDowell's work; and that McDowell himself has said nothing that would call those strategies seriously into question (as I argued in section 1). There is a tendency among recent advocates of an Aristotelian conception of ethics to play Aristotle off against a rather crude and unappealing interpretation of modern conceptions of morality—especially Kantian conceptions.[50] At the same time those working within the Kantian tradition in particular have been developing increasingly sophisticated and attractive accounts of what a Kantian account might look like, which are hardly vulnerable to all the standard objections.[51] McDowell has done us the service of sketching an interpretation of the Aristotelian conception of practical reason which relates it to a broader paradigm of a rational process, and distinguishes it from prevailing Kantian and Humean approaches. But the final assessment of his Aristotelian conception is going to require a much more serious engagement with Kantian and Humean alternatives than McDowell and other neo-Aristotelians have so far essayed.

[49] Thomas Nagel aims to establish this conclusion, in *The Possibility of Altruism*.

[50] Though there is not the space to argue the point here, I believe this is a common failing of the following works: Philippa Foot, 'Morality as a System of Hypothetical Imperatives', reprinted in her *Virtues and Vices* (Oxford: Blackwell, 1978), 157–73; MacIntyre, *After Virtue*; Martha Nussbaum, *The Fragility of Goodness* (Cambridge, England: Cambridge University Press, 1986); Bernard Williams, 'Persons, Character, and Morality' and 'Moral Luck', both reprinted in his *Moral Luck*, 1–39; also his *Ethics and the Limits of Philosophy* (Cambridge, Mass.: Harvard University Press, 1985).

[51] In addition to the works cited in n. 29, above, see e.g. Barbara Herman, 'On the Idea of Acting from the Motive of Duty', *Philosophical Review*, 90 (1981), 359–82; Christine Korsgaard, 'Skepticism about Practical Reason', *Journal of Philosophy* (1986), 5–25; O'Neill, *Constructions of Reason*; and the papers collected in Otfried Höffe (ed.), *Grundlegung zur Metaphysik der Sitten: Ein kooperativer Kommentar* (Frankfurt am Main: Vittorio Klostermann, 1989). Because of its obvious Kantian inspiration, Scanlon's contractualism might also be considered in this connection; certainly it seems to me more promising than utilitarianism as a way of developing a Humean alternative to the connoisseurship model. See also, more recently, T.M. Scanlon, *What We Owe to Each Other* (Cambridge, Mass.: Harvard University Press, 1998).

12

Scanlon's Contractualism

T. M. Scanlon's magisterial book *What We Owe to Each Other* is surely one of the most sophisticated and important works of moral philosophy to have appeared for many years. It raises fundamental questions about all the main aspects of the subject, and I hope and expect that it will have a decisive influence on the shape and direction of moral philosophy in the years to come. In this essay I shall focus on four sets of issues raised by Scanlon's systematic argument, with the aim of clarifying some of Scanlon's central assumptions and presenting alternatives at several key points. The perspective from which I offer these comments is that of a reader who is sympathetic to Scanlon's general approach but not yet convinced on various points of detail.

Before taking up particular issues, however, it will be well to say a few words about the basic thrust of Scanlon's book. Scanlon characterizes his theory as a form of contractualism, one whose roots can be traced to the social contract approach of Rousseau (p. 5). Contractualism in this form is an account of the 'subject matter' of morality (p. 1), or at least of one central strand in moral thinking, which Scanlon identifies as the morality of right and wrong. The leading idea is that moral reflection of this kind is essentially concerned with what we can justify to other people; 'thinking about right and wrong is, at the most basic level, thinking about what could be justified to others on grounds that they, if appropriately motivated, could not reasonably reject' (p. 5).

Originally published in *Ethics*, 112 (April 2002), 429–70. Copyright © 2002 by The University of Chicago. All rights reserved. Reprinted by permission. This paper is a discussion of T. M. Scanlon, *What We Owe to Each Other* (Cambridge, Mass.: Harvard University Press, 1998). Unless otherwise noted, all page citations in this essay refer to Scanlon's book. Many thanks to the participants in my colloquium in ethics at the Humboldt-Universität zu Berlin in the Sommersemester of 1999 for extremely helpful discussion of Scanlon's book. I have also profited greatly from discussions of this article, and of Scanlon's book more generally, with permanent and visiting members of the philosophy program in the Research School of Social Sciences at the Australian National University from February through April 2000 (especially Brad Hooker, Karen Jones, Sue Mendus, Philip Pettit, Mike Ridge, Michael Smith, and Susan Wolf). Further helpful discussion was provided by the participants in the Göttingener Workshop on practical reason in the summer of 2000. In addition, I would like to thank the following people for extensive and incisive written comments on earlier drafts of this article, which have led (I hope) to numerous improvements: Monika Betzler, Jochen Boldt, John Deigh, Samuel Freeman, Logi Gunnarsson, Ulrike Heuer, Rahul Kumar, Samuel Scheffler, and Michael Smith.

Scanlon's sustained and rigorous development of this idea pushes out in two different directions. First, as Scanlon sees it, contractualism offers an appealing response to traditional philosophical concerns about the authority of moral standards to govern the deliberations of individual agents. It does this by characterizing moral motivation in such a way as to render transparent and intelligible both the importance of moral reasons and their deliberative priority over other kinds of normative consideration. Second, Scanlon understands the kind of contractualism he favors as an account of the structure of the morality of right and wrong. That is, the idea of justifiability to others on grounds they could not reasonably reject is said to be what guides substantive reflection about particular moral issues, imparting to the plurality of moral considerations the unity of a single normative domain or 'subject matter'. These two aspects of Scanlon's contractualism are pursued (respectively) in chapters 4 and 5 of *What We Owe to Each Other*, which together present the central positive argument of the book. The three chapters that make up part 1, together with the appendix, discuss general issues in the theory of practical reason and of value that bear on both aspects of the contractualist project, while chapters 6 through 8 explore particular moral issues through the lens of the theory, and pursue its implications for traditional questions about responsibility and relativism.

As this brief synopsis makes plain, Scanlon sees contractualism as a systematic response to a range of philosophical problems; the same theory that lays bare the structure of the morality of right and wrong is also meant to illuminate the authority of moral considerations in practical reflection about how we are to act. In this respect, Scanlon's version of contractualism can be seen as a worthy successor to the classical moral theories of the modern tradition, such as Kantianism and utilitarianism. Much contemporary work in ethics exhibits a kind of fragmentation of focus. There are detailed discussions in so-called normative ethics, often built around variations of imaginary cases, which seem to ignore the implications of substantive moral conclusions for traditional questions about the authority and objectivity of moral requirements. Conversely, many treatments of the latter issues are conducted in virtually complete abstraction from details about the structure of moral thinking, rather as if moral philosophy were just a special branch of metaphysics and epistemology. There is nothing necessarily objectionable about this, but Scanlon's book serves as a useful reminder of the connections between the substantive and the more theoretical sides of moral philosophy;[1] it is in this respect a kind of paradigm of systematic ethical theory.

A further respect in which Scanlon's book seems to me exemplary concerns its strategy of argument. The book is the result of many years of reflection about moral philosophy, focused not only on working out the details of his own

---

[1] In a more old-fashioned idiom, one might refer to the relations between normative ethics and metaethics, though I find these categories problematic and so prefer the admittedly vague expressions in the text.

preferred approach, but also on understanding the questions to which his approach represents a response. Scanlon begins each stage of his argument with a judicious analysis of the particular issues that are at stake, distinguishing the points of genuine controversy from less important side issues, and trying to get as clear as possible about the questions he is addressing before advancing his favored solution. His discussion of relativism and disagreement in chapter 8, for instance, is presented not simply as a response to a philosophical question that is taken to be antecedently well understood but, rather, as an interpretation of the threats posed by diversity in moral thought and practice, in the light of which we can appreciate the advantages of contractualism for understanding such diversity. The resulting density of content makes heavy demands on the reader, who is asked to think simultaneously about contractualism and about the terms of the problems to which a philosophical account of morality is addressed; undoubtedly those will profit most from Scanlon's discussion who have themselves already engaged in independent reflection about the issues of moral philosophy, and who are well versed in the extensive literature to which Scanlon (often rather allusively) responds. But the demands are amply rewarded, as the book stimulates one to think in fresh terms about virtually all of the many issues it addresses.

1. REASONS AND MOTIVATION

At the end of the introduction Scanlon characterizes *What We Owe to Each Other* 'as a book dealing with three concentric and successively narrower normative domains: reasons, values, and what we owe to each other' (p. 13). The treatment of reasons occupies chapter 1 and the appendix of the book. Scanlon's overall position on this issue, which provides an important foundation for his defense of contractualism in the later chapters, is distinguished by two main commitments (p. 17). First, Scanlon takes the idea of a reason as primitive; in both the theoretical and the practical sphere reasons are considerations that speak for or against something, and there is no prospect of analyzing this relation in terms that are more fundamental. Second, Scanlon holds that this primitive idea of a reason is also one that is basically in good order. Philosophers have often supposed that reasons in the practical domain—that is, reasons for action—raise special philosophical problems; on account of their distinctive connection with motivation, reasons of this kind have been thought to require a subjective grounding in the agent's desires, of a sort that has no analogue in the case of reasons for belief. But Scanlon rejects this suggestion, contending that the link between reasons for action and motivation presents no special philosophical problem.

The position Scanlon develops within the framework of these commitments might be called a kind of cognitivism about reasons. The attitude of taking a given consideration to be a reason, holding it to count for or against some action or belief, can itself be counted a belief that is susceptible of truth or falsity in the ordinary ways (ch. 1, sect. 12).[2] This attitude is not, to be sure, like empirical beliefs in requiring a metaphysics of objects that are at a spatial distance from the subject who judges that something is the case, but there is no reason to suppose that attitudes can count as genuine beliefs only if they resemble empirical judgments in this respect (pp. 62–3). The most serious questions about the status of claims about reasons concern not the metaphysical and epistemological commitments of such claims but the availability of substantive standards for assessing them as correct or incorrect (pp. 63–4).

Particularly in regard to claims about reasons for action, it might be thought that reliable intersubjective standards of this kind are lacking. But Scanlon argues that this is not the case, sketching a general procedure for reflecting about such reasons that generates commitments in which we have a high degree of confidence and which exhibit significant interpersonal stability (ch. 1, sect. 13). Practical deliberation often begins with states in which it seems to us that it would be good in some way to perform a given action. Critical reflection about reasons for action is a process of characterizing more exactly the reason putatively grasped in a state of this kind, and exploring its implications for other, related situations and cases (pp. 65–9). Those commitments that survive this process of critical reflection, earning the confidence not only of the agent but of others who undertake to reflect about the matter, can be considered to be correct or true judgments about what is the case. We might also think of this position as a kind of procedural realism about reasons (p. 380 n. 48)—procedural, because the credentials of our judgments regarding what there is reason to do are secured not by their standing in the right relation to an independent realm of objects, but by their resilience within the procedures of critical reflection relevant to judgments of this kind.

It is an important consequence of this general approach that it encourages us to take very seriously the conclusions of deliberative reflection about what there is reason to do. Such conclusions may be thought of as principles (p. 197), specifying (in schematic terms) that considerations of kind c provide sufficient reason for performing an action of kind x. To accept a principle of this sort is not merely to have a pro-attitude toward x-ing, in circumstances of the specified variety, but to judge that those circumstances ordinarily speak conclusively in favor of doing x. Judgments about reasons for action thus have an implicit generality; we cannot endorse a judgment about what we have reason to do without accepting a principle that is at least potentially applicable to other cases, setting out what any agent would have reason to do in circumstances that are relevantly similar (pp. 73–4). This in turn suggests an important constraint on philosophical reflection about

---

[2] Actually Scanlon leaves open the question whether a 'special attitude' theory of the stance of taking something to be a reason might be correct (pp. 58–9), while advancing considerations that favor the view that this stance is an ordinary belief with a distinctively normative content (pp. 59–62). Since Scanlon makes it clear that he himself accepts the latter position, it seems fair to characterize his view as a kind of cognitivism or realism.

reasons for action, which we might call the priority of deliberative judgment. The conclusions of first-personal deliberation are not to be treated as mere pieces of phenomenological biography, which impinge on philosophical theorizing (at best) as data to be explained psychologically. Assuming that such deliberation can survive the heuristic procedures of critical assessment mentioned above, its results represent sound and perfectly generalizable verdicts about what there is reason for anybody to do,[3] and philosophical theory must so far as possible respect and seek to accommodate these verdicts on their own normative terms.

The significance of this approach becomes especially apparent in Scanlon's exceptionally interesting discussion of the relations between reasons for action and desires. As I mentioned above, it is very common to contend that reasons of this kind stand in a special relation to the desires of the agent to whom the reasons apply, deriving from those desires, or being contingent on them in some way. But, Scanlon argues, it is hard to reconcile this contention with the thesis of the priority of deliberative judgment. For one thing, when we reflect carefully on the kinds of considerations that seem to us, from the deliberative perspective, to supply concrete justifications for acting in one way or another, it emerges that desires almost never have this role to play (ch. 1, sect. 9). Even in the cases that would seem most congenial to the connection between reasons and desires, involving a person's tastes and preferences, it is not desires *per se* that function as reasons (in the basic, normative sense of considerations that speak in favor of a given course of action). My reason for eating chocolate ice cream for dessert is not, strictly speaking, that I want to do so, but that it would be pleasant or satisfying in some way; it is thus the intrinsic quality of the experience of eating the ice cream that recommends this course of action, rather than the fact that it would formally satisfy my occurrent desire (pp. 44–5).

In cases of this kind, of course, our reasons are contingent in some more general manner on what might be called subjective conditions, pertaining to our tastes, preferences, interests, and so on. Even if my occurrent desire for chocolate ice cream is not itself what recommends eating some for dessert, still I have reason to do so only because it happens to be true of me that I like the stuff and that eating it would therefore be a source of culinary pleasure. Moreover, this contingency of my reason on subjective conditions is something that I can affirm within deliberative reflection. But, Scanlon argues, with many of our most significant reasons for action things are otherwise. From the deliberative point of view, for instance, it does not strike us that moral reasons are contingent on subjective facts about us in the way they clearly seem to be in matters of taste. The considerations that speak against, say, manipulation or duplicity are the specific features of these ways of

---

[3] This does not mean that all agents have reason to act in precisely the same way but merely that anyone who is in the relevant respects in the same situation as I am, and who has relevantly similar projects and interests and commitments and so on, will have the same reasons for action that I have.

interacting with people that make them wrong,[4] and these wrong-making features are not contingent on subjective facts about the *agent's* desires, preferences, interests, or tastes (p. 367; cf. pp. 41–2). Internalism in the sense introduced by Bernard Williams—that is, the thesis that all reasons for action require a basis in the agent's subjective motivational set—thus cannot be reconciled with the priority of deliberative judgment (cf. the appendix).[5]

Those who are attracted to this kind of internalism would presumably respond that, even if their favored thesis strains against our deliberative self-understanding in some cases, it is the only way to make sense of the capacity of practical reason to move us to action. Rational reflection on our reasons typically gives rise to a corresponding motivation, and internalists contend that this motivating dimension of reasons for action can be accounted for only on the assumption that such reasons are appropriately grounded in our desires. But Scanlon's discussion of reasons includes a highly sophisticated response to this influential line of thought. The response has two main parts. First, Scanlon points out that it is a perfectly general mark of rationality that we form attitudes in response to our own views about reasons in the primitive normative sense (ch. 1, sects. 2–3). Virtually nobody finds problematic, for instance, the idea that rational agents modify their beliefs in accordance with their assessment of the considerations that speak for and against particular conclusions about what is the case; beliefs are states that are intrinsically sensitive to judgments about reasons of this kind, and for the most part rational believers automatically modify their beliefs to bring them into alignment with their judgments about the balance of reasons. But, Scanlon contends, the states of intention that typically move us to act are similarly 'judgment-sensitive attitudes', exhibiting the same kind of intrinsic responsiveness to our assessment of reasons that is uncontroversially present in the sphere of theoretical rationality (pp. 21–2). We are perhaps inclined to think of practical reason as a peculiarly mysterious capacity to set the body in motion, requiring the postulation of forces (such as desire) that go beyond anything necessary to account for the rational modification of our beliefs. But this picture is a caricature. The problem of rational motivation is to explain how the states of intention that move us to action could themselves be produced by reflection on what we have reason to do. But since those states are judgment-sensitive attitudes, their responsiveness to this kind of reasoning can be accounted for in exactly the same way that we explain the capacity of theoretical reflection to produce changes in our beliefs. There is thus no *special* problem that is posed by the connection of practical reason with intentional action.

---

[4] Or, in Scanlon's terms, that make it reasonable to reject principles that permit these ways of acting. I return to the question of how to characterize the reason-giving force of moral considerations in sect. 4, below.

[5] See Bernard Williams, 'Internal and External Reasons', as reprinted in his *Moral Luck* (Cambridge: Cambridge University Press, 1981), 101–13. In the discussion that follows I shall use the expressions 'internalism' and 'externalism' in Williams's sense, to denote accounts that affirm and deny (respectively) the dependence of reasons on elements in the agent's subjective motivational set.

The second part of Scanlon's response to the internalist challenge is to question widespread assumptions about the way in which desires produce motivations to action. Those attracted to internalism, like those attracted to noncognitivist and expressivist accounts in ethics, must assume that desires are intrinsically and directly motivating in a way mere beliefs (about, say, reasons for action) cannot be. Furthermore, in a central class of cases to desire something is to be in an occurrent state of attraction to some particular object or course of action—Scanlon refers to this as desire in the 'directed attention sense' (pp. 38–9)—and desires of this familiar kind certainly seem to be sources of motivation to action. But how exactly are we to understand the motivating power of such desires? Scanlon makes a compelling case for the conclusion that the motivating force of desires in the directed attention sense must be traced to their cognitive content, in particular to the agent's grasp of some consideration as a reason (ch. 1, sect. 8). Thus the element of attraction that is characteristic of such desires cannot be understood as a brute force to which the agent is subject, impelling the body directly in one way or another. The motivating tendency of desires is connected to their distinctive phenomenology, the focusing of one's attention onto an object or possibility for action as something that would be good along some dimension. Thus when I am in the grip of a desire for (say) a piece of chocolate, I will find myself dwelling on the possibility of eating the chocolate, and the imagined pleasure of this experience will present itself to me as something that counts in favor of putting the chocolate in my mouth. The phenomenological attraction, in other words, can be traced to the normative content of the cognitions involved in the state of desire, indeed to the very same kind of cognition that is distinctively involved in our judgments about what there is reason to do.

It thus emerges that the motivating power of desires relies on the more basic mechanism whereby our attitudes are sensitive to our normative judgments or cognitions about what there is reason to do. Noncognitivists and expressivists tend to deny that such normative commitments can be counted genuine thoughts or cognitions, arguing that their motivating potential requires us to suppose that they give expression to desires or pro-attitudes of some kind. But if Scanlon is correct, this position has things exactly the wrong way around.[6] Far from representing a source of motivation to action that is independent of normative cognitions, and in terms of which the distinctive features of such cognitions can be explained, desire itself seems to presuppose the availability of motivating cognitions about what there is reason to do. We need to appeal to such cognitions to capture both

---

[6] I should perhaps mention that this is not a conclusion Scanlon himself explicitly endorses; indeed, he leaves open the question of whether a 'special attitude' theory of the stance of taking something to be a reason might be correct (see n. 3, above). But Scanlon's reflections about phenomenal motivation or attraction seem to raise a doubt about one of the considerations typically advanced in favor of such 'special attitude' theories.

the distinctive phenomenology and the motivating potential of the most central and familiar examples of the phenomenon of desire.[7]

Scanlon's position on reasons represents a systematic and formidable challenge to a wide range of views that remain extremely influential in contemporary moral philosophy. I believe his thesis of the priority of deliberative judgment to be profoundly correct, and agree with his reflections on the motivating and justificatory role of desires. But puzzles remain; I should like to raise two questions about this part of Scanlon's theory. The first and less significant question has to do with the implications of Scanlon's account of the motivating force of desires for our understanding of the behavior of animals and very young infants. On the one hand, it certainly seems as if we can make sense of such behavior by postulating desires that move animals and infants to rudimentary forms of action. It is plausible to say (for instance) that the dog is pushing its dish around the kitchen because it wants something to eat, or that the child's removal of all objects from its crib expresses the desire to bring its nap time to an end. On the other hand, if Scanlon's basic strategy is correct the motivating force of desire should be traced to a kind of cognition that we may be reluctant to suppose children and animals to be capable of. Even if we are prepared to accept that such creatures have a capacity for basic representations of the world around them, it is unclear that they are capable of distinctively normative thoughts, about what counts in favor of various ways of acting; yet it is cognitions of this kind, Scanlon maintains, that provide the basic impetus to action when we (adult humans) are in the grip of desire. Moreover in reflecting about these kinds of cases we seem to understand well enough the attribution of motivating desires to children and animals. It is very tempting to suppose that there is a primitive, inarticulate experience of wanting something, which stands in a characteristic relation to behavior aimed at bringing about the state that one desires. Indeed this widespread thought lends some credence to the noncognitivist contention that the phenomenon of desire is more basic and elemental than that of normative cognition, so that the latter can be accounted for in terms of the former.

Particularly since I am inclined to agree with Scanlon's account of the motivating dimension of desires, it seems to me that something more needs to be said about the motivating role of desire in connection with animal and infant behavior, and about the connections between desire in this context and in the context of adult human motivation. But I shall put this issue to the side in order to focus on a second and to my mind more serious difficulty. This is raised by cases of

---

[7] This position might seem to rule out the possibility of what Nagel has called 'unmotivated desires', which just come over us and are not grounded in our prior evaluative judgments. But if we emphasize the distinction between genuine judgments and mere cognitions, we can make room for unmotivated desires of this kind. These will be cases in which we are assailed by the thought that it would be good to pursue some particular course of action, without our sincerely judging (either antecedently or concurrently) that this is in fact the case.

irrationality in the sphere of action. By irrationality here I mean precisely the phenomenon to which Scanlon himself refers by use of this term. In a very important discussion he suggests that claims about what a given agent has reason to do should be distinguished from claims about the conditions under which the agent is guilty of irrationality (ch. 1, sect. 4). Thus, if Scanlon is right in holding that moral reasons, for instance, do not have subjective conditions, then there is reason for virtually any person to comply with the basic standards that define the morality of right and wrong. It does not follow from this, however, that agents who act immorally thereby open themselves automatically to the charge of irrationality. The natural thing to say about agents of this kind is that they are (say) cruel, or inconsiderate, or unfair, or self-absorbed, not that they are irrational (pp. 27–9, 366–7). A verdict of irrationality becomes appropriate only in a small and rather special subset of cases, in which the agent in question acknowledges the force of the rational requirement that they flout. This suggestion seems independently plausible, insofar as it brings allegations of practical irrationality into alignment with our use of this notion in connection with beliefs. Moreover, it frees externalist approaches to reasons for action from the absurdly heavy burden of holding that those who fail to act on their reasons are thereby automatically irrational. One can thus maintain that moral and other reasons apply to persons regardless of their antecedent motivations, without having to draw the conclusion that immoral agents necessarily suffer from a defect of rationality.

Especially in the sphere of action, however, there are many cases in which this more specialized charge would seem to be warranted. These are cases to which the traditional categories of *akrasia* and weakness of will apply, in which an agent freely and intentionally acts in a given way, while acknowledging that it would really be better to do something else instead. I believe that a successful account of rational motivation needs to leave open the possibility of cases of this kind; but it is not clear to me that Scanlon's account succeeds in satisfying this constraint. As we have seen, that account appeals to the general tendency of rational subjects to acquire judgment-sensitive attitudes in accordance with their irreducibly normative beliefs about reasons. This approach amounts to a kind of cognitivism about motivation, and the question arises whether a cognitivism of this variety leaves room for deliberate action at variance with one's beliefs about what there is most reason to do. The motivation to act against one's better judgment, it appears, must be traced to the agent's normative thought that doing so would be good or recommended, a thought that is perhaps associated with some wayward desire to which the agent is subject. But if it is really a normative thought of this kind that motivates *akratic* action (together with the agent's basic tendency to form attitudes that are sensitive to such judgments), it becomes difficult to see how the agent can really have believed, at the time of action, that it would be better to do something else. Given the basic tendency to adjust one's attitudes to one's judgments about one's reasons, we should surely expect that the agent's belief about what it would be best to do, all things considered, would produce a corresponding intention to act, if indeed that belief is both sincerely held and clearly before the mind of the agent at the relevant time. This suggests that the normative cognition latent in the wayward desire on which the *akrates* acts must somehow have clouded their grasp of what there is most reason to do—a pattern of explanation reminiscent of Aristotelian skepticism about the possibility of clear-eyed *akrasia*.

Scanlon recognizes that there can be 'a distinction between an agent's assessment of the reason-giving force of a consideration and the influence that that consideration has on the agent's thought and action' (p. 36). He makes two observations about this distinction. First, it applies no less in the sphere of belief than in the sphere of action; there is, in other words, room for one's beliefs to diverge from one's judgment about what there is reason to think in a way that is strictly analogous to *akrasia* of action (pp. 35–6). Second, if we are to make sense of this distinction we must view it in relation to the abilities that make rationality possible in the first place: 'Akratic actions (and irrational beliefs) are cases in which a person's rational capacities have malfunctioned, not cases in which these capacities are overmastered by something else, called desire' (p. 40).

I agree with Scanlon that *akratic* action should not be conceptualized on the model of overmastery by some desiderative force that is strictly foreign to reason itself. But it is not clear to me that this represents the only alternative to the cognitivist picture that Scanlon himself favors. He accounts for the distinction between a normative judgment about one's reasons and the effects of that judgment on one's thought and behavior by appealing to the way in which circumstances can affect (for instance) the degree to which the content of the normative judgment is vividly before one's mind (pp. 34–5). Presumably wayward desires (of the directed-attention variety) are among the circumstances that have this kind of effect, making one vividly aware of certain potentially reason-giving considerations (such as short-term opportunities for pleasure) in a way that causes one's assessment of what there is most reason to do to go out of focus. As explained above, I think this amounts to an Aristotelian denial of the possibility of clear-eyed *akrasia*. But quite apart from this issue Scanlon's approach seems at odds with our experience in a wide range of cases in which our motivations are not merely a function of the degree to which relevant normative considerations are vividly present to consciousness. In cases of strength of will, for instance, agents succeed in doing what they believe best in the face of extremely vivid temptations to go astray.[8]

Scanlon might reply that this is possible only to the extent that the strong-willed person manages to focus on or attend to the reasons that properly ought to prevail in the situation at hand. Even when this is the right way to describe what is going on, however, facts pertaining to the focus of the agent's thoughts do not seem to be mere facts about the circumstances in which the agent is placed, on a

---

[8] Indeed, if we are to believe Aristotle, strong-willed persons hold out in the face of temptations that are much stronger and more vivid than most people are able to resist, whereas *akratic* persons succumb to temptations that ordinary agents can readily cope with; see the *Nicomachean Ethics*, 1150a9–16.

par with facts about their desires and emotions. Rather, focusing on the right set of reasons seems to be something that the strong-willed agent *does*, part of the strategy whereby they bring it about that they act well despite the vivid temptation to which they are subject. This seems to point in the direction of an executive capacity for self-determination in the realm of action, one whose operations cannot be reconstructed solely in terms of the combined effects of normative cognition and the basic sensitivity of our attitudes to such cognition. Perhaps a moral psychology that takes the *will* more seriously is needed if we are to account adequately both for the motivational effects of normative judgment and for the peculiar human capacity for deliberate action that flouts such judgment.

To follow this path would be to introduce an important disanalogy in accounts of rationality in the theoretical and practical domains, for I see no reason to suppose that we must postulate a similar capacity for self-determination in regard to belief. As I explained above, Scanlon stresses the continuities between theoretical and practical reason. In particular, he suggests that the very same susceptibility to judgment-sensitive attitudes can account for rational belief-revision and rational motivation, and he maintains that analogous possibilities for strict irrationality are present in the two domains. But the example he deploys to illustrate the latter point seems unconvincing: 'I may know . . . that despite Jones's pretensions to be a loyal friend, he is merely an artful deceiver. Yet when I am with him I may find the appearance of warmth and friendship so affecting that I find myself thinking, although I know better, that he can be relied on after all' (p. 35).[9] Here we find a person, in the presence of what appears to be appropriate evidence, entertaining the thought that something is the case, while knowing that it is not. This is indeed analogous to a phenomenon connected with action, but the phenomenon is not *akrasia* but, rather, temptation: being subject to a strong desire to do something, while simultaneously believing that it would be best on the whole not to. Temptation turns into *akrasia* when the agent decides to give in to the wayward desire, despite continuing to believe that doing so would not be best. The corresponding phenomenon in the theoretical case would be to form the belief that Jones is sincere and reliable, while continuing to know that he is merely a deceiver; but as this description makes plain, it is extremely difficult to imagine something like this taking place. It seems to be ruled out by fundamental constraints on the attribution of beliefs.[10] We have, I maintain, no comparable difficulty imagining

---

[9] I discuss this example at greater length in my paper 'Normativity, Commitment, and Instrumental Reason', Chapter 5 in this volume.

[10] Constraints of this kind do not prevent us from postulating conflicts between a person's conscious and unconscious attitudes (as in certain cases of self-deception) or from distinguishing between different senses of belief or knowledge. Thus one may believe in one sense (e.g. insofar as one would assent to the proposition on reflection) that Jones is a deceiver, while believing in another sense (e.g. insofar as the proposition is vividly present to consciousness) that he is basically reliable. The point is that analogous moves do not need to be made in order to make sense of irrationality in the domain of action. The *akrates*, it seems, can know or believe in the fullest sense of the word that it would be best to do *x*, while deliberately and consciously choosing, also in the fullest sense of the word, to do not-*x*.

the possibility of clear-eyed *akrasia*, and this leads me to suspect that Scanlon has overstrained the analogy between theoretical and practical rationality. There may, after all, be special problems raised by the motivational effects of reasons for action.

2. RESPONSIBILITY AND VALUE

The suspicion raised at the end of the preceding section seems to be confirmed by a pair of further claims that Scanlon endorses in regard to desires in the directed attention sense. On the one hand, Scanlon remarks that these desires are states with respect to which we are in some sense passive; they are unreflective elements in our practical thinking, assailing us unbidden, and often persisting in the face of conflicting considered judgments about what there is reason to do (pp. 39–40, 65). In these ways, our desires often do not seem to be fully subject to our voluntary control (p. 400 n. 13). On the other hand, in virtue of their cognitive content, their standing as states that are within the broad domain of reason rather than as forces wholly external to it, Scanlon contends that desires are attributable to the agent in all the ways that render moral appraisal appropriate (pp. 21–2, 273–4). Thus it is fully appropriate to hold persons accountable for their wayward desires, criticizing them on this basis in the distinctive manner that gives expression to blame.

To my mind, these two claims are in tension with each other. If we concede that desires are not subject to a person's voluntary control, then it seems misguided to blame the person merely on account of them. To take Scanlon's own example: someone who judges correctly that they do not need a new computer, and who succeeds in acting in accordance with this judgment, should not be subject to criticism just because the desire for a new computer persists (cf. pp. 43–4). Of course, wayward desires of this kind must in some sense be attributable to the agent, otherwise there would be no special need for the agent to struggle against them. We may also concede that such desires form an appropriate basis for certain kinds of evaluative and moral assessment of persons. People who are persistently subject to strong desires to acquire new consumer products, irrespective of their real usefulness or value, may in that respect have an unlovely character. But to the extent that the desires in question elude the voluntary control of the person subject to them, to blame the person for them would seem to me to be the wrong kind of response. Furthermore, it remains an inappropriate response even in those cases in which the wayward desires in question have a significant interpersonal dimension. My involuntary strong aversion to reading the student papers on my desk, or my temporary lack of sympathy for the person I am in a unique position to help (think of Kant's 'friend of man'), are not themselves blameworthy moral faults.

We blame people in the first instance for their decisions and choices, and for their actions to the extent that these reflect questionable decisions and choices. The presupposition of this practice is that states of these kinds are subject to the direct control of the agent, in a way that mere desires do not necessarily seem to be; they are central examples of the class of volitional attitudes to which I adverted at the end of the preceding section, as the locus of self-determining agency. A moral psychology that leaves room for attitudes of this kind will thus have a principled basis for distinguishing between the forms of moral assessment appropriate to mere desires and emotions, on the one hand, and to actions and decisions, on the other hand.

Scanlon apparently takes a more catholic view of the states that are appropriate targets of strong moral criticism, resulting in a wider conception of what we are in the first instance morally responsible for. His position on these issues is supported by an interesting account of the special force of moral criticism, as distinguished from criticism of other kinds (ch. 6, sect. 4). According to Scanlon's account, the special force of moral appraisal can be traced to the significance that violations of moral principles have for an agent's relations with other people. Failure to comply with such principles is not something to which other persons can afford to be indifferent, because it essentially betrays a kind of disregard, a failure to recognize and respond appropriately to their value as persons (pp. 271–2; cf. pp. 103–7, 158–60). Moral faults introduce basic rifts into the social fabric, and this gives criticism in moral terms a force and significance that set it apart from other forms of appraisal (in, say, aesthetic or intellectual terms). Scanlon's account of the distinctive force of moral assessment points toward a corresponding restriction on the scope of such assessment. This is properly directed, Scanlon suggests, only toward rational creatures, and only in regard to their judgment-sensitive attitudes, which are in principle subject to rational control (p. 272). Moral appraisal can be understood as a request to reconsider the attitudes expressed in an agent's action and to modify or withdraw the attitudes accordingly, but this request seems to make sense only on the condition that the attitude in question belongs to the class of states that are open to these kinds of rational modification (pp. 275–6).

Scanlon takes his account of the force and scope of moral appraisal to show that such appraisal can appropriately be applied to our desires, since these belong to the general class of judgment-sensitive attitudes. But I believe the account in fact supports a different and narrower conclusion: namely, that moral appraisal of desires is in order only to the extent that the desires in question prove susceptible to direct rational control. In the cases of wayward desire considered above, this condition is not satisfied, insofar as those desires persist even in the face of conflicting reflective judgments about what there is reason to do, and require to be struggled against. Though wayward desires of this type have a conceptual structure, their persistence in the presence of conflicting normative judgments suggests that they are not in fact open to direct rational control by the agent; this in turn makes the request to withdraw or modify the attitude latent in moral criticism seem misdirected.[11] In cases in which our desires fail to respond to our own normative reflection, it makes sense to say that we are alienated or estranged from states that are at some literal level ours.[12] We are not identified with these states in the way we may be identified with the judgments we arrive at through normative reflection, or (I would add) with the decisions or choices we make on the basis of such judgments. They thus do not seem to be attributable to us in the way that would render moral blame appropriate.

Scanlon's position on responsibility for wayward desires runs parallel to his stance on a different but related issue, concerning the general conditions of moral accountability. Some philosophers—Susan Wolf and I are recent examples—hold that it is only fair or fitting to hold responsible those agents who exhibit what might be called moral competence: the general capacity to grasp distinctively moral reasons and to act in accordance with reasons of this kind.[13] But Scanlon rejects this condition. He apparently concedes that it can make sense to speak of a distinctively moral competence of this kind and to suppose that this narrow competence might be lacking in persons who possess the more general capacity to make judgments about what there is reason to do. But he argues that moral criticism and blame can appropriately be directed toward the judgment-sensitive attitudes of persons who are morally incompetent, so long as the more general capacity for practical reason is present (ch. 6, sect. 5, esp. pp. 287–90). Agents who satisfy this more general condition are able to act in ways that disregard our standing and value as persons, and so their moral failures exhibit the special significance for interpersonal relations that moral appraisal and blame distinctively signal.

But what about the idea that appraisal of this kind represents an appeal to the transgressor to modify or withdraw the attitudes that are subject to criticism? How can such an appeal be warranted if the agent is not capable of understanding the moral principles upon which the appeal rests? Scanlon acknowledges that this

---

[11] Of course, it would not necessarily be misdirected to request that the agent take steps to reduce their susceptibility to such wayward desires in the future. Alternatively, Scanlon might say that a request to modify or withdraw these attitudes is always appropriate; even if such a request proves ineffective, 'there's no harm in asking', as one might say. Interpreted in this way, however, his discussion of moral criticism becomes correspondingly implausible as an account of the special force of blame, which seems distinctively connected with the reactive attitudes that find expression in sanctioning behavior. To respond to offenses in this way is not merely to issue an idle request for modification of the offensive attitudes, but to demand their modification or withdrawal (cf. pp. 289–90).

[12] It is a leitmotiv of the work of Harry Frankfurt and Gary Watson that persons can be subject to motivating attitudes with which they are not fully identified; see e.g. Harry Frankfurt, 'Identification and Wholeheartedness', as reprinted in his *The Importance of What We Care About* (Cambridge, England: Cambridge University Press, 1988), 159–76; and Gary Watson, 'Free Agency', as reprinted in Watson (ed.), *Free Will* (Oxford: Oxford University Press, 1982), 96–110.

[13] See Susan Wolf's *Freedom within Reason* (New York: Oxford University Press, 1990), ch. 4; and my *Responsibility and the Moral Sentiments* (Cambridge, Mass.: Harvard University Press, 1994), ch. 6.

line of thought may explain our attraction to the idea that moral competence is a further condition of accountability. But he thinks the idea nevertheless mistaken, urging that what matters is the more basic fact that moral criticism is applied to attitudes that are in general sensitive to the agent's judgments (pp. 288–9). As we saw in discussing wayward desires, however, this more basic fact does not really seem to be enough. That my desires belong to a class of attitudes that is in general sensitive to normative judgments does not make me responsible for them in cases in which the desires in question escape my best efforts to control them. Nor does this condition suffice in cases in which I cannot grasp the terms in which the criticism that is directed at my attitudes and actions is couched. Scanlon himself makes the useful suggestion that morality can be thought of as a 'system of co-deliberation' (p. 268), but this suggestion seems to me only to reinforce the thought that moral competence should be an additional condition of accountability. How can it be reasonable to blame people for violating moral principles when they are not capable of participating in the system of codeliberation which it is the function of those principles to define?[14]

With respect to the issue of moral competence, this disagreement with Scanlon over the commitments of his own view may not have much practical significance. We typically assume that there are persons—the psychopaths of the philosophical imagination—who, though subject to judgment-sensitive attitudes and in general capable of practical deliberation, are somehow blind to moral reasons in particular; but it is not clear how many actual people are really like this. The disagreement is possibly more consequential in regard to wayward desires, for I take it (and Scanlon would agree) that we are all frequently subject to desires that defy our own reflective conclusions about what there is most reason to do. Against Scanlon, I would contend that desires of this kind are not attributable to us in the way that would justify strong moral appraisal and blame. Scanlon's different line on these cases may reflect the assumption that, if we cannot hold people to account for their wayward desires, we may not be able to blame them even in the most central cases in which they are morally at fault. Such cases typically display some *de facto* failure to respond to moral reasons, at least dimly perceived, and this may suggest that what properly grounds moral appraisal is not the actual sensitivity of our attitudes to our judgments, but their belonging to a broader class of attitudes that exhibits this kind of sensitivity—a condition equally satisfied by wayward desires. But this assumption can be questioned. As I suggested in the preceding section, there seems to be a distinctive kind of volitional state, exemplified by decisions and choices, that is subject to our direct control in ways mere desire

---

[14] On pp. 347–8 of ch. 8, Scanlon comes close to acknowledging this point. There, he remarks that when it is difficult for people to appreciate the moral facts or to see the force of moral reasons, we rightly qualify the kind of criticism and blame that we direct at them for the wrong actions they perform. This seems to presuppose that moral competence is a condition of full-scale blame, since the inability to appreciate moral facts or to grasp moral reasons would be a paradigm case of impaired moral competence.

in the directed attention sense is not. When we apply moral criticism to attitudes of this kind, our request for modification or withdrawal of the attitude thus seems peculiarly appropriate to its target, as it does not when a request of this kind is directed at mere desires.

There is one further general issue I should like to touch on briefly before moving to Scanlon's account of moral reasons. This issue concerns the relations between reasons and the good, and it is raised by Scanlon's impressive discussion of values in chapter 2 of *What We Owe to Each Other*. There Scanlon presents an abstract account of the structure of the idea of value, an account that contains two distinct and independent elements: 'One is the idea . . . that value is not a purely teleological notion. The other is the claim that being valuable is not a property that provides us with reasons. Rather, to call something valuable is to say that it has other properties that provide reasons for behaving in certain ways in regard to it' (p. 96). It is probably the first of these two elements that is more important for Scanlon's larger purposes. Many philosophers view it as something close to a conceptual truth that value has a basically teleological structure; according to this teleological conception, states of affairs are the sole bearers of intrinsic value, and the reasons for action that are provided by values are exclusively reasons to promote or to bring about such states of affairs (pp. 79–81). If we accept this teleological conception, it becomes extremely difficult to resist a consequentialist interpretation of the structure of moral reasoning in particular. Any proposal about (say) the value of actions will get interpreted as a claim about the kinds of states of affairs that are to be promoted or discouraged, and this provides one basis for skepticism about the very idea that there could be distinctively agent-centered prohibitions or requirements. Scanlon mounts a convincing case against the teleological conception of value, attending to a range of examples in which it distorts rather than illuminates our reasons to force them into a teleological framework (ch. 2, sects. 2–3). The reasons provided by friendship, for example, are not in the first instance reasons to promote states of affairs that involve friendship, but to structure one's interactions with the individuals who are one's friends in ways that display loyalty, attention, concern, solicitude, and so on (pp. 88–90).

Scanlon refers to the second element in his abstract account of value as the 'buck-passing' theory of the good (p. 96). The root idea here is that goodness or value is not some substantive nonnatural property that itself provides us with reasons for action. Reasons are instead provided by the natural properties that make things valuable along different concrete dimensions, and to say that something is good is just a way of signaling that there are some such substantive reasons for choosing, preferring, recommending, or admiring it. Scanlon advances two considerations in favor of this buck-passing account (pp. 97–8). First, reflection on cases suggests that it is the natural properties of actions and things that constitute our concrete reasons for choosing or preferring them. Second, there is a vast diversity of things that we take to be good or valuable, and Scanlon finds it implausible that there should be a single reason-providing property common to everything that falls within this range.

This second consideration seems persuasive to me, but I remain somewhat unclear whether it really justifies the buck-passing account that Scanlon favors. For one thing, it seems to me striking that a buck- passing account can with equal plausibility be formulated for the case of reasons for action. According to such an account, the property of being a reason for some action (or counting in favor of it) is not to be understood as a substantive property that itself makes the action in question good; rather, to say that there is a reason of this kind is a way of signaling that the action has other concrete properties, which differ from case to case, in virtue of which the action is good or worthy of performing.

Scanlon's preferred version of the buck-passing strategy suggests that what is at issue is the explanatory priority of reasons vis-à-vis values, or (as we might put it) of the normative vis-à-vis the evaluative. But his own discussion of the normative domain in chapter 1 raises a doubt about whether this really could be what is at issue. There, Scanlon represents both desires and judgments about reasons as involving what he himself calls a distinctively 'evaluative element' (p. 38), or an appeal to some 'evaluative category' (p. 65), and he suggests that the task of practical reflection about our reasons is to 'characterize' precisely the concrete ways in which particular actions would be good or desirable (pp. 65–9). In the same spirit, Scanlon contends in chapter 4 that the reason-giving force of moral judgments can be explained 'by characterizing more fully, in substantive terms, the particular form of value that we respond to in acting rightly and violate by doing what is wrong' (p. 150). This important strand in Scanlon's discussion strongly suggests that the task of understanding reasons for action goes hand in hand with the task of clarifying the concrete forms of value that can be achieved or realized in action. At least as far as the epistemology of reasons and values is concerned, in other words, neither domain can claim priority vis-à-vis the other.[15] If there is an issue of priority, it would seem to concern instead the relation between general and specific concepts, and this distinction cuts across the divide between the normative and the evaluative.[16] Scanlon's version of the buck-passing account expresses the point that goodness does not represent a nonnatural master property that constitutes or explains our specific reasons for action in particular cases. The alternative version of the buck-passing account that I formulated above expresses the complementary point that being a reason is similarly not a general property that constitutes or explains the concrete value of the specific things we have reason to

[15] One might try to distinguish the broadly epistemological issue of the terms in which reflection about reasons and values is conducted from the metaphysical or constitutive issue about the relation between evaluative and normative properties of things. But given Scanlon's procedural realism about reasons, this kind of distinction does not seem very promising: if the objective credentials of judgments about reasons are established by their surviving the relevant procedures of reflection, then the fact that such reflection is conducted in evaluative terms would seem to tell against the suggestion that normative properties are somehow metaphysically more basic.

[16] The issue of the priority and independence of general concepts vis-à-vis specific ones is discussed by S. L. Hurley under the heading of 'centralism' in her *Natural Reasons: Personality and Polity* (New York: Oxford University Press, 1989), ch. 1.

do. General normative and evaluative claims can thus be understood as ways of signaling that there is some specific reason for action in the offing, a reason that can be characterized by specifying the particular way in which the action in question would be valuable.

It goes without saying, I believe, that this kind of position can be reconciled with Scanlon's anti-teleological strictures about the good. To claim that reasons for action represent concrete ways in which an action would be valuable is not to maintain that actions derive their value exclusively from their contribution to states of affairs that are intrinsically good. But the position just sketched raises a different question about Scanlon's presentation of the buck-passing account. As I mentioned above, Scanlon takes reflection on cases to count in favor of such an account, arguing that our concrete reasons for action are typically provided by the natural properties of things and not by any special properties of goodness and value. As examples he mentions the following cases: 'The fact that a resort is pleasant is a reason to visit it or to recommend it to a friend, and the fact that a discovery casts light on the causes of cancer is a reason to applaud it and to support further research of that kind' (p. 97). But it is not entirely clear how these observations are to be reconciled with Scanlon's own favored account of deliberative reflection on our reasons. As I explained above, Scanlon takes such reflection to be a matter of characterizing the concrete values that can be achieved or realized in action, and this strains against the contention that reasons are 'provided by' the perfectly natural properties of things.

The examples Scanlon himself brings forward, however, raise an independent doubt about this contention. To say that a resort is 'pleasant', for instance, is a way of adverting to the distinctively positive qualities of experience that are enjoyed by a visitor to the resort. It is not merely an evaluatively neutral description of the natural properties of the resort or of the experiences induced by the resort in its visitors, and this is what makes it appropriate to think of pleasure itself as a concrete category of evaluation (cf. p. 43). Similarly, in the context of decision making about the kind of research that should be pursued or supported, the statement that a certain discovery 'casts light' on a phenomenon such as cancer does not seem to be an evaluatively neutral representation of the natural properties of the discovery. It is, rather, a way of pointing to a particular form of value that is particularly relevant to questions regarding the conduct and funding of research, insofar as research precisely aims at enhancing our understanding of important phenomena (a contrastive description of the discovery would be that it is boring or irrelevant to our understanding of how cancer works). This interpretation is anyway in line with Scanlon's description of deliberative reflection as a matter of 'characterizing' the concrete forms of value that bear on action. Since concrete modalities of value are closely aligned with the natural properties of objects and actions, perhaps Scanlon means to be referring to such values when he claims that reasons are provided by natural properties rather than by properties of goodness or value themselves. The pertinent contrast would then not be between the evaluative and the entirely natural, but (again) between the abstract property of goodness, and the concrete modalities of value that provide our reasons for action in particular contexts of decision.

3. MORAL REASONS

Chapter 4 of *What We Owe to Each Other* offers a contractualist account of 'the reason-giving and motivating force of judgments of right and wrong' (p. 149). The general task that Scanlon sets himself here is to explain the normativity of moral judgments, to show why facts about the morality of right and wrong provide us with reasons for action. This goal is probably the holy grail of traditional moral philosophy, and so the reader is particularly anxious to see whether and how Scanlon's methodological sophistication will yield improvements in understanding. Scanlon begins by setting out constraints on an adequate solution to the problem of reason-giving force. Such an account must illuminate both the priority and the importance of moral reasons; it should explain why moral considerations take precedence over other kinds of reason and value, and why the failure to comply with moral reasons represents a specially serious kind of shortcoming (pp. 148–9). Furthermore, in accounting for these matters the theory we seek must avoid getting impaled on the horns of Prichard's dilemma (p. 150). It will not do merely to assert that rightness and wrongness are themselves sources of reasons; that would be uninformative as an answer to the question of reason-giving force, presupposing what was to be explained. But, on the other hand, the reasons morality provides must not exhibit a merely contingent connection with the things that make actions right and wrong. An account with this form would not succeed in illuminating the nature of distinctively moral reasons.

Scanlon himself proposes to satisfy these constraints by developing a substantive account of the reason-giving force of morality. In line with his general views about the procedures appropriate to reflection about reasons, he thinks we need to characterize in substantive terms the particular kind of value that people respond to in acting rightly and that they violate when they do what is wrong (p. 150). Moreover, he believes that contractualism provides a characterization of precisely the sought-after variety. According to contractualism, 'an act is wrong if its performance under the circumstances would be disallowed by any set of principles for the general regulation of behavior that no one could reasonably reject as a basis for informed, unforced general agreement' (p. 153). This formula does not itself describe a concrete form of value to which people might be responding when they do what they take to be morally right, but Scanlon believes that a description of this kind can easily be extracted from the formula. The substantive value that is realized by moral behavior consists in a certain kind of relation to one's fellow humans, the terms of which are equally acceptable to all, insofar as they are specified by principles that no one could reasonably reject (p. 155). Scanlon later refers to this form of relation as 'mutual recognition' (p. 162). At issue is not necessarily actual recognition of one's standing by others (since they may not themselves always be moved by moral concerns) but, rather, a kind of idealized reciprocity of respect. Morality is to be viewed, not as the instrument whereby we achieve some concrete emotional benefit from others but, rather, as the condition for the possibility of relationships based on fully reciprocal recognition (p. 168). Scanlon's argument is that this is a form of relationship whose concrete positive value we can appreciate and affirm through reflection—the contractualist account is in this way accurate to what Scanlon calls the 'phenomenology' of moral motivation (pp. 155, 163, 187–8). Moreover, it specifies a reason for acting morally that promises to illuminate both the importance and the priority of moral considerations.

Before turning to these issues, it may help to consider briefly the version of contractualism that Scanlon defended in his now classic paper 'Contractualism and Utilitarianism'.[17] There Scanlon accounted for the reason-giving force of moral considerations by appealing to the desire to be able to justify oneself to others on grounds no one could reasonably reject. But Scanlon's aims in the earlier paper were different from and more modest than his aims in chapter 4 of *What We Owe to Each Other*. In the paper, he set out to bypass traditional worries about the normative priority and importance of moral principles. Instead of showing how morality can be a source of unconditional reasons for action that properly defeat other, potentially competing kinds of normative consideration, Scanlon there contented himself with observations about the distribution and strength of the desire to be able to justify oneself to others. The suggestion seemed to be that it is enough if a theory of morality can identify a distinctive pattern of motivation that, as a matter of fact, is both grounded in human nature and strong enough to provide those who have it with a generally reliable incentive to do the right thing.

But the theory of reasons that Scanlon develops in his book necessitates a change in strategy (cf. pp. 7–8).[18] As we saw above, he now rejects the view that desires represent independent sources either of motivation or of reasons, holding that what moves us to action are our normative judgments and that reasons are almost never constituted by desires. This means that it is no longer open to Scanlon to appeal to facts about the distribution and strength of a certain class of desires in accounting for moral motivation. If as a matter of fact many people are strongly motivated to justify themselves to others on grounds no one could reasonably reject, this must be because they take such justifiability to count in favor of actions that secure it or to represent a concrete form of value that is worth

---

[17] T. M. Scanlon, 'Contractualism and Utilitarianism', in Amartya Sen and Bernard Williams (eds.), *Utilitarianism and Beyond* (Cambridge, England: Cambridge University Press, 1982), 103–28.

[18] I do not mean to suggest that this consideration must have been the original impetus for the change in strategy I go on to describe. It may be that there are internal tensions in 'Contractualism and Utilitarianism' that motivated both the new theory of reasons and the associated changes in response to the problems of importance and priority.

pursuing. Moreover, the motivation that is produced by these normative judgments will be reputable only if the judgments themselves satisfy the standards that properly regulate our practical deliberation about what there is reason to do. The task, as we have seen, is thus to characterize the concrete form of value that is realized when we comply with moral demands, and this Scanlon attempts to achieve by appealing to the ideal of mutual recognition sketched above.

But how does this ideal help us with the problems of importance and priority? Scanlon's treatment of importance is comparatively straightforward (ch. 4, sect. 4). The question to be answered is why the failure to be moved by moral considerations strikes us as a specially significant kind of shortcoming, different in kind from other cases in which people do not happen to share our interests and motivations. Scanlon contends that the importance of moral concern becomes clear once we grasp the contractualist interpretation of the content of morality. It follows from that interpretation that to lack moral concern is to fail to see any need to justify oneself to those who are potentially affected by one's behavior, something that is tantamount to the failure to appreciate their value as persons (cf. ch. 2, sect. 6). This is unnerving in a way other motivational eccentricities are not, since it has immediate implications for the amoral agent's relations with others (pp. 159–60). An unbridgeable abyss seems to open up between amoral agents and those who must live and interact with them.

The problem of priority is different and in many ways harder, because it is posed from the agent's own point of view. At issue here is not the significance for others of my failure to appreciate moral considerations, but the capacity of such considerations to prevail in practical reflection about what I myself have most reason to do. It is perhaps at this point in his discussion of reason-giving force that the differences between Scanlon's book and his earlier paper become most pronounced. So long as our reasons to act morally were traced to the desire to justify ourselves to others, their capacity to prevail in competition with reasons of other kinds could be established by an appeal to their causal force.[19] But this option is no longer open to Scanlon, who must now explain in more explicitly normative terms the capacity of morality to stand up in deliberative conflict with other kinds of reasons and values.

Scanlon's approach to this normative problem is complex and subtle, and I am not certain that I understand all its details. But the basic strategy is to articulate a general schema for thinking about the relation between moral requirements and the other kinds of reasons and values with which they might seem to come into conflict (ch. 4, sect. 5). It is customary and (I believe) correct to suppose that the most interesting potential challenges are posed by what Bernard Williams has called our 'projects':[20] the interests and activities that define our deepest sense of self, including above all our friendships and our abiding personal and professional

[19] Compare Scanlon, 'Contractualism and Utilitarianism', 117.
[20] See Bernard Williams, 'Persons, Character, and Morality', as reprinted in his *Moral Luck*, 1–19.

ambitions. Scanlon proposes a three-part strategy for establishing that moral considerations have priority over reasons that are grounded in projects of this kind (p. 166). The first stage is to argue that the morality of right and wrong can itself make room for the pursuit of individual projects, insofar as it would be reasonable to reject principles that do not allow for such pursuits (cf. pp. 224–5); contractualism can thus accommodate directly the importance of projects to our lives, in a way some other moral theories (such as direct utilitarianism) arguably cannot. This reduces, but does not altogether eliminate, the potential for conflict between morality and individual projects. The second and third stages in Scanlon's strategy apply in cases in which these residual conflicts threaten to break out and pertain, respectively, to the moral and the personal sides of the conflict. Specifically, Scanlon points to the 'great importance' of the value of mutual recognition that is secured by complying with moral principles, and to the idea that personal projects themselves have a 'built-in sensitivity to the demands of right and wrong' (p. 166).

It is not entirely clear, however, how effective the second and third stages of this strategy are likely to be. The insistence on the importance of distinctively moral values at stage 2 looks to be potentially question-begging in the context of a demonstration of the priority of moral reasons. Scanlon should probably be understood as launching an appeal to his readers to reflect carefully for themselves on the concrete value of being able to enter into relationships with people on terms of mutual recognition. The idea, I suppose, is that they will come through such reflection to grasp the value of complying with moral principles, in a way that was not clear to them before their encounter with the contractualist theory of morality. But this appears to be a response to a different kind of challenge. If we are puzzled as to how morality could possibly be valuable in its own terms (as opposed to being a kind of collective fetish or a neurotic compulsion, say),[21] then it may be helpful to learn that moral ends can be characterized in a way that makes them recognizable and intelligible as concrete modalities of the good. But this seems less helpful in connection with the essentially comparative problem of priority. If we are concerned about this problem, we will want to know why we should accord moral considerations deliberative priority by contrast with the reasons that are grounded in our personal projects. To be reminded that the values realized by morality seem to us to be important, on reflection, does little to reassure us that we are right to accord them this kind of deliberative priority. Indeed, the 'reminder' seems likely to misfire, given that we are supposed to be in the mood of questioning the deliberative priority of moral reasons in the first place.

---

[21] Compare Scanlon, 'Contractualism and Utilitarianism', 106; and John Rawls, *A Theory of Justice* (Cambridge, Mass.: Harvard University Press, 1971), 514–16. This 'fetishism' objection seems properly directed against certain forms of intuitionism, which leave it mysterious why anyone should care about moral considerations in the first place. The problem, in Scanlon's terms, is to explain how rightness can be a reason—a consideration that speaks in favor of actions that are right—not to explain the priority or deliberative importance of this reason compared with reasons of other kinds.

At stage 3 in his schematic approach, Scanlon turns to the personal side of potential conflicts, illustrating his strategy with some suggestive observations about the cases of friendship and scientific achievement. The general idea is that, properly understood, the concrete values embodied in these cases display an intrinsic sensitivity to the requirements of morality, so that their conflict with morality is more apparent than real. Again, however, there is some reason to doubt how far this kind of approach will take us. In discussing friendship, for instance, Scanlon begins with remarks which suggest that genuine friendship is itself an inherently moral form of relationship, involving a recognition of the independent moral standing of the persons with whom we are befriended (pp. 164–5). He immediately qualifies this conclusion, however, suggesting that it will suffice to establish the availability of a conception or form of friendship that exhibits this distinctively moral structure (p. 165). But will this really suffice for the person who is in the grip of the problem of priority? Such a person may concede the value of standing in the relation of mutual recognition with their friends[22] but wonder whether the logic of friendship equally requires them to value this kind of relationship with other persons (whom they may find neither appealing nor admirable). The fact that there exist forms of friendship that have this moralized structure will not alone cut much ice, so long as it is conceded that thoroughly moralized friendship is not the only kind.[23]

The difficulty with both the second and the third stages in Scanlon's schematic argument is that they seem potentially out of touch with the deliberative perspective from which the problem of priority is characteristically posed. This problem is not to explain how morality can be valuable in its own terms, but whether and how it can attain the kind of importance exhibited by friendships, professional ambitions, and other personal projects. Only if morality is important in something like this way, it may be thought, will it be capable of standing up rationally in competition with our projects (when, for instance, the demands of honesty or fairness place constraints on our relationships and pursuits). This is a matter about which it is easy to be skeptical. How, we may wonder, can the abstract goods realized by compliance with moral principles possibly prevail in competition with the contingent ambitions and relationships that give meaning and texture to our lives?

Scanlon's contractualism initially seems ill-suited to provide a satisfying answer to this skeptical question. The idealized value of mutual recognition that he ascribes to morality is rather bloodless, detached as it is from such tangible benefits as warmth and understanding and human emotional support. The explanation

---

[22] Something, incidentally, that need not be grounded in mere 'liking': cf. p. 165.

[23] Analogous questions arise about Scanlon's discussion of the value of scientific discovery (pp. 166–7). There he makes the sound point that proper respect for scientific activity commits one to a kind of truthfulness incompatible with (say) falsifying scientific data. But we are all familiar with the type of the scrupulous but very ambitious investigator who is prepared to tyrannize subordinates and students in the pursuit of important results. Can it so clearly be maintained that this kind of behavior is a betrayal of the values latent in scientific activity itself?

of moral reasons in terms of mutual recognition thus seems to invite the question of priority rather than to settle it. Seen from a different angle, however, I believe that Scanlon's contractualism contains the seeds of a promising response to that question. We may begin by thinking about the special kind of importance that we naturally attach to our basic personal projects. I believe that we intuitively take such projects to be significant because they contribute directly to making our lives good from our own point of view. They may not result in a net increase in our happiness or well-being, but as Scanlon convincingly argues in chapter 3, this is not anyway a category of evaluation that is significant in first-personal deliberation. What does matter to us in thinking about our own lives is that they are worthwhile or meaningful, and the manifest significance of personal projects lies in their ability to make our lives good in precisely these ways.[24] If this is right, however, it suggests that a successful treatment of the priority issue must show that morality too can make this kind of contribution. The challenge is to explain how compliance with moral principles can be among the things that make our lives worthwhile from our own point of view.

It is in this context, I believe, that the distinctive contribution of Scanlon's contractualism to the priority problem comes into focus. As we have seen, his theory has the consequence that agents attain a distinctive social standing when they do the right thing, rendering themselves fit to participate in relationships with others on grounds of mutual recognition. This may be understood as a specific way in which the agent's own life is made better or more worthy, from their own point of view, by their compliance with moral principles. What is needed to respond to the problem of priority is an elucidation of the concrete contribution that morality can make to the meaning and goodness of the agent's own life, showing how the agent's life is itself transformed when it is conducted on moral terms. Scanlon's appeal to the value of mutual recognition appears to be a response of precisely this kind.

By contrast, the appeal to mutual recognition does not seem nearly as persuasive as a general account of the reason-giving force of morality. Given Scanlon's own background theory of reasons and motivation, one would expect such an account to make transparent the concrete considerations that count in favor of doing the right thing in specific situations of action and decision, considerations which in turn motivate the agent to do what morality requires when they are grasped. But the value of mutual recognition does not seem cut out to play this role, for the simple reason that virtuous agents rarely structure their practical reflection around this particular modality of the good. What typically 'motivates'

---

[24] Compare p. 132, where Scanlon concedes that there is a perspective from which we ask intelligible questions about the goodness of human lives. He is not inclined to view this perspective as particularly important, but it may well be the standpoint that matters when it comes to thinking about the issue of priority. On the concern to lead a meaningful life, compare Susan Wolf, 'Happiness and Meaning: Two Aspects of the Good Life', in Ellen Frankel Paul, Fred D. Miller, Jr., and Jeffrey Paul (eds.), *Self-Interest* (Cambridge, England: Cambridge University Press, 1997), 207–25.

us to do the right thing are not thoughts about rightness or wrongness themselves, nor thoughts about our ability to live in unity with our fellow creatures (cf. p. 163) but, rather, thoughts about the kinds of consideration that render particular options right or wrong: that a given action would hurt someone's feelings, say, or be demeaning or cruel or helpful. To attempt to extract from the value of mutual recognition a general account of the reason-giving force of moral considerations thus seems false to the phenomenology of moral deliberation and action, ascribing to it a self-directed focus that it does not ordinarily seem to exhibit.

Scanlon is of course well aware of these facts. He attempts to accommodate them by appeal to the idea that contractualism does not seek principles merely for the assessment of first-order actions but also for the construction of suitable procedures of reflection (pp. 155–8). Specifically, it 'provides a higher-order reason to shape our process of practical thinking in the ways that are necessary to make it one that others could reasonably be asked to license us to use' (p. 156). This passage (and others like it) raises large questions whose discussion I shall postpone until the next section. But as a response to the present problem, it does not seem fully satisfying. If, as Scanlon proposes, the real reason-giving force of moral considerations is to be traced to the value of mutual recognition, then processes of motivating reflection that exclude this distinctive value, and feature instead such specific moral categories as fairness, danger, harm, and cruelty, look like forms of false consciousness. Contractualist morality may applaud deliberation that is conducted in these terms, but in doing so it starts to resemble those unstable and artificially compartmentalized forms of indirect consequentialism that recommend (on consequentialist grounds) the inculcation of distinctively nonconsequentialist dispositions of thought and motivation.[25]

A more satisfying contractualist treatment of the general problem of reason-giving force might begin from the observation that the basic ideal of justifiability to others has various aspects. In particular, we can distinguish between other-directed and self-directed aspects of this ideal. Scanlon himself proposes that the aspiration to treat people in ways justifiable to them (on terms no one could reasonably reject) is a proper response to their value as persons (pp. 103–7, 168–9). This suggests what is to my mind a plausible treatment of the general reason-giving force of moral considerations. What speaks in favor of doing the right thing, in the first instance, is the fact that those affected by one's behavior would have a reasonable ground for complaint if one does not. One's attention is thus focused outward, onto the concrete implications of one's actions for others; this in turn makes it natural to say that one is responding to their value as humans in bringing one's behavior into conformity with moral principles.

Of course, in practice what is often uppermost in one's mind are thoughts that are couched in terms of the concrete categories of moral assessment alluded to

---

[25] Compare T. M. Scanlon, 'Levels of Moral Thinking', D. Seanor and N. Fotion (eds.), in *Hare and Critics: Essays on 'Moral Thinking'* (Oxford: Clarendon Press, 1988), 129–46.

above, such as harm, fairness, danger, cruelty, and help. But the contractualist can say that the reason-giving force of such thoughts is derivative from the more basic idea of justifiability to others. On Scanlon's view, it is not (strictly speaking) the fact that a given action would be cruel that gives me moral reason to avoid it, but the different fact that it would be reasonable for the victim of cruelty to object to such behavior.[26] The contractualist could maintain that our responsiveness to these concrete moral categories is guided by our internalized understanding of the ways in which they provide grounds for reasonable rejection in particular cases. This seems to me to promise a less compartmentalized accommodation of the ordinary phenomenology of moral deliberation than Scanlon's appeal to higher-order reasons. The content and focus of actual moral thought do not need to be traced to the application of contractualist reasoning in second-order reflection about our processes of deliberation themselves; they can instead be explained in terms of our implicit understanding of the ways in which familiar categories of action ordinarily provide people with a reasonable basis for complaint.

As I said above, however, the ideal of justifiability to others has a different, self-directed aspect, and this second aspect becomes prominent in those specialized deliberative contexts in which the question of priority is at issue. Thus, instead of concentrating on the specific ways in which one's actions could affect other people, providing them with reasonable bases for objection, one can focus on the positive value of being a person who is able to relate to others on terms of mutual recognition. This is a specific way in which acting morally makes one's own life go better, and reflection about this dimension of the ideal of justifiability can help to render less mysterious the ability of moral considerations to prevail rationally in competition with one's defining personal projects. Of course, more will need to be said to silence all doubts about the priority issue. We might think of the contractualist argument I have presented as an improved version of the second stage in Scanlon's three-stage strategy, to be supplemented by the considerations Scanlon himself advances at the first and—to a perhaps more limited extent—third stages.

Two brief comparisons will complete this reconstructed contractualist response to the priority issue. One is to utilitarianism, which Scanlon sees as offering a substantive account of moral motivation in terms of the idea of the greatest happiness (pp. 151–2). This idea, like the ideal of justifiability to others, can be viewed under two aspects, which it seems to me important to distinguish when thinking about utilitarian treatments of moral motivation. One can in the first place focus outward, concentrating on the specific implications of the actions available to one for the overall well-being of human and other sentient creatures. This way of thinking about the general happiness seems to offer the most plausible utilitarian response to the issue of the general reason-giving force of morality, but it does not

---

[26] For present purposes I shall accept without comment this important and potentially controversial claim. Some critical questions are raised about the claim in sect. 4, below.

provide much assistance with the problem of priority. Someone who is worried about the ability of moral demands to stand up in competition with personal projects will want to understand better how acting morally could possibly contribute to making their own life worthwhile or meaningful. Here, it seems to me, utilitarians can and sometimes do point to a different aspect of the idea of general happiness; specifically, they urge that contributing to the general happiness can have a distinctive and valuable effect on one's own life, enabling one to transcend one's narrow concerns, or to participate in a plane of value that is somehow larger than oneself.[27] No doubt many actual utilitarians are unclear about this distinction, or run together the two aspects of the idea of general happiness that I have tried to keep apart. My point is merely that the utilitarian strategy seems more promising when the two aspects of the substantive value that it celebrates are distinguished, and that in this respect the utilitarian account of moral motivation resembles the reconstructed contractualist account sketched above.

The second comparison is to the goods of friendship. In his discussion of the priority issue Scanlon begins with the case of friendship, arguing that it can be viewed not merely as a potential competitor to morality, but also as a paradigm for thinking about how a response to the priority problem for the case of morality can avoid Prichard's dilemma (pp. 161–2). The task, Scanlon suggests, is to characterize friendship in a way that makes intelligible the following two ideas: first, that friends are willing to do things simply because loyalty requires it; and second, that being a friend involves many additional benefits as well (such as companionship and support). In Scanlon's own words:

By bringing these two elements together as aspects of a single value, such an account enables us to see that the analogue of Prichard's 'dilemma' is not really a dilemma at all. It merely appears to be one because it presents two essential aspects of friendship as if they were two competing answers to the same question. A person who was loyal to a friend simply to have the benefits of friendship would not be a true friend. On the other hand, a person who did not regard friendship as a good to him, did not enjoy it and see it as an important ingredient in a good life, would not be a real friend either, but only following a strangely cold imperative. (pp. 161–2)

I trust that the parallels between Scanlon's discussion of this paradigm and the reconstructed contractualist account of moral motivation I have presented do not require to be belabored. Indeed, they seem to me sufficiently striking that the question arises whether the reconstructed account I have offered might not capture at least part of what Scanlon himself had in mind all along.

---

[27] Compare the ideal of transcendence discussed (though not endorsed) in Samuel Scheffler, *Human Morality* (New York: Oxford University Press, 1992), 120–1. A similar ideal is both elaborated and endorsed in Peter Singer, *How Are We to Live? Ethics in an Age of Self-Interest* (Oxford: Oxford University Press, 1997).

4. THE UNITY OF MORALITY

Scanlon presents contractualism as a 'unified account' of the subject matter of morality (p. 218). More precisely, it offers a unified account of the subject matter of one central part of morality, which Scanlon dubs the morality of right and wrong. Scanlon himself emphasizes that morality as it is conventionally understood includes a plurality of normative domains (ch. 4, sect. 7). As we have seen, the morality of right and wrong can be thought of as fixing our proper response to the inherent value of human life. But there are other values, to some extent independent from the value of human life, about which recognizably moral issues can be raised— Scanlon mentions as examples the values of friendship, parenthood, achievement, and sex (pp. 173–6). The moral issues posed by such examples center around the question of how the values at stake in them are to be understood and responded to. Thus people who utterly lack the aspiration to meet high standards in their work, or who concentrate single-mindedly on professional achievement to the exclusion of all else, could be said to have a deficient understanding of the value of work and achievement, where this would be a form of moral criticism in the broadest sense.

Scanlon's thesis of the fragmentation of the moral seems to me quite plausible. By emphasizing the diversity of normative domains conventionally included within morality, Scanlon is able both to insulate his contractualism from the objection that it is incomplete (since the theory only aspires to cover the morality of right and wrong) and to supplement the theory at certain important points (e.g., in his discussions of the scope of morality and of relativism: cf. ch. 4, sect. 8 and ch. 8, sect. 4). But the fragmentation that Scanlon detects within the broader moral realm threatens to bleed over into the central domain of right and wrong that is his primary concern. If morality writ large represents a hodgepodge of values and ideals, how can we be certain that the morality of right and wrong exhibits the unity of a single subject matter? This question raises large issues, not only about contractualism but also about moral theory more generally, that are well worth thinking about in some detail.

There are a number of things that might be meant by talk about the 'unity' of morality, and accordingly a number of ways of challenging the thesis that morality constitutes a unified subject matter. One might, for instance, question the assumption that the very same considerations that determine what it is for actions to be right or wrong also provide us with corresponding reasons for action. Those who deny that morality is an inherently normative domain (in the sense of being an immediate source of reasons for action) might contend that no single theory can hope to illuminate both what makes actions right and wrong and what gives particular agents reason to do as morality prescribes (cf. pp. 169–70).[28] But I think a more

---

[28] For tentative doubts of this kind, see (e.g.) David O. Brink, *Moral Realism and the Foundations of Ethics* (Cambridge, England: Cambridge University Press, 1988), ch. 3; and Peter Railton, 'Moral Realism', as reprinted in Stephen Darwall, Allan Gibbard, and Peter Railton (eds.), *Moral Discourse and Practice* (New York: Oxford University Press, 1997), 137–63.

interesting challenge can be posed within the framework of a normative conception of morality, by questioning whether there is any unified, general story to tell either about what makes actions right and wrong or about what gives us reason to act accordingly. Consider, for instance, the concrete moral concepts that (as Scanlon agrees) figure saliently in much everyday moral reasoning, concepts such as suffering, fairness, loyalty, need, and help. Scanlon can concede that concepts such as these are often necessary to explain what makes particular actions right and wrong (cf. p. 391 n. 21). On his account, however, this is just a reflection of the fact that the concepts in question help us to understand which candidate principles it would be reasonable to reject. For example, aiming to inflict gratuitous and unwanted suffering on a person both makes an action wrong and provides us with a reason to avoid the action, because any principle that permitted actions with this property could reasonably be rejected. Without recourse to the idea of justifiability to others, we can understand neither what it is for actions to be right and wrong, nor our reasons for doing what is right and avoiding what is wrong.

Against this, however, it might be maintained that the constitutive role that Scanlon ascribes to the idea of justifiability to others is specious. What really guides normative reflection, the objection would go, is not our sense of the conditions under which candidate principles could reasonably be rejected but, rather, our prior understanding of the concrete values to which the kind of specific concepts introduced above—'thick' concepts, as Bernard Williams would call them—refer.[29] Someone who takes this line could agree with the contractualist intuition that wrong actions would be disallowed by those principles no one could reasonably reject. But they would explain this intuition by appeal to our prior understanding of the values and reasons associated with comparatively thick predicates and concepts. It would be reasonable for people to reject principles allowing, say, torture, because a proper understanding of such evaluative concepts as suffering and humiliation leads to the conclusion that actions that aim at these states should be avoided. To say that torture is wrong is just a summary way of alluding to these substantive reasons; and since our grasp of the relevant reasons is prior to and independent of the idea that corresponding principles could reasonably be rejected, that idea cannot be said to play a constitutive role in determining what it is for torture to be wrong.[30]

---

[29] See Bernard Williams, *Ethics and the Limits of Philosophy* (Cambridge, Mass.: Harvard University Press, 1985), esp. ch. 8.

[30] This line of thought is superficially reminiscent of a 'circularity' objection sometimes brought against Scanlon's theory. This objection alleges that the contractualist procedure cannot illuminate the morality of right and wrong, since our grounds for rejecting many candidate principles precisely consist in the fact that the actions they prescribe would be wrong. This objection does not seem to me very serious, and so it is important to stress that the pluralist position I am sketching in the text has a very different basis. It does not accuse Scanlon of circularity, but questions whether considerations of moral right and wrong have a substantive role to play in practical deliberation. This pluralist stance regarding moral right and wrong seems analogous to the position Scanlon himself takes regarding the role of well-being within first-personal deliberation; cf. p. 133, where Scanlon suggests that well-being functions in this context as a kind of 'evaluative Trojan horse'.

Ultimately, a position of this kind—thoroughgoing pluralism, as we might refer to it—calls into question the unity that Scanlon attributes to the morality of right and wrong. It holds that this moral domain exhibits the very same kind of heterogeneity that Scanlon himself attributes to morality in the broader sense. At the fundamental level, there are only questions about the proper appreciation of specific modalities of value. We can say that actions that betray such concrete values are wrong, if we like, but a charge of this kind will pertain equally to violations within and without the central core that Scanlon is concerned to demarcate. There is thus no coherent normative domain that is specially concerned with moral right and wrong, or with justifiability to others. It may seem to us as if morality in the narrower sense constitutes a distinctive and unified set of normative considerations. But the pluralist I am concerned with might suggest that this sense is a historical relic—a remnant, perhaps, of religious attitudes that once made adherence to a selected subset of norms seem a matter of particular urgency, but that have since lost their grip on us.[31]

I go into this kind of pluralism at some length, because there are strains within Scanlon's contractualism that seem congenial to the pluralist position. One of these is his buck-passing theory of the good. Scanlon presents this theory as an account of the relation between values and reasons, but as I explained in section II, above, the examples and arguments Scanlon himself deploys suggest that what is really at issue is the relation between general and specific normative and evaluative concepts. There is no master property of goodness or being a reason that constitutes or explains the concrete value of particular actions or the considerations that speak in favor of performing them. Rather, general normative and evaluative claims indicate the presence of concrete modalities of value, which are both metaphysically and epistemologically basic. But if this is indeed Scanlon's position in regard to general normative and evaluative commitments, one might expect him to be attracted to an analogous position in regard to moral rightness, which is equally a thin or abstract concept. The analogous position would hold that rightness is not a substantive master concept that itself provides us with reasons but, rather, a way of signaling the presence of concrete reasons that are bound up with specific modalities of moral value.[32] But this position, of course, is precisely the pluralist view sketched above!

The second aspect of Scanlon's theory that appears congenial to the pluralist position is his (procedural) realism about reasons and values. As we saw in section I, Scanlon holds that reflection about reasons is subject to sophisticated internal standards of correctness in which we have great confidence, and he inclines to the view that when our normative judgments satisfy these standards, they may be considered straightforwardly true. Scanlon himself accordingly engages in first-order

---

[31] Compare Williams's discussion of 'the morality system' in *Ethics and the Limits of Philosophy*, ch. 10.

[32] This is in fact the conclusion about rightness that Hurley extracts from her general 'anti-centralism', in *Natural Reasons*, ch. 1.

normative reflection at numerous points throughout *What We Owe to Each Other*, characterizing a range of concrete values that are relevant to action, and venturing conclusions about how these values are properly understood and responded to. There are, for instance, reflections about the 'proper' or 'plausible' way to understand and respond to the values embodied in such phenomena as human life (p. 106), art and science (p. 167), children and work (pp. 173–4), sexual relations (p. 176), sentient beings (p. 181), the Grand Canyon (p. 220), and right conduct (p. 325). Scanlon also appeals to such normative judgments in illustrating the structure of contractualism, observing that the theory requires us to make assumptions about the 'generic' reasons that pertain to the various representative standpoints from which candidate moral principles are to be assessed (pp. 204–6). At issue here are judgments about the (agent-centered) reasons that persons in the various affected positions might have for rejecting candidate principles. But, the pluralist will suggest, if reliable procedures are available for thinking about such a wide and diverse range of values, perhaps those same procedures could be deployed in reflection about the concrete values that make up the morality of right and wrong. Why do moral agents require special procedures for deliberating about what to do? Won't it suffice to apply our general procedures of normative reflection to such concrete values (and dis-values) as loyalty, suffering, betrayal, need, dependence, autonomy, and choice, deriving conclusions about our reasons for action by clarifying the proper way of understanding and responding to these values?[33]

Scanlon, of course, does not seem to think that these general procedures suffice. He holds that the morality of right and wrong constitutes a unified domain of reasons and values, defined by distinctive methods of practical reflection, which the contractualist formula describes. Indeed, it is significant that his discussions of the structure of contractualism are couched in what appear to be constructivist terms. We have already encountered an important example of this in the preceding section, in connection with Scanlon's claim that contractualism provides second-order reasons to shape our processes of practical thinking in certain ways (cf. pp. 156–8). In this passage Scanlon does not represent contractualism as a procedure for thinking directly about what there is moral reason to do; rather it is depicted as a method for determining which considerations people should be licensed to *count* as reasons (p. 157). Similarly constructivist imagery appears in the subsequent sections of *What We Owe to Each Other* (cf. pp. 201, 203–4, 220). The suggestion in these passages seems to be that moral reasons are in some sense the products of idealized reflection about moral issues. Such reflection is concerned to establish those principles for the general regulation of behavior that no one could reasonably reject, where principles in turn are general statements about reasons

---

[33] Joseph Raz seems to advocate a pluralist position of this kind; see the papers collected in his *Engaging Reason: On the Theory of Value and Action* (Oxford: Oxford University Press, 1999), esp. chs. 11–13.

that shape the deliberations of those who accept and internalize them (cf. ch. 5, sect. 3). Moral reasons are thus 'constructed' through an idealized procedure of contractualist reflection about principles.

Of course, like other forms of constructivism this position is easily misunderstood. Note in particular that at no point does Scanlon suggest that moral reasons are constructed by our actual deliberations about moral problems. In thinking about such problems we may assume that there is an objectively correct answer, prior to and independent of our actual deliberations, to questions about the morality of right and wrong.[34] We could therefore equally characterize Scanlon's approach to moral reasons in the terms Scanlon deploys to describe his general account of reasons, namely, as a form of procedural realism. Still, two features distinguish his attitude toward moral reasons from his position on reasons more generally. The most salient is the fact that Scanlon proposes special procedures of reflection about moral reasons (in the narrow sense); as we have seen, this is connected with his contention that the morality of right and wrong represents a distinctive and unified normative domain. Second, the special procedures of moral reflection that Scanlon proposes require us to determine what there is moral reason to do *by* thinking about the rejectability of candidate principles. By contrast, in normative deliberation more generally there appears to be no need for this detour through the question of reasonable rejectability. A proposed principle for regulating, say, sexual conduct or attitudes toward the natural world can be assessed directly, by reference to the question of whether it reflects a proper understanding of the concrete values at issue; questions about the rejectability of such principles are secondary, and can be resolved only on the basis of our direct assessment of the principles themselves.

In calling attention to these special features of Scanlon's treatment of moral reasons I do not wish to suggest that his position is internally inconsistent. There would perhaps be advantages of theoretical simplicity and elegance if it could be shown that the very same procedures used in ordinary normative reflection also determine what we are morally required to do. This might, among other things, make it easier to establish the authority of moral principles to regulate the deliberations of individual agents.[35] But these theoretical advantages hardly require us to postulate a continuity of procedures for moral and nonmoral reflection. Even if his position is not inconsistent, however, the combination of realist and constructivist

---

[34] This would be to assume that there is an independent fact of the matter about whether it would be reasonable to reject a given principle for the general regulation of behavior.

[35] Hobbesians and Kantians in ethics offer different versions of this approach. For an example of the Hobbesian variety, see David Gauthier, *Morals by Agreement* (Oxford: Clarendon Press, 1986). A recent example of the Kantian approach is Christine M. Korsgaard, *The Sources of Normativity* (Cambridge, England: Cambridge University Press, 1996), esp. lectures 3 and 4. Scanlon's remarks about 'formal' accounts of moral motivation on pp. 150–1 suggest that he appreciates the strategic advantages of these kinds of approach, but doubts their ability to illuminate the distinctive force and content of moral reasons. (Note, however, that Hobbesians and Kantians build much more structure into their accounts of the general procedures of normative reflection than the pluralist I discuss in the text.)

methods that Scanlon advocates is striking, and raises questions about his special treatment of moral reasons. Given the availability of the thoroughgoing pluralism sketched above, and the apparent similarities between that position and Scanlon's own general approach to reasons, why should we believe that the morality of right and wrong constitutes a distinctive and internally unified normative domain? What motivates or justifies this important assumption?

I have already touched in passing on two possible answers to this question on Scanlon's behalf. The first derives from considerations regarding the reason-giving force of morality. As we saw in the preceding section, Scanlon holds that contractualism provides a substantive account of moral motivation that is uniquely true to the phenomenology of moral experience. The suggestion seems to be that we only really understand what counts in favor of complying with moral demands when we appreciate the connection between such demands and the idea of justification to others, which is intuitively intelligible as a concrete form of value. If correct, this suggestion would strongly support a unified treatment of the morality of right and wrong in contractualist terms; in particular, it follows from Scanlon's proposal that the pluralist alternative would leave us with no explanation of the ultimate reason-giving force of the divers considerations collected under the rubric of moral right and wrong.[36] The cogency of this argument, however, seems to me somewhat undermined by Scanlon's concession that it is the various thick moral concepts appealed to by the pluralist that are ordinarily the focus of motivating moral consciousness (pp. 155–6). As I explained in the preceding section, I believe that this point can be reconciled with the general contractualist theory of moral motivation, insofar as the thick moral concepts can be understood as considerations that typically provide grounds for rejecting candidate principles. In the context of the debate between contractualism and pluralism concerning the unity of morality, however, the concession that moral deliberation is typically structured around the thick moral concepts seems to weaken the contractualist position. The pluralist can contend that the phenomenology of moral deliberation and action actually supports the idea that there is no unified explanation to be had of what counts in favor of all the various actions that may be considered morally right; the substantive values that recommend such actions are to be specified instead in terms of the various thick concepts that figure saliently in our deliberative experience.

A second potential motivation for Scanlon's conception of the unity of morality is provided by the internal structure of moral thought itself. On Scanlon's view,

---

[36] Scanlon could concede that the considerations collected under thick predicates have some independent reason-giving force. Just as they provide persons, within the contractualist procedure, with reasons for rejecting candidate principles, they may also provide agents directly with reasons for acting. But Scanlon would insist, I take it, that these reasons for action are distinct from the specifically moral reasons that contractualism aims to illuminate. The fact that an act would be treacherous, say, may speak against performing it. But in addition, it also speaks against such an act that principles allowing it could reasonably be rejected.

contractualism illuminates both the normative force of moral considerations and the content of the morality of right and wrong. The idea of justifiability to others thus does not merely account for moral motivation, it also serves to shape our substantive thinking about what makes actions right and wrong: 'Particular moral arguments seem to establish that an action is wrong just when, and *just because*, they show that so acting could not be justified to others on grounds they could not reasonably reject' (p. 170, emphasis mine; cf. p. 189). If this further claim is correct, it means that the proof of the unity of morality is in the pudding, so to speak. The way in which we conduct moral arguments about concrete cases will reveal both that there is a common set of terms in which such arguments are conducted and that these terms center around the notion of justifiability to others.

Like the first motivation discussed above, however, this argument is very hard to assess. On the one hand, it seems to me striking how naturally moral arguments can be couched in terms of the notion of rejectability of principles from various representative standpoints. In Scanlon's impressive discussion of promising in chapter 7, for example, the interpretation of the wrong involved in promise breaking and related forms of behavior is advanced by considering the reasons affected parties would have for rejecting candidate principles; moreover, this seems a perfectly intuitive way to proceed, illuminating the underlying moral issues. On the other hand, the pluralist could contend that, while it seems natural to couch moral arguments in terms of the issue of justifiability to others, this is not really the consideration that shapes those arguments at the level of substantive reflection. Scanlon himself must agree that whenever a candidate principle is reasonably rejectable, there will be some more concrete value or reason at issue that makes it reasonable to reject the principle. For instance, in the promising case Scanlon appeals to the 'value of assurance' to explain why it would be reasonable to reject principles that permit people (in the absence of special justification) not to fulfill the expectations they have voluntarily and intentionally raised in others (pp. 302–5). But the pluralist could claim that it is this substantive dimension of the good, and not the more abstract notion of reasonable rejectability, that is doing the real work in argument about the morality of promise keeping. That is, what really shapes our practical reflection about this issue is our prior understanding of the concrete value of assurance, our sense that it would not be a proper response to this value to disappoint the expectations we have deliberately raised in other people. The fact that principles that permit this response could reasonably be rejected merely follows from this more basic kind of normative understanding and is not what guides moral argument in the first instance.

Against this, Scanlon might maintain that we do not really have a grip on the question of how properly to respond to the value of assurance if we abstract from the question of whether this value provides a reasonable basis for rejecting candidate principles for the general regulation of behavior. He could claim, for instance, that (narrowly) moral reflection about this value differs from reflection about such values as sex and scientific achievement in having an essentially comparative dimension. Thus a morally adequate response to the good of assurance must also take into account the other values potentially in conflict with it (such as the convenience and flexibility that promisers would gain if they could provide compensation in lieu of fulfilling the literal terms of the promises they have voluntarily entered into). Comparative reflection of this kind, it could be suggested, requires us to assess the values in question as representative grounds for rejecting alternative principles (cf. p. 195). This response seems to me to have some plausibility, but the underlying issues remain difficult and elusive.[37]

A third possible motivation for Scanlon's conception of the unity of morality is suggested by his discussion of the value of human life (ch. 2, sect. 6). As we have already seen, Scanlon proposes that moral requirements in the narrow sense can be understood as determining what it is to respond properly to the value of persons, and this seems to me to offer an interpretation of the morality of right and wrong that is both intuitive and deeply appealing. It is a central legacy of the Enlightenment that there are certain things we owe others just in virtue of their standing as persons, and Scanlon can claim that morality in the narrow sense has the job of spelling out what these requirements are. Its principles do not merely specify what it would be right and wrong to do in a generic sense; they fix, more specifically, what we owe to others in virtue of their standing as persons, and what we must do if we are to avoid *wronging* them. If this is right, however, it provides at least an abstract reason for thinking of the morality of right and wrong as a unified normative domain, one whose divers demands hang together as responses to a single central value. Further support for this kind of conception is provided by Scanlon's more tentative suggestion that we respond properly to the value of human life precisely by striving to comply with principles that no one could reasonably reject (p. 106). This would motivate the distinctive contractualist interpretation of the unity of morality, its claim that the search for (nonrejectable) principles plays a constitutive role in determining our moral reasons that has no direct analogue in practical reflection more generally.

In the end, I find myself strongly attracted to Scanlon's contractualist vision of the unity of morality, but the inconclusiveness of the arguments sketched above leaves me somewhat uncertain about the issue. There is a pluralist alternative to Scanlon's position, anchored in Scanlon's own broader reflections about reasons and values, that poses a serious and interesting challenge to his interpretation of the morality of right and wrong. To be sure, if the pluralist position is correct, moral reflection will be a rather messy and indeterminate business, exhibiting all the difficulty and unclarity characteristic of normative reflection more generally. This might seem to represent a further consideration in favor of contractualism, pointing to the need for a special domain of normative principles that are relatively immune from the disagreement that characterizes normative thought more

---

[37] For instance, is it really plausible to suppose that there is not equally an implicitly comparative dimension involved in determining the 'proper' response to such values as sex and scientific achievement?

generally, and hence suited to figure in public justification and interpersonal criticism. But this does not represent a clear advantage for contractualism, since Scanlon is at pains to emphasize that the moral principles his theory delivers 'leave wide room for interpretation and judgment' (p. 199; cf. pp. 218, 242–7, 356–60). He does not share Sidgwick's ambition to formulate the first principles of morality in terms that are maximally precise and unambiguous (and hence 'scientific'). Moral theory, on Scanlon's conception of it, should be construed not as an attempt to eliminate the difficulty and contentiousness of actual moral thought, but to characterize the terms in which such thought is conducted. If this is right, however, it suggests that the dispute between pluralism and contractualism cannot be decided on grounds of the comparative publicity or interpersonal appeal of the normative principles the theories deliver.

The advantages of contractualism emerge more clearly when it is contrasted not with pluralism but with other substantive accounts of the morality of right and wrong (construed as a unified normative domain). As Scanlon notes (pp. 151–2), utilitarianism has provided the most influential modern account of this kind (at least in the English-speaking philosophical world). But contractualism seems to me more plausible than utilitarianism and its consequentialist relatives, both in respect to the issue of moral motivation and in respect to the internal structure of the morality of right and wrong. I shall conclude by mentioning two important strengths of the contractualist approach to the latter issue. One of these is the ability of contractualism to do justice to the diversity of considerations relevant to moral deliberation within the context of the unified moral framework that it describes. Contractualist reflection needs to take into account all the considerations that potentially provide people with a reasonable basis for objecting to candidate principles, and as Scanlon persuasively argues, these include not only the effects of such principles on individual well-being but also many other factors as well (including considerations of fairness, responsibility, choice, and so on; cf. pp. 211–12, 216–17, ch. 6, sect. 3). To the extent that this is the case, contractualism seems to reflect more accurately than classical utilitarianism the complexity and sophistication of moral life and thought. Indeed it seems superior in this respect even to those consequentialist moral theories that depart from classical utilitarianism in postulating a plurality of intrinsic goods. Such theories pay homage to the genuine diversity of considerations that are directly relevant to moral reflection, but the unifying framework into which those considerations are forced seems to distort rather than to illuminate their normative significance. Thus as Scanlon argues in chapter 2, many values are not well represented in the teleological terms recommended by consequentialism, as states of affairs that it is our task as agents to promote.

The second salient strength of contractualism in regard to the structure of moral thought is its focus on the standpoint of individual persons. The question of the acceptability of a given principle is made to depend on a one-by-one assessment of the strength of the reasons that individuals would have for rejecting the principle, compared with the alternatives to it. This captures in a direct and attractive way a distinctive feature of ordinary moral thought, and helps to render plausible the suggestion that contractualist procedures of reflection represent an appropriate response to the value of persons (pp. 229–30). Thus it is virtually a paradigm of moral thought to allow the grave objections of a single individual to defeat a project or plan that would otherwise be expedient for many; a willingness to defer to the standpoint of individuals in such cases seems to be required by their standing as ends in themselves (as Kantians would put the point). Utilitarian approaches, by contrast, have always seemed problematic in this respect, since the emphasis they place on maximizing a sum allows weighty burdens on individuals to be justified by comparatively minor advantages to others, so long as those advantages accrue to a sufficiently large number of persons. Of course, there are situations—certain rescue cases, for example, that present an agent with a choice between saving a larger and a smaller group of persons from a comparable loss or injury—in which aggregative considerations seem to matter to moral reflection. But Scanlon has an ingenious and illuminating discussion of the resources contractualism can offer for thinking about such situations without departing from the individualistic framework that makes contractualism intuitively appealing (ch. 5, sect. 9).

There is much more to be said about Scanlon's account of the structure of moral thought, which raises fundamental issues about a host of concrete moral problems. I hope I have said enough, however, to make clear why I regard Scanlon's contractualism as a remarkable philosophical achievement. It is, quite simply, the most promising unified account of the morality of right and wrong on the contemporary scene. If Scanlon is wrong, it is not because there is some alternative theory of this normative domain that is superior to his contractualism, but because an assumption common to all such theories turns out to be mistaken: the assumption, namely, that the morality of right and wrong represents a unified normative subject matter. It is not the smallest virtue of Scanlon's book that it helps us to appreciate the significance of this issue for the traditional project of ethical theory, even while it extends that tradition in powerful and illuminating ways.

13

The Rightness of Acts and the Goodness of Lives

A prominent tendency in recent work of Joseph Raz's has been to deny that there is any interesting philosophical problem about the authority of moral considerations to govern our lives. Philosophers who address this problem typically suppose that morality designates a domain of putatively normative considerations that hang together in some nonvacuous way. They then ask whether the considerations within this unified domain really do constitute reasons for action, and how they stack up compared to reasons of other kinds in respect of their normative importance. Thus it is common to contrast moral considerations with considerations of rational self-interest, and to ask whether and why we should conform to the former when they conflict with the latter.

Raz rejects this whole picture. He accepts a thoroughgoing pluralism about the domain of reasons, which denies that there is any context-independent way of classifying normative considerations as moral rather than nonmoral.[1] If morality does not constitute a unified normative domain, however, then the general question about the normative force of 'moral' considerations will fail to get a grip—it will be basically unclear what we are even asking about. Raz equally denies that self-interest represents a significant class of reasons for action.[2] Individual well-being

Originally published in in R. Jay Wallace, Philip Pettit, Samuel Scheffler, and Michael Smith (eds.), *Reason and Value: Themes from the Moral Philosophy of Joseph Raz* (Oxford: Clarendon Press, 2004), 385–411. Reprinted by permission of Oxford University Press. I have profited from stimulating discussions of predecessors of this paper at the following institutions: the Free University in Berlin; the Ludwig Maximilian University in Munich; the University of South Carolina; the Central Division Meetings of the American Philosophical Association; the Workshop in Law, Philosophy, and Political Theory at Berkeley; and the US Naval Academy. I am especially grateful to Janet Broughton, Logi Gunnarsson, and Nicholas Sturgeon for thoughtful written feedback on early versions of the paper, and to Niko Kolodny and Samuel Scheffler for very helpful comments on the penultimate draft.

[1] Joseph Raz, 'On the Moral Point of View', reprinted in his *Engaging Reason: On the Theory of Value and Action* (Oxford: Oxford University Press, 1999), 247–72; also 'The Amoralist', reprinted in his *Engaging Reason*, 273–302.

[2] Joseph Raz, 'The Central Conflict: Morality and Self-Interest', reprinted in his *Engaging Reason*, 303–32. Compare T. M. Scanlon, *What We Owe to Each Other* (Cambridge, Mass.: Harvard University Press, 1998), ch. 3.

consists in the successful pursuit of valuable ends, but this kind of consideration lacks deliberative significance for the agent to whom it applies. In place of the modern moral philosopher's contrast between morality and self-interest, Raz recommends a 'classical' conception of agency and normative reasons.[3] This holds that reasons are anchored in the value of ends and activities, and that they reflect directly the diversity and plurality that characterize the realm of value. The global question about the normativity of the moral thus gives way to an indefinite succession of first-order deliberative questions that confront individual agents as they make their way through life, questions that can be resolved only by reflection on the nature and significance of the concrete values that are at stake.

There is much to commend in this general approach to the relation between reasons and value. Nevertheless, I am not quite convinced by Raz's arguments that the traditional problem of understanding the normative force of moral considerations can so easily be dismissed or dissolved. To explain my doubts, I will begin by considering some of Raz's own examples, and show how they very naturally suggest a philosophical question about the deliberative significance of ethical[4] requirements. In the sections that follow I shall try to develop a framework to make sense of this question, one that is capable of standing up to the doubts expressed by Raz. While agreeing with Raz that narrow self-interest does not constitute an interesting normative domain, I contend that there is a broader class of 'eudaimonistic' considerations that is significant for practical deliberation. My aim is to explain the challenge that can be posed to morality in terms of this class of reasons, and to make some observations about the resources available within moral philosophy for dealing with the challenge.

1. GOODNESS FOR THE AGENT

Concern about the normative standing of moral considerations is encouraged by cases in which morality demands forms of conduct that do not promise any apparent benefit to the agent. We must be faithful to our promises, provide emergency assistance to those in need, refrain from exploiting the vulnerable, etc., even when doing these things is inconvenient for us, or otherwise renders difficult the pursuit of our private aims and goals. Situations of this kind seem to raise a general question about the normative significance of moral requirements, whose grip on us can start to appear puzzling or mysterious.

Raz contends that this appearance is a mere illusion. One of his several arguments for this conclusion begins from reflection on what it is for something to be good *for* a given agent. Thus he suggests that we justify claims to the effect that something is good for a given agent by showing '(*a*) that the thing is good,

---

[3] See Joseph Raz, 'Agency, Reason, and the Good', in his *Engaging Reason*, 22–45.
[4] I shall use the expressions 'ethical' and 'moral' interchangeably in what follows.

and (*b*) that the agent has the ability and the opportunity to have that good'.[5] This is a schema that can easily be satisfied even in the case of morally required actions that are inconvenient for the agent. An act of helping another person in need, for instance, is clearly good, so when we have the ability and the opportunity to perform such an act, our doing so will be good for us. Granted, it will not be good for us in the same way the act will be good for its direct beneficiary, namely instrumentally; but an act can be good for us without benefiting us in the manner characteristic of instrumental goods.

As Raz himself notes, however, the actions required by morality still seem significantly different from many of the activities that are paradigmatically good for their agents. Take teaching, for instance: we can readily make sense of this as something that can be good not just for the student but also for the teacher, because it is 'a challenging, complex activity which can be fulfilling to those engaging in it'.[6] Such moral actions as keeping a promise or providing emergency assistance, by contrast, hardly seem to resemble the paradigm case of teaching in these respects; they do not seem to be intrinsically good for their agents, just in virtue of being morally good in the ways they are. But this, Raz suggests, would be the wrong lesson to draw from the contrast between teaching and morality. What is at issue here is the contrast not between things that are good for the agent and the requirements of morality, but rather between two different kinds of intrinsic good: namely, the intrinsic good of *activities* and the intrinsic good of *acts*.[7] With activities, such as teaching, what is intrinsically good for the agent lies in the complex, challenging pattern of behavior over time that the activity itself consists in. With morally required acts, by contrast, the value of the behavior that is required lies principally in the results to be achieved. If I help somebody by giving to charity, for example, the value of what I am doing does not inhere in my writing out a cheque, placing it in an envelope, etc., but rather in the end that is brought about through my donation.

This will address our original worry about the normative standing of moral considerations, of course, only if things that are valuable in the way that acts are can be good *for* the agent who does them. Raz argues that this is in fact the case, using the example of a world-record sprinter to make his point. Running 100 metres in record time is not valuable in virtue of the physical processes and bodily exertions that it involves—which in themselves might well be far from enjoyable for the sprinter—but rather for its result, the setting of a new record. 'Those who achieve it cannot complain that they do not enjoy the activity of racing which led to the result as well. Their reward is in the result.'[8] Similarly for moral acts: the agent who writes out a cheque to a charitable cause is doing something whose reward does not lie in the processes and exertions of writing the cheque, but in the

---

[5] Raz, 'On the Moral Point of View', 260.   [6] Ibid. 266.   [7] Ibid. 267–8.
[8] Ibid. 267.

valuable result that those processes achieve. The general schema remains in place that something is good for an agent if it is good and the agent has the ability and opportunity to achieve it. What is distinctive of the things that morality requires of us, at least in a range of central cases, is that they fit into this general schema in the way characteristic of acts rather than activities.

This response, however, does not succeed in removing the worry to which it was addressed. The worry is that what morality requires does not seem to be valuable for the agent in the way our most important endeavors and activities can be. The example of the sprinter is a helpful one, because world-class athletic competition is an enterprise that can clearly contribute to one's own well-being—engaging in this activity well is something that can be better for the person who goes in for it. If the value of the activity lies in the result of setting a record, this is something that seems intelligible as a *reward* for the agent, an *achievement* of the kind that makes their own life better. But the valuable results that moral acts may bring about do not seem to contribute in a similar way to enriching the life of the agents who perform them, as Raz's schematic argument would require. At least, it is not obvious how one's own life is made better through one's performing acts whose value lies in results external to the acts themselves, which redound to the benefit of persons other than oneself.

Curiously, Raz seems to concede precisely this point in a separate treatment of the relation between morality and individual well-being.[9] He describes a case involving a young person confronted with a choice between accepting a scholarship to study at university and volunteering to drive a lorry in an emergency operation to bring food to the victims of a severe famine. Raz supposes that the moral reasons in favor of the latter option defeat the considerations that speak in favor of beginning a course of study at the university; they are categorical reasons, whose stringency is grounded in the importance of the lives that are to be saved, in a way that is unaffected by whether or not acting on the reasons would subserve the agent's personal goals. In so far as driving the lorry in the food convoy represents a good that the agent has the ability and the opportunity to realize, choosing that option will be good for the agent. But Raz grants that it will not contribute as greatly to the agent's well-being as would going to university. He explains this by invoking, again, the distinction between acts and activities, noting that the former are typically of shorter duration than the latter, and that assessments of well-being take the 'person's life as a whole as the measure'.[10] The upshot is that the morally required acts involved in driving the lorry, though more valuable than the activity of studying at a university, will make less of a contribution to the agent's well-being, because they ramify less extensively through the agent's life. This seems correct, but it only reinforces the question posed above. Once we are clear that the

[9] Raz, 'Central Conflict', §§ 2–4.   [10] Ibid. 320.

acts that morality often requires contribute less significantly to our well-being than the alternatives that are open to us, it appears puzzling that they should be categorical in their stringency.

I do not believe this is a decisive objection to the normative significance of moral considerations. My point is rather that there is an intelligible and gripping question about the normativity of moral requirements in this vicinity, and that the question does not seem to be foreclosed by Raz's general animadversions on the concept of something's being good for an agent. Not all of the goods whose realization a given agent has the capacity and the opportunity to achieve are things whose realization is intrinsically good for the agent, in the way the acts and activities involved in our most important personal relationships and projects typically seem to be. In particular, the goods that are realized by many of the actions that morality requires us to perform do not seem to be important in this way. Perhaps this kind of personal importance is not a general condition of ethical normativity, something without which an agent cannot have reason to perform an action that morality requires. Even if this is correct, however, there is bound to be a question about the capacity of moral reasons to prevail in competition with the acts and activities that are more directly and obviously good for the agent who performs them. This, at any rate, is the idea that I propose to develop in the remainder of the present essay. In doing so, I hope to vindicate, in a limited way, one aspect of the traditional normative project of ethical theory against Raz's attempts at dissolution.

2. FACILITATING GOODS

First we will need to get a bit clearer about what morality is. As I mentioned above, Raz himself is skeptical about the idea that morality is a unified normative domain, a set of reasons and values that stand apart from other kinds of normative consideration, and that can be characterized in terms that are both substantive and context-independent. Skepticism about this issue is part of what leads Raz to doubt that there is an interesting general question to be joined about the authority of moral reasons and values. For the record, I am less skeptical than Raz that the moral realm exhibits any interesting kind of unity. It seems to me that we can acknowledge the plurality of considerations that go to determining whether acts are right or wrong, while providing an informative account of what these considerations have in common—what makes them determinants of moral right and wrong.[11]

This is an issue to which I shall return below. For the present, however, it seems to me that we can proceed to formulate a question about the normative authority

---

[11] See my 'Scanlon's Contractualism', Chapter 12 in this volume, sect. 4.

of moral considerations even without having in hand a substantive characterization of the unity of the moral realm. It will suffice if we can identify a group of salient and central moral considerations that both demand sacrifices of us, and appear to be deficient by comparison with the activities and projects that are paradigmatically good for the agent who engages in them. Whatever else they may or may not have in common, there seems to be a range of moral requirements that satisfy these two conditions, including (for instance) requirements of fidelity to agreements, fairness, mutual aid, veracity, and nonmaleficence.

Now I do not wish to question whether these kinds of moral consideration are genuine reasons for action, or whether they are correctly understood as requirements in some sense or other. There are questions that might be raised at the most fundamental level about the normative standing of these moral considerations, their claim to significance in the deliberations of agents about what they are to do. For purposes of this discussion, however, I would like to put those questions to the side, and focus on an issue that arises even after the normative significance of basic moral requirements has been granted or established.

The issue is raised very clearly by a way of thinking about the values implicated in these central cases of moral requirements that Raz himself has proposed. He suggests that many moral values are what he calls 'facilitating' or 'enabling' values, in that their 'good is in making possible or facilitating the instantiation of other values'.[12] Thus moral requirements such as justice or fidelity or veracity are good, at least in part, in so far as adherence to them facilitates the collective pursuit of other ends that are valuable. Our ability to act effectively to realize complex and valuable goals is clearly enhanced, for example, if we can rely on other people to keep their agreements and fulfill the expectations they lead others to have about what they are going to do, as fidelity requires people to do. Raz notes that enabling or facilitating values can also be valuable in a different way, in so far as acting on them is partly constitutive (for instance) of valuable personal relationships. Let us abstract, however, from situations in which this is the case, to focus on the pure examples of moral requirements whose value lies in their contribution to facilitating the pursuit of other values. Let us also grant that this kind of pure facilitating value provides people with corresponding moral reasons to comply with the requirements in question.

Granting that this is the case, however, does not suffice to remove all basis for questioning the authority of moral principles to govern our lives. For morality often requires us to make significant personal sacrifices, compromising or curtailing the pursuit of our individual projects in order to do the right thing. It is typically understood as a kind of highest-level end, laying down fundamental ground rules that are to be complied with as we fashion our more particular plans and decisions.[13] To allow morality to play this role is to structure one's practical reflection

---

[12] Joseph Raz, *The Practice of Value*, ed. R. Jay Wallace (Oxford: Oxford University Press, 2003), 34.
[13] See Joseph Raz, *The Morality of Freedom* (Oxford: Oxford University Press, 1986), 292–93, on the hierarchical structure of human goals.

in terms of its requirements. Morality leaves room for the pursuit of personal ends, but only within the parameters that are set by moral requirements; it thus functions as a set of constraints on our individual, nonmoral activities. If we focus on the central cases in which morality is grounded in facilitating goods, however, there is room to question whether the reasons it provides could possibly be serious enough to constrain our personal attachments and concerns in this way. It does not seem reasonable to grant its requirements this kind of *priority* in shaping our lives.

A worry of this kind seems to me to lie behind some of the more interesting recent critiques of modern morality. Bernard Williams's influential objections to the 'morality system', for instance, turn in part on the idea that no set of purely impartial requirements could hope to prevail in competition with the kinds of 'ground projects' that give our lives meaning and point.[14] A standard response to this suggestion has been to assert that morality itself may be among a person's ground projects, and so at least on a par with the other sorts of commitments over which it is supposed to prevail.[15] But this cannot simply be taken for granted. At least a part of what Williams is trying to question, I believe, is whether impartial morality is the sort of thing to which it would be reasonable to be committed in the way one is committed to one's personal projects and relationships. This question seems especially pressing when we reflect on those central moral requirements that represent facilitating values. The fact that justice and fidelity facilitate or enable the pursuit of valuable ends might well make these things good themselves, and give us some reason to respond to and to care about them. But offhand, it hardly seems very sensible to care about the facilitating goods of morality in anything like the way we care about the ground projects that give texture and substance to our own lives.

This is not, it should be emphasized, merely because the values in question stand in a facilitating relation to other goods.[16] There are cases in which it might well seem sensible to be devoted to a facilitating value in the manner of a ground project or a personal relationship. There are many professional roles, for instance, that primarily involve facilitating the pursuit of other valuable ends or goals— think of the job of an office administrator or a city traffic engineer—and it would not seem unintelligible to us that someone might be committed to performing well in these roles, as a kind of ground project in life. But the facilitating values at

---

[14] See Bernard Williams, 'Persons, Character and Morality' and 'Moral Luck', both reprinted in his *Moral Luck* (Cambridge, England: Cambridge University Press, 1981), 1–19 and 20–39, respectively. See also Susan Wolf's reflections on the relations between impartial morality and partial attachments, in 'Morality and Partiality', *Philosophical Perspectives*, 6 (1992), 243–59.

[15] See e.g. Peter Railton, 'Alienation, Consequentialism, and the Demands of Morality', as reprinted in Samuel Scheffler (ed.), *Consequentialism and its Critics* (Oxford: Oxford University Press, 1988), 93–133, at 112–13, and Thomas Nagel, *The View from Nowhere* (New York: Oxford University Press, 1986), 198.

[16] I owe this point to a very helpful discussion with Niko Kolodny.

issue in morality seem different in this respect. For one thing, they are defined in terms of requirements whose demands on us are episodic rather than continuous; to borrow the distinction from Raz introduced above, we comply with them through a series of apparently disconnected acts, rather than through a pattern of ongoing activity. For another thing, there is a generic quality to the central requirements of morality, in so far as they apply indifferently to all human agents. Acting in conformity with these requirements therefore does not seem to give expression to anything distinctive about the agent's personality or character or outlook on life. This combination of features seems to disqualify impartial morality from acquiring the significance for an agent of personal relationships and ground projects.

If the facilitating values at the heart of morality are not important to us in this way, however, then their capacity to stand up in rational competition with the claims of our projects and relationships may seem insecure. There will be a basis within practical reason for questioning the *priority* that moral requirements are typically taken to possess.

3. GOODNESS FOR: NARROW AND BROAD

The comparison with ground projects returns us to the question of whether the acts that are required by morality can be good for their agent. For the challenge posed by the work of such critics of impartial morality as Williams is frequently understood in these terms—most notably by Thomas Nagel, who represents Williams as raising a question about the relation between the moral life and the good life.[17] But this way of putting things requires further interpretation. The notion of what is good for an agent is notoriously elastic, but perhaps the most natural way of interpreting it is in prudential terms, as referring to what is in the agent's interests or conducive to the agent's own welfare, where this in turn is understood, in familiar if elusive ways, as a matter of health, material comfort, psychic satisfaction, and so on.[18]

This prudential interpretation seems too narrow, however, to ground an interesting challenge to the deliberative importance of morality. Thus as parents and friends, people involved in our work and committed to various projects and institutions, we are often perfectly willing to put up with sacrifices in our own interests or well-being, narrowly construed; nor does it seem irrational of us to do so.[19] If this attitude is in general not open to rational criticism, there seems no reason to

---

[17] See Nagel, *View from Nowhere*, ch. 10.

[18] For further discussion, see Derek Parfit, *Reasons and Persons* (Oxford: Oxford University Press, 1984), app. I, and James Griffin, *Well-Being: Its Meaning, Measurement, and Moral Importance* (Oxford: Oxford University Press, 1986).

[19] Compare Parfit's arguments against the self-interest theory in *Reasons and Persons*, pt. II.

find it objectionable when the ends for which we are willing to make personal sacrifices are moral ones. The narrow or prudential interpretation of the good life, in terms of the agent's own welfare, thus does not look very promising as a basis for challenging the importance of impartial morality. If we reject this interpretation of the question, however, it begins to look as if there is no longer any ground at all for the skeptical challenger to stand on. We might follow Raz in proposing a broader interpretation of 'goodness for', according to which a pursuit is good for an agent just in case it is valuable, and also something that the agent has the ability and opportunity to go in for. But this interpretation is *too* broad for the purposes at hand. Any value, including the merely facilitating values at the heart of morality, is one whose successful pursuit would automatically be good for the agent, and this leaves no basis for a contrast with the kinds of values involved in Williams's ground projects.[20] We seem to lack terms to articulate the intuitive sense that morality might be rationally deficient by comparison with the personal relationships and endeavours around which we structure our lives.

The intuitive concern raised by this contrast is perhaps most naturally expressed in the language of importance. Ground projects in Williams's sense are the sorts of things that are of obvious importance to us; they generate rational claims that are central to our understanding of ourselves, and that we intelligibly and naturally respond to as things that make compelling demands on our attention and concern. The intuitive importance of these kinds of requirements seems to reflect the fact that the values in which they are grounded are things whose pursuit can be made sense of as something that is good for the agent. As we have seen, however, an interpretation of 'goodness for' that is adequate to this intuitive understanding of ground projects seems elusive. The narrow interpretation in terms of prudential self-interest is too narrow to include many of the central cases, whereas Raz's extremely generic interpretation seems too broad to enable us to articulate the central intuition.[21] Is there a third alternative?

I would like to explore the following suggestion: one way in which an activity or pursuit might be good for the agent engaged in it is by making the agent's life *worthwhile* or *meaningful* from the agent's own point of view. Furthermore, being good for the agent in this way is something that has normative significance for the agent's own deliberations. Thus there is a standpoint of practical reflection,

---

[20] As we saw above, Raz at one point qualifies this view, allowing that moral values might contribute less to the agent's well-being than the values whose pursuit occupies a more extensive segment of the agent's life; see, again, 'Central Conflict', § 4. This does not provide a basis for questioning the significance of moral ends, in Raz's view, because 'normally an agent's well-being is not, for him, a reason for action' (ibid. 322). A challenge to the authority of morality requires not merely a demonstration that there are other ends with which morality might conflict, but also that those other ends are themselves deliberatively significant.

[21] Compare Donald H. Regan, 'Why Am I My Brother's Keeper?', in R. Jay Wallace, Philip Pettit, Samuel Scheffler, and Michael Smith (eds.), *Reason and Value: Themes from the Moral Philosophy of Joseph Raz* (Oxford: Clarendon Press, 2004), 202–30, for an expression of deep skepticism about the idea that there is a notion of 'goodness for' that is both coherent and normatively significant.

reasonably familiar to most of us, which is reached by stepping back from our basic first-order pursuits, and asking whether it is good that we are engaged in these pursuits. In raising this question, we are not asking whether it is good for other people, or humanity as a whole, that we should be engaged in the pursuits we are; nor are we asking whether doing so is good for us in the narrowly prudential sense I have already discussed. We are asking, rather, whether engaging in these pursuits is *worthwhile*, something that makes our own lives choiceworthy as human lives. We are asking whether our life is made meaningful or worth living as a result of our being engaged in these pursuits.[22] For want of a less misleading expression, we might refer to the point of view from which we pose these questions as the standpoint of eudaimonistic reflection. My suggestion is that our sense of the importance of relationships and ground projects is connected to their salience within eudaimonistic reflection of this kind; they are good for us as individual agents insofar as they can be made sense of as direct contributions to the choice-worthiness of our own lives.

To this it may be objected that any activity that is good in some way, or that we have reason to engage in, will be capable of satisfying this condition. But this does not seem to be correct. A low-level employee's willingness to put in long hours performing inherently uninteresting tasks for the firm may be a response that is grounded in reasons, also one that is valuable in some way or other (e.g., for the firm and its shareholders). But it is far from obvious that it is valuable *for the agent* in the distinctive way I have been trying to characterize: namely, as something that itself contributes directly to making the agent's life meaningful or choiceworthy. Or consider again the facilitating values at the centre of impartial morality. The fact that fidelity or nonmaleficence facilitates the collective pursuit of valuable ends makes these moral requirements valuable, and perhaps gives us reason to comply with them as well. But these dimensions of value do not *seem* to render compliance with moral requirements good for the agent in anything like the way our important personal projects and relationships appear to do. This is a thought that Raz himself gives clear expression to in the following passage: 'being a nonmurderer, or a non-rapist, or a person who simply gives away everything he has . . . is not something that can give meaning to life'.[23]

A brief survey of some particular kinds of activities that we ordinarily take to be of great personal importance may help to illustrate the notion of 'goodness for' that is at issue here, illuminating both its distinction from the narrower notion of

---

[22] Compare Susan Wolf, 'Happiness and Meaning: Two Aspects of the Good Life', in Ellen Frankel Paul, Fred D. Miller, Jr., and Jeffrey Paul (eds.), *Self-Interest* (Cambridge, England: Cambridge University Press, 1997), 207–25.

[23] Raz, *Practice of Value*, 36. Compare Harry Frankfurt, 'Preface' to *Necessity, Volition, and Love* (Cambridge, England: Cambridge University Press, 1999), p. x: 'For most people, the relevance of their moral obligations as legitimately binding constraints or as proper determinants of choice and conduct is quite limited. What morality has to say concerning how to live and what to do is important, but its importance is often exaggerated.'

prudential self-interest and its direct significance for practical deliberation. Consider first the example of personal relationships. People are clearly willing to make fairly great sacrifices for the sake of those they feel attached to as friends, lovers, spouses, and so on. But, just as clearly, having relationships of these kinds is among the things that make life interesting and worthwhile. Our lives would be impoverished in all kinds of ways if we did not have the opportunity to experience intimacies of these kinds, and this is itself a powerful reason to nourish and cultivate our personal ties.

A different example involves our professional commitments. There are lots of cases in which people seem quite reasonably willing to make large sacrifices in terms of their own interests and welfare for the sake of professional goals to which they are committed. To take a case of this kind familiar to most of us, there is the scientist or scholar who is willing to put in exceptionally long and grinding hours working on projects that are unlikely to bring fame or financial reward, that render it difficult to develop the range of interests important for a balanced human life, and that introduce their own forms of psychic conflict and distress. Sacrifices of these kinds may without infelicity be said to be good for the agent who makes them, but what renders this conclusion plausible is that the activities in question are direct contributions to the goodness of human lives. Highly structured and complex scientific and artistic pursuits are, after all, characteristically human forms of *achievement*, directed at an appropriate and worthwhile object, and distinguishing oneself in these activities is therefore one way of distinguishing oneself as a human being (compare Raz's example of the sprinter). To the extent that this is the case, engaging well in complex scientific or artistic activities may contribute directly to the goodness of the agent's life, making it choiceworthy and meaningful from the agent's point of view, and this consideration can supply a compelling reason to put up with great sacrifices for the sake of such activities.

There are other kinds of cases, however, in which one has reason to make sacrifices in respect of one's own interests, despite the fact that the activities that impose such sacrifices do not themselves seem to be forms of human accomplishment of this kind. Many people labor virtually to the point of exhaustion in activities that are intrinsically mechanical and unrewarding, such that it is extremely implausible to represent the activities themselves as contributing directly to the choiceworthiness of their lives. Dedication of this sort can nevertheless be good for the agent, if it is a condition for the person's engaging, perhaps at some later point in life, in other meaningful activities. This is a familiar enough pattern: people can have reason to tolerate years of sacrifice and drudgery—law school and the unrelenting grunt work of legal practice, or a long stretch of tedious factory labor—if doing so enables them later to pursue other, more worthwhile endeavors.

In a still different kind of case, a person will toil at an exceptionally tedious and unrewarding occupation not in order to achieve other or later advantages for themselves, but to make possible a better and more choiceworthy life for (say) their offspring. This might of course be a perfectly reasonable thing to do, as a special case of the relationship-based sacrifices already touched on above. But I would maintain that it can remain good for the agent, even when the occupation in question is so consuming that it leaves little time for the person to develop a real relationship with the child whose prospects are to be improved. The condition for its being important in this way, however, is that the agent be able to view the intrinsically tedious activities in a different light: perhaps as a way of participating in something greater than oneself, contributing to a value that will live on when one is gone. Seeing one's activities in this kind of light can enable one to appreciate them as constitutive parts of a life that is worth living. One's own life acquires meaning in so far as it is connected in this radical way to values that lie outside the self, and this supplies a powerful reason to commit oneself to the intrinsically uninteresting acts that fill out the life, which would otherwise be intolerable.[24]

This seems to me recognizable, perhaps as a limiting case, as a way in which a life can be worthwhile from the agent's point of view; but the self-transcending form of value in question is by its nature one that is probably capable of being appreciated only by those who are subject to the transforming effects of personal love or quasi-religious devotion. Outside such personal or religious contexts, most of us would be unable to recognize or endorse the values of self-transcendence in eudaimonistic reflection as sources of meaning. We typically need to see more substantial values embodied in our lives.

4. EUDAIMONISTIC REFLECTION

In the last section, I appealed to intuitive convictions about whether the sacrifice of one's own interests could or could not be said to be good for the agent making the sacrifice, and about the relevance of this kind of goodness to practical deliberation. It will now be well to try to be more systematic about these convictions. I have spoken of a standpoint of eudaimonistic reflection, from which we are concerned with the question of the contribution of our activities to the goodness of our own lives. Furthermore, I have suggested that being good for the agent in this way is connected to our sense of the importance of the ends and requirements that stem from our relationships and ground projects. In these terms, the worry that I am trying to articulate about morality is that the facilitating values at its heart do not seem capable of taking on this kind of importance. Compliance with such moral requirements does not appear to be good for the agent in the way that personal values and requirements clearly are—namely, as direct contributions to the goodness or meaning of the agent's own life. To the extent this is the case, and

---

[24] This is an extreme case of a more general phenomenon to which Harry Frankfurt has called attention, in which the intrinsic value to us of certain activities is a function of their instrumental contribution to an end that we care about; see his 'On the Usefulness of Final Ends', as reprinted in his *Necessity, Volition, and Love*, 82–94.

to the extent this dimension of goodness has normative significance, there seems to be a basis *within practical reason* for questioning the deliberative priority of impartial morality, its claim to define a comprehensive framework within which our personal projects and activities are to be pursued.

The appeal to the standpoint of eudaimonistic reflection is an attempt to make out a point of view from which a serious skeptical challenge to the rational authority of morality might be raised. Thus I am in agreement with Raz that the context of amoralist skepticism about morality—defined by the assumption that we are concerned exclusively with our own well-being in the narrow, prudential sense— is not one that defines a serious class of reasons for action; so the suggestion that it might not be prudentially rational to be moral should not be troubling to us. By contrast, the context defined by the standpoint of eudaimonistic reflection is both readily accessible and deliberatively significant; it is important that we are able to justify our most basic projects from this point of view, as things that make our lives worthwhile.

This is not to say that the eudaimonistic point of view is the only one we are capable of occupying for purposes of practical reflection. In addition, there is also (for instance) the point of view of impartial morality itself. As interpreted in the most significant moral theories of the last centuries, such as Kantianism and utilitarianism, impartial morality defines a distinctive way of looking at and thinking about practical questions, one characterized by a kind of abstraction from personal concerns. In certain versions of utilitarianism, and in Nagel's moral theory, for instance, one steps back in moral reflection to a standpoint of impersonality, thinking about practical questions not merely from the first-personal point of view of a particular agent, but as far as possible from the 'point of view of the universe'.[25] In Kant's theory, the moral point of view is defined by a concern with the universalizability of one's maxims or intentions; while some contractualist accounts characterize this perspective in terms of the aim of acting in a way that can be justified to those potentially affected by what we do.[26] Furthermore, all of these theories hold that the characteristically moral point of view is also a comprehensive one, in so far as a moral justification can in principle be demanded for any activity we might be engaged in.

To follow the tradition of modern moral philosophy in this respect is to grant that moral dispositions characteristically enable agents to deliberate about practical problems in a distinctive way. If we go down this route, however, then an important question looms about the intelligibility of moral skepticism. Granting that morality defines a characteristic point of view, a challenge to its rational status must apparently be formulated in terms of a standpoint of practical reflection that

---

[25] See Henry Sidgwick, *The Methods of Ethics*, 7th edn. (Indianapolis: Hackett Publishing Co., 1981), and Nagel, *View from Nowhere*, chs. 8–9. (Nagel's view is qualified by the recognition that the impersonal point of view takes in only part of the moral landscape.)

[26] See Scanlon, *What We Owe to Each Other*.

is distinctively nonmoral,[27] and this raises the issue of why the status of moral norms should be answerable to considerations that are external to moral thought itself. (This is a version of Prichard's question, in his influential paper 'Does Moral Philosophy Rest on a Mistake?'[28]) Furthermore, this is an objection to which Raz too should be sympathetic—despite his skepticism about the unity of anything that might be described as the 'moral point of view'. On the classical account that he favors, there is no interesting context-independent way of classifying reasons and values as distinctively moral. But the classical approach remains deeply pluralistic, acknowledging profound differences between the values in which our various reasons for action are grounded. In the spirit of this approach, one might emphasize the categorial discrepancy between the facilitating moral values that have been my main focus to this point and the personal projects and relationships that are significant within eudaimonistic reflection. Even if it should turn out to be misleading to characterize this discrepancy by talking about two distinct, comprehensive points of view, the question arises as to why the normative significance of facilitating values should be answerable to the distinct kinds of value at the bottom of personal projects and relationships.

One way to develop this point is in terms of the notion of importance. I have appealed to the eudaimonistic value of a meaningful or worthwhile life (from the agent's point of view) to elucidate what intuitively seems to be important about the values implicated in personal projects and relationships. But it might be argued that there is more than one kind of importance. An action that is not itself important as a direct contribution to the goodness of the agent's own life might still be important in some other way, say as a contribution to facilitating the general pursuit by humans of valuable ends and activities. If moral values and requirements can be important in the latter way, however, it might be wondered why it should matter if they are not also important in the former. Why should the failure of moral actions to contribute directly to the meaning or choiceworthiness of the agent's own life in any way impugn their claim to determine what the agent is to do? We do not, after all, similarly worry that the claims of our projects and relationships are threatened if they cannot be shown to be important in the distinctive ways characteristic of central moral requirements (i.e., as contributions to facilitating the collective pursuit of valuable ends).

It is far from obvious, however, that these two kinds of importance carry with them equal significance for practical deliberation. The impersonal importance exhibited by facilitating moral values is a function of their relation to the general pursuit of valuable ends by human agents; but things that are valuable and important in this way need not be important *to me*. Personal projects and relationships,

---

[27] I pass over here the possibility of an 'internal' critique of the status of moral norms, of the sort often attributed (for instance) to Friedrich Nietzsche in the first essay of *On the Genealogy of Morals*.

[28] Reprinted in J. O. Urmson and W. D. Ross (eds.), *Moral Obligation and Duty and Interest: Essays and Lectures by H. A. Prichard* (Oxford: Oxford University Press, 1968), 1–17.

by contrast, are things that are paradigmatically important *to* the agents whose projects and relationships they are, in so far as they are good for those agents in the manner I have been trying to trace—that is, as conditions for a meaningful or worthwhile life. It seems manifest that this species of importance *to* the agent is one that has great deliberative significance. Thus we would scarcely know how to interpret someone who conceded that doing *x* was of great importance to him, but went on to ask why he should care about doing *x*. The corresponding question posed about the impersonal importance of facilitating moral values, however, seems eminently intelligible. Someone might well grant that fidelity to agreements, for instance, would facilitate the general pursuit of valuable ends by human agents, but wonder why exactly she ought to care about *that*. The intelligibility of this question suggests that the kind of importance exhibited by facilitating moral values does not play the same prominent role within practical reason that importance *to* the agent seems to play.

In saying this I do not mean to deny that we have reason to comply with moral requirements, or to care about the ends that such compliance subserves. But *how much* should we care about doing what is good or important in these ways? If the skeptical challenge I have been trying to articulate goes unanswered, there may be no clear answer to this question at the end of the day. On the one hand, when we reflect on the objective importance of facilitating values for human agents, it seems that moral requirements ought to be given very high deliberative priority, fundamentally structuring the most basic life pursuits of the agents to whom they apply. For it is hardly possible for them to achieve their function if they are not accorded this kind of significance in the lives of individual agents. On the other hand, when we compare moral values with the personal values at the heart of projects and relationships, it appears puzzling that the former should attain the highest deliberative priority. It does not seem to be good for the agent to comply with moral requirements, in the way it clearly can be to comply with the demands that stem from personal values.

We might borrow Sidgwick's image of a dualism of practical reason to express this skeptical aporia.[29] When we attend to the values that define the moral point of view (to the extent there is such a thing), it seems plausible to suppose that moral requirements should have the status of highest-level ends, fundamentally structuring our deliberations and actions. From the standpoint of eudaimonistic reflection, however, it seems doubtful that moral requirements should have this kind of deliberative priority; compliance with them does not appear to be good for the agent, or important to the agent, in the way that is characteristic of the projects and relationships that are of paramount deliberative significance. If this is the problem, however, then the solution would seem to consist in showing that the differing standpoints can be brought into substantive alignment, so that the

---

[29] See Sidgwick, *Methods of Ethics*, 507–9 (e.g.).

verdicts arrived at within each are in harmony with one another. To answer the skeptical challenge, it needs to be shown that—contrary to initial appearances— there is a congruence between the standpoint from which the challenge is mounted and the standpoint of morality itself.[30]

To see how this kind of congruence might be brought about, it will be necessary to consider further the standpoint of eudaimonistic reflection from which, on my account, the skeptical challenge is posed. One thing I have already touched on is that this standpoint is not concerned, in the first instance, with the value of particular actions, but rather with our fundamental priorities. Eudaimonistic reflection is reflexive, and focused on our basic projects and comprehensive life goals, the kind of projects and goals that provide the context within which our more particular decisions are posed. It follows from this, perhaps, that the standpoint of eudaimonistic reflection is not one that we actually project ourselves into all that often. Indeed, if things are going well for us—that is, if we are actually engaged in activities that make our lives meaningful from our own point of view—there may be little practical need to stop and reflect about what makes this the case. The reflexive standpoint is nevertheless available to us, and especially in situations in which our projects require sacrifices of us, there will be occasion to make those projects themselves the object of reflection, asking whether it is reasonable to structure our lives in terms of them.

Reflection of this kind involves, as we have seen, fixing our sense of what is important to us.[31] By framing the question of whether we are engaged in pursuits that make our lives worthwhile as we live them, we help to clarify for ourselves what really matters to us, and the degree to which what matters to us is adequately reflected in the most basic priorities we have set for ourselves. Thus, not everything that one invests a lot of time and energy in is something that, upon reflection, one really turns out to care about all that much. That one is prepared to invest time and energy in an activity is a necessary condition, perhaps, of the activity's being important, but it is not sufficient; the lesson of a certain kind of mid-life crisis, for example, is that one's actual priorities can be out of alignment with one's sense of what really matters. If this kind of result is to be avoided, the agent herself must be able to endorse her actual patterns of activity reflectively, as an adequate expression of her own sense of what is important in life. We may think of this further, normative condition as a condition of articulation: reflection about our activities must make transparent to us the ways in which our *de facto* priorities contribute to the choiceworthiness of our lives, and the dimensions of value thus articulated must be ones that we can actually succeed in caring about.

---

[30] For the basic strategy of establishing the congruence between the constitutive standpoints of practical reason, see above all John Rawls, *A Theory of Justice* (Cambridge, Mass.: Harvard University Press, 1971), pt. 3.

[31] On the general idea of what is important to a person, see Harry Frankfurt, 'The Importance of What We Care About', as reprinted in his *The Importance of What We Care About* (Cambridge: Cambridge University Press, 1988), 80–94.

Once a conception of what is important is fixed in this way, it establishes a framework for further eudaimonistic reasoning, the task of which can best be characterized in terms of integration. One does not necessarily weigh the various things that matter to one in a balance, with the objective of maximizing the value of something (the goodness or meaningfulness of one's life, say). Rather, one tries to find ways of integrating the various objectives that matter, bringing them together into a single life that makes appropriate room for each. To take the most obvious kind of example, when it comes to degree of importance, many of us would have no trouble concluding that certain intimate personal relationships are more important to us than our professional goals. It in no way follows from this, however, that practical reasoning should be concerned primarily to adjust our priorities in life to reflect precisely this difference in comparative importance of the professional and the personal. The salient desideratum for practical reason is not that the professional is less important than the personal, but that both matter to us greatly (if we are lucky). Given that this is the case, our primary practical objective is to find ways of doing justice to the concrete demands of both spheres within the parameters of a single life. It is only when integrative reasoning of this kind cannot go forward, because circumstances do not allow the demands of the two different spheres to be satisfied together, that considerations of comparative importance may become relevant. And even here, one's decision is apt to have the character of a radical choice or a tragic conflict, rather than of a simple problem of maximization.

That this is the case can be traced to the fact that our most important projects present themselves to us as making claims on us. As friends, lovers, Oakland A's fans, and teachers of philosophy, there are certain things that one simply has to do: provide support for the friend during a difficult phase in her life, follow the playoffs, prepare one's classes, and so on. Each of these projects functions as a highest-level end, defining constraints that structure our more particular deliberations, and partly define who we are.[32] My suggestion is that, once eudaimonistic reflection has determined that these various aspects of one's identity are all of them important, the immediate problem for practical reason is to devise a plan that will enable the various claims to be fulfilled together. Our conception of what is important in this way sets the terms in which practical reasoning about our more particular decisions will go forward.

5. MEANING AND MORALITY

Let us now return to morality and the problem of its congruence with the eudaimonistic point of view. The skeptical challenge that I have been concerned

---

[32] Compare the discussion of practical identity and its link with obligation in Christine M. Korsgaard, *The Sources of Normativity* (Cambridge, England: Cambridge University Press, 1996), 101–2.

to articulate in this paper begins from the worry that, considered from the perspective of eudalmonistic reflection, compliance with moral norms cannot be endorsed as contributing directly to the goodness of one's own life. The remarks of the previous section suggest that this challenge may be answered if it can be shown that compliance with moral requirements is among the things that matter to us when it comes to determining our basic priorities, defining one of the groups of claims that must be incorporated into the fixed structure of our life plans. If this condition can be satisfied, then one will be able to agree, from the standpoint of eudaimonistic reason, that the meaning and value of one's life will depend in part on the extent to which one succeeds in finding ways of pursuing one's personal goals and projects that are compatible with the requirements of impartial morality. In these terms, the concern articulated earlier in this paper is that impartial morality isn't the sort of end to which we should ascribe this kind of importance.

An adequate response to this challenge would have two parts, one philosophical and one practical. The philosophical aspect of the response would consist in a redescription of the object of moral motivation, which reveals our moral activities to be the sorts of things that make intelligible contributions to the goodness of our own lives. In the terms of my earlier discussion, this would involve showing how compliance with moral norms can contribute directly to making our lives worthwhile or meaningful, so that we ourselves live better to the extent we achieve such compliance. One might, for instance, seek to establish that compliance with moral principles is a universally necessary condition for a meaningful human life, such that no life can be counted worthwhile which lacks a commitment to moral ends. But this is only the most ambitious version of the kind of argument I have in mind. A more modest version might aim to establish that acting rightly *can* make a direct contribution to the value of the agent's own life; this requires that we articulate the effects of a commitment to moral ends on the life of one who is so committed, so that it becomes transparent to us in what ways such a life is rendered worthwhile by that very commitment. The moral life may not be the only kind of life that can be meaningful from the agent's point of view, but it should at least be on the short list of candidates for such a life.

The second, practical part of the response would consist in bringing it about that the agent whose life is in question actually cares about the relevant dimension of value. After all, not everything that is potentially good for an agent, or that it would be reasonable to attach personal importance to, is something that actually matters to us in fact; so it is possible that we might be left cold by the goods of impartial morality in our own eudaimonistic reflection about our lives. To the extent this is the case, we will face a practical problem about the authority of moral norms to govern our activities, in so far as the eudaimonistic and the moral standpoints will continue to diverge from each other. No moral theory can by itself solve this practical problem—it is in the first instance a social and psychological problem, not a philosophical one. But a philosophical contribution will be satisfying only to the degree that the species of eudaimonistic value it identifies is one that people, as a practical matter, find it comparatively natural to care about.

A brief look at utilitarian and contractualist approaches will serve both to illustrate these observations and to conclude my discussion.[33] On a utilitarian view, the fundamental touchstone for moral rightness lies in the value of the consequences of that which is to be assessed; actions are morally right, on this account, just in case their consequences are better, on the whole, than those of the alternative actions that are open to the agent at the time of action. Views of this kind deliver an interpretation of moral norms that initially makes it seem puzzling how compliance with such norms could possibly be endorsed from within eudaimonistic reflection. Direct versions of utilitarianism are notoriously demanding, apparently leaving little space in life for the agent to devote to the kind of personal projects that give most of us reason to go on. Indirect versions attempt to address this defect, but with questionable success: either they end up 'ushering themselves from the scene', or they relocate the problem of alienation from one's personal projects by subjecting those projects to a systematic requirement of impartial justification.

I nevertheless believe that utilitarian theories are animated in part by a conception of the goodness of the moral agent's life. They remind us of something that we are perhaps inclined to forget or underemphasize when we think of morality as a set of generic requirements that facilitate human agency: namely, that more is at stake in morality than mere coordination of private activities. On the utilitarian approach, morality fundamentally guides us to maximize that which is intrinsically valuable in the world, where this in turn is the sort of aim that could intelligibly become an object of personal devotion. Its teleological structure potentially transforms the moral life into something more than a collection of disconnected episodic acts, imbuing its practical expressions with the coherence and continuity characteristic of ongoing activities that are systematically organized in the way of a project. Seen in this light, moral values begin to seem intelligible, as things whose pursuit could make a direct contribution to the choiceworthiness of the agent's own life.

Here we should recall the example I cited earlier of parents willing to subordinate their own interests radically to the project of improving the lot of their children—to a degree, that is, that precludes their enjoying the normal goods of personal relationship with the children. Thinking about this kind of example, I suggested that it might be recognizable, as a kind of limiting case, as a project that contributes directly to the meaning of the agent's own life, in so far as the agent achieves through the project a kind of self-transcendence, a connection to values that are outside the self, and that will live on when the agent is gone. Utilitarianism seems to me to appeal to a similar ideal of self-transcendence, insofar as moral conduct is seen as an ongoing project of promoting what is ultimately good in

---

[33] For more on these issues, see my 'Scanlon's Contractualism', Chapter 12 in this volume, sect. 3.

the world. Acting rightly may impose immense sacrifices on us in terms of our own interests and welfare, but there is nevertheless something to endorse in it from the standpoint of eudaimonistic reflection: it embodies an attitude of dedication to a higher plane of value.[34]

At this point, however, we need to consider the second, practical aspect of the problem of importance. If congruence in practical reason is really to be attained by a given individual, then not only must it be the case that moral conduct contributes in a recognizable way to the choiceworthiness of the agent's life. It must also be the case that the agent should care about the value in question, taking the incorporation of the value into their life to be a matter of personal importance. In this respect, the utilitarian account of the eudaimonistic significance of morality is deficient. As I mentioned earlier, the value of self-transcendence seems to be something that we tend to care about only if we have a direct and personal interest in the external goods to which our own lives are to be subordinated. Thus it matters to parents that their life should be dedicated to improving the prospects of their children—that it should be choiceworthy as a contribution to this end— because they love their children directly. Similarly, religious love and devotion can make it possible for an agent to take absolute dedication to the divine will to be a matter of supreme importance, in thinking about what it is to live well. In the case of utilitarianism, however, this kind of personal connection to the larger end to which one's life is to be subordinated is seldom present. We are perhaps not indifferent to the greatest good of the greatest number (or however else the impartial values promoted by morality are characterized), but—moral saints apart—most of us don't care enough about those values to make supreme dedication to them important *to us*, as a respect in which our own lives become choiceworthy.

Utilitarianism is often thought of as the paradigmatic secular moral theory. Its account of moral rightness is couched in terms that are utterly congenial to the progressive scientific temperament, and its proponents are notoriously dismissive of the metaphysical and religious baggage that is carried by other moral theories. In light of this, it is a matter of considerable irony that utilitarianism itself should implicitly rely, in its ideal of the goodness of a life, on the idea that the moral personality has an essentially religious structure: the utilitarian agent must be sufficiently attached to a transcendent value outside the self that systematic devotion to that end makes their own life good itself.[35]

In this respect, contractualism seems to me to offer a more attractive response to the problem of the priority of moral requirements. According to contractualism,

---

[34] Compare the ideal of transcendence discussed—though not endorsed—in Samuel Scheffler, *Human Morality* (New York: Oxford University Press, 1992), 120–1. A similar ideal is both elaborated and endorsed in Peter Singer, *How Are We to Live? Ethics in an Age of Self-interest* (Oxford: Oxford University Press, 1997).

[35] Compare Bernard Williams, 'Replies', in J. E. J. Altham and Ross Harrison (eds.), *World Mind, and Ethics. Essays on the Ethical Philosophy of Bernard Williams* (Cambridge, England: Cambridge University Press, 1995), 203.

moral rightness is essentially a matter of justification: what makes an act right is not, say, the value of its consequences, but rather that the act is required by principles that no one concerned to devise a common set of principles could reasonably reject.[36] Acting in accord with principles of this kind can be seen as a way of treating other persons with respect; by striving to comply with moral requirements, we take seriously the status of others as sources of claims, regarding them as people to whom justification is owed. We may put this in Kantian terms by saying that moral conduct represents an appropriate response to the value of persons (as 'ends in themselves').

But the contractualist approach offers at the same time an account of the contribution of moral conduct to the value of the agent's own life. Compliance with moral principles, understood along contractualist lines, not only acknowledges the value of other persons as sources of claims; it also affects directly the agent's own status. By acting in accordance with moral requirements, we enter into a distinctive kind of relationship with other people, one that is based on mutual recognition or acknowledgement, and that involves essentially a form of interpersonal justification. One stands in relationships with other people on this basis to the extent that one can give an acceptable account of oneself to them—that is, an account acceptable to those people themselves. According to contractualism, it is the business of impartial morality to define the terms on which interpersonal justification of this kind is possible. By complying with those terms, then, we ensure that we are able to give an account of ourselves to others—a status that we fall short of when we fail to do what impartial morality requires.

Now it seems to me that attainment of this status is the sort of thing that it is reasonable to care about in contexts of eudaimonistic reflection. It is a respect in which one's own life is transformed by one's compliance with moral principles, and it seems plausible to regard this transformation as a positive dimension of eudaimonistic value, a respect in which one's own life is made more meaningful and worthwhile. If utilitarianism attributes eudaimonistic value to morality by assimilating it to the paradigm of a quasi-religious project, contractualism sees the contribution of morality to the goodness of our lives in the dimension of human relationships. Insofar as compliance with moral requirements is constitutive of mutual recognition, such compliance need not be thought of as a series of disconnected episodic performances; instead it is given coherence through the ongoing pursuit of an ideal form of relationship to one's fellows. As a practical matter, it seems that many people care fairly strongly about this dimension of value, taking it to be a matter of considerable importance whether or not they stand to other people in relationships of mutual recognition.[37] This concern is not, perhaps, the immediate motivation to moral conduct in most of us. But it develops very

---

[36] See (again) Scanlon, *What We Owe to Each Other*.
[37] Compare ibid. 163, on the attitudes of Americans in the 1960s.

naturally in people who are responsive to moral ends, as a kind of reflexive refinement of our inherent sociability. Granted, mutual recognition lacks the texture and emotional complexity of the personal relationships that we enter into with other people, and that contribute so manifestly to enriching our lives.[38] But it has a personal aspect, in so far as it turns on the possibility of justifying oneself specifically *to* the individuals who might be affected by one's actions. To the extent that morality is connected to this way of relating to other people as individuals, it seems that we both can and should ascribe to it considerable importance within the context of eudaimonistic reflection.

My present aim, however, is not to defend the contractualist answer to the question of the eudaimonistic value of the moral life. I will be content if I have established that there is a question here to be answered, and that philosophical accounts of morality can help us in coming to terms with it. Raz has rightly urged us to reject the simplistic picture of a fundamental opposition between morality and self-interest. Even if we are not egoists, however, we reasonably want to lead meaningful and significant lives, and it is an ongoing and important problem—both for philosophy and for life—to understand how morality might relate to this aspiration.

[38] Compare the discussion of 'relationship-dependent reasons' in Samuel Scheffler, 'Projects, Relationships, and Reasons', in Wallace, Pettit, Scheffler, and Smith (eds.), *Reason and Value*, 247–69.

14

Moral Reasons and Moral Fetishes:
Rationalists and Anti-Rationalists
on Moral Motivation

Ethical rationalism, to a first approximation, is the thesis that moral requirements are requirements of practical reason. This thesis has a long tradition in moral philosophy, but it also has long met with philosophical resistance. A particular crux for thinking about ethical rationalism is the phenomenon of moral motivation. It has been argued, in particular, that rationalism alone can provide a plausible interpretation of the motivations characteristic of the virtuous agent, and that those who reject rationalism treat the concern to act morally as a kind of fetish. My aim in this paper is to consider and assess this charge.

The essay is written in the spirit of sympathetic reconstruction. The larger aim is to explain the strength and appeal of rationalism as a framework for thinking about moral motivation. I begin in section 1 by considering the rationalist approach to motivation of this kind. Central to this approach is the idea that moral motivation is potentially grounded in the agent's own deliberative reflection about morality and its normative significance. This idea needs to be developed, however, in a way that leaves room for a variety of possible divergences between motivation and the agent's deliberative point of view. In sections 2 and 3, I take up the charge that anti-rationalists are saddled with a fetishistic account of moral motivation. I argue that the charge of fetishism turns on the basic idea that the anti-rationalist position lacks the resources for understanding moral motivation as a response that is warranted by its objects. If this is correct, then the question of fetishism is connected to more basic issues about the alleged normative significance of various kinds of moral considerations, in ways that I try to spell out. In section 4, I consider some moves that are open to the anti-rationalist in response to the objection from fetishism. To meet the objection, it is necessary for the anti-rationalist either to defend a kind of global nihilism about reasons for action—something, I suggest,

Not previously published. I have received very helpful feedback on distant predecessors of this paper from audiences in Berkeley (BAFFLE), Minnesota (Conference on Moral Psychology), Chicago (Central Division Meeting of the APA), Oxford (Moral Philosophy Seminar), Adelaide (departmental colloquium), Canberra (Conference on Reasons and Rationality), Åarhus (departmental colloquium), Rotterdam (public lecture), and Canterbury, New Zealand (Erskine Lecture).

that may be difficult to pull off—or to abandon the distinctively anti-rationalist conception of moral motivation. To see why this is the case should help us to appreciate the force and interest of the complaint that the anti-rationalist account of moral motivation is fetishistic.

1. REASONS AND MOTIVATION

Let us begin by considering the rationalist interpretation of moral motivation. The central rationalist tenet is the claim that morality is a normative domain, providing reasons for action to all agents, regardless of their contingent desires, dispositions, and concerns. The reasons in question are normative reasons, of the sort that count for or against prospective actions in contexts of deliberation and advice.[1] It is the proper function of such reasons, we might say, to figure in contexts of deliberation and advice, as the considerations that agents reflect on in order to arrive at sound conclusions about what they ought to do. Acknowledging this fact, the rationalist will suggest that moral motivation can be grounded in deliberative reflection that is couched in moral terms, and that we respond correctly to the moral considerations we take to obtain only to the extent we are motivated accordingly.[2]

This is a rough formulation, which leaves room for a variety of ways in which normative reflection and moral motivation might come apart. There are three possibilities of this kind that should be kept in mind. First, even if moral considerations are suited to figure explicitly in the deliberation of the agents to whom they apply, such agents in practice often comply unreflectively with the moral requirements that govern their actions. Well-habituated agents will typically have internalized a policy of treating people fairly and with respect, so that they do not need to reflect anew on the normative significance of such considerations in deliberating about what to do. For such agents, morality may function to filter out prospective options for action before they even enter the deliberative field, in a way that obviates conscious attention to moral reasons within practical reflection itself.

Nothing in the rationalist picture is at odds with these possibilities. The rationalist insists that moral considerations are suited to appear in the practical deliberation of the agents to whom they apply, insofar as they constitute genuine reasons for action. But considerations can satisfy this condition without figuring continuously in the foreground of the agent's deliberative consciousness. Even when moral motivation does not result immediately from an episode of moral reasoning, however, the rationalist can still say that it is grounded in the agent's deliberative point of view. This will be true in a weak sense if it is counterfactually

---

[1] On reasons in this basic normative sense, see T. M. Scanlon, *What We Owe to Each Other* (Cambridge, Mass.: Harvard University Press, 1999), ch. 1.

[2] This is, for instance, a common commitment in the rationalist positions of Christine Korsgaard, *The Sources of Normativity* (Cambridge, England: Cambridge University Press, 1996), and Michael Smith, *The Moral Problem* (Oxford: Basil Blackwell, 1994).

the case that the agent would affirm the role of moral considerations as internalized filters for deliberation, if they were to reflect explicitly on the question of how their practical thinking should be structured. And it will be true in a more robust sense if the agent actually does engage, on other occasions, in episodes of reflection through which the general structuring role of moral considerations is explicitly affirmed.

Even when moral considerations are directly acknowledged in this kind of deliberation, however, they do not always succeed in engaging the will of the agent who reflects on them. There are in fact two possibilities that need to be left open here. To see this, it will be helpful to introduce a distinction between moral judgments on the one hand, and normative judgments on the other. A moral judgment is a judgment that is couched in moral terms, to the effect (for instance) that doing *x* would be morally right, or thoughtful or considerate or helpful or just. A normative judgment, by contrast, expresses the generic acknowledgment that a consideration of some other, substantive kind constitutes a reason for action, counting in favor of or against a prospective policy or course of action. Now it seems to be a general truth about normativity that at least some of the considerations that are normative for human thought and action can be acknowledged to obtain, without acknowledging *that* those considerations are normative. Many of the things that count as normative reasons in ordinary discourse and practice, for instance, include what Hume might have called matters of fact and existence. That a contribution to my pension fund would enhance my financial security in old age is, in itself, merely an interesting empirical truth about that course of action. It is perfectly possible for a cogent, clear-eyed, and otherwise rational agent to concede that this fact obtains, yet deny that the consideration in question counts in favor of making a contribution to the pension fund. Furthermore, this remains the case even if we grant what anyway seems very plausible, namely that enhancement of financial security in one's old age really is a reason for making contributions to one's pension fund.

With moral considerations, things may appear otherwise. Some metaethical positions, in particular, seem to blur the distinction between moral judgments and what I have called normative judgments, holding that one sincerely endorses a moral judgment only if one also acknowledges the normative significance of the moral considerations that are judged to obtain.[3] For the record, these positions seem to me to go too far in the direction of building normativity into the meaning of the moral predicates. It is perhaps plausible to say that morality aspires to normative significance, insofar as moral considerations are widely taken to count as reasons in contexts of deliberation and advice. Many people suppose that morality collects considerations that have direct relevance for the practical question of what they are to do, and these considerations are routinely cited when we criticize the

---

[3] See e.g. Michael Smith, *The Moral Problem*. I say more about Smith's metaethical views in sect. 3 below.

actions of others, and attempt to engage with them in collective deliberation. The rationalist will suppose that these activities are basically in good order, insofar as they reflect the fact that moral considerations really do have normative significance for practical reflection. Even if it is not the case that morality is normative in this way, however, it is generally taken to have this status, and this has no doubt left some residue in moral language. Consider someone who denies that the moral wrongness of *x*-ing—or its cruelty or injustice or humiliating effects on others— are considerations that count against doing *x*. If such a person did not have some sense, in drawing this conclusion, that they were going against the grain of moral discourse, and using moral language in ways that are at odds with widespread social practices, then they would probably not have a firm grasp on the meaning of the predicates that they were deploying. To the extent this is the case, we can say that morality intrinsically aspires to normative significance.

As I suggested above, however, some will want to go further than this, holding that the acknowledgment of normative significance is built into the meaning of the moral predicates. On a view of this kind, it will not strictly be possible to arrive at the sincere conclusion that *x*-ing would be morally wrong, but to deny that its wrongness counts against doing *x*. Discourse about morality would then differ in this respect from discourse about some other normative domains (such as the reasons involved in the case of the pension contribution mentioned above). For present purposes, nothing of substance hangs on this metaethical question. Even if rationalism is correct, I want to say that it is possible to acknowledge that moral considerations obtain, but to fail to be motivated accordingly, because one denies their standing as genuine reasons for action. This is the position occupied by the conventional skeptic about morality, someone who understands moral discourse, and is prepared to grant that doing *x* would be (say) morally wrong—or unjust or unkind or cruel—but wonders why they should care.[4] It seems perfectly intelligible that someone might take up a stance of this kind; the question that the skeptic is posing locates a genuine issue, one of the defining questions for the traditional subject of moral philosophy. Of course, if a firm commitment to normativity is built into the meaning of the moral predicates, then the question will have to be reformulated slightly. It will not be the question whether moral considerations constitute normative reasons, but instead the question whether what are ordinarily called moral considerations constitute normative reasons. But nothing of real substance seems to me to hang on whether we choose to formulate the question in one or the other of these ways.

Moral skepticism thus represents one scenario in which an agent who acknowledges moral considerations in reflection might fail to be motivated accordingly. This scenario involves a gap between putatively moral judgments and normative

---

[4] On skepticism in this form, see David Brink, *Moral Realism and the Foundations of Ethics* (Cambridge, England: Cambridge University Press, 1989), ch. 3. I differ from Brink in thinking that the possibility of skepticism in this form does not rule out 'internalist' metaethical views.

judgments; the skeptic grants, in effect, that moral considerations apply (that, say, *x*-ing would be morally wrong, or unjust or cruel etc.[5]), but denies, or at least does not yet concede, that these considerations are genuine reasons. Furthermore, because skeptics challenge the normative significance of morality in this way, they will typically fail to be motivated accordingly. Of course, if rationalism is true, then the person who occupies this position will be making a substantive mistake.[6] Rationalism is the view that moral considerations are normative reasons, so the person who denies that this is the case, or who questions its truth, will be missing something, and thereby going astray in their deliberative reflection about the landscape of reasons. But substantive error is rampant in human intellectual life, and there is no reason to think it less likely in relation to practical questions than in relation to theoretical issues of various kinds (on the contrary). The rationalist should therefore leave room for the stance of the moral skeptic, noting that it represents one way of acknowledging (putatively) moral considerations without being motivated to act on them.[7]

Let us now contrast moral skepticism with a third kind of case in which moral judgment and motivation come apart. This is the case that we might call moral weakness, in which agents concede the normative significance of the moral considerations that apply to their situation, but still fail to act on them. Weakness of this kind is of course a special instance of a more general phenomenon, whose distinguishing feature is that an agent freely and intentionally acts contrary to their own best judgment about what they have reason to do. If rationalism is correct, then the moral version of this general phenomenon will include cases in which agents are not making any substantive mistakes in their deliberative reflection. If moral considerations really do apply in the way the agent takes them to— if, for instance, *x*-ing really would be wrong, or unjust or inconsiderate or cruel—then the agent will be correct to conclude that they have reason to avoid doing *x*. And yet, despite arriving at the correct conclusion about the bearing of morality on their deliberative situation, agents who are morally weak fail to act in accordance with their normative judgments. They go astray by their own lights, as it were, and to the extent this is the case they seem to be peculiarly irrational, in a way that potentially contrasts with the outlook of the moral skeptic.[8] (The skeptic may be mistaken to judge that moral considerations are without

---

[5] Or, at least, that *x*-ing would ordinarily be considered morally wrong, etc.

[6] Substantive error of this kind might be epistemically blameless. Someone who for whatever reason is not in a position to see that *x* is wrong, or that *x*'s wrongness is a reason, may not be deliberating incorrectly in failing to accept either of these judgments.

[7] A different possibility that is opened up by the potential divergence between moral and normative judgment is a scenario in which an agent is motivated in accordance with moral considerations that they recognize to obtain, despite believing that those considerations are without normative significance. Possibilities of this kind are interestingly explored by Nomy Arpaly in *Unprincipled Virtue* (New York: Oxford University Press, 2002).

[8] Here I follow Scanlon's suggestion about irrationality; see *What We Owe to Each Other*, ch. 1, sect. 4.

normative significance, but there is no obvious irrationality in making a substantive mistake of this kind.)

Taking these various possibilities into account, how should we characterize the rationalist approach to moral motivation? The basic rationalist thesis is that morality is a normative domain. Insofar as moral considerations constitute reasons for all agents, they will be capable of figuring in practical deliberation, as considerations that count for and against prospective actions that it is open to agents to perform. Those agents who deliberate correctly, and who are not otherwise irrational, will acknowledge the normative significance of morality, and be motivated in accordance with their moral and normative conclusions. Rationalism thus suggests a conception of moral motivation as potentially grounded in the agent's own deliberative reflection.

This general conception allows, however, for various kinds of divergence between practical deliberation and moral motivation. We have considered three forms that this divergence can take:

(a) Habituated or automatic responsiveness to moral reasons, where the agent is motivated to act in accordance with moral reasons without reflecting on them. The rationalist should allow that morally admirable agents internalize their commitment to moral ends, in ways that often obviate explicit moral reflection. Motivational structures of this kind may still be grounded in the agent's deliberative point of view, however, insofar as the agent does or would affirm their role through reflection.

(b) Moral skepticism, in which a lack of moral motivation can be traced to the agent's denial of the normative significance of morality. On the rationalist view, this position, though possible, involves a substantive mistake about the landscape of reasons.

(c) Moral weakness, involving the failure to act on moral considerations whose normative significance one explicitly affirms. The rationalist will say that this kind of case represents a paradigm of practical irrationality.

2. RIGHTNESS AND THE FETISHISM OBJECTION

It is a consequence of the rationalist approach that motivation will tend to track moral judgment. People can by and large be expected to be moved to do what they believe it would be morally right to do, and changes in a given person's moral beliefs will be correlated reliably with corresponding changes in their motivations. Thus someone who comes to the view that it would be wrong to support a politics of tax cuts for the affluent will typically be moved to adjust their political activities and preferences accordingly. Of course, a typical relation of this kind is not an infallible relation, and we must leave room for the kind of backsliding that can inhibit the reliable connection between moral judgment and motivation, and also for the moral skepticism that denies the normative significance of morality. But rationalism allows for these sorts of phenomena. The relation that it postulates between moral judgment and motivation 'typically' holds, just insofar as agents are typically not subject to the kinds of substantive errors and defects of reasoning that are present when the link between moral judgment and moral motivation is severed, or when the reason-giving force of moral considerations is called into question.

If we reject the rationalist account of the demands made by morality on motivation, how might we explain the reliable connection between moral judgment and motivating attitudes? One possibility would be to opt for an expressivist treatment of moral judgment, holding that judgments of this kind are necessarily motivating, insofar as they function to give expression to motivating noncognitive attitudes. This kind of metaethical position is compatible with the view that moral considerations do not constitute independent reasons for action, and so it represents one route the anti-rationalist could take for making sense of the reliable connection between moral judgment and moral motivation. But for reasons already adverted to, this approach does not strike me as very promising. In effect, it makes the connection between moral judgment and moral motivation *too* reliable, ruling out from the start the kinds of moral weakness and moral skepticism that can occur in agents who are capable of making sincere judgments about morality. A plausible account of the connection between moral judgment and moral motivation must leave room for these possibilities, in ways that noncognitivist accounts notoriously fail to do.

The natural alternative strategy that is open to the anti-rationalist would be to concede that moral judgments do not function essentially to express motivating attitudes, but to contend that such attitudes are nevertheless present whenever agents are in fact motivated to act in accordance with their moral beliefs. Thus we might postulate a contingent concern to do the right thing on the part of agents who take morality seriously, whose motivations would adjust in virtue of this concern to changes in their judgments about what it would be morally right to do. We might then say that having a concern of this kind to do the right thing is partly constitutive of being a morally good or admirable person. It is a contingent concern, because having it is not itself a requirement of reason. In particular, the nonderivative concern to do what is right will not be present in those agents who are (for instance) skeptical or cynical about moral discourse, agents who will not in fact tend to be motivated to do what they understand to be morally right. But in the morally virtuous agents whose motivations do track their moral judgments, we might explain this psychological fact by appeal to a concern for morality that precisely distinguishes the morally admirable from the cynics, skeptics, and rogues of this world.[9]

---

[9] For an example of this strategy, see David O. Brink, *Moral Realism and the Foundations of Ethics*, ch. 3.

This explanation has a certain surface plausibility. There is little doubt that morally admirable agents differ from other people in part in having a special concern to do what is morally right, and it would be possible to account in terms of such a concern for the reliable connection between moral judgment and moral motivation in such agents. Furthermore, precisely insofar as this concern for rightness is contingent, the approach leaves room for the kind of divergences between moral judgment and moral motivation canvassed in the preceding section. Michael Smith has argued, however, that this way of accounting for moral motivation is deeply flawed.[10] He points out that the concern to do what is right will produce motivations that track an agent's changing beliefs about what it is right to do only if it is interpreted in a distinctive way: as a concern for rightness in itself, where this is understood *de dicto* and not *de re*. But, Smith argues, this kind of concern is hardly characteristic of morally admirable agents. They are moved by nonderivative concerns for the variety of concrete ends that morality prescribes, such as justice, honesty, the flourishing of their friends, and so on. Pursuit of such ends may in fact be morally right, but if so the virtuous agent's interest in them is not derivative from that fact; in this way, their concern to do what is right can be interpreted *de re*. By contrast, a person whose concern for moral rightness were properly understood as *de dicto* would exhibit a kind of moral fetishism, a preoccupation with rightness of the sort that would alienate them from the myriad concrete ends that are morally important. The anti-rationalist approach to moral motivation should therefore be rejected, Smith suggests, as incompatible with our understanding of the structures of care and concern that genuinely distinguish those agents who are morally admirable.

Two different strategies initially suggest themselves for responding to this argument. The first is to point out that there is nothing in the anti-rationalist account that would preclude morally virtuous agents from developing the kinds of nonderivative concern for concrete moral ends that Smith takes to be exemplary of a nonfetishistic outlook.[11] It is true that morally virtuous agents have a concern to do what is right, where this is properly understood *de dicto* and not *de re*, and that it is this concern that accounts for their tendency to be motivated in accordance with their moral judgments. But it is also true that a direct concern for rightness of this kind can coexist with a nonderivative concern for the variety of first-order ends that morality approves of. Thus someone who has long been indifferent to considerations of social equality might change their view about the moral permissibility of inegalitarian arrangements, and thereby acquire a new concern about the lack of equality in their society. This new concern would initially be derivative from the agent's general desire to do what is right. But over time it could

---

[10] See his *The Moral Problem*, sect. 3.5.

[11] See e.g. Sigrun Svavarsdóttir, 'Moral Cognitivism and Motivation', *Philosophical Review*, 108 (1999), 161–219, at 215–18.

develop into a self-standing or nonderivative motivational structure, of the sort that Smith takes to be characteristic of those agents whose characters we admire.

The basic point upon which this argument insists is surely correct: there is no reason why a general concern for rightness of the *de dicto* kind could not coexist with a variety of nonderivative concerns for the different ends whose pursuit the virtuous agent believes to be right.[12] But this point is not by itself an adequate response to Smith's basic objection. The objection turns on the idea that it would be fetishistic to exhibit a concern for rightness as such (as contrasted with an interest in such concrete substantive values as justice, equality, honesty, and loyalty to one's friends). But if this is correct, then the anti-rationalist account will be defective in appealing to such a concern to explain the virtuous agent's initial motivation to pursue the ends that they believe to be morally right. Nor is the objection undermined by the observation that such agents could come to develop over time nonderivative interests in the first-order moral ends that they believe to be morally right. If a *de dicto* concern for rightness is fetishistic, then the anti-rationalist's reliance on such a concern at any point in their account of moral motivation would seem problematic, for the basic reason that we should not ascribe to the morally admirable agent a form of motivation that is distinctively fetishistic.

A second line of argument addresses this worry head-on. The gist of it is to deny that a *de dicto* concern for moral rightness would be a fetishistic form of motivation. Thus it might be observed that a general concern to do the right thing has a venerable history in moral philosophy. A version of this form of motivation seems to lie at the heart of Kant's ethical theory, for example, in the guise of the motive of duty that distinguishes the good will. The Kantian motive of duty is a nonderivative concern to act rightly, and Kant holds that one achieves a good will only when this concern is operative in leading one to do what duty prescribes. But if a Kantian conception of the good will represents a plausible ideal of moral motivation, it can hardly be objected that the anti-rationalist's appeal to the general desire to act rightly is incompatible with our conception of moral virtue. The morally admirable agent is someone who is moved by a general concern to do what is right, and this is precisely in line with the anti-rationalist's account.

Of course, there are many philosophers who do not find the Kantian conception of the good will attractive as an ideal of character or action. It is thought to leave too little room for the sorts of emotional satisfactions that may be experienced by the virtuous person in acting well, enjoining a dour moralism that

---

[12] In a later development of his fetishism objection Smith contends that the anti-rationalist should not in fact approve of the cultivation of such nonderivative concerns, since they would potentially inhibit right action in the case of revised beliefs about what it would be right to do; see Smith, 'In Defense of *The Moral Problem*: A Reply to Brink, Copp, and Sayre-McCord', *Ethics*, 108 (1997), 84–119, at 113. But this point does not strike me as very powerful. Someone who believes that it is right to keep agreements, or to support one's friends, might reasonably be confident enough in these convictions to make it reasonable for them to cultivate supporting nonderivative dispositions to act in these ways—even granting the slight risk that might be involved in so doing.

precludes direct concern for the ends that morality promotes (such as the welfare of other persons). Perhaps, then, Smith's objection to the anti-rationalist approach would apply equally to the Kantian conception of the good will. That is, he might reject Kant's account of the value of acting from the motive of duty for the same reasons that he rejects the anti-rationalist's suggestion that moral motivation derives from a general concern for moral rightness. The basic complaint in both cases would be that the accounts on offer ascribe to the morally admirable agent a fetishistic concern with rightness for its own sake, a concern whose operation would alienate the agent from the several valuable ends that the virtuous characteristically pursue.

There is an important difference between the Kantian and anti-rationalist approaches that this line of argument overlooks, however. For the anti-rationalist, the basic concern to do what is right that explains moral motivation is rationally contingent. After all, it is distinctive of the anti-rationalist position that it denies that moral considerations constitute reasons or rational requirements; the whole point of postulating a general concern to do what is right is to make sense of the reliable connection between moral judgment and moral motivation without assuming that moral rightness (say) is something we all have reason to care about. But Kant's ethical theory is different in precisely this respect. He is perhaps the paradigmatic rationalist in the tradition of moral philosophy, insofar as he believes that moral requirements are rational requirements on action. The categorical imperative, which articulates the normative structure of morality, is on Kant's view itself a principle of practical reason. To the extent this is the case, it can be said that moral rightness has independent normative significance; it is a reason for action, a consideration that will be attended to by any agent who is deliberating correctly about action.

This difference between the Kantian and the anti-rationalist positions, however, would seem to determine a corresponding difference in their vulnerability to the charge of fetishism. On the anti-rationalist picture, moral motivation gets traced to a general concern to do what is right that is arbitrary from the point of view of reason. Rightness does not itself count in favor of actions that have that property, so someone who is moved by the concern to do what is right is attaching significance to a consideration that is, by hypothesis, of no independent normative importance. To the extent this is the case, the charge of fetishism would seem to be justified, for one way to think of fetishism is as the investment of attention and interest in objects that do not intrinsically merit such responses. The general concern to do what is right is not something that is called for by the nature of rightness; rather it is an optional psychological extra that some agents just happen to have, on the order of a taste for clams or the color azure.

For Kantians, by contrast, the concern to do what is right is precisely a subjective response to a consideration that is independently understood as a reason or a normative requirement. According to this way of seeing things, those who have a concern to act rightly are not investing attention and interest in objects that do not merit such responses. Insofar as rightness is an independent reason for action, the concern to do what is right is a form of motivation that is called for by its proper object, and we would be open to rational criticism if we were to lack that distinctive concern. This is a crucial difference between the anti-rationalist and the Kantian approaches, despite the superficial similarities in their accounts of moral motivation, and it suggests that the former could be vulnerable to the fetishism objection in a way the Kantian account would not be.

3. DIGRESSION: SMITH ON 'RIGHT'

Now a Kantian position of this kind will be successful only if it is correct to maintain that moral rightness is itself a reason-giving consideration. It appears, however, that Michael Smith is committed to denying precisely this claim. On his metaethical account, judgments about moral rightness are not to be understood as identifying a consideration that itself constitutes a reason for action. Rather they amount to claims to the effect that there is reason of some other kind to perform the action that is said to be right.[13] (To adopt Smith's preferred terminology, their content is given by the claim that one would desire to perform the right action in the agent's situation, if one were fully rational, where claims of this kind are claims about one's normative reasons for action.) We might think of this as a summary or 'buck-passing' account of rightness, insofar as it construes rightness not as a normatively significant kind or property in its own right, but as the property of being an action of a certain substantive kind that the agent has other, independent reasons for performing. To say that *x* would be right is to say that *x*-ing is something one has good reason to do, not to identify the reason why one ought to do it. Insofar as reasons to do *x* are in the picture, they are provided not by the consideration that *x*-ing would be right, but by the features that make *x*-ing the right thing to do under the agent's circumstances: for instance, that it would maximize impartial utility, or be the honest or just or considerate course of action.[14] Rightness will accordingly be transparent in the deliberations of the person who is reasoning correctly about action, which will be focused instead on concrete right-making features of this kind.

As a characterization of Smith's position this is correct as far as it goes. But within the framework of his metaethical theory it would in fact be possible to articulate and defend a position of the broadly Kantian kind. To see this, we need only note that Smith's account of the concept of rightness leaves completely open the question of what the substantive right-making features are. Here it may be useful to distinguish between two different kinds of position. There are, first, pluralist accounts of the structure of the normative domain, which hold that there are

---

[13] See Smith, *The Moral Problem*, ch. 6.
[14] Compare Smith, 'In Defense of *The Moral Problem*', 116–17.

no interesting unities to be found at the level of the right-making features of peoples' actions and circumstances. In particular, there is no independent property that is held in common by a subset of the right-making features, by reference to which we can identify those features as distinctively moral, and which set them apart from other, nonmoral reasons for action. A second kind of position, by contrast, maintains that there is a unity of this kind at the level of the right-making features of actions. According to these positions, we can isolate an interesting substantive property that is held in common by a subset of the right-making features, a property that is normatively significant in its own right, and that also sets the reasons in the unified class apart, as specially moral in character.[15] Thus a utilitarian might hold that moral reasons have in common the property of maximizing impartial utility, while a contractualist would characterize the unifying property in terms of principles that it would be unreasonable for people to reject. In the same spirit, a Kantian might characterize the distinctively moral reasons by reference to the categorical imperative, identifying a certain sort of universalizability as the normatively significant property that is held in common by all and only the specifically moral reasons for action. We see, then, that Smith's metaethical theory does not after all commit him to the view that Kantians have a fetishistic conception of moral motivation. His summary account of the concept of rightness leaves open the possibility that there is a substantive unity at the level of the right-making features of precisely the sort the Kantian would need there to be to avoid the charge of fetishism.

The most basic point to have emerged from this discussion is that the charge of fetishism is in place when a source of moral motivation is posited that cannot be understood as a proper response to its object, a response that is rendered appropriate by independent facts about what one has reason to do. The anti-rationalist account in terms of a general concern to do what is right seems fetishistic in this sense, insofar as the account starts from the assumption that rightness is not itself a reason-giving consideration. This assumption is a defining commitment of the anti-rationalist's own position, and so its avowed source of moral motivation is fetishistic on grounds that would be accepted by anti-rationalists themselves.

Beyond this, we have seen that concerns about fetishism will go hand-in-hand with differing substantive views about normative reasons for action. Thus anti-rationalists and Kantians may appear to have similar accounts of the basic structure of moral motivation, postulating a class of desires or concerns whose content is characterized in terms of an abstract moral concept, such as that of duty or of the moral law. The accounts strikingly differ, however, on precisely the issue that is paramount for the issue of fetishism. Kantians affirm that the general properties to which morally admirable agents are responsive are normatively significant; they

---

[15] These accounts, if convincing, would provide an answer to the interesting challenge to 'nonverdictive' interpretations of rightness posed by Garrett Cullity, in 'Sympathy, Discernment, and Reasons', *Philosophy and Phenomenological Research*, 68 (2004), 37–62, sect. 4.

constitute reasons for anyone to act accordingly, and to the extent this is the case the Kantian can avoid the charge of fetishism to which the anti-rationalist's superficially similar account seems vulnerable.

One way to put this point is to recall that, on the rationalist position as I have presented it, there are two distinct judgments that will be involved in moral motivation, when its reflective structure is made fully explicit. To see this, let us take as an example a contractualist account of the unity of the moral domain, which characterizes moral reasons in terms of the idea of principles for the general regulation of behavior that no one could reasonably reject. Deliberated moral motivation, given the contractualist picture, will involve the belief that this property obtains—that, for instance, x-ing would be required by principles for the general regulation of behavior that no one could reasonably reject. If we are anti-rationalists, this judgment must exhaust the cognitive content of the motivation to act morally, which will involve a brute desire to perform actions that have the property in question. For the rationalist, by contrast, there is a further and distinct judgment that is at issue, the normative judgment, namely, that the fact that x-ing is required by contractualist principles is a reason. The truth of this second judgment is what makes it the case that moral motivation, on the rationalist account, is not a merely fetishistic fixation, but rather a response that is warranted by its proper object. Moreover, as I have developed the rationalist position moral motivation at least potentially involves the acknowledgment, on the part of the agent, that this distinctively normative truth obtains. It is the endorsement of the normative judgment, for example, that distinguishes morally admirable agents from the moral skeptics that the rationalist should acknowledge to be possible.

If this is on the right lines, however, it raises a question about Smith's presentation of the fetishism objection. He puts the objection by charging that we should not think of moral motivation as a desire to do what is right, where this is construed as *de dicto* rather than *de re*. But now it looks as if the rationalist too will think of moral motivation in a way that involves a *de dicto* belief on the agent's part about the rightness of what they do, and a responsiveness to this consideration. Reflective moral agents judge that a property obtains that makes x-ing, morally speaking, the thing to do; but—to express the point in Smith's terms—they also judge that it is right to do x because it has that property, and their motivation to do x is in some way responsive to their acknowledgment that x-ing would be right. If it is fetishistic to have a *de dicto* concern to do what is right, why doesn't this render the rationalist's account of moral motivation vulnerable to the fetishism objection?

There are a couple of points to be made about Smith's own position that might help to answer this question. One is that he does not himself posit a *desire* to act rightly of the *de dicto* kind in his story about how reflective agency gives rise to moral action. Fully reflective agents will grasp that x-ing would be right, in a way that gives rise to the motivation to do x. What produces this motivation, however, is not a *de dicto* desire to do what is right, but rather a disposition to coherence, of the same general kind that is operative whenever we revise our attitudes in compliance with requirements of rationality.[16] So it is misleading to suggest that rationalism, at least as Smith construes it, requires a *de dicto* desire to do what is right. (The point generalizes, I believe, to other ways of developing a rationalist position.) Second, it should be noted that Smith and the anti-rationalist give different accounts of the content of the *de dicto* judgments of rightness that they each take to be involved somehow in moral motivation. For the anti-rationalist, these judgments are what we might call substantive judgments about the morally right, to the effect (for instance) that some general property is instantiated, such as the maximizing of impartial utility, that holds the moral considerations together as a class. For Smith, by contrast, the rightness that figures in the rational agent's judgments is the summary concept we encountered earlier; the *de dicto* judgment that *x*-ing would be right plays the role that other rationalists might take to be played by the unanalyzed normative judgment that there is conclusive reason to do *x*. There is no inconsistency involved in saying that a *de dicto* judgment of rightness of one of these kinds would be a problematic component in the thoughts that give rise to moral motivation, while affirming a role for *de dicto* judgments of rightness of the other kind.

This is still not quite right, however. For on Smith's view, too, it looks as if *de dicto* judgments about rightness of both kinds will have a role to play in moral motivation. That is, if—as Smith himself seems to leave open—the anti-pluralists about morality are correct, so that there are general properties held in common by all of the distinctively moral reasons, then the *de dicto* judgment that those properties obtain will have a perfectly respectable role to play in the reflections of morally admirable agents. Their motivations, in other words, will be focused not just on the fact that *x*-ing would be kind or just or helpful, but also on the fact that *x*-ing would maximize impartial utility, or be required by principles for the general regulation of behavior that no one could reasonably reject. What is crucial, for the fetishism objection, is not merely whether general *de dicto* judgments of substantive moral rightness of this kind figure in moral deliberation, but whether such judgments can be combined with further, normative judgments (whose content will also be *de dicto*) about the reason-giving force of the substantive moral considerations in question.

I conclude that the question of whether *de dicto* thoughts about rightness figure in moral motivation is a red herring. Smith is correct to suggest that anti-rationalists interpret moral motivation as a kind of fetish. What makes this the case, however, is not the fact that accounts of this kind trace moral motivation to *de dicto* judgments of rightness. It is the different and more basic fact that anti-rationalists deny the independent normative significance of such moral properties as they are willing to countenance.

---

[16] See Smith, 'In Defense of *The Moral Problem*'.

4. THREE ANTI-RATIONALIST RESPONSES

To this point I have mainly been concerned to get clear about what the fetishism objection comes to. In the present section I would like to test the strength of the objection, by considering three lines of response that it is open to the anti-rationalist to pursue. My hope is that these considerations will help us to understand the deep attractions of the rationalist approach as a way of thinking about the motivations of moral agents.

The fetishism objection turns on the idea that moral motivation is not a response that is merited by its object, if we think of it in anti-rationalist terms. But anti-rationalists might reply that on their account no less than that of the rationalist, moral motivation can be considered a response that is merited by its object. Agents who lack the desire to do what is right open themselves to certain distinctive forms of criticism; they are (for instance) cads, or bastards, or selfish and insensitive louts. Insofar as criticism of these kinds is warranted when agents lack the desire to do what is right, that response does not seem to be on all fours with purely subjective tastes and preferences, such as those of a culinary or aesthetic variety. It is a proper way of responding to the morally right, precisely in the sense that those who lack the response render themselves vulnerable to moral censure.

It is not obvious, however, that moral motivation, on the anti-rationalist account of it, really does differ in this respect from preferences regarding foods and colors. Those who do not appreciate certain foods and wines may be said to have an unsophisticated palette, and there are preferences in the domain of color that are clear expressions of bad taste. This is not, to be sure, *moral* censure, but the anti-rationalist argument turns on the vulnerability to criticism of those who lack moral motivations, not on the nature of the criticism that is called for in these cases. The more fundamental point, however, is that our ability to criticize those who lack moral motivations does not alone suffice to render those motivations proper responses to their characteristic objects. The central anti-rationalist thesis is that there is no independent reason for people to care about moral ends. If this thesis is true, then those who lack the desire to do what is right cannot be said to be deliberating incorrectly. They may be nasty and unjust, but we cannot say that they are mistaken in their reasoning about what to do—not even if they are epistemically well positioned to see that their actions are wrong, and to grasp what makes them morally objectionable. The moral criticism that the anti-rationalist may direct at those who lack moral motivations is in this way superficial. It does not vindicate the basic suggestion that the desire to do what is right is a response that is called for by the intrinsic nature of its object.

On the rationalist picture, our most basic point of view as agents is that of practical deliberation, a perspective from which we attempt to make out what we have reason to do in ways that lead to justified modifications of our intentions. It follows from this picture that criticism in terms of reasons is inescapable, in a way that merely moral censure (considered simply as such) need not be; to be mistaken in one's judgments about one's reasons, or to fail to be motivated in accordance with those judgments, is to fail at what one is most fundamentally endeavoring to do (insofar as one is engaged in practical reflection). Here a comparison with fetishism in the sexual domain may be instructive. A fetish of this kind involves the investment of sexual interest and energy in objects that are not intrinsically erotic, such as socks or elbows. We have here a kind of subjective response—sexual arousal—that is by its nature aimed at objects of a certain category, together with an independent way of ascertaining whether objects really do fall into that category or not. Analogously, the rationalist understands intentions as responses that—by our nature as practical reasoners—are out to track our reasons for action. Against this background, an account that does not anchor moral motivation in independent normative considerations may quite rightly be considered fetishistic.

A second and more radical response on behalf of anti-rationalism would be to question a basic feature of the rationalist position that gives the fetishism objection purchase. This is the assumption that there are reasons for action, in the normative sense that I have been appealing to throughout this paper. Thus if we deny this assumption, then the distinction between fetishistic and nonfetishistic forms of motivation would seem to lack application. There will be *no* motivations that can be said to be presumptively warranted or fitting responses to their objects, because at the end of the day there are no facts of the matter about what anyone has reason to do. The desire to do what is right is not a response to something that we have independent reason to care about, but in this respect it is no different from any other motivation. All motivations would appear to be equally fetishistic, which is to say that the charge of fetishism is without any critical bite. The analogy, in the sexual case, would be the position that there is no property of being erotic that we have a handle on, independently of considering the responses of particular agents. On this view, neither reproductive organs nor breasts (say) can be considered intrinsically erotic zones of the body. These zones may be ones that people, as a matter of fact, often take a sexual interest in, but if so that is a fact of merely statistical significance. There is no interesting contrast to be drawn between objects in respect of their being intrinsically erotic or not, and to the extent this is the case there will be no critical bite to the characterization of a particular sexual preference as fetishistic.

Now as it happens I believe that a view along these general lines has some plausibility in the case of sexual arousal. That is, I concede the attractions of the position that holds that no conceivable objects of sexual desire can truly be said to be intrinsically erotic, in a way that sets them interestingly apart from other such objects. (Of course, some parts of the body have starring roles to play, as it were, in connection with the processes of reproduction, but it is not clear that this functional fact about them vindicates the claim that the bodily parts in question are intrinsically erotic.) If this is right, then fetishism in the domain of sexual response will be at best a statistical concept, one whose application is utterly devoid of critical animus or force. In a similar vein, anti-rationalists might contend that there are no facts of the matter about normative reasons for action, of the sort that might make some motivations rather than others presumptively warranted responses to their proper objects. And indeed there are at least hints of such a view that can be discerned in the work of some anti-rationalists, who write about moral and other kinds of motivation as if there are merely objective facts of a quotidian or nonnormative kind on the one hand, and the subjective desires of various agents on the other hand.[17] A view of this kind might be developed by maintaining that distinctively normative judgments are, as a class, somehow conceptually confused, so that we do not even know what is being asserted when it is claimed that a given agent has a normative reason to do *x*. Or it might be contended that judgments of this class, though not meaningless in this fashion, are all of them false, right across the board. This would effectively defuse the fetishism objection in a way precisely analogous to the denial of intrinsically erotic facts or properties in the sexual case.

This seems to me to be a coherent position, one that, if correct, would in fact rebut the charge of fetishism as an objection to the anti-rationalist account of moral motivation. But the rebuttal turns on an extreme and wide-ranging view about normative reasons for action, something tantamount to a kind of nihilism about the whole normative domain. Certainly, it would be surprising if anti-rationalism turned out to involve an extreme commitment of this kind. The central anti-rationalist thesis concerns the normative significance of distinctively moral considerations, and on the surface a view of this sort would seem to leave room for the acknowledgment that there are normative reasons of other, non-moral kinds (reasons for agents to avoid actions that would cause them extreme pain, for example). So if anti-rationalism is committed to what I have called normative nihilism, this is not something about it that has been very clearly expressed by anti-rationalists themselves. Moreover, the further commitment that is in question here is one that seems highly problematic, considered just on its own terms. It is at odds, for instance, with the whole of our deliberative experience, which seems fundamentally structured around the assumption that there are reasons that speak for and against the various actions that are open to us; the very point of deliberation would seem to be to get clear about what these reasons are in the case at hand, and to arrive at some kind of assessment of their overall balance and direction. If normative nihilism is correct, however, then all of this is an illusion, something that must be explained away in psychological terms. Given the centrality of the deliberative point of view to our sense of ourselves as agents and persons, I find myself very skeptical that something like global normative nihilism could be true.

---

[17] See e.g. Nick Zangwill, 'Externalist Moral Motivation', *American Philosophical Quarterly*, 40 (2003), 143–54, sects. 5–6. Zangwill's view appears to shift between skepticism about 'normativity' (when this is construed as something that goes beyond the applicability of moral predicates), and a kind of instrumentalism or 'internalism' about reasons for action.

For the present, however, my point is merely that the anti-rationalist takes on a surprising and very heavy burden of argument in appealing to normative nihilism to defuse the objection from fetishism.

A third and less extreme response to the fetishism charge would concede that there are normative reasons for action, but offer a more refined interpretation of the reasons that are involved in the moral case. In particular, it would be open to anti-rationalists to make the following modification in their account of moral motivation. The concern to do what is right is indeed arbitrary from the point of view of reason, insofar as rightness is not a consideration that provides all agents with reasons for action and attention. But those agents in whom this concern is present, it might be said, do have reason to strive to act in accordance with moral requirements. For them, the fact that x-ing would be right, together with the subjective fact that they are concerned to act rightly, combine to speak in favor of doing x. The motivation to do what is right, on this account, need not be fetishistic in the way the original anti-rationalist position seemed to represent moral motivation as being, since that motivation can be understood as an appropriate response to normative reasons—albeit reasons that apply only to those agents in whom the contingent concern to act rightly is present. The resulting position concedes that the distinction between fetishistic and nonfetishistic forms of motivation has critical animus, but attempts to show that moral motivations fall on the right side of that distinction after all.

This revised position seems to avoid the objection of fetishism. But does it retain the defining claim of anti-rationalism, which is the denial that moral considerations represent requirements of reason? I believe it does. The revised position holds that virtuous agents have reason to do what morality requires. But the reasons in question are not provided by moral considerations alone. On this view, it is not simply the fact that x-ing would be wrong that gives me reason to refrain from x-ing, but that fact together with the fact that I have a concern to avoid acting wrongly.[18] To the extent this is the case, the revised position remains committed to the idea that moral considerations are not independent requirements of reason. In the idiom introduced by Bernard Williams, they supply internal rather than external reasons, counting in favor of acting rightly only for those whose subjective motivational sets are appropriately aligned.[19] A view of this kind can still be counted a form of anti-rationalism, even if it is not quite as radically anti-rationalist as the position considered earlier.

---

[18] Alternatively, the fact that I have a concern to avoid acting wrongly might be said to be, not a constituent in my normative reason (when it is fully spelled out), but merely a condition of my having the reason. But on this version of the position as well, moral considerations are not independent reasons for action, insofar as their standing as reasons for a given agent precisely depends on the presence of appropriate desires in the agent's subjective motivational set. The distinction between these two interpretations of the role of desires in an internal reasons account will play no role in the discussion that follows, which applies equally to both versions of the position.

[19] Bernard Williams, 'Internal and External Reasons', as reprinted in his *Moral Luck* (Cambridge, England: Cambridge University Press, 1981), 101–13.

The Kantian and contractualist approaches discussed earlier, by contrast, are strongly rationalist views. They hold that moral considerations are reasons for anybody, regardless of the constitution of their subjective motivational set. The fact that an action would be uniquely universalizable, or required by principles that no one could reasonably reject, is itself a consideration that speaks strongly in favor of doing it, and it has this normative standing regardless of whether the agent in question happens to care about doing the right thing. To the extent this is the case, the general moral properties have what I earlier referred to as independent normative significance, and it is this fact about them that immunizes the Kantian and contractualist approaches from the potential charge that they are fetishistic in their conceptions of moral motivation.

The revised position I have sketched thus differs from the paradigm rationalist accounts, in a way that renders the anti-rationalist label appropriate. It also provides a way of answering the charge of fetishism, showing that moral motivation, on a suitably anti-rationalist account of it, can after all be understood as a response that is in the relevant way warranted by the normative character of its proper objects. This nonfetishistic interpretation can be sustained, however, only at the cost of abandoning the anti-rationalist's original and distinctive account of moral motivation. According to that account, it is the concern to do what is morally right, interpreted in a *de dicto* way, that is the virtuous agent's fundamental motivation to do what morality requires. In the revised, internal reasons theory, by contrast, that concern comes to play a very different kind of role; it figures not as the source of moral motivation, but as a condition for having reason to act rightly. If the account is to avoid the charge of fetishism, then it must represent morally admirable agents as responding to reasons that they can acknowledge to obtain, and this acknowledgment would appear to go by way of second-order reflection on the subjective concern to act rightly that is a condition or constituent in their reason for action.

What moves fully reflective moral agents to action, then, is not the general concern to do what is right. It is rather the acknowledgment, arrived at through reflexive thought about their own possession of such a general concern, that they have reason to act rightly. This account of moral motivation is in its essentials the rationalist account. Agents who act morally have reasons for so acting, and their motivations implicate their general rational capacities for grasping and responding to the facts about what they have reason to do. The disagreement between rationalists and anti-rationalists, on this way of developing the anti-rationalist view, is not about the general psychic structures that make moral motivation possible, but about the content and truth conditions of the normative judgments on which moral agents distinctively act. Rationalists, for their part, should be very happy with this outcome, since it concedes their basic point that moral motivation is grounded in the deliberative reflections of the agent.

But the situation is still worse for the anti-rationalist position than this might suggest. If we follow the route just described, then anti-rationalism, in taking on board the rationalist account of motivation, threatens to become an internally unstable collection of views. Proponents of the internal reasons model have typically defended the idea that reasons depend on our desires by saying that those desires are what make it possible for us to act on our reasons. Normative reasons are grounded in desires that are rationally contingent, the thought goes, because such desires are the ultimate source of our motivations to action; they account for the capacity of normative considerations to engage the will of rational agents. On the position just sketched, however, it turns out that this claim is false. Motivation has its source not in our contingent desires and dispositions, but in independent capacities for deliberative reflection about the normative. By conceding the rationalist account of motivation, anti-rationalists thus undermine the line of thought that purportedly gave support to the internal reasons view in the first place.[20]

There are, to be sure, other ways in which an internal reasons approach to moral normativity might be developed. The anti-rationalist might insist that the concern to do what is right functions not merely as a condition of the virtuous agent's reason to act morally, but also as the psychic structure that directly enables moral motivation. On this kind of position, agents in whom the concern to act rightly is present will indeed have reason to act as morality prescribes. But when they do the right thing, their actions will be motivated not by their acknowledgment that these reasons obtain, but rather by the basic concern to act rightly that conditions their moral reasons in the first place. This kind of position restores the anti-rationalist's distinctive account of moral motivation, tracing it to a concern for moral rightness that is arbitrary from the point of view of reason. Precisely insofar as it interprets moral motivation in this way, however, the revised position abandons its claim to have overcome the fetishism objection. Moral motivation is once again understood as a response that is not merited by its proper objects, insofar as it is constituted by a brute and unmotivated desire to act in ways that are morally right, rather than by the agent's reflexive acknowledgment of reasons to act morally that are constituted or conditioned by such brute desires.

The anti-rationalist might respond that even if moral motivation remains in this way fetishistic, the *actions* it gives rise to are not. Agents who are moved by the brute concern for moral rightness will end up doing what they have reason to do, and to the extent this is the case we can say that their actions are merited responses to normative facts about their situation. It is just that these responses are produced by psychic structures that are not themselves sensitive to the normative fact that the actions they motivate are merited in this way. The anti-rationalist might maintain that this much fetishism is unavoidable for any position that wishes to reject the distinctively rationalist picture of moral motivation as potentially grounded in normative reflection.[21]

[20] Compare my 'Three Conceptions of Rational Agency', chapter 2 in this volume, sect. 1.

[21] There is perhaps a hint of this kind of position in Bernard Williams's suggestion that we cannot in deliberation acknowledge fully the role that our own dispositions play as conditions of our normative outlook on action; see e.g. his *Ethics and the Limits of Philosophy* (Cambridge, Mass.: Harvard University Press, 1985), 51–3.

Once anti-rationalists have maneuvered themselves into the position of conceding that there are reasons for the actions that moral agents perform, however, it seems highly artificial to insist that those reasons should not register in the deliberation of the agents to whom they apply. As I suggested in section 1, reasons are precisely considerations that are suited to figure in contexts of deliberative reflection and advice, counting for and against options for action that it is open to the agent to perform. A position that makes room for such reasons, and appeals to them to explain why the actions of moral agents are not merely arbitrary responses, should leave room for the possibility of motivation that is based on reflection about these normative considerations. There is thus a kind of natural dynamic that pushes the internal reasons theorist back to the rationalist account of moral motivation.

I do not suppose that these considerations alone decide the issue between rationalists and their opponents. But I believe they locate a real challenge for the anti-rationalist approach. If we reject the idea that morality constitutes an independent normative domain, then it will be much harder than theorists may have supposed to come up with an account of moral motivation that is both attractive and independently stable.

Index